# THE LOSS OF THE S. S. TITANIC
## Its Story And Its Lessons
*by*
Lawrence Beesley

# THE TRUTH ABOUT THE TITANIC
*by*
Colonel Archibald Gracie

# TITANIC
*by*
Commander Lightoller

# THE THRILLING TALE BY TITANIC'S SURVIVING WIRELESS MAN

from The New York Times, April 28, 1912
*by*
Harold Bride

# THE STORY OF
# THE TITANIC

*As Told by Its Survivors*

Lawrence Beesley

Archibald Gracie

Commander Lightoller

Harold Bride

*Edited by*

Jack Winocour

DOVER PUBLICATIONS, INC.
New York

Published in Canada by General Publishing Company, Ltd., 30 Lesmill Road, Don Mills, Toronto,
Ontario.
Published in the United Kingdom by Constable
and Company, Ltd.

This Dover edition, first published in 1960, contains the following:

*The Loss of the S. S. Titanic,* by Lawrence Beesley
in unabridged, unaltered republication as originally
published by Houghton Mifflin Company in 1912.

*The Truth about the Titanic,* by Archibald Gracie
in unabridged, unaltered republication as originally
published by Mitchell Kennerley in 1913.

*Titanic and Other Ships,* by Commander Lightoller. The author's chapters on the Titanic (30, 31,
32, 33, 34, 35) have been selected and are given in
unabridged, unaltered republication. The original
book was published by Ivor Nicholson and Watson
in 1935.

*Thrilling Tale by Titanic's Surviving Wireless
Man.* An unbridged, unaltered reprinting of Harold
Bride's account as reproduced in the *New York
Times* of April 28, 1912.

Illustrations have been selected from the above
books and from the Souvenir Number of *The Shipbuilder* for June, 1911.

*International Standard Book Number: 0-486-20610-6*
*Library of Congress Catalog Card Number: 60-1462*

Manufactured in the United States of America
Dover Publications, Inc.
180 Varick Street
New York, N. Y. 10014

# PREFACE TO THE DOVER EDITION

i

What really happened on board the *Titanic* on the morning of April 15, 1912? Why did a ship that responsible naval architects and builders proclaimed unsinkable sink so easily and so rapidly? Is it true that the captain was drunk? Was the White Star Line trying to establish a speed record through waters that were known to be studded with icebergs? Did the band really play "Nearer My God to Thee" as the ship towered on end for its plunge into the sea? Was the crew heroic, or did hordes of panic-stricken stewards pile into the lifeboats and have to be rowed away from the ship by women? Did an American millionaire try to buy his way into one of the boats, and did another disguise himself as a woman to escape? Why did the *California* stand some four miles away, watching distress signals, yet make no move to save the fifteen hundred men, women, and children?[1]

Draw your own conclusions from the documents presented in this book. Here, in this reader about the *Titanic*, are reprinted for the first time all of the most significant accounts by survivors of the great ship's destruction: the full text of Beesley's book *The Loss of the S. S. Titanic*, Colonel Gracie's book *The Truth about the Titanic*, and the narratives of Second Officer Lightoller and Assistant Radio Operator Bride.

*The Loss of the S. S. Titanic, Its Story and Its Lessons*, by Lawrence Beesley, appeared in 1912. The first major analysis of the disaster, it not only relates Beesley's experiences during the foundering and in his lifeboat but also presents the most thorough non-technical account of the structural defects of the vessel. Its author, Lawrence Beesley, was a young science master from a British public school, on his way to the United States for a vacation.

---

[1] The widely held opinion, based on the findings of the 1912 inquiries, that the *Californian* was the ship seen near the sinking *Titanic*, has been strongly challenged by the Mercantile Marine Service Association. This society of British Shipmasters, to which Captain Lord of the *Californian* belonged from 1898 until his death in 1962, is pledged to continue to press for an official reversal of the original inquiry findings and the issuing of an authoritative statement that is was another ship—possibly the Norwegian sealing vessel *Samson*—which was actually seen from the *Titanic*, the *Californian* herself being some 25 to 30 miles away.

*The Truth about the Titanic*, by Colonel Archibald Gracie, U. S. Army, Ret., tells of Gracie's nearly miraculous underwater escape from the sinking *Titanic*. It is also the most exhaustive and most spirited collection of survivors' accounts. It enables you to experience, through the senses of several dozen men and women, the first shock of collision, the incredulous awareness of disaster, confusion and despair, and finally the death of two-thirds of the ship's passengers.

Colonel Gracie was probably the last man to leave the *Titanic*. He never recovered from the exposure and shock he suffered, however, and did not live to see his book published in 1913. He died on December 4, 1912, about eight months after the disaster, as much a victim of the *Titanic* as those who drowned in the North Atlantic.

Charles Lightoller was Second Officer of the *Titanic*. The only officer to survive the catastrophe, he had directed the loading of the lifeboats. It is easy to be harsh upon Lightoller, as you will discover when you read his account of the "whitewashing" (his own term) inquiries after the disaster. Indeed, Lightoller has been criticized, despite his unquestioned bravery, for having evolved the strange ethical algebra which decided that one female, travelling first-class, deserved life some six times as much as one male, travelling third-class. In justice to Lightoller, however, it must be remembered that some selection of survivors had to be made, since there were far too few lifeboats. There was no time for lots, and a first-come-first-saved policy would probably have resulted in panic and even greater loss of life.

Like Colonel Gracie, Lightoller went down with the ship; but the same gigantic funnel whose falling crushed scores of humans struggling in the 28° water flipped him away from the ship to safety. We have quoted six pertinent chapters from his autobiography, *Titanic and Other Ships*, printed in England in 1935. It has never before been printed in America.

Harold Bride was Assistant Radio Operator on board the *Titanic*. His account appeared in the so-called "Titanic issue" of the *New York Times*, April 28, 1912. It has never before appeared in book form.

Certain of the illustrations in this book have been reproduced from the Souvenir Number of the periodical *The Shipbuilder* (Midsummer, 1911), which was devoted to the sister ships *Olympic* and *Titanic*. As their captions indicate, some of these illustrations are of the *Olympic*, which was finished earlier than the *Titanic* and was more extensively photographed. These pictures are in no material way misleading, however, since the two ships were nearly identical, differing only in some minor details of decoration.

ii

These accounts and illustrations may convey to you something of the emotional pang that the foundering of the *Titanic* caused. Beyond the personal discomfort of the survivors, and the pain of the mourners, beyond the sinking of a gigantic vessel, the destruction of the *Titanic* was felt as something bewildering and almost sacrilegious. Even to-day, forty-seven years later, the *Titanic* overshadows more recent sea disasters like the *Lusitania* or the *Morro Castle*.

Why was the loss of the *Titanic* such a shattering experience? Part of the answer, probably, lies in our superstitious heritage. The builders of the ship (it was commonly felt) had tempted Fate by their loud shouting that the vessel could not be sunk. A press campaign had alerted the world for the *Titanic*'s triumphal sea-flight to New York, perhaps even for a speed record. Animistically inclined writers, ever since, have totalled up the many bad omens that took place as the ship left her pier, and have spoken solemnly of the ship's death wish. Many stories have also been told of the passengers (and missed passengers) who had prophetic dreams warning them against sailing on the *Titanic*. The supernatural has always tried to claim a share of the *Titanic*.

A larger share of the answer to the question why the *Titanic* still arouses so much interest, however, may lie in the position that the *Titanic* held in the world of 1912. The *Titanic* was not simply a means of conveying people from a place they wished to leave to a place they wanted to be, as is the case with most modern ships. It was a floating symbol of status, almost a materialized article of social faith. Its owners had succeeded admirably in establishing it as a symbol of safety, luxury, exclusiveness, and social privilege.

This world was smashed in an evening, indeed, in a matter of hours. The watertight compartments which the owners had puffed so extensively turned out to be worthless. The pride of twentieth-century technology floundered and plunged like the weakest seventeenth-century pink.

Millionaires and immigrants from the third-class shared the common experience of death. Death, it was suddenly recognized, could strike down a Rothschild or a Guggenheim as quickly as it could a stoker. All in all, the sinking of the *Titanic* was a demonstration of man's fate in microcosm. It also showed that the heroism of a few could outweigh the panic of many. The names of Astor, Widener, and Straus were singled out as much for the way their bearers acted minutes before death as for the vast fortunes they left behind them

The *Titanic* disaster combined the inevitability of a Greek tragedy with the ominous warning of the medieval morality play. It marked the end of an era, and with the *Titanic* sank the snugness and smugness of the Edwardian illusion that there were no limits to man's ingenuity and progress. In place of this hard-lost illusion came the harsh recognition of the onset of the age of insecurity, of which the *Titanic* offered the first forebodings. The *Titanic* disaster marks a partition in human history, and for this reason, in addition to its essential drama, it will always arouse interest as a tragedy of historic and epic magnitude.

1960                                                    DOVER PUBLICATIONS, INC.

# CONTENTS

# ILLUSTRATIONS

# The S. S. Titanic

Wednesday, April 10, 1912—the *Titanic* leaves Southampton on her maiden voyage.

# THE LOSS OF THE
# S. S. TITANIC
## Its Story and Its Lessons

*By*

Lawrence Beesley

# PREFACE

The circumstances in which this book came to be written are as follows. Some five weeks after the survivors from the *Titanic* landed in New York, I was the guest at luncheon of Hon. Samuel J. Elder and Hon. Charles T. Gallagher, both well-known lawyers in Boston. After luncheon I was asked to relate to those present the experiences of the survivors in leaving the *Titanic* and reaching the *Carpathia*.

When I had done so, Mr. Robert Lincoln O'Brien, the editor of the *Boston Herald*, urged me as a matter of public interest to write a correct history of the *Titanic* disaster, his reason being that he knew several publications were in preparation by people who had not been present at the disaster, but from newspaper accounts were piecing together a description of it. He said that these publications would probably be erroneous, full of highly colored details, and generally calculated to disturb public thought on the matter. He was supported in his request by all present, and under this general pressure I accompanied him to Messrs. Houghton Mifflin Company, where we discussed the question of publication.

Messrs. Houghton Mifflin Company took at that time exactly the same view that I did, that it was probably not advisable to put on record the incidents connected with the *Titanic*'s sinking: it seemed better to forget details as rapidly as possible.

However, we decided to take a few days to think about it. At our next meeting we found ourselves in agreement again—but this time on the common ground that it would probably be a wise thing to write a history of the *Titanic* disaster as correctly as possible. I was supported in this decision by the fact that a short account, which I wrote at intervals on board the *Carpathia*, in the hope that it would calm public opinion by stating the truth of what happened as nearly as I could recollect it, appeared in all the American, English, and Colonial papers and had exactly the effect it was intended to have. This encourages me to hope that the effect of this work will be the same.

Another matter aided me in coming to a decision—the duty that we, as survivors of the disaster, owe to those who went down with the ship, to see that the reforms so urgently needed are not allowed to be forgotten.

Whoever reads the account of the cries that came to us afloat on the sea from those sinking in the ice-cold water must remember that they were addressed to him just as much as to those who heard them, and that the duty of seeing that reforms are carried out devolves on every one who knows that such cries were heard in utter helplessness the night the *Titanic* sank.

# CONTENTS

CHAPTER I

# CONSTRUCTION AND PREPARA-
# TIONS FOR THE FIRST VOYAGE

The history of the R. M. S. *Titanic*, of the White Star Line, is one of
the most tragically short it is possible to conceive. The world had
waited expectantly for its launching and again for its sailing; had read
accounts of its tremendous size and its unexampled completeness and
luxury; had felt it a matter of the greatest satisfaction that such a comfortable and above all such a safe boat had been designed and built—
the "unsinkable lifeboat"—and then in a moment to hear that it had
gone to the bottom as if it had been the veriest tramp steamer of a few
hundred tons; and with it fifteen hundred passengers, some of them
known the world over! The improbability of such a thing ever happening was what staggered humanity.

If its history had to be written in a single paragraph it would be somewhat as follows:

"The R. M. S. *Titanic* was built by Messrs. Harland & Wolff at their
well-known shipbuilding works at Queen's Island, Belfast, side by side
with her sister ship the *Olympic*. The twin vessels marked such an
increase in size that specially laid-out joiner and boiler shops were prepared to aid in their construction, and the space usually taken up by
three building slips was given up to them. The keel of the *Titanic* was
laid on March 31, 1909, and she was launched on May 31, 1911; she
passed her trials before the Board of Trade officials on March 31, 1912,
at Belfast, arrived at Southampton on April 4, and sailed the following
Wednesday, April 10, with 2,208 passengers and crew, on her maiden
voyage to New York. She called at Cherbourg the same day, Queenstown Thursday, and left for New York in the afternoon, expecting to
arrive the following Wednesday morning. But the voyage was never
completed. She collided with an iceberg on Sunday at 11.45 p. m. in
Lat. 41° 46′ N. and Long. 50° 14′ W., and sank two hours and a half
later; 815 of her passengers and 688 of her crew were drowned and 705
rescued by the *Carpathia*."

9

Such is the record of the *Titanic*, the largest ship the world had ever seen—she was three inches longer than the *Olympic* and one thousand tons more in gross tonnage—and her end was the greatest maritime disaster known. The whole civilized world was stirred to its depths when the full extent of loss of life was learned, and it has not yet recovered from the shock. And that is without doubt a good thing. It should not recover from it until the possibility of such a disaster occurring again has been utterly removed from human society, whether by separate legislation in different countries or by international agreement. No living person should seek to dwell in thought for one moment on such a disaster except in the endeavor to glean from it knowledge that will be of profit to the whole world in the future. When such knowledge is practically applied in the construction, equipment, and navigation of passenger steamers—and not until then—will be the time to cease to think of the *Titanic* disaster and of the hundreds of men and women so needlessly sacrificed.

A few words on the ship's construction and equipment will be necessary in order to make clear many points that arise in the course of this book. A few figures have been added which it is hoped will help the reader to follow events more closely than he otherwise could.

The considerations that inspired the builders to design the *Titanic* on the lines on which she was constructed were those of speed, weight of displacement, passenger and cargo accommodation. High speed is very expensive, because the initial cost of the necessary powerful machinery is enormous, the running expenses entailed very heavy, and passenger and cargo accommodation have to be fined down to make the resistance through the water as little as possible and to keep the weight down. An increase in size brings a builder at once into conflict with the question of dock and harbor accommodation at the ports she will touch: if her total displacement is very great while the lines are kept slender for speed, the draft limit may be exceeded. The *Titanic*, therefore, was built on broader lines than the ocean racers, increasing the total displacement; but because of the broader build, she was able to keep within the draft limit at each port she visited. At the same time she was able to accommodate more passengers and cargo, and thereby increase largely her earning capacity. A comparison between the *Mauretania* and the *Titanic* illustrates the difference in these respects:

|  | *Displacement* | *Horse power* | *Speed in knots* |
| --- | --- | --- | --- |
| *Mauretania* | 44,640 | 70,000 | 26 |
| *Titanic* | 60,000 | 46,000 | 21 |

The vessel when completed was 883 feet long, 92½ feet broad; her height from keel to bridge was 104 feet. She had 8 steel decks, a cellular double bottom, 5¼ feet through (the inner and outer "skins" so-called), and with bilge keels projecting 2 feet for 300 feet of her length amidships. These latter were intended to lessen the tendency to roll in a sea; they no doubt did so very well, but, as it happened, they proved to be a weakness, for this was the first portion of the ship touched by the iceberg and it has been suggested that the keels were forced inwards by the collision and made the work of smashing in the two "skins" a more simple matter. Not that the final result would have been any different.

Her machinery was an expression of the latest progress in marine engineering, being a combination of reciprocating engines with Parsons's low-pressure turbine engine—a combination which gives increased power with the same steam consumption, an advance on the use of reciprocating engines alone. The reciprocating engines drove the wing-propellers and the turbine a mid-propeller, making her a triple-screw vessel. To drive these engines she had 29 enormous boilers and 159 furnaces. Three elliptical funnels, 24 feet 6 inches in the widest diameter, took away smoke and water gases; the fourth one was a dummy for ventilation.

She was fitted with 16 lifeboats 30 feet long, swung on davits of the Welin double-acting type. These davits are specially designed for dealing with two, and, where necessary, three, sets of lifeboats—i. e., 48 altogether; more than enough to have saved every soul on board on the night of the collision. She was divided into 16 compartments by 15 transverse watertight bulkheads reaching from the double bottom to the upper deck in the forward end and to the saloon deck in the after end (Fig. 2), in both cases well above the water line. Communication between the engine rooms and boiler rooms was through watertight doors, which could all be closed instantly from the captain's bridge: a single switch, controlling powerful electro-magnets, operated them. They could also be closed by hand with a lever, and in case the floor below them was flooded by accident, a float underneath the flooring shut them automatically. These compartments were so designed that if the two largest were flooded with water—a most unlikely contingency in the ordinary way—the ship would still be quite safe. Of course, more than two were flooded the night of the collision, but exactly how many is not yet thoroughly established.

Her crew had a complement of 860, made up of 475 stewards, cooks, etc., 320 engineers, and 65 engaged in her navigation

The machinery and equipment of the *Titanic* was the finest obtainable and represented the last word in marine construction. All her structure was of steel, of a weight, size, and thickness greater than that of any ship yet known: the girders, beams, bulkheads, and floors all of exceptional strength. It would hardly seem necessary to mention this, were it not that there is an impression among a portion of the general public that the provision of Turkish baths, gymnasiums, and other so-called luxuries involved a sacrifice of some more essential things, the absence of which was responsible for the loss of so many lives. But this is quite an erroneous impression. All these things were an additional provision for the comfort and convenience of passengers, and there is no more reason why they should not be provided on these ships than in a large hotel. There were places on the *Titanic*'s deck where more boats and rafts could have been stored without sacrificing these things. The fault lay in not providing them, not in designing the ship without places to put them. On whom the responsibility must rest for their not being provided is another matter and must be left until later.

When arranging a tour round the United States, I had decided to cross in the *Titanic* for several reasons—one, that it was rather a novelty to be on board the largest ship yet launched, and another that friends who had crossed in the *Olympic* described her as a most comfortable boat in a seaway, and it was reported that the *Titanic* had been still further improved in this respect by having a thousand tons more built in to steady her. I went on board at Southampton at 10 a. m. Wednesday, April 10, after staying the night in the town. It is pathetic to recall that as I sat that morning in the breakfast room of an hotel, from the windows of which could be seen the four huge funnels of the *Titanic* towering over the roofs of the various shipping offices opposite, and the procession of stokers and stewards wending their way to the ship, there sat behind me three of the *Titanic*'s passengers discussing the coming voyage and estimating, among other things, the probabilities of an accident at sea to the ship. As I rose from breakfast, I glanced at the group and recognized them later on board, but they were not among the number who answered to the roll-call on the *Carpathia* on the following Monday morning.

Between the time of going on board and sailing, I inspected, in the company of two friends who had come from Exeter to see me off, the various decks, dining-saloons and libraries; and so extensive were they that it is no exaggeration to say that it was quite easy to lose one's way on such a ship. We wandered casually into the gymnasium on the boat-deck, and were engaged in bicycle exercise when the instructor came in with two photographers and insisted on our remaining there while his friends—as we thought at the time—made a record for him of his apparatus in use. It was only later that we discovered that they were the photographers of one of the illustrated London papers. More passengers came in, and the instructor ran here and there, looking the very picture of robust, rosy-cheeked health and "fitness" in his white flannels, placing one passenger on the electric "horse" another on the "camel," while the laughing group of onlookers watched the inexperienced riders vigorously shaken up and down as he controlled the little motor which made the machines imitate so realistically horse and camel exercise.

It is related that on the night of the disaster, right up to the time of the *Titanic*'s sinking, while the band grouped outside the gymnasium doors played with such supreme courage in face of the water which rose foot by foot before their eyes, the instructor was on duty inside, with passengers on the bicycles and the rowing-machines, still assisting and encouraging to the last. Along with the bandsmen it is fitting that his name, which I do not think has yet been put on record—it is McCawley —should have a place in the honorable list of those who did their duty faithfully to the ship and the line they served.

# CHAPTER II

# FROM SOUTHAMPTON TO THE NIGHT OF THE COLLISION

Soon after noon the whistles blew for friends to go ashore, the gangways were withdrawn, and the *Titanic* moved slowly down the dock, to the accompaniment of last messages and shouted farewells of those on the quay. There was no cheering or hooting of steamers' whistles from the fleet of ships that lined the dock, as might seem probable on the occasion of the largest vessel in the world putting to sea on her maiden voyage; the whole scene was quiet and rather ordinary, with little of the picturesque and interesting ceremonial which imagination paints as usual in such circumstances. But if this was lacking, two unexpected dramatic incidents supplied a thrill of excitement and interest to the departure from dock. The first of these occurred just before the last gangway was withdrawn: a knot of stokers ran along the quay, with their kit slung over their shoulders in bundles, and made for the gangway with the evident intention of joining the ship. But a petty officer guarding the shore end of the gangway firmly refused to allow them on board; they argued, gesticulated, apparently attempting to explain the reasons why they were late, but he remained obdurate and waved them back with a determined hand, the gangway was dragged back amid their protests, putting a summary ending to their determined efforts to join the *Titanic*. Those stokers must be thankful men to-day that some circumstance, whether their own lack of punctuality or some unforeseen delay over which they had no control, prevented their being in time to run up that last gangway! They will have told—and will no doubt tell for years—the story of how their lives were probably saved by being too late to join the *Titanic*.

The second incident occurred soon afterwards, and while it has no doubt been thoroughly described at the time by those on shore, perhaps a view of the occurrence from the deck of the *Titanic* will not be without interest. As the *Titanic* moved majestically down the dock, the crowd of friends keeping pace with us along the quay, we came together

14

level with the steamer *New York* lying moored to the side of the dock along with the *Oceanic*, the crowd waving "good-byes" to those on board as well as they could for the intervening bulk of the two ships. But as the bows of our ship came about level with those of the *New York*, there came a series of reports like those of a revolver, and on the quay side of the *New York* snaky coils of thick rope flung themselves high in the air and fell backwards among the crowd, which retreated in alarm to escape the flying ropes. We hoped that no one was struck by the ropes, but a sailor next to me was certain he saw a women carried away to receive attention. And then, to our amazement the *New York* crept towards us, slowly and stealthily, as if drawn by some invisible force which she was powerless to withstand. It reminded me instantly of an experiment I had shown many times to a form of boys learning the elements of physics in a laboratory, in which a small magnet is made to float on a cork in a bowl of water and small steel objects placed on neighboring pieces of cork are drawn up to the floating magnet by magnetic force. It reminded me, too, of seeing in my little boy's bath how a large celluloid floating duck would draw towards itself, by what is called capillary attraction, smaller ducks, frogs, beetles, and other animal folk, until the menagerie floated about as a unit, oblivious of their natural antipathies and reminding us of the "happy families" one sees in cages on the seashore. On the *New York* there was shouting of orders, sailors running to and fro, paying out ropes and putting mats over the side where it seemed likely we should collide; the tug which had a few moments before cast off from the bows of the *Titanic* came up around our stern and passed to the quay side of the *New York*'s stern, made fast to her and started to haul her back with all the force her engines were capable of; but it did not seem that the tug made much impression on the *New York*. Apart from the serious nature of the accident, it made an irresistibly comic picture to see the huge vessel drifting down the dock with a snorting tug at its heels, for all the world like a small boy dragging a diminutive puppy down the road with its teeth locked on a piece of rope, its feet splayed out, its head and body shaking from side to side in the effort to get every ounce of its weight used to the best advantage. At first all appearance showed that the sterns of the two vessels would collide; but from the stern bridge of the *Titanic* an officer directing operations stopped us dead, the suction ceased, and the *New York* with her tug trailing behind moved obliquely down the dock, her stern gliding along the side of the *Titanic* some few yards away. It gave an extraordinary impression of the absolute helplessness of a big liner in the absence of any motive power to guide her. But all excitement was not yet over: the *New York* turned her bows inward towards the quay, her stern swinging just clear of and passing in front of our bows, and moved slowly head on for the *Teutonic* lying moored to the side; mats were quickly got out and so deadened the force of the collision, which from where we were seemed to be too slight to cause any damage. Another tug came up and took hold of the *New York* by the bows; and between the two of them they dragged her round the corner of the quay which just here came to an end on the side of the river.

We now moved slowly ahead and passed the *Teutonic* at a creeping pace, but notwithstanding this, the latter strained at her ropes so much that she heeled over several degrees in her efforts to follow the *Titanic*: the crowd were shouted back, a group of gold-braided officials, probably the harbor-master and his staff, standing on the sea side of the moored ropes, jumped back over them as they drew up taut to a rigid line, and urged the crowd back still farther. But we were just clear, and as we slowly turned the corner into the river I saw the *Teutonic* swing slowly back into her normal station, relieving the tension alike of the ropes and of the minds of all who witnessed the incident.

Unpleasant as this incident was, it was interesting to all the passengers leaning over the rails to see the means adopted by the officers and crew of the various vessels to avoid collision, to see on the *Titanic*'s docking-bridge (at the stern) an officer and seamen telephoning and ringing bells, hauling up and down little red and white flags, as danger of collision alternately threatened and diminished. No one was more interested than a young American kinematograph photographer, who, with his wife, followed the whole scene with eager eyes, turning the handle of his camera with the most evident pleasure as he recorded the unexpected incident on his films. It was obviously quite a windfall for him to have been on board at such a time. But neither the film nor those who exposed it reached the other side, and the record of the accident from the *Titanic*'s deck has never been thrown on the screen.

As we steamed down the river, the scene we had just witnessed was the topic of every conversation: the comparison with the *Olympic–Hawke* collision was drawn in every little group of passengers, and it seemed to be generally agreed that this would confirm the suction theory which was so successfully advanced by the cruiser *Hawke* in the law courts, but which many people scoffed at when the British Admiralty first suggested it as the explanation of the cruiser ramming the *Olympic*. And since this is an attempt to chronicle facts as they happened on board the *Titanic*, it must be recorded that there were among the passengers and such of the crew as were heard to speak on the matter, the direct misgivings at the incident we had just witnessed. Sailors are

The *Titanic* narrowly escapes collision with the steamer *New York* in Southampton Water.

The main staircase and entrance hall on the promenade deck of the *Olympic*, nearly identical sister ship of the *Titanic*, show the elegance of the luxury liners.

proverbially superstitious; far too many people are prone to follow their lead, or, indeed, the lead of any one who asserts a statement with an air of conviction and the opportunity of constant repetition; the sense of mystery that shrouds a prophetic utterance, particularly if it be an ominous one (for so constituted apparently is the human mind that it will receive the impress of an evil prophecy far more readily than it will that of a beneficent one, possibly through subservient fear to the thing it dreads, possibly through the degraded, morbid attraction which the sense of evil has for the innate evil in the human mind), leads many people to pay a certain respect to superstitious theories. Not that they wholly believe in them or would wish their dearest friends to know they ever gave them a second thought; but the feeling that other people do so and the half-conviction that there "may be something in it, after all," sways them into tacit obedience to the most absurd and childish theories. I wish in a later chapter to discuss the subject of superstition in its reference to our life on board the *Titanic*, but will anticipate events here a little by relating a second so-called "bad omen" which was hatched at Queenstown. As one of the tenders containing passengers and mails neared the *Titanic*, some of those on board gazed up at the liner towering above them, and saw a stoker's head, black from his work in the stokehold below, peering out at them from the top of one of the enormous funnels—a dummy one for ventilation—that rose many feet above the highest deck. He had climbed up inside for a joke, but to some of those who saw him there the sight was seed for the growth of an "omen," which bore fruit in an unknown dread of dangers to come. An American lady—may she forgive me if she reads these lines!—has related to me with the deepest conviction and earnestness of manner that she saw the man and attributes the sinking of the *Titanic* largely to that. Arrant foolishness, you may say! Yes, indeed, but not to those who believe in it; and it is well not to have such prophetic thoughts of danger passed round among passengers and crew: it would seem to have an unhealthy influence.

We dropped down Spithead, past the shores of the Isle of Wight look-ing superbly beautiful in new spring foliage, exchanged salutes with a White Star tug lying-to in wait for one of their liners inward bound, and saw in the distance several warships with attendant black destroyers guarding the entrance from the sea. In the calmest weather we made Cherbourg just as it grew dusk and left again about 8.30, after taking on board passengers and mails. We reached Queenstown about 12 noon on Thursday, after a most enjoyable passage across the Channel, although the wind was almost too cold to allow of sitting out on deck on Thursday morning.

The coast of Ireland looked very beautiful as we approached Queens-town Harbour, the brilliant morning sun showing up the green hillsides and picking out groups of dwellings dotted here and there above the rugged grey cliffs that fringed the coast. We took on board our pilot, ran slowly towards the harbor with the sounding-line dropping all the time, and came to a stop well out to sea, with our screws churning up the bottom and turning the sea all brown with sand from below. It had seemed to me that the ship stopped rather suddenly, and in my ignor-ance of the depth of the harbor entrance, that perhaps the sounding-line had revealed a smaller depth than was thought safe for the great size of the *Titanic*: this seemed to be confirmed by the sight of sand churned up from the bottom—but this is mere supposition. Passengers and mails were put on board from two tenders, and nothing could have given us a better idea of the enormous length and bulk of the *Titanic* than to stand as far astern as possible and look over the side from the top deck, forwards and downwards to where the tenders rolled at her bows, the merest cockle-shells beside the majestic vessel that rose deck after deck above them. Truly she was a magnificent boat! There was something so graceful in her movement as she rode up and down on the slight swell in the harbor, a slow, stately dip and recover, only notice-able by watching her bows in comparison with some landmark on the coast in the near distance; the two little tenders tossing up and down like corks beside her illustrated vividly the advance made in comfort of motion from the time of the small steamer.

Presently the work of transfer was ended, the tenders cast off, and at 1.30 p. m., with the screws churning up the sea bottom again, the *Titanic* turned slowly through a quarter-circle until her nose pointed down along the Irish coast, and then steamed rapidly away from Queens-town, the little house on the left of the town gleaming white on the hillside for many miles astern. In our wake soared and screamed hundreds of gulls, which had quarrelled and fought over the remnants of lunch pouring out of the waste pipes as we lay-to in the harbor entrance; and now they followed us in the expectation of further spoil. I watched them for a long time and was astonished at the ease with which they soared and kept up with the ship with hardly a motion of their wings: picking out a particular gull, I would keep him under observation for minutes at a time and see no motion of his wings downwards or upwards to aid his flight. He would tilt all of a piece to one side or another as the gusts of wind caught him: rigidly unbendable, as an airplane tilts side-ways in a puff of wind. And yet with graceful ease he kept pace with the *Titanic* forging through the water at twenty knots: as the wind met him he would rise upwards and obliquely forwards, and come down slantingly again, his wings curved in a beautiful arch and his tail feathers outspread as a fan. It was plain that he was possessed of a secret we are only just beginning to learn—that of utilizing air-currents as escalators up and down which he can glide at will with the expenditure of the minimum amount of energy, or of using them as a ship does when it sails within one or two points of a head wind. Aviators, of course, are imitating the gull, and soon perhaps we may see an airplane or a glider dipping gracefully up and down in the face of an opposing wind and all the time forging ahead across the Atlantic Ocean. The gulls were still behind us when night fell, and still they screamed and dipped down into the broad wake of foam which we left behind; but in the morning they were gone: perhaps they had seen in the night a steamer bound for their Queenstown home and had escorted her back.

All afternoon we steamed along the coast of Ireland, with grey cliffs guarding the shores, and hills rising behind gaunt and barren; as dusk fell, the coast rounded away from us to the northwest, and the last we saw of Europe was the Irish mountains dim and faint in the dropping darkness. With the thought that we had seen the last of land until we set foot on the shores of America, I retired to the library to write letters, little knowing that many things would happen to us all—many experiences, sudden, vivid and impressive to be encountered, many perils to be faced, many good and true people for whom we should have to mourn—before we saw land again.

There is very little to relate from the time of leaving Queenstown on Thursday to Sunday morning. The sea was calm—so calm, indeed, that very few were absent from meals: the wind westerly and southwesterly —"fresh" as the daily chart described it—but often rather cold, generally too cold to sit out on deck to read or write, so that many of us spent a good part of the time in the library, reading and writing. I wrote a large number of letters and posted them day by day in the box outside the library door: possibly they are there yet.

Each morning the sun rose behind us in a sky of circular clouds, stretching round the horizon in long, narrow streaks and rising tier upon tier above the sky-line, red and pink and fading from pink to white, as the sun rose higher in the sky. It was a beautiful sight to one who had not crossed the ocean before (or indeed been out of sight of the shores of England) to stand on the top deck and watch the swell of the sea extending outwards from the ship in an unbroken circle until it met the sky-line with its hint of infinity: behind, the wake of the vessel white with foam where, fancy suggested, the propeller blades had cut up the long Atlantic rollers and with them made a level white road bounded on either side by banks of green, blue, and blue-green waves that would

presently sweep away the white road, though as yet it stretched back
to the horizon and dipped over the edge of the world back to Ireland
and the gulls, while along it the morning sun glittered and sparkled.
And each night the sun sank right in our eyes along the sea, making an
undulating glittering pathway, a golden track charted on the surface of
the ocean which our ship followed unswervingly until the sun dipped
below the edge of the horizon, and the pathway ran ahead of us faster
than we could steam and slipped over the edge of the sky-line—as if
the sun had been a golden ball and had wound up its thread of gold too
quickly for us to follow.

From 12 noon Thursday to 12 noon Friday we ran 386 miles, Friday
to Saturday 519 miles, Saturday to Sunday 546 miles. The second day's
run of 519 miles was, the purser told us, a disappointment, and we
should not dock until Wednesday morning instead of Tuesday night,
as we had expected; however, on Sunday we were glad to see a longer
run had been made, and it was thought we should make New York,
after all, on Tuesday night. The purser remarked: "They are not pushing her this trip and don't intend to make any fast running: I don't
suppose we shall do more than 546 now; it is not a bad day's run for
the first trip." This was at lunch, and I remember the conversation
then turned to the speed and build of Atlantic liners as factors in
their comfort of motion: all those who had crossed many times were
unanimous in saying the *Titanic* was the most comfortable boat they
had been on, and they preferred the speed we were making to that of
the faster boats, from the point of view of lessened vibration as well as
because the faster boats would bore through the waves with a twisted,
screw-like motion instead of the straight up-and-down swing of the
*Titanic*. I then called the attention of our table to the way the *Titanic*
listed to port (I had noticed this before), and we all watched the sky-line
through the portholes as we sat at the purser's table in the saloon: it was
plain she did so, for the sky-line and sea on the port side were visible
most of the time and on the starboard only sky. The purser remarked
that probably coal had been used mostly from the starboard side. It is
no doubt a common occurrence for all vessels to list to some degree;
but in view of the fact that the *Titanic* was cut open on the starboard
side and before she sank listed so much to port that there was quite a
chasm between her and the swinging lifeboats, across which ladies had
to be thrown or to cross on chairs laid flat, the previous listing to port
may be of interest.

Returning for a moment to the motion of the *Titanic*, it was interesting
to stand on the boat-deck, as I frequently did, in the angle between
lifeboats 13 and 15 on the starboard side (two boats I have every reason

to remember, for the first carried me in safety to the *Carpathia*, and it seemed likely at one time that the other would come down on our heads as we sat in 13 trying to get away from the ship's side), and watch the general motion of the ship through the waves resolve itself into two motions—one to be observed by contrasting the docking-bridge, from which the log-line trailed away behind in the foaming wake, with the horizon, and observing the long, slow heave as we rode up and down. I timed the average period occupied in one up-and-down vibration, but do not now remember the figures. The second motion was a side-to-side roll, and could be calculated by watching the port rail and contrasting it with the horizon as before. It seems likely that this double motion is due to the angle at which our direction to New York cuts the general set of the Gulf Stream sweeping from the Gulf of Mexico across to Europe; but the almost clock-like regularity of the two vibratory movements was what attracted my attention: it was while watching the side roll that I first became aware of the list to port. Looking down astern from the boat-deck or from B deck to the steerage quarters, I often noticed how the third-class passengers were enjoying every minute of the time: a most uproarious skipping game of the mixed-double type was the great favorite, while "in and out and roundabout" went a Scotchman with his bagpipes playing something that Gilbert says "faintly resembled an air." Standing aloof from all of them, generally on the raised stern deck above the "playing field," was a man of about twenty to twenty-four years of age, well-dressed, always gloved and nicely groomed, and obviously quite out of place among his fellow-passengers: he never looked happy all the time. I watched him, and classified him at hazard as the man who had been a failure in some way at home and had received the proverbial shilling plus third-class fare to America: he did not look resolute enough or happy enough to be working out his own problem. Another interesting man was traveling steerage, but had placed his wife in the second cabin: he would climb the stairs leading from the steerage to the second deck and talk affectionately with his wife across the low gate which separated them. I never saw him after the collision, but I think his wife was on the *Carpathia*. Whether they ever saw each other on the Sunday night is very doubtful: he would not at first be allowed on the second-class deck, and if he were, the chances of seeing his wife in the darkness and the crowd would be very small, indeed. Of all those playing so happily on the steerage deck I did not recognize many afterwards on the *Carpathia*.

Coming now to Sunday, the day on which the *Titanic* struck the iceberg, it will be interesting, perhaps, to give the day's events in some detail, to appreciate the general attitude of passengers to their surroundings just before the collision. Service was held in the saloon by the purser in the morning, and going on deck after lunch we found such a change in temperature that not many cared to remain to face the bitter wind—an artificial wind created mainly, if not entirely, by the ship's rapid motion through the chilly atmosphere. I should judge there was no wind blowing at the time, for I had noticed about the same force of wind approaching Queenstown, to find that it died away as soon as we stopped, only to rise again as we steamed away from the harbor.

Returning to the library, I stopped for a moment to read again the day's run and observe our position on the chart; the Rev. Mr. Carter, a clergyman of the Church of England, was similarly engaged, and we renewed a conversation we had enjoyed for some days: it had commenced with a discussion of the relative merits of his university—Oxford —with mine—Cambridge—as world-wide educational agencies, the opportunities at each for the formation of character apart from mere education as such, and had led on to the lack of sufficiently qualified men to take up the work of the Church of England (a matter apparently on which he felt very deeply) and from that to his own work in England as a priest. He told me some of his parish problems and spoke of the impossibility of doing half his work in his Church without the help his wife gave. I knew her only slightly at that time, but meeting her later in the day, I realized something of what he meant in attributing a large part of what success he had as a vicar to her. My only excuse for mentioning these details about the Carters—now and later in the day—is that, while they have perhaps not much interest for the average reader, they will no doubt be some comfort to the parish over which he presided and where I am sure he was loved. He next mentioned the absence of a service in the evening and asked if I knew the purser well enough to request the use of the saloon in the evening where he would like to have a "hymn sing-song"; the purser gave his consent at once, and Mr. Carter made preparations during the afternoon by asking all he knew— and many he did not—to come to the saloon at 8.30 p. m.

The library was crowded that afternoon, owing to the cold on deck: but through the windows we could see the clear sky with brilliant sunlight that seemed to augur a fine night and a clear day to-morrow, and the prospect of landing in two days, with calm weather all the way to New York, was a matter of general satisfaction among us all. I can look back and see every detail of the library that afternoon—the beautifully furnished room, with lounges, armchairs, and small writing- or card-tables scattered about, writing-bureaus round the walls of the room, and the library in glass-cased shelves flanking one side—the whole finished in mahogany relieved with white fluted wooden columns that supported the deck above. Through the windows there is the covered corridor, reserved by general consent as the children's playground, and here are playing the two Navatril children with their father—devoted to them, never absent from them. Who would have thought of the dramatic history of the happy group at play in the corridor that afternoon!—the abduction of the children in Nice, the assumed name, the separation of father and children in a few hours, his death and their subsequent union with their mother after a period of doubt as to their parentage! How many more similar secrets the *Titanic* revealed in the privacy of family life, or carried down with her untold, we shall never know.

In the same corridor is a man and his wife with two children, and one of them he is generally carrying: they are all young and happy: he is dressed always in a grey knickerbocker suit—with a camera slung over his shoulder. I have not seen any of them since that afternoon.

Close beside me—so near that I cannot avoid hearing scraps of their conversation—are two American ladies, both dressed in white, young, probably friends only: one had been to India and is returning by way of England, the other is a school-teacher in America, a graceful girl with a distinguished air heightened by a pair of *pince-nez*. Engaged in conversation with them is a gentleman whom I subsequently identified from a photograph as a well-known resident of Cambridge, Massachusetts, genial, polished, and with a courtly air towards the two ladies, whom he has known but a few hours; from time to time as they talk, a child acquaintance breaks in on their conversation and insists on their taking notice of a large doll clasped in her arms; I have seen none of this group since then. In the opposite corner are the young American kinematograph photographer and his young wife, evidently French, very fond of playing patience, which she is doing now, while he sits back in his chair watching the game and interposing from time to time with suggestions. I did not see them again. In the middle of the room are two Catholic priests, one quietly reading—either English or Irish, and probably the latter—the other, dark, bearded, with broad-brimmed hat, talking earnestly to a friend in German and evidently explaining some verse in the open Bible before him; near them a young fire engineer on his way to Mexico, and of the same religion as the rest of the group. None of them were saved. It may be noted here that the percentage of men saved in the second-class is the lowest of any other division—only eight per cent.

Many other faces recur to thought, but it is impossible to describe them all in the space of a short book: of all those in the library that Sunday afternoon, I can remember only two or three persons who found their way to the *Carpathia*. Looking over this room, with his back to the library shelves, is the library steward, thin, stooping, sad-faced, and generally with nothing to do but serve out books; but this afternoon he is busier than I have ever seen him, serving out baggage declaration-forms for passengers to fill in. Mine is before me as I write: "Form for nonresidents in the United States. Steamship *Titanic*: No. 31444, D," etc. I had filled it in that afternoon and slipped it in my pocket-book instead of returning it to the steward. Before me, too, is a small cardboard square: "White Star Line. R. M. S. *Titanic*. 208. This label must be given up when the article is returned. The property will be deposited in the Purser's safe. The Company will not be liable to passengers for the loss of money, jewels, or ornaments, by theft or otherwise, not so deposited." The "property deposited" in my case was money, placed in an envelope, sealed, with my name written across the flap, and handed to the purser; the "label" is my receipt. Along with other similar envelopes it may be still intact in the safe at the bottom of the sea, but in all probability it is not, as will be seen presently.

After dinner, Mr. Carter invited all who wished to the saloon, and with the assistance at the piano of a gentleman who sat at the purser's table opposite me (a young Scotch engineer going out to join his brother fruit-farming at the foot of the Rockies), he started some hundred passengers singing hymns. They were asked to choose whichever hymn they wished, and with so many to choose, it was impossible for him to do more than have the greatest favorites sung. As he an-nounced each hymn, it was evident that he was thoroughly versed in their history: no hymn was sung but that he gave a short sketch of its author and in some cases a description of the circumstances in which it was composed. I think all were impressed with his knowledge of hymns and with his eagerness to tell us all he knew of them. It was curious to see how many chose hymns dealing with dangers at sea. I noticed the hushed tone with which all sang the hymn, "For those in peril on the Sea."

The singing must have gone on until after ten o'clock, when, seeing the stewards standing about waiting to serve biscuits and coffee before going off duty, Mr. Carter brought the evening to a close by a few words of thanks to the purser for the use of the saloon, a short sketch of the happiness and safety of the voyage hitherto, the great confidence all felt on board this great liner with her steadiness and her size, and the happy outlook of landing in a few hours in New York at the close of a delightful voyage; and all the time he spoke, a few miles ahead of us lay the "peril on the sea" that was to sink this same great liner with many of those on board who listened with gratitude to his simple, heartfelt words. So much for the frailty of human hopes and for the confidence reposed in material human designs.

Think of the shame of it, that a mass of ice of no use to any one or anything should have the power fatally to injure the beautiful *Titanic*! That an insensible block should be able to threaten, even in the smallest degree, the lives of many good men and women who think and plan and hope and love—and not only to threaten, but to end their lives. It is unbearable! Are we never to educate ourselves to foresee such dangers and to prevent them before they happen? All the evidence of history shows that laws unknown and unsuspected are being discovered day by day: as this knowledge accumulates for the use of man, is it not certain that the ability to see and destroy beforehand the threat of danger will be one of the privileges the whole world will utilize? May that day come soon. Until it does, no precaution too rigorous can be taken, no safety appliance, however costly, must be omitted from a ship's equipment.

After the meeting had broken up, I talked with the Carters over a cup of coffee, said good-night to them, and retired to my cabin at about quarter to eleven. They were good people and this world is much poorer by their loss.

It may be a matter of pleasure to many people to know that their friends were perhaps among that gathering of people in the saloon, and that at the last the sound of the hymns still echoed in their ears as they stood on the deck so quietly and courageously. Who can tell how much it had to do with the demeanor of some of them and the example this would set to others?

# CHAPTER III

# THE COLLISION AND EMBARKATION IN LIFEBOATS

I had been fortunate enough to secure a two-berth cabin to myself —D 56—quite close to the saloon and most convenient in every way for getting about the ship; and on a big ship like the *Titanic* it was quite a consideration to be on D deck, only three decks below the top or boat-deck. Below D again were cabins on E and F decks, and to walk from a cabin on F up to the top deck, climbing five flights of stairs on the way, was certainly a considerable task for those not able to take much exercise. The *Titanic* management has been criticized, among other things, for supplying the boat with lifts: it has been said they were an expensive luxury and the room they took up might have been utilized in some way for more life-saving appliances. Whatever else may have been superfluous, lifts certainly were not: old ladies, for example, in cabins on F deck, would hardly have got to the top deck during the whole voyage had they not been able to ring for the lift-boy. Perhaps nothing gave one a greater impression of the size of the ship than to take the lift from the top and drop slowly down past the different floors, discharging and taking in passengers just as in a large hotel. I wonder where the lift-boy was that night. I would have been glad to find him in our boat, or on the *Carpathia* when we took count of the saved. He was quite young—not more than sixteen, I think—a bright-eyed, handsome boy, with a love for the sea and the games on deck and the view over the ocean—and he did not get any of them. One day, as he put me out of his lift and saw through the vestibule windows a game of deck quoits in progress, he said, in a wistful tone, "My! I wish I could go out there sometimes!" I wished he could, too, and made a jesting offer to take charge of his lift for an hour while he went out to watch the game; but he smilingly shook his head and dropped down in answer to an imperative ring from below. I think he was not on duty with his lift after the collision, but if he were, he would smile at his passengers all the time as he took them up to the boats waiting to leave the sinking ship.

After undressing and climbing into the top berth, I read from about quarter-past eleven to the time we struck, about quarter to twelve. During this time I noticed particularly the increased vibration of the ship, and I assumed that we were going at a higher speed than at any other time since we sailed from Queenstown. Now I am aware that this is an important point, and bears strongly on the question of responsibility for the effects of the collision; but the impression of increased vibration is fixed in my memory so strongly that it seems important to record it. Two things led me to this conclusion—first, that as I sat on the sofa undressing, with bare feet on the floor, the jar of the vibration came up from the engines below very noticeably; and second, that as I sat up in the berth reading, the spring mattress supporting me was vibrating more rapidly than usual: this cradle-like motion was always noticeable as one lay in bed, but that night there was certainly a marked increase in the motion. Referring to the plan,[1] it will be seen that the vibration must have come almost directly up from below, when it is mentioned that the saloon was immediately above the engines as shown in the plan, and my cabin next to the saloon. From these two data, on the assumption that greater vibration is an indication of higher speed—and I suppose it must be—then I am sure we were going faster that night at the time we struck the iceberg than we had done before, i. e., during the hours I was awake and able to take note of anything.

And then, as I read in the quietness of the night, broken only by the muffled sound that came to me through the ventilators of stewards talking and moving along the corridors, when nearly all the passengers were in their cabins, some asleep in bed, others undressing, and others only just down from the smoking-room and still discussing many things, there came what seemed to me nothing more than an extra heave of the engines and a more than usually obvious dancing motion of the mattress on which I sat. Nothing more than that—no sound of a crash or of anything else: no sense of shock, no jar that felt like one heavy body meeting another. And presently the same thing repeated with about the same intensity. The thought came to me that they must have still further increased the speed. And all this time the *Titanic* was being cut open by the iceberg and water was pouring in her side, and yet no evidence that would indicate such a disaster had been presented to us. It fills me with astonishment now to think of it. Consider the question of list alone. Here was this enormous vessel running starboard-side onto an iceberg, and a passenger sitting quietly in bed, reading, felt no motion or list to the opposite or port side, and this must have been felt had it been more than the usual roll of the ship—never very

[1]See Fig. 2, facing p. 28.

much in the calm weather we had all the way. Again, my bunk was fixed to the wall on the starboard side, and any list to port would have tended to fling me out on the floor: I am sure I should have noted it had there been any. And yet the explanation is simple enough: the *Titanic* struck the berg with a force of impact of over a million foot-tons; her plates were less than an inch thick, and they must have been cut through as a knife cuts paper: there would be no need to list; it would have been better if she had listed and thrown us out on the floor, for it would have been an indication that our plates were strong enough to offer, at any rate, some resistance to the blow, and we might all have been safe to-day.

And so, with no thought of anything serious having happened to the ship, I continued my reading; and still the murmur from the stewards and from adjoining cabins, and no other sound: no cry in the night; no alarm given; no one afraid—there was then nothing which could cause fear to the most timid person. But in a few moments I felt the engines slow and stop; the dancing motion and the vibration ceased suddenly after being part of our very existence for four days, and that was the first hint that anything out of the ordinary had happened. We have all "heard" a loud-ticking clock stop suddenly in a quiet room, and then have noticed the clock and the ticking noise, of which we seemed until then quite unconscious. So in the same way the fact was suddenly brought home to all in the ship that the engines—that part of the ship that drove us through the sea—had stopped dead. But the stopping of the engines gave us no information: we had to make our own calculations as to why we had stopped. Like a flash it came to me: "We have dropped a propeller blade: when this happens the engines always race away until they are controlled, and this accounts for the extra heave they gave"; not a very logical conclusion when considered now, for the engines should have continued to heave all the time until we stopped, but it was at the time a sufficiently tenable hypothesis to hold. Acting on it, I jumped out of bed, slipped on a dressing-gown over pajamas, put on shoes, and went out of my cabin into the hall near the saloon. Here was a steward leaning against the staircase, probably waiting until those in the smoke-room above had gone to bed and he could put out the lights. I said, "Why have we stopped?" "I don't know, sir," he replied, "but I don't suppose it is anything much." "Well," I said, "I am going on deck to see what it is," and started towards the stairs. He smiled indulgently at me as I passed him, and said, "All right, sir, but it is mighty cold up there." I am sure at that time he thought I was rather foolish to go up with so little reason, and I must confess I felt rather absurd for not remaining in the cabin: it seemed like making a needless

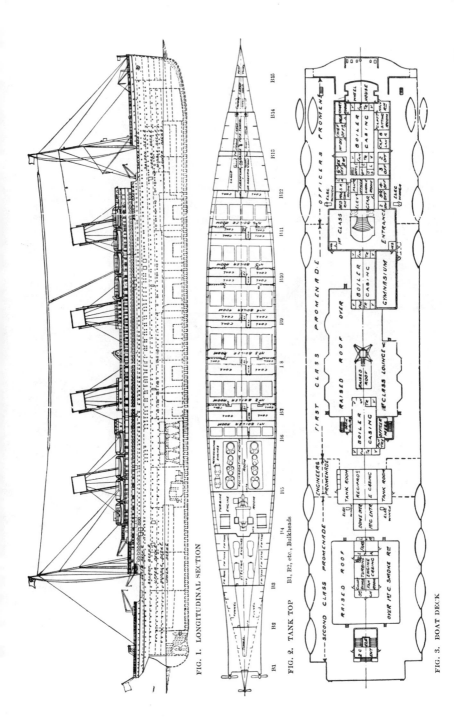

FIG. 1. LONGITUDINAL SECTION

FIG. 2. TANK TOP    B1, B2, etc, Bulkheads

FIG. 3. BOAT DECK

fuss to walk about the ship in a dressing-gown. But it was my first trip across the sea; I had enjoyed every minute of it and was keenly alive to note every new experience; and certainly to stop in the middle of the sea with a propeller dropped seemed sufficient reason for going on deck. And yet the steward, with his fatherly smile, and the fact that no one else was about the passages or going upstairs to reconnoiter, made me feel guilty in an undefined way or breaking some code of a ship's régime—an Englishman's fear of being thought "unusual," perhaps!

I climbed the three flights of stairs, opened the vestibule door leading to the top deck, and stepped out into an atmosphere that cut me, clad as I was, like a knife. Walking to the starboard side, I peered over and saw the sea many feet below, calm and black; forward, the deserted deck stretching away to the first-class quarters and the captain's bridge; and behind, the steerage quarters and the stern bridge; nothing more: no iceberg on either side or astern as far as we could see in the darkness. There were two or three men on deck, and with one—the Scotch engineer who played hymns in the saloon—I compared notes of our experiences. He had just begun to undress when the engines stopped and had come up at once, so that he was fairly well-clad; none of us could see anything, and all being quiet and still, the Scotchman and I went down to the next deck. Through the windows of the smoking-room we saw a game of cards going on, with several onlookers, and went in to enquire if they knew more than we did. They had apparently felt rather more of the heaving motion, but so far as I remember, none of them had gone out on deck to make any enquiries, even when one of them had seen through the windows an iceberg go by towering above the decks. He had called their attention to it, and they all watched it disappear, but had then at once resumed the game. We asked them the height of the berg and some said one hundred feet, others, sixty feet; one of the on-lookers—a motor engineer traveling to America with a model carbur-eter (he had filled in his declaration form near me in the afternoon and had questioned the library steward how he should declare his patent)—said, "Well, I am accustomed to estimating distances and I put it at between eighty and ninety feet." We accepted his estimate and made guesses as to what had happened to the *Titanic*: the general impression was that we had just scraped the iceberg with a glancing blow on the starboard side, and they had stopped as a wise precaution, to examine her thoroughly all over. "I expect the iceberg has scratched off some of her new paint," said one, "and the captain doesn't like to go on until she is painted up again." We laughed at his estimate of the captain's care for the ship. Poor Captain Smith!—he knew by this time only too well what had happened.

One of the players, pointing to his glass of whiskey standing at his elbow, and turning to an onlooker, said, "Just run along the deck and see if any ice has come aboard: I would like some for this." Amid the general laughter at what we thought was his imagination—only too realistic, alas! for when he spoke the forward deck was covered with ice that had tumbled over—and seeing that no more information was forthcoming, I left the smoking-room and went down to my cabin, where I sat for some time reading again. I am filled with sorrow to think I never saw any of the occupants of that smoking-room again: nearly all young men full of hope for their prospects in a new world; mostly unmarried; keen, alert, with the makings of good citizens. Presently, hearing people walking about the corridors, I looked out and saw several standing in the hall talking to a steward—most of them ladies in dressing-gowns; other people were going upstairs, and I decided to go on deck again, but as it was too cold to do so in a dressing-gown, I dressed in a Norfolk jacket and trousers and walked up. There were now more people looking over the side and walking about, questioning each other as to why we had stopped, but without obtaining any definite information. I stayed on deck some minutes, walking about vigorously to keep warm and occasionally looking downwards to the sea as if something there would indicate the reason for delay. The ship had now resumed her course, moving very slowly through the water with a little white line of foam on each side. I think we were all glad to see this: it seemed better than standing still. I soon decided to go down again, and as I crossed from the starboard to the port side to go down by the vestibule door, I saw an officer climb on the last lifeboat on the port side—number 16— and begin to throw off the cover, but I do not remember that any one paid any particular attention to him. Certainly no one thought they were preparing to man the lifeboats and embark from the ship. All this time there was no apprehension of any danger in the minds of passengers, and no one was in any condition of panic or hysteria; after all, it would have been strange if they had been, without any definite evidence of danger.

As I passed to the door to go down, I looked forward again and saw to my surprise an undoubted tilt downwards from the stern to the bows: only a slight slope, which I don't think anyone had noticed—at any rate, they had not remarked on it. As I went downstairs a confirmation of this tilting forward came in something unusual about the stairs, a curious sense of something out of balance and of not being able to put one's feet down in the right place: naturally, being tilted forward, the stairs would slope downwards at an angle and tend to throw one forward. I could not see any visible slope of the stairway: it was perceptible only by the sense of balance at this time.

On D deck were three ladies—I think they were all saved, and it is a good thing at least to be able to chronicle meeting some one who was saved after so much record of those who were not—standing in the passage near the cabin. "Oh! why have we stopped?" they said. "We did stop," I replied, "but we are now going on again." "Oh, no," one replied; "I cannot feel the engines as I usually do, or hear them. Listen!" We listened, and there was no throb audible. Having noticed that the vibration of the engines is most noticeable lying in a bath, where the throb comes straight from the floor through its metal sides—too much so ordinarily for one to put one's head back with comfort on the bath—I took them along the corridor to a bathroom and made them put their hands on the side of the bath: they were much reassured to feel the engines throbbing down below and to know we were making some headway. I left them and on the way to my cabin passed some stewards standing unconcernedly against the walls of the saloon: one of them, the library steward again, was leaning over a table, writing. It is no exaggeration to say that they had neither any knowledge of the accident nor any feeling of alarm that we had stopped and had not yet gone on again full speed: their whole attitude expressed perfect confidence in the ship and officers.

Turning into my gangway (my cabin being the first in the gangway), I saw a man standing at the other end of it fastening his tie. "Anything fresh?" he said. "Not much," I replied; "we are going ahead slowly and she is down a little at the bows, but I don't think it is anything serious." "Come in and look at this man," he laughed; "he won't get up." I looked in, and in the top bunk lay a man with his back to me, closely wrapped in his bedclothes and only the back of his head visible. "Why won't he get up? Is he asleep?" I said. "No," laughed the man dressing, "he says ——" But before he could finish the sentence the man above grunted: "You don't catch me leaving a warm bed to go up on that cold deck at midnight. I know better than that." We both told him laughingly why he had better get up, but he was certain he was just as safe there and all this dressing was quite unnecessary; so I left them and went again to my cabin. I put on some underclothing, sat on the sofa, and read for some ten minutes, when I heard through the open door, above, the noise of people passing up and down, and a loud shout from above: "All passengers on deck with lifebelts on."

I placed the two books I was reading in the side pockets of my Norfolk jacket, picked up my lifebelt (curiously enough, I had taken it down for the first time that night from the wardrobe when I first retired to my cabin) and my dressing-gown, and walked upstairs tying on the lifebelt. As I came out of my cabin, I remember seeing the purser's assistant, with his foot on the stairs about to climb them, whisper to a steward and jerk his head significantly behind him; not that I thought anything of it at the time, but I have no doubt he was telling him what had happened up in the bows, and was giving him orders to call all passengers.

Going upstairs with other passengers—no one ran a step or seemed alarmed—we met two ladies coming down: one seized me by the arm and said, "Oh! I have no lifebelt; will you come down to my cabin and help me to find it?" I returned with them to F deck—the lady who had addressed me holding my arm all the time in a vise-like grip, much to my amusement—and we found a steward in her gangway who took them in and found their lifebelts. Coming upstairs again, I passed the purser's window on F deck, and noticed a light inside; when halfway up to E deck, I heard the heavy metallic clang of the safe door, followed by a hasty step retreating along the corridor towards the first-class quarters. I have little doubt it was the purser, who had taken all valuables from his safe and was transferring them to the charge of the first-class purser, in the hope they might all be saved in one package. That is why I said above that perhaps the envelope containing my money was not in the safe at the bottom of the sea: it is probably in a bundle, with many others like it, waterlogged at the bottom.

Reaching the top deck, we found many people assembled there—some fully dressed, with coats and wraps, well-prepared for anything that might happen; others who had thrown wraps hastily round them when they were called or heard the summons to equip themselves with lifebelts—not in much condition to face the cold of that night. Fortunately there was no wind to beat the cold air through our clothing: even the breeze caused by the ship's motion had died entirely away, for the engines had stopped again and the *Titanic* lay peacefully on the surface of the sea—motionless, quiet, not even rocking to the roll of the sea; indeed, as we were to discover presently, the sea was as calm as an inland lake save for the gentle swell which could impart no motion to a ship the size of the *Titanic*. To stand on the deck many feet above the water lapping idly against her sides, and looking much farther off than it really was because of the darkness, gave one a sense of wonderful security: to feel her so steady and still was like standing on a large rock in the middle of the ocean. But there were now more evidences of the coming catastrophe to the observer than had been apparent when on deck last: one was the roar and hiss of escaping steam from the boilers, issuing out of a large steam pipe reaching high up one of the funnels: a harsh, deafening boom that made conversation difficult and no doubt increased the apprehension of some people merely because of the volume of noise: if one imagines twenty locomotives blowing off steam in a low key it would give some idea of the unpleasant sound that met us as we climbed out on the top deck.

But after all it was the kind of phenomenon we ought to expect: engines blow off steam when standing in a station, and why should not a ship's boilers do the same when the ship is not moving? I never heard any one connect this noise with the danger of boiler explosion, in the event of the ship sinking with her boilers under a high pressure of steam, which was no doubt the true explanation of this precaution. But this is perhaps speculation; some people may have known it quite well, for from the time we came on deck until boat 13 got away, I heard very little conversation of any kind among the passengers. It is not the slightest exaggeration to say that no signs of alarm were exhibited by any one: there was no indication of panic or hysteria; no cries of fear, and no running to and fro to discover what was the matter, why we had been summoned on deck with lifebelts, and what was to be done with us now we were there. We stood there quietly looking on at the work of the crew as they manned the lifeboats, and no one ventured to interfere with them or offered to help them. It was plain we should be of no use; and the crowd of men and women stood quietly on the deck or paced slowly up and down waiting for orders from the officers.

Now, before we consider any further the events that followed, the state of mind of passengers at this juncture, and the motives which led each one to act as he or she did in the circumstances, it is important to keep in thought the amount of information at our disposal. Men and women act according to judgment based on knowledge of the conditions around them, and the best way to understand some apparently inconceivable things that happened is for any one to imagine himself or herself standing on deck that night. It seems a mystery to some people that women refused to leave the ship, that some persons retired to their cabins, and so on; but it is a matter of judgment, after all.

So that if the reader will come and stand with the crowd on deck, he must first rid himself entirely of the knowledge that the *Titanic* has sunk —an important necessity, for he cannot see conditions as they existed there through the mental haze arising from knowledge of the greatest maritime tragedy the world has known: he must get rid of any fore-knowledge of disaster to appreciate why people acted as they did. Secondly, he had better get rid of any picture in thought painted either by his own imagination or by some artist, whether pictorial or verbal, "from information supplied." Some are most inaccurate (these, mostly word-pictures), and where they err, they err on the highly dramatic side. They need not have done so: the whole conditions were dramatic enough in all their bare simplicity, without the addition of any high coloring.

Having made these mental erasures, he will find himself as one of the crowd faced with the following conditions: a perfectly still atmosphere; a brilliantly beautiful starlight night, but no moon, and so with little light that was of any use; a ship that had come quietly to rest without any indication of disaster—no iceberg visible, no hole in the ship's side through which water was pouring in, nothing broken or out of place, no sound of alarm, no panic no movement of any one except at a walking pace; the absence of any knowledge of the nature of the accident, of the extent of damage, of the danger of the ship sinking in a few hours, of the numbers of boats, rafts, and other lifesaving appliances available, their capacity, what other ships were near or coming to help —in fact, an almost complete absence of any positive knowledge on any point. I think this was the result of deliberate judgment on the part of the officers, and perhaps, it was the best thing that could be done. In particular, he must remember that the ship was a sixth of a mile long, with passengers on three decks open to the sea, and port and starboard sides to each deck: he will then get some idea of the difficulty presented to the officers of keeping control over such a large area, and the impossibility of any one knowing what was happening except in his own immediate vicinity. Perhaps the whole thing can be summed up best by saying that, after we had embarked in the lifeboats and rowed away from the *Titanic*, it would not have surprised us to hear that all passengers would be saved: the cries of drowning people after the *Titanic* gave the final plunge were a thunderbolt to us. I am aware that the experiences of many of those saved differed in some respects from the above: some had knowledge of certain things, some were experienced travelers and sailors, and therefore deduced more rapidly what was likely to happen; but I think the above gives a fairly accurate representation of the state of mind of most of those on deck that night.

All this time people were pouring up from the stairs and adding to the crowd: I remember at that moment thinking it would be well to return to my cabin and rescue some money and warmer clothing if we were to embark in boats, but looking through the vestibule windows and seeing people still coming upstairs, I decided it would only cause confusion passing them on the stairs, and so remained on deck.

I was now on the starboard side of the top boat deck; the time about 12.20. We watched the crew at work on the lifeboats, numbers 9, 11, 13, 15, some inside arranging the oars, some coiling ropes on the deck— the ropes which ran through the pulleys to lower to the sea—others with cranks fitted to the rocking arms of the davits. As we watched, the cranks were turned, the davits swung outwards until the boats hung clear of the edge of the deck. Just then an officer came along from the first-class deck and shouted above the noise of escaping steam, "All women and children get down to deck below and all men stand back from the boats." He had apparently been off duty when the ship struck, and was lightly dressed, with a white muffler twisted hastily round his neck. The men fell back and the women retired below to get into the boats from the next deck. Two women refused at first to leave their husbands, but partly by persuasion and partly by force they were separated from them and sent down to the next deck. I think that by this time the work on the lifeboats and the separation of men and women impressed on us slowly the presence of imminent danger, but it made no difference in the attitude of the crowd: they were just as prepared to obey orders and to do what came next as when they first came on deck. I do not mean that they actually reasoned it out: they were the average Teutonic crowd, with an inborn respect for law and order and for traditions bequeathed to them by generations of ancestors: the reasons that made them act as they did were impersonal, instinctive, hereditary.

But if there were any one who had not by now realized that the ship was in danger, all doubt on this point was to be set at rest in a dramatic manner. Suddenly a rush of light from the forward deck, a hissing roar that made us all turn from watching the boats, and a rocket leapt upwards to where the stars blinked and twinkled above us. Up it went, higher and higher, with a sea of faces upturned to watch it, and then an explosion that seemed to split the silent night in two, and a shower of stars sank slowly down and went out one by one. And with a gasping sigh one word escaped the lips of the crowd: "Rockets!" Anybody knows what rockets at sea mean. And presently another, and then a third. It is no use denying the dramatic intensity of the scene: separate it if you can from all the terrible events that followed, and picture the calmness of the night, the sudden light on the decks crowded with people in different stages of dress and undress, the background of huge funnels and tapering masts revealed by the soaring rocket, whose flash illumined at the same time the faces and minds of the obedient crowd, the one with mere physical light, the other with a sudden revelation of what its message was. Every one knew without being told that we were calling for help from any one who was near enough to see.

The crew were now in the boats, the sailors standing by the pulley ropes let them slip through the cleats in jerks, and down the boats went till level with B deck; women and children climbed over the rail into the boats and filled them; when full, they were lowered one by one, beginning with number 9, the first on the second-class deck, and working backwards towards 15. All this we could see by peering over the edge of the boat-deck, which was now quite open to the sea, the four boats which formed a natural barrier being lowered from the deck and leaving it exposed.

About this time, while walking the deck, I saw two ladies come over from the port side and walk towards the rail separating the second-class from the first-class deck. There stood an officer barring the way. "May we pass to the boats?" they said. "No madam," he replied politely, "your boats are down on your own deck," pointing to where they swung below. The ladies turned and went towards the stairway, and no doubt were able to enter one of the boats: they had ample time. I mention this to show that there was, at any rate, some arrangement—whether official or not—for separating the classes in embarking in boats; how far it was carried out, I do not know, but if the second-class ladies were not expected to enter a boat from the first-class deck, while steerage passengers were allowed access to the second-class deck, it would seem to press rather hardly on the second-class men, and this is rather supported by the low percentage saved.

Almost immediately after this incident, a report went round among men on the top deck—the starboard side—that men were to be taken off on the port side; how it originated, I am quite unable to say, but can only suppose that as the port boats, numbers 10 to 16, were not lowered from the top deck quite so soon as the starboard boats (they could still be seen on deck), it might be assumed that women were being taken off on one side and men on the other; but in whatever way the report started, it was acted on at once by almost all the men, who crowded across to the port side and watched the preparation for lowering the boats, leaving the starboard side almost deserted. Two or three men remained, however: not for any reason that we were consciously aware of; I can personally think of no decision arising from reasoned thought that induced me to remain rather than to cross over. But while there was no process of conscious reason at work, I am convinced that what was my salvation was a recognition of the necessity of being quiet and waiting in patience for some opportunity of safety to present itself.

Soon after the men had left the starboard side, I saw a bandsman—the 'cellist—come round the vestibule corner from the staircase entrance and run down the now deserted starboard deck, his 'cello trailing behind him, the spike dragging along the floor. This must have been about 12.40 a. m. I suppose the band must have begun to play soon after this and gone on until after 2 a. m. Many brave things were done that night, but none more brave than by those few men playing minute after minute as the ship settled quietly lower and lower in the sea and the sea rose higher and higher to where they stood; the music they played serving alike as their own immortal requiem and their right to be recorded on the rolls of undying fame.

Looking forward and downward, we could see several of the boats now in the water, moving slowly one by one from the side, without confusion or noise, and stealing away in the darkness which swallowed them in turn as the crew bent to the oars. An officer—I think First Officer Murdock—came striding along the deck, clad in a long coat, from his manner and face evidently in great agitation, but determined and resolute; he looked over the side and shouted to the boats being lowered: "Lower away, and when afloat, row around to the gangway and wait for orders." "Aye, aye sir," was the reply; and the officer passed by and went across the ship to the port side.

Almost immediately after this, I heard a cry from below of, "Any more ladies?" and looking over the edge of the deck, saw boat 13 swinging level with the rail of B deck, with the crew, some stokers, a few men passengers and the rest ladies—the latter being about half the total number; the boat was almost full and just about to be lowered. The call for ladies was repeated twice again, but apparently there were none to be found. Just then one of the crew looked up and saw me looking over. "Any ladies on your deck?" he said. "No," I replied. "Then you had better jump." I sat on the edge of the deck with my feet over, threw the dressing-gown (which I had carried on my arm all of the time) into the boat, dropped, and fell in the boat near the stern.

As I picked myself up, I heard a shout: "Wait a moment, here are two more ladies," and they were pushed hurriedly over the side and tumbled into the boat, one into the middle and one next to me in the stern. They told me afterwards that they had been assembled on a lower deck with other ladies, and had come up to B deck not by the usual stairway inside, but by one of the vertically upright iron ladders that connect each deck with the one below it, meant for the use of sailors passing about the ship. Other ladies had been in front of them and got up quickly, but these two were delayed a long time by the fact that one of them—the one that was helped first over the side into boat 13 near the middle—was not at all active: it seemed almost impossible for her to climb up a vertical ladder. We saw her trying to climb the swinging rope ladder up the *Carpatha*'s side a few hours later, and she had the same difficulty.

As they tumbled in, the crew shouted, "Lower away"; but before the order was obeyed, a man with his wife and a baby came quickly to the side: the baby was handed to the lady in the stern, the mother got in near the middle and the father at the last moment dropped in as the boat began its journey down to the sea many feet below.

# CHAPTER IV

# THE SINKING OF THE *TITANIC* SEEN FROM A LIFEBOAT

L ooking back now on the descent of our boat down the ship's side, it is a matter of surprise, I think, to all the occupants to remember how little they thought of it at the time. It was a great adventure, certainly: it was exciting to feel the boat sink by jerks, foot by foot, as the ropes were paid out from above and shrieked as they passed through the pulley blocks, the new ropes and gear creaking under the strain of a boat laden with people, and the crew calling to the sailors above as the boat tilted slightly, now at one end, now at the other, "Lower aft!" "Lower stern!" and "Lower together!" as she came level again—but I do not think we felt much apprehension about reaching the water safely. It certainly was thrilling to see the black hull of the ship on one side and the sea, seventy feet below, on the other, or to pass down by cabins and saloons brilliantly lighted; but we knew nothing of the apprehension felt in the minds of some of the officers whether the boats and lowering-gear would stand the strain of the weight of our sixty people. The ropes, however, were new and strong, and the boat did not buckle in the middle as an older boat might have done. Whether it was right or not to lower boats full of people to the water—and it seems likely it was not—I think there can be nothing but the highest praise given to the officers and crew above for the way in which they lowered the boats one after the other safely to the water; it may seem a simple matter, to read about such a thing, but any sailor knows, apparently, that it is not so. An experienced officer has told me that he has seen a boat lowered in practise from a ship's deck, with a trained crew and no passengers in the boat, with practised sailors paying out the ropes, in daylight, in calm weather, with the ship lying in dock—and has seen the boat tilt over and pitch the crew headlong into the sea. Contrast these conditions with those obtaining that Monday morning at 12.45 a. m., and it is impossible not to feel that, whether the lowering crew were trained or not, whether they had or had not drilled since coming on board, they did their duty in a way that argues the greatest efficiency. I cannot help feeling the deepest gratitude to the two sailors who stood at the ropes above and lowered us to the sea: I do not suppose they were saved.

Perhaps one explanation of our feeling little sense of the unusual in leaving the *Titanic* in this way was that it seemed the climax to a series of extraordinary occurrences: the magnitude of the whole thing dwarfed events that in the ordinary way would seem to be full of imminent peril. It is easy to imagine it—a voyage of four days on a calm sea, without a single untoward incident; the presumption, perhaps already mentally half realized, that we should be ashore in forty-eight hours and so complete a splendid voyage—and then to feel the engine stop, to be summoned on deck with little time to dress, to tie on a lifebelt, to see rockets shooting aloft in call for help, to be told to get into a lifeboat—after all these things, it did not seem much to feel the boat sinking down to the sea: it was the natural sequence of previous events, and we had learned in the last hour to take things just as they came. At the same time, if any one should wonder what the sensation is like, it is quite easy to measure seventy-five feet from the windows of a tall house or a block of flats, look down to the ground and fancy himself with some sixty other people crowded into a boat so tightly that he could not sit down or move about, and then picture the boat sinking down in a continuous series of jerks, as the sailors pay out the ropes through cleats above. There are more pleasant sensations than this! How thankful we were that the sea was calm and the *Titanic* lay so steadily and quietly as we dropped down her side. We were spared the bumping and grinding against the side which so often accompanies the launching of boats: I do not remember that we even had to fend off our boat while we were trying to get free.

As we went down, one of the crew shouted, "We are just over the condenser exhaust: we don't want to stay in that long or we shall be swamped; feel down on the floor and be ready to pull up the pin which lets the ropes free as soon as we are afloat." I had often looked over the side and noticed this stream of water coming out of the side of the *Titanic* just above the water-line: in fact so large was the volume of water that as we ploughed along and met the waves coming towards us, this stream would cause a splash that sent spray flying. We felt, as well as we could in the crowd of people, on the floor, along the sides, with no idea where the pin could be found—and none of the crew knew where it was, only of its existence somewhere—but we never found it. And all the time we got closer to the sea and the exhaust roared nearer and nearer—until finally we floated with the ropes still holding us from above, the exhaust washing us away and the force of the tide driving us back against the side—the latter not of much account in influencing the direction, however. Thinking over what followed, I imagine we must have touched the water with the condenser stream at our bows, and not in the middle as I thought at one time: at any rate, the resultant of these three forces was that we were carried parallel to the ship, directly under the place where boat 15 would drop from her davits into the sea. Looking up we saw her already coming down rapidly from B deck: she must have filled almost immediately after ours. We shouted up, "Stop lowering 14," [1] and the crew and passengers in the boat above, hearing us shout and seeing our position immediately below them, shouted the same to the sailors on the boat deck; but apparently they did not hear, for she dropped down foot by foot—twenty feet, fifteen, ten—and a stoker and I in the bows reached up and touched her bottom swinging above our heads, trying to push away our boat from under her. It seemed now as if nothing could prevent her dropping on us, but at this moment another stoker sprang with his knife to the ropes that still held us and I heard him shout, "One! Two!" as he cut them through. The next moment we had swung away from underneath 15, and were clear of her as she dropped into the water in the space we had just before occupied. I do not know how the bow ropes were freed, but imagine that they were cut in the same way, for we were washed clear of the *Titanic* at once by the force of the stream and floated away as the oars were got out.

I think we all felt that that was quite the most exciting thing we had yet been through, and a great sigh of relief and gratitude went up as we swung away from the boat above our heads; but I heard no one cry aloud during the experience—not a woman's voice was raised in fear or hysteria. I think we all learnt many things that night about the bogey called "fear", and how the facing of it is much less than the dread of it.

The crew was made up of cooks and stewards, mostly the former, I think; their white jackets showing up in the darkness as they pulled away, two to an oar: I do not think they can have had any practise in rowing, for all night long their oars crossed and clashed; if our safety had depended on speed or accuracy in keeping time it would have gone hard with us. Shouting began from one end of the boat to the other as to what we should do, where we should go, and no one seemed to have any knowledge how to act. At last we asked, "Who is in charge of this boat?" but there was no reply. We then agreed by general consent that the stoker who stood in the stern with the tiller should act as captain,

---

[1] In an account which appeared in the newspapers of April 19 I have described this boat as 14, not knowing they were numbered alternately.

and from that time he directed the course, shouting to other boats and keeping in touch with them. Not that there was anywhere to go or anything we could do. Our plan of action was simple: to keep all the boats together as far as possible and wait until we were picked up by other liners. The crew had apparently heard of the wireless communications before they left the *Titanic*, but I never heard them say that we were in touch with any boat but the *Olympic*: it was always the *Olympic* that was coming to our rescue. They thought they knew even her distance, and making a calculation, we came to the conclusion that we ought to be picked up by her about two o'clock in the afternoon. But this was not our only hope of rescue: we watched all the time the darkness lasted for steamers' lights, thinking there might be a chance of other steamers coming near enough to see the lights which some of our boats carried. I am sure there was no feeling in the minds of any one that we should not be picked up next day: we knew that wireless messages would go out from ship to ship, and as one of the stokers said: "The sea will be covered with ships to-morrow afternoon: they will race up from all over the sea to find us." Some even thought that fast torpedo boats might run up ahead of the *Olympic*. And yet the *Olympic* was, after all, the farthest away of them all; eight other ships lay within three hundred miles of us.

How thankful we should have been to know how near help was, and how many ships had heard our message and were rushing to the *Titanic*'s aid. I think nothing has surprised us more than to learn so many ships were near enough to rescue us in a few hours.

Almost immediately after leaving the *Titanic* we saw what we all said was a ship's lights down on the horizon on the *Titanic*'s port side: two lights, one above the other, and plainly not one of our boats; we even rowed in that direction for some time, but the lights drew away and disappeared below the horizon.

But this is rather anticipating: we did none of these things first. We had no eyes for anything but the ship we had just left. As the oarsmen pulled slowly away we all turned and took a long look at the mighty vessel towering high above our midget boat, and I know it must have been the most extraordinary sight I shall ever be called upon to witness; I realize now how totally inadequate language is to convey to some other person who was not there any real impression of what we saw.

But the task must be attempted: the whole picture is so intensely dramatic that, while it is not possible to place on paper for eyes to see the actual likeness of the ship as she lay there, some sketch of the scene will be possible. First of all, the climatic conditions were extraordinary. The night was one of the most beautiful I have ever seen: the sky without a single cloud to mar the perfect brilliance of the stars, clustered so thickly together that in places there seemed almost more dazzling points of light set in the black sky than background of sky itself; and each star seemed, in the keen atmosphere, free from any haze, to have increased its brilliance tenfold and to twinkle and glitter with a staccato flash that made the sky seem nothing but a setting made for them in which to display their wonder. They seemed so near, and their light so much more intense than ever before, that fancy suggested they saw this beautiful ship in dire distress below and all their energies had awakened to flash messages across the black dome of the sky to each other; telling and warning of the calamity happening in the world beneath. Later, when the *Titanic* had gone down and we lay still on the sea waiting for the day to dawn or a ship to come, I remember looking up at the perfect sky and realizing why Shakespeare wrote the beautiful words he puts in the mouth of Lorenzo:

> Jessica, look how the floor of heaven
> Is thick inlaid with patines of bright gold.
> There's not the smallest orb which thou behold'st
> But in his motion like an angel sings,
> Still quiring to the young-eyed cherubims;
> Such harmony is in immortal souls;
> But whilst this muddy vesture of decay
> Doth grossly close it in, we cannot hear it.

But it seemed almost as if we could—that night: the stars seemed really to be alive and to talk. The complete absence of haze produced a phenomenon I had never seen before: where the sky met the sea the line was as clear and definite as the edge of a knife, so that the water and the air never merged gradually into each other and blended to a softened rounded horizon, but each element was so exclusively separate that where a star came low down in the sky near the clear-cut edge of the water-line, it still lost none of its brilliance. As the earth revolved and the water edge came up and covered partially the star, as it were, it simply cut the star in two, the upper half continuing to sparkle as long as it was not entirely hidden, and throwing a long beam of light along the sea to us.

In the evidence before the United States Senate Committee the captain of one of the ships near us that night said the stars were so extraordinarily bright near the horizon that he was deceived into thinking that they were ships' lights: he did not remember seeing such a night before. Those who were afloat will all agree with that statement: *we* were often deceived into thinking they were lights of a ship.

And next the cold air! Here again was something quite new to us: there was not a breath of wind to blow keenly round us as we stood in the boat, and because of its continued persistence to make us feel cold; it was just a keen, bitter, icy, motionless cold that came from nowhere and yet was there all the time; the stillness of it—if one can imagine "cold" being motionless and still—was what seemed new and strange.

And these—the sky and the air—were overhead; and below was the sea. Here again something uncommon: the surface was like a lake of oil, heaving gently up and down with a quiet motion that rocked our boat dreamily to and fro. We did not need to keep her head to the swell: often I watched her lying broadside on to the tide, and with a boat loaded as we were, this would have been impossible with anything like a swell. The sea slipped away smoothly under the boat, and I think we never heard it lapping on the sides, so oily in appearance was the water. So when one of the stokers said he had been to sea for twenty-six years and never yet seen such a calm night, we accepted it as true without comment. Just as expressive was the remark of another—"It reminds me of a bloomin' picnic!" It was quite true; it did: a picnic on a lake, or a quiet inland river like the Cam, or a backwater on the Thames.

And so in these conditions of sky and air and sea, we gazed broadside on the *Titanic* from a short distance. She was absolutely still—indeed from the first it seemed as if the blow from the iceberg had taken all the courage out of her and she had just come quietly to rest and was settling down without an effort to save herself, without a murmur of protest against such a foul blow. For the sea could not rock her: the wind was not there to howl noisily round the decks, and make the ropes hum; from the first what must have impressed all as they watched was the sense of stillness about her and the slow, insensible way she sank lower and lower in the sea, like a stricken animal.

The mere bulk alone of the ship viewed from the sea below was an awe-inspiring sight. Imagine a ship nearly a sixth of a mile long, 75 feet high to the top decks, with four enormous funnels above the decks, and masts again high above the funnels; with her hundreds of portholes, all her saloons and other rooms brilliant with light, and all round her, little boats filled with those who until a few hours before had trod her decks and read in her libraries and listened to the music of her band in happy content; and who were now looking up in amazement at the enormous mass above them and rowing away from her because she was sinking

I had often wanted to see her from some distance away, and only a few hours before, in conversation at lunch with a fellow-passenger, had registered a vow to get a proper view of her lines and dimensions when we landed at New York: to stand some distance away to take in a full view of her beautiful proportions, which the narrow approach to the dock at Southampton made impossible. Little did I think that the opportunity was to be found so quickly and so dramatically. The background, too, was a different one from what I had planned for her: the black outline of her profile against the sky was bordered all round by stars studded in the sky, and all her funnels and masts were picked out in the same way: her bulk was seen where the stars were blotted out. And one other thing was different from expectation: the thing that ripped away from us instantly, as we saw it, all sense of the beauty of the night, the beauty of the ship's lines, and the beauty of her lights—and all these taken in themselves were intensely beautiful—that thing was the awful angle made by the level of the sea with the rows of porthole lights along her side in dotted lines, row above row. The sea level and the rows of lights should have been parallel—should never have met—and now they met at an angle inside the black hull of the ship. There was nothing else to indicate she was injured; nothing but this apparent violation of a simple geometrical law—that parallel lines should "never meet even if produced ever so far both ways"; but it meant the *Titanic* had sunk by the head until the lowest portholes in the bows were under the sea, and the portholes in the stern were lifted above the normal height. We rowed away from her in the quietness of the night, hoping and praying with all our hearts that she would sink no more and the day would find her still in the same position as she was then. The crew, however, did not think so. It has been said frequently that the officers and crew felt assured that she would remain afloat even after they knew the extent of the damage. Some of them may have done so—and perhaps, from their scientific knowledge of her construction, with more reason at the time than those who said she would sink—but at any rate the stokers in our boat had no such illusion. One of them —I think he was the same man that cut us free from the pulley ropes— told us how he was at work in the stoke-hole, and in anticipation of going off duty in quarter of an hour—thus confirming the time of the collision as 11.45—had near him a pan of soup keeping hot on some part of the machinery; suddenly the whole side of the compartment came in, and the water rushed him off his feet. Picking himself up, he sprang for the compartment doorway and was just through the aperture when the watertight door came down behind him, "like a knife," as he said; "they work them from the bridge." He had gone up on deck but was ordered down again at once and with others was told to draw the fires from under the boiler, which they did, and were then at liberty to come on deck again. It seems that this particular knot of stokers must have known almost as soon as any one of the extent of injury. He added mournfully, "I could do with that hot soup now"—and indeed he could: he was clad at the time of the collision, he said, in trousers and singlet, both very thin on account of the intense heat in the stoke-hole; and although he had added a short jacket later, his teeth were chattering with the cold. He found a place to lie down underneath the tiller on the little platform where our captain stood, and there he lay all night with a coat belonging to another stoker thrown over him and I think he must have been almost unconscious. A lady next to him, who was warmly clad with several coats, tried to insist on his having one of hers—a fur-lined one—thrown over him, but he absolutely refused while some of the women were insufficiently clad; and so the coat was given to an Irish girl with pretty auburn hair standing near, leaning against the gunwale—with an "outside berth" and so more exposed to the cold air. This same lady was able to distribute more of her wraps to the passengers, a rug to one, a fur boa to another; and she has related with amusement that at the moment of climbing up the *Carpathia's* side, those to whom these articles had been lent offered them all back to her; but as, like the rest of us, she was encumbered with a lifebelt, she had to say she would receive them back at the end of the climb. I had not seen my dressing-gown since I dropped into the boat, but some time in the night a steerage passenger found it on the floor and put it on.

It is not easy at this time to call to mind who were in the boat, because in the night it was not possible to see more than a few feet away, and when dawn came we had eyes only for the rescue ship and the icebergs; but so far as my memory serves the list was as follows: no first-class passengers; three women, one baby, two men from the second cabin; and the other passengers steerage—mostly women; a total of about 35 passengers. The rest, about 25 (and possibly more), were crew and stokers. Near to me all night was a group of three Swedish girls, warmly clad, standing close together to keep warm, and very silent; indeed there was very little talking at any time.

One conversation took place that is, I think, worth repeating: one more proof that the world after all is a small place. The ten-months-old baby which was handed down at the last moment was received by a lady next to me—the same who shared her wraps and coats. The mother had found a place in the middle and was too tightly packed to come through to the child, and so it slept contentedly for about an hour in a stranger's arms; it then began to cry and the temporary nurse said: "Will you feel down and see if the baby's feet are out of the blanket! I don't know much about babies but I think their feet must be kept warm." Wriggling down as well as I could, I found its toes exposed to the air and wrapped them well up, when it ceased crying at once: it was evidently a successful diagnosis! Having recognized the lady by her voice—it was much too dark to see faces—as one of my *vis-à-vis* at the purser's table, I said—"Surely you are Miss ——?" "Yes," she replied, "and you must be Mr. Beesley; how curious we should find ourselves in the same boat!" Remembering that she had joined the boat at Queenstown, I said, "Do you know Clonmel? a letter from a great friend of mine who is staying there at —— [giving the address] came aboard at Queenstown." "Yes, it is my home: and I was dining at —— just before I came away." It seemed that she knew my friend, too; and we agreed that of all places in the world to recognize mutual friends, a crowded lifeboat afloat in mid-ocean at 2 a. m. twelve hundred miles from our destination was one of the most unexpected.

And all the time, as we watched, the *Titanic* sank lower and lower by the head and the angle became wider and wider as the stern porthole lights lifted and the bow lights sank, and it was evident she was not to stay afloat much longer. The captain-stoker now told the oarsmen to row away as hard as they could. Two reasons seemed to make this a wise decision: one that as she sank she would create such a wave of suction that boats, if not sucked under by being too near, would be in danger of being swamped by the wave her sinking would create—and we all knew our boat was in no condition to ride big waves, crowded as it was and manned with untrained oarsmen. The second was that an explosion might result from the water getting to the boilers, and débris might fall within a wide radius. And yet, as it turned out, neither of these things happened.

At about 2.15 a. m. I think we were any distance from a mile to two miles away. It is difficult for a landsman to calculate distance at sea but we had been afloat an hour and a half, the boat was heavily loaded, the oarsmen unskilled, and our course erratic: following now one light and now another, sometimes a star and sometimes a light from a port lifeboat which had turned away from the *Titanic* in the opposite direction and lay almost on our horizon; and so we could not have gone very far away.

About this time, the water had crept up almost to her sidelight and the captain's bridge, and it seemed a question only of minutes before she sank. The oarsmen lay on their oars, and all in the lifeboat were motionless as we watched her in absolute silence—save some who would not look and buried their heads on each other's shoulders. The lights still shone with the same brilliance, but not so many of them: many were now below the surface. I have often wondered since whether they

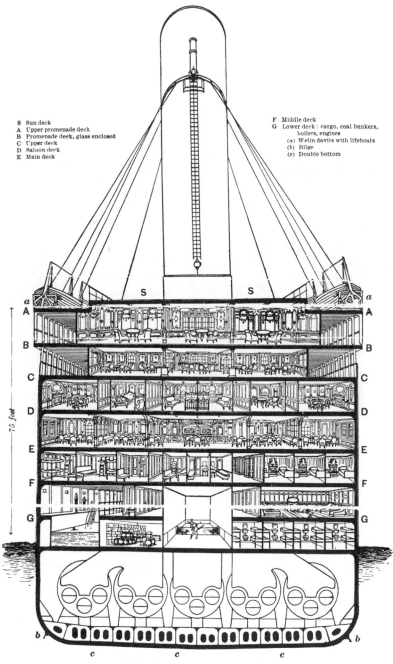

8  Sun deck
A  Upper promenade deck
B  Promenade deck, glass enclosed
C  Upper deck
D  Saloon deck
E  Main deck

F  Middle deck
G  Lower deck: cargo, coal bunkers,
   boilers, engines
   (a) Welin davits with lifeboats
   (b) Bilge
   (c) Double bottom

75 feet

FIG. 4.  TRANSVERSE (AMIDSHIP) SECTION OF THE TITANIC

continued to light up the cabins when the portholes were under water; they may have done so.

And then, as we gazed awe-struck, she tilted slowly up, revolving apparently about a center of gravity just astern of amidships, until she attained a vertically upright position; and there she remained— motionless! As she swung up, her lights, which had shone without a flicker all night, went out suddenly, came on again for a single flash, then went out altogether. And as they did so, there came a noise which many people, wrongly I think, have described as an explosion; it has always seemed to me that it was nothing but the engines and machinery coming loose from their bolts and bearings, and falling through the compartments, smashing everything in their way. It was partly a roar, partly a groan, partly a rattle, and partly a smash, and it was not a sudden roar as an explosion would be: it went on successively for some seconds, possibly fifteen to twenty, as the heavy machinery dropped down to the bottom (now the bows) of the ship: I suppose it fell through the end and sank first, before the ship. But it was a noise no one had heard before, and no one wishes to hear again: it was stupefying, stupendous, as it came to us along the water. It was as if all the heavy things one could think of had been thrown downstairs from the top of a house, smashing each other and the stairs and everything in the way.

Several apparently authentic accounts have been given, in which definite stories of explosions have been related—in some cases even with wreckage blown up and the ship broken in two; but I think such accounts will not stand close analysis. In the first place the fires had been withdrawn and the steam allowed to escape some time before she sank, and the possibility of explosion from this cause seems very remote. Then, as just related, the noise was not sudden and definite, but prolonged—more like the roll and crash of thunder. The probability of the noise being caused by engines falling down will be seen by referring to Fig. 2, where the engines are placed in compartments 3, 4, and 5. As the *Titanic* tilted up they would almost certainly fall loose from their bed and plunge down through the other compartments.

No phenomenon like that pictured in some American and English papers occurred—that of the ship breaking in two, and the two ends being raised above the surface. I saw these drawings in preparation on board the *Carpathia*, and said at the time that they bore no resemblance to what actually happened.

When the noise was over the *Titanic* was still upright like a column: we could see her now only as the stern and some 150 feet of her stood outlined against the star-specked sky, looming black in the darkness, and in this position she continued for some minutes—I think as much as five minutes, but it may have been less. Then, first sinking back a little at the stern, I thought, she slid slowly forwards through the water and dived slantingly down; the sea closed over her and we had seen the last of the beautiful ship on which we had embarked four days before at Southampton.

And in place of the ship on which all our interest had been concentrated for so long and towards which we looked most of the time because it was still the only object on the sea which was a fixed point to us—in place of the *Titanic*, we had the level sea now stretching in an unbroken expanse to the horizon: heaving gently just as before, with no indication on the surface that the waves had just closed over the most wonderful vessel ever built by man's hand; the stars looked down just the same and the air was just as bitterly cold.

There seemed a great sense of loneliness when we were left on the sea in a small boat without the *Titanic*: not that we were uncomfortable (except for the cold) nor in danger: we did not think we were either, but the *Titanic* was no longer there.

We waited head on for the wave which we thought might come— the wave we had heard so much of from the crew and which they said had been known to travel for miles—and it never came. But although the *Titanic* left us no such legacy of a wave as she went to the bottom, she left us something we would willingly forget forever, something which it is well not to let the imagination dwell on—the cries of many hundreds of our fellow-passengers struggling in the ice-cold water.

I would willingly omit any further mention of this part of the disaster from this book, but for two reasons it is not possible—first, that as a matter of history it should be put on record; and secondly, that these cries were not only an appeal for help in the awful conditions of danger in which the drowning found themselves—an appeal that could never be answered—but an appeal to the whole world to make such conditions of danger and hopelessness impossible ever again; a cry that called to the heavens for the very injustice of its own existence: a cry that clamored for its own destruction.

We were utterly surprised to hear this cry go up as the waves closed over the *Titanic*: we had heard no sound of any kind from her since we left her side; and, as mentioned before, we did not know how many boats she had or how many rafts. The crew may have known, but they probably did not, and if they did, they never told the passengers: we should not have been surprised to know all were safe on some life-saving device.

So that unprepared as we were for such a thing, the cries of the drowning floating across the quiet sea filled us with stupefaction: we longed to return and rescue at least some of the drowning, but we knew it was impossible. The boat was filled to standing-room, and to return would mean the swamping of us all, and so the captain-stoker told his crew to row away from the cries. We tried to sing to keep all from thinking of them; but there was no heart for singing in the boat at that time.

The cries, which were loud and numerous at first, died away gradually one by one, but the night was clear, frosty and still, the water smooth, and the sounds must have carried on its level surface free from any obstruction for miles, certainly much farther from the ship than we were situated. I think the last of them must have been heard nearly forty minutes after the *Titanic* sank. Lifebelts would keep the survivors afloat for hours; but the cold water was what stopped the cries.

There must have come to all those safe in the lifeboats, scattered round the drowning at various distances, a deep resolve that, if anything could be done by them in the future to prevent the repetition of such sounds, they would do it—at whatever cost of time or other things. And not only to them are those cries an imperative call, but to every man and woman who has known of them. It is not possible that ever again can such conditions exist; but it is a duty imperative on one and all to see that they do not. Think of it! a few more boats, a few more planks of wood nailed together in a particular way at a trifling cost, and all those men and women whom the world can so ill afford to lose would be with us to-day, there would be no mourning in thousands of homes which now are desolate, and these words need not have been written.

# CHAPTER V

# THE RESCUE

All accounts agree that the *Titanic* sunk about 2.20 a. m.: a watch in our boat gave the time as 2.30 a. m. shortly afterwards. We were then in touch with three other boats: one was 15, on our starboard quarter, and the others I have always supposed were 9 and 11, but I do not know definitely. We never got into close touch with each other, but called occasionally across the darkness and saw them looming near and then drawing away again; we called to ask if any officer were aboard the other three, but did not find one. So in the absence of any plan of action, we rowed slowly forward—or what we thought was forward, for it was in the direction the *Titanic*'s bows were pointing before she sank. I see now that we must have been pointing northwest, for we presently saw the Northern Lights on the starboard, and again, when the *Carpathia* came up from the south, we saw her from behind us on the southeast, and turned our boat around to get to her. I imagine the boats must have spread themselves over the ocean fanwise as they escaped from the *Titanic:* those on the starboard and port sides forward being almost dead ahead of her and the stern boats being broadside from her; this explains why the port boats were so much longer in reaching the *Carpathia*—as late as 8.30 a. m.—while some of the starboard boats came up as early as 4.10 a. m. Some of the port boats had to row across the place where the *Titanic* sank to get to the *Carpathia*, through the débris of chairs and wreckage of all kinds.

None of the other three boats near us had a light—and we missed lights badly: we could not see each other in the darkness; we could not signal to ships which might be rushing up full speed from any quarter to the *Titanic*'s rescue; and now we had been through so much it would seem hard to have to encounter the additional danger of being in the line of a rescuing ship. We felt again for the lantern beneath our feet, along the sides, and I managed this time to get down to the locker below the tiller platform and open it in front by removing a board, to find nothing but the zinc airtank which renders the boat unsinkable when upset. I do not think there was a light in the boat. We felt also for food and water, and found none, and came to the conclusion that none had been put in; but here we were mistaken. I have a letter from Second Officer Lightoller in which he assures me that he and Fourth Officer Pitman examined every lifeboat from the *Titanic* as they lay on the *Carpathia*'s deck afterwards and found biscuits and water in each. Not that we wanted any food or water then: we thought of the time that might elapse before the *Olympic* picked us up in the afternoon.

Towards 3 a. m. we saw a faint glow in the sky ahead on the starboard quarter, the first gleams, we thought, of the coming dawn. We were not certain of the time and were eager perhaps to accept too readily any relief from darkness—only too glad to be able to look each other in the face and see who were our companions in good fortune; to be free from the hazard of lying in a steamer's track, invisible in the darkness. But we were doomed to disappointment: the soft light increased for a time, and died away a little; glowed again, and then remained stationary for some minutes! "The Northern Lights"! It suddenly came to me, and so it was: presently the light arched fanwise across the northern sky, with faint streamers reaching towards the Pole-star. I had seen them of about the same intensity in England some years ago and knew them again. A sigh of disappointment went through the boat as we realized that the day was not yet; but had we known it, something more comforting even than the day was in store for us. All night long we had watched the horizon with eager eyes for signs of a steamer's lights; we heard from the captain-stoker that the first appearance would be a single light on the horizon, the masthead light, followed shortly by a second one, lower down, on the deck; if these two remained in vertical alignment and the distance between them increased as the lights drew nearer, we might be certain it was a steamer. But what a night to see that first light on the horizon! We saw it many times as the earth revolved, and some stars rose on the clear horizon and others sank down to it: there were "lights" on every quarter. Some we watched and followed until we saw the deception and grew wiser; some were lights from those of our boats that were fortunate enough to have lanterns, but these were generally easily detected, as they rose and fell in the near distance. Once they raised our hopes, only to sink them to zero again. Near what seemed to be the horizon on the port quarter we saw two lights close together, and thought this must be our double light; but as we gazed across the miles that separated us, the lights slowly drew apart and we realized that they were two boats' lanterns at different distances from us, in line, one behind the other. They were probably the forward port boats that had to return so many miles next morning across the *Titanic*'s graveyard.

But notwithstanding these hopes and disappointments, the absence of lights, food and water (as we thought), and the bitter cold, it would not be correct to say we were unhappy in those early morning hours: the cold that settled down on us like a garment that wraps close around was the only real discomfort, and that we could keep at bay by not thinking too much about it as well as by vigorous friction and gentle stamping on the floor (it made too much noise to stamp hard!). I never heard that any one in boat B had any after-effects from the cold—even the stoker who was so thinly clad came through without harm. After all, there were many things to be thankful for: so many that they made insignificant the temporary inconvenience of the cold, the crowded boat, the darkness and the hundred-and-one things that in the ordinary way we might regard as unpleasant. The quiet sea, the beautiful night (how different from two nights later when flashes of lightning and peals of thunder broke the sleep of many on board the *Carpathia*!), and above all the fact of being in a boat at all when so many of our fellow-passengers and crew—whose cries no longer moaned across the water to us—were silent in the water. Gratitude was the dominant note in our feelings then. But grateful as we were, our gratitude was soon to be increased a hundred-fold. About 3.30 a. m., as nearly as I can judge, some one in the bow called our attention to a faint far-away gleam in the southeast. We all turned quickly to look and there it was certainly: streaming up from behind the horizon like a distant flash of a warship's searchlight; then a faint boom like guns afar off, and the light died away again. The stoker who had lain all night under the tiller sat up suddenly as if from a dream, the overcoat hanging from his shoulders. I can see him now, staring out across the sea, to where the sound had come from, and hear him shout, "That was a cannon!" But it was not: it was the *Carpathia*'s rocket, though we did not know it until later. But we did know now that something was not far away, racing up to our help and signaling to us a preliminary message to cheer our hearts until she arrived.

With every sense alert, eyes gazing intently at the horizon and ears open for the least sound, we waited in absolute silence in the quiet night. And then, creeping over the edge of the sea where the flash had been, we saw a single light, and presently a second below it, and in a few minutes they were well above the horizon and they remained in line! But we had been deceived before, and we waited a little longer before we allowed ourselves to say we were safe. The lights came up rapidly: so rapidly it seemed only a few minutes (though it must have been longer) between first seeing them and finding them well above the horizon and bearing down rapidly on us. We did not know what sort of a vessel was coming, but we knew she was coming quickly, and we searched for paper, rags—anything that would burn (we were quite prepared to burn our coats if necessary). A hasty paper torch was twisted out of letters found in someone's pocket, lighted, and held aloft by the stoker standing on the tiller platform. The little light shone in flickers on the faces of the occupants of the boat, ran in broken lines for a few yards along the black oily sea (where for the first time I saw the presence of that awful thing which had caused the whole terrible disaster—ice— in little chunks the size of one's fist, bobbing harmlessly up and down), and spluttered away to blackness again as the stoker threw the burning remnants of paper overboard. But had we known it, the danger of being run down was already over, one reason being that the *Carpathia* had already seen the lifeboat which all night long had shown a green light, the first indication the *Carpathia* had of our position. But the real reason is to be found in the *Carpathia*'s log:—"Went full speed ahead during the night; stopped at 4 a. m. with an iceberg dead ahead." It was a good reason.

With our torch burnt and in darkness again we saw the headlights stop, and realized that the rescuer had hove to. A sigh of relief went up when we thought no hurried scramble had to be made to get out of her way, with a chance of just being missed by her, and having to meet the wash of her screws as she tore by us. We waited and she slowly swung round and revealed herself to us as a large steamer with all her port-holes alight. I think the way those lights came slowly into view was one of the most wonderful things we shall ever see. It meant deliverance at once: that was the amazing thing to us all. We had thought of the afternoon as our time of rescue, and here only a few hours after the *Titanic* sank, before it was yet light, we were to be taken aboard. It seemed almost too good to be true, and I think everyone's eyes filled with tears, men's as well as women's, as they saw again the rows of lights one above the other shining kindly to them across the water, and "Thank God!" was murmured in heartfelt tones round the boat. The boat swung round and the crew began their long row to the steamer; the captain called for a song and led off with "Pull for the shore, boys." The crew took it up quaveringly and the passengers joined in, but I think one verse was all they sang. It was too early yet, gratitude was too deep and sudden in its overwhelming intensity, for us to sing very steadily. Presently, finding the song had not gone very well, we tried a cheer, and that went better. It was more easy to relieve our feelings with a noise, and time and tune were not necessary ingredients in a cheer.

In the midst of our thankfulness for deliverance, one name was mentioned with the deepest feeling of gratitude: that of Marconi. I wish that he had been there to hear the chorus of gratitude that went out to him for the wonderful invention that spared us many hours, and perhaps many days, of wandering about the sea in hunger and storm and cold. Perhaps our gratitude was sufficiently intense and vivid to "Marconi" some of it to him that night.

All around we saw boats making for the *Carpathia* and heard their shouts and cheers. Our crew rowed hard in friendly rivalry with other boats to be among the first home, but we must have been eighth or ninth at the side. We had a heavy load aboard, and had to row round a huge iceberg on the way.

And then, as if to make everything complete for our happiness, came the dawn. First a beautiful, quiet shimmer away in the east, then a soft golden glow that crept up stealthily from behind the sky-line as if it were trying not to be noticed as it stole over the sea and spread itself quietly in every direction—so quietly, as if to make us believe it had been there all the time and we had not observed it. Then the sky turned faintly pink and in the distance the thinnest, fleeciest clouds stretched in thin bands across the horizon and close down to it, becoming every moment more and more pink. And next the stars died, slowly—save one which remained long after the others just above the horizon; and near by, with the crescent turned to the north, and the lower horn just touching the horizon, the thinnest, palest of moons.

And with the dawn came a faint breeze from the west, the first breath of wind we had felt since the *Titanic* stopped her engines. Anticipating a few hours—as the day drew on to 8 a. m., the time the last boats came up—this breeze increased to a fresh wind which whipped up the sea, so that the last boat laden with people had an anxious time in the choppy waves before they reached the *Carpathia*. An officer remarked that one of the boats could not have stayed afloat another hour: the wind had held off just long enough.

The captain shouted along our boat to the crew, as they strained at the oars—two pulling and an extra one facing them and pushing to try to keep pace with the other boats—"A new moon! Turn your money over, boys! That is, if you have any!" We laughed at him for the quaint superstition at such a time, and it was good to laugh again, but he showed his disbelief in another superstition when he added. "Well, I shall never say again that 13 is an unlucky number. Boat 13 is the best friend we ever had."

If there had been among us—and it is almost certain that there were, so fast does superstition cling—those who feared events connected with the number thirteen, I am certain they agreed with him, and never again will they attach any importance to such a foolish belief. Perhaps the belief itself will receive a shock when it is remembered that boat 13 of the *Titanic* brought away a full load from the sinking vessel, carried them in such comfort all night that they had not even a drop of water on them, and landed them safely at the *Carpathia*'s side, where they climbed aboard without a single mishap. It almost tempts one to be the thirteenth at table, or to choose a house numbered 13 fearless of any croaking about flying in the face of what is humorously called "Providence."

Looking towards the *Carpathia* in the faint light, we saw what seemed to be two large fully rigged sailing ships near the horizon, with all sails set, standing up near her, and we decided that they must be fishing vessels off the Banks of Newfoundland which had seen the *Carpathia* stop and were waiting to see if she wanted help of any kind. But in a few minutes more the light shone on them and they stood revealed as huge icebergs, peaked in a way that readily suggested a ship. When the sun rose higher, it turned them pink, and sinister as they looked towering like rugged white peaks of rock out of the sea, and terrible as was the disaster one of them had caused, there was an awful beauty about them which could not be overlooked. Later, when the sun came above the horizon, they sparkled and glittered in its rays; deadly white, like frozen snow rather than translucent ice.

As the dawn crept towards us there lay another almost directly in the line between our boat and the *Carpathia*, and a few minutes later, another on her port quarter, and more again on the southern and western horizons, as far as the eye could reach: all differing in shape and size and tones of color according as the sun shone through them or was reflected directly or obliquely from them.

We drew near our rescuer and presently could discern the bands on her funnel, by which the crew could tell she was a Cunarder; and already some boats were at her side and passengers climbing up her ladders. We had to give the iceberg a wide berth and make a détour to the south: we knew it was sunk a long way below the surface with such things as projecting ledges—not that it was very likely there was one so near the surface as to endanger our small boat, but we were not inclined to take any risks for the sake of a few more minutes when safety lay so near.

Once clear of the berg, we could read the Cunarder's name— C A R P A T H I A—a name we are not likely ever to forget. We shall see her sometimes, perhaps, in the shipping lists—as I have done already once when she left Genoa on her return voyage—and the way her lights climbed up over the horizon in the darkness, the way she swung and showed her lighted portholes, and the moment when we read her name on her side will all come back in a flash; we shall live again the scene of rescue, and feel the same thrill of gratitude for all she brought us that night.

We rowed up to her about 4.30, and sheltering on the port side from the swell, held on by two ropes at the stern and bow. Women went up the side first, climbing rope ladders with a noose round their shoulders to help their ascent; men passengers scrambled next, and the crew last of all. The baby went up in a bag with the opening tied up: it had been quite well all the time, and never suffered any ill effects from its cold journey in the night. We set foot on deck with very thankful hearts, grateful beyond the possibility of adequate expression to feel a solid ship beneath us once more.

# CHAPTER VI

# THE SINKING OF THE *TITANIC* SEEN FROM HER DECK

The two preceding chapters have been to a large extent the narrative of a single eye-witness and an account of the escape of one boat only from the *Titanic*'s side. It will be well now to return to the *Titanic* and reconstruct a more general and complete account from the experiences of many people in different parts of the ship. A considerable part of these experiences was related to the writer first hand by survivors, both on board the *Carpathia* and at other times, but some are derived from other sources which are probably as accurate as first-hand information. Other reports, which seemed at first sight to have been founded on the testimony of eye-witnesses, have been found on examination to have passed through several hands, and have therefore been rejected. The testimony even of eye-witnesses has in some cases been excluded when it seemed not to agree with direct evidence of a number of other witnesses or with what reasoned judgment considered probable in the circumstances. In this category are the reports of explosions before the *Titanic* sank, the breaking of the ship in two parts, the suicide of officers. It would be well to notice here that the *Titanic* was in her correct course, the southerly one, and in the position which prudence dictates as a safe one under the ordinary conditions at that time of the year: to be strictly accurate she was sixteen miles south of the regular summer route which all companies follow from January to August.

Perhaps the real history of the disaster should commence with the afternoon of Sunday, when Marconigrams were received by the *Titanic* from the ships ahead of her, warning her of the existence of icebergs. In connection with this must be taken the marked fall of temperature observed by everyone in the afternoon and evening of this day as well as the very low temperature of the water. These have generally been taken to indicate that without any possibility of doubt we were near an iceberg region, and the severest condemnation has been poured on the heads of the officers and captain for not having regard to these climatic conditions; but here caution is necessary. There can be little doubt now that the low temperature observed can be traced to the icebergs and ice-field subsequently encountered, but experienced sailors are aware that it might have been observed without any icebergs being near. The cold Labrador current sweeps down by Newfoundland across the track of Atlantic liners, but does not necessarily carry icebergs with it; cold winds blow from Greenland and Labrador and not always from icebergs and ice-fields. So that falls in temperature of sea and air are not *prima facie* evidence of the close proximity of icebergs. On the other hand, a single iceberg separated by many miles from its fellows might sink a ship, but certainly would not cause a drop in temperature either of the air or water. Then, as the Labrador current meets the warm Gulf Stream flowing from the Gulf of Mexico across to Europe, they do not necessarily intermingle, nor do they always run side by side or one on top of the other, but often interlaced, like the fingers of two hands. As a ship sails across this region the thermometer will record within a few miles temperatures of 34°, 58°, 35,° 59°, and so on.

It is little wonder then that sailors become accustomed to place little reliance on temperature conditions as a means of estimating the probabilities of encountering ice in their track. An experienced sailor has told me that nothing is more difficult to diagnose than the presence of icebergs, and a strong confirmation of this is found in the official sailing directions issued by the Hydrographic Department of the British Admiralty. " No reliance can be placed on any warning being conveyed to the mariner, by a fall in temperature, either of sea or air, of approaching ice. Some decrease in temperature has occasionally been recorded, but more often none has been observed."

But notification by Marconigram of the exact location of icebergs is a vastly different matter. I remember with deep feeling the effect this information had on us when it first became generally known on board the *Carpathia*. Rumors of it went round on Wednesday morning, grew to definite statements in the afternoon, and were confirmed when one of the *Titanic* officers admitted the truth of it in reply to a direct question. I shall never forget the overwhelming sense of hopelessness that came over some of us as we obtained definite knowledge of the warning messages. It was not then the unavoidable accident we had hitherto supposed: the sudden plunging into a region crowded with icebergs which no seaman, however skilled a navigator he might be, could have avoided! The beautiful *Titanic* wounded too deeply to recover, the cries of the drowning still ringing in our ears and the thousands of homes that mourned all these calamities—none of all these things need ever have been!

It is no exaggeration to say that men who went through all the experiences of the collision and the rescue and the subsequent scenes on the quay at New York with hardly a tremor, were quite overcome by this knowledge and turned away, unable to speak; I for one, did so, and I know others who told me they were similarly affected.

I think we all came to modify our opinions on this matter, however, when we learnt more of the general conditions attending trans-Atlantic steamship services. The discussion as to who was responsible for these warnings being disregarded had perhaps better be postponed to a later chapter. One of these warnings was handed to Mr. Ismay by Captain Smith at 5 p. m. and returned at the latter's request at 7 p. m., that it might be posted for the information of officers; as a result of the messages they were instructed to keep a special lookout for ice. This, Second Officer Lightoller did until he was relieved at 10 p. m. by First Officer Murdock, to whom he handed on the instructions. During Mr. Lightoller's watch, about 9 p. m., the captain had joined him on the bridge and discussed "the time we should be getting up towards the vicinity of the ice, and how we should recognize it if we should see it, and refreshing our minds on the indications that ice gives when it is in the vicinity." Apparently, too, the officers had discussed among themselves the proximity of ice and Mr. Lightoller had remarked that they would be approaching the position where ice had been reported during his watch. The lookouts were cautioned similarly, but no ice was sighted until a few minutes before the collision, when the lookout man saw the iceberg and rang the bell three times, the usual signal from the crow's nest when anything is seen dead-ahead.

By telephone he reported to the bridge the presence of an iceberg, but Mr. Murdock had already ordered Quartermaster Hichens at the wheel to starboard the helm, and the vessel began to swing away from the berg. But it was far too late at the speed she was going to hope to steer the huge *Titanic*, over a sixth of a mile long, out of reach of danger. Even if the iceberg had been visible half a mile away it is doubtful whether some portion of her tremendous length would not have been touched, and it is in the highest degree unlikely that the lookout could have seen the berg half a mile away in the conditions that existed that night, even with glasses. The very smoothness of the water made the presence of ice a more difficult matter to detect. In ordinary conditions the dash of the waves against the foot of an iceberg surrounds it with a circle of white foam visible for some distance, long before the iceberg itself; but here was an oily sea sweeping smoothly round the deadly monster and causing no indication of its presence.

There is little doubt, moreover, that the crow's nest is not a good place from which to detect icebergs. It is proverbial that they adopt to a large extent the color of their surroundings; and seen from above at a high angle, with the black, foam-free sea behind, the iceberg must have been almost invisible until the *Titanic* was close upon it. I was much struck by a remark of Sir Ernest Shackleton on his method of detecting icebergs—to place a lookout man as low down near the water-line as he could get him. Remembering how we had watched the *Titanic* with all her lights out, standing upright like "an enormous black finger," as one observer stated, and had only seen her thus because she loomed black against the sky behind her, I saw at once how much better the sky was than the black sea to show up an iceberg's bulk.

And so in a few moments the *Titanic* had run obliquely on the berg, and with a shock that was astonishingly slight—so slight that many passengers never noticed it—the submerged portion of the berg had cut her open on the starboard side in the most vulnerable portion of her anatomy—the bilge.[1] The most authentic accounts say that the wound began at about the location of the foremast and extended far back to the stern, the brunt of the blow being taken by the forward plates, which were either punctured through both bottoms directly by the blow, or through one skin only, and as this was torn away it ripped out some of the inner plates. The fact that she went down by the head shows that probably only the forward plates were doubly punctured, the stern ones being cut open through the outer skin only. After the collision, Murdock had at once reversed the engines and brought the ship to a standstill, but the iceberg had floated away astern. The shock, though little felt by the enormous mass of the ship, was sufficient to dislodge a large quantity of ice from the berg: the forecastle deck was found to be covered with pieces of ice.

Feeling the shock, Captain Smith rushed out of his cabin to the bridge, and in reply to his anxious enquiry was told by Murdock that ice had been struck and the emergency doors instantly closed. The officers roused by the collision went on deck: some to the bridge; others, while hearing nothing of the extent of the damage, saw no necessity for doing so. Captain Smith at once sent the carpenter below to sound the ship, and Fourth Officer Boxhall to the steerage to report damage. The latter found there a very dangerous condition of things and reported to Captain Smith, who then sent him to the mail-room; and here again, it was easy to see, matters looked very serious. Mail-bags were floating about and the water rising rapidly. All this was reported to the captain, who ordered the lifeboats to be got ready at once. Mr. Boxhall went to the chart-room to work out the ship's position, which

[1]See Fig. 4, facing p. 46.

he then handed to the Marconi operators for transmission to any ship near enough to help in the work of rescue.

Reports of the damage done were by this time coming to the captain from many quarters, from the chief engineer, from the designer—Mr. Andrews—and in a dramatic way from the sudden appearance on deck of a swarm of stokers who had rushed up from below as the water poured into the boiler-rooms and coal-bunkers: they were immediately ordered down below to duty again. Realizing the urgent heed of help, he went personally to the Marconi room and gave orders to the operators to get into touch with all the ships they could and to tell them to come quickly. The assistant operator Bride had been asleep, and knew of the damage only when Phillips, in charge of the Marconi room, told him ice had been encountered. They started to send out the well-known "C. Q. D." message—which interpreted means: C. Q. "all stations attend," and D, "distress," the position of the vessel in latitude and longitude following. Later, they sent out "S. O. S.," an arbitrary message agreed upon as an international code-signal.

Soon after the vessel struck, Mr. Ismay had learnt of the nature of the accident from the captain and chief engineer, and after dressing and going on deck had spoken to some of the officers not yet thoroughly acquainted with the grave injury done to the vessel. By this time all those in any way connected with the management and navigation must have known the importance of making use of all the ways of safety known to them—and that without any delay. That they thought at first that the *Titanic* would sink as soon as she did is doubtful; but probably as the reports came in they knew that her ultimate loss in a few hours was a likely contingency. On the other hand, there is evidence that some of the officers in charge of boats quite expected the embarkation was a precautionary measure and they would all return after daylight. Certainly the first information that ice had been struck conveyed to those in charge no sense of the gravity of the circumstances: one officer even retired to his cabin and another advised a steward to go back to his berth as there was no danger.

And so the order was sent round, "All passengers on deck with lifebelts on"; and in obedience to this a crowd of hastily dressed or partially dressed people began to assemble on the decks belonging to their respective classes (except the steerage passengers who were allowed access to other decks), tying on lifebelts over their clothing. In some parts of the ship women were separated from the men and assembled together near the boats, in others men and women mingled freely together, husbands helping their own wives and families and then other women and children into the boats. The officers spread themselves about the decks, superintending the work of lowering and loading the boats, and in three cases were ordered by their superior officers to take charge of them. At this stage great difficulty was experienced in getting women to leave the ship, especially where the order was so rigorously enforced, "Women and children only." Women in many cases refused to leave their husbands, and were actually forcibly lifted up and dropped in the boats. They argued with the officers, demanding reasons, and in some cases even when induced to get in were disposed to think the whole thing a joke, or a precaution which it seemed to them rather foolish to take. In this they were encouraged by the men left behind, who, in the same condition of ignorance, said good-bye to their friends as they went down, adding that they would see them again at breakfast-time. To illustrate further how little danger was apprehended—when it was discovered on the first-class deck that the forward lower deck was covered with small ice, snowballing matches were arranged for the following morning, and some passengers even went down to the deck and brought back small pieces of ice which were handed round.

Below decks too was additional evidence that no one thought of immediate danger. Two ladies walking along one of the corridors came across a group of people gathered round a door which they were trying vainly to open, and on the other side of which a man was demanding in loud terms to be let out. Either his door was locked and the key not to be found, or the collision had jammed the lock and prevented the key from turning. The ladies thought he must be afflicted in some way to make such a noise, but one of the men was assuring him that in no circumstances should he be left, and that his (the bystander's) son would be along soon and would smash down his door if it was not opened in the mean time. "He has a stronger arm than I have," he added. The son arrived presently and proceeded to make short work of the door: it was smashed in and the inmate released, to his great satisfaction and with many expressions of gratitude to his rescuer. But one of the head stewards who came up at this juncture was so incensed at the damage done to the property of his company, and so little aware of the infinitely greater damage done the ship, that he warned the man who had released the prisoner that he would be arrested on arrival in New York.

It must be borne in mind that no general warning had been issued to passengers: here and there were experienced travelers to whom collision with an iceberg was sufficient to cause them to make every preparation for leaving the ship, but the great majority were never enlightened as to the amount of damage done, or even as to what had happened. We knew in a vague way that we had collided with an iceberg, but there our knowledge ended, and most of us drew no deductions from that fact alone. Another factor that prevented some from taking to the boats was the drop to the water below and the journey into the unknown sea: certainly it looked a tremendous way down in the darkness, the sea and the night both seemed very cold and lonely; and here was the ship, so firm and well lighted and warm.

But perhaps what made so many people declare their decision to remain was their strong belief in the theory of the *Titanic*'s unsinkable construction. Again and again was it repeated, "This ship cannot sink; it is only a question of waiting until another ship comes up and takes us off." Husbands expected to follow their wives and join them either in New York or by transfer in mid-ocean from steamer to steamer. Many passengers relate that they were told by officers that the ship was a lifeboat and could not go down; one lady affirms that the captain told her the *Titanic* could not sink for two or three days; no doubt this was immediately after the collision.

It is not any wonder, then, that many elected to remain, deliberately choosing the deck of the *Titanic* to a place in a lifeboat. And yet the boats had to go down, and so at first they went half-full: this is the real explanation of why they were not as fully loaded as the later ones. It is important then to consider the question how far the captain was justified in withholding all the knowledge he had from every passenger. From one point of view he should have said to them, "This ship will sink in a few hours: there are the boats, and only women and children can go to them." But had he the authority to enforce such an order? There are such things as panics and rushes which get beyond the control of a handful of officers, even if armed, and where even the bravest of men get swept off their feet—mentally as well as physically.

On the other hand, if he decided to withhold all definite knowledge of danger from all passengers and at the same time persuade—and if it was not sufficient, compel—women and children to take to the boats, it might result in their all being saved. He could not foresee the tenacity of their faith in the boat: there is ample evidence that he left the bridge when the ship had come to rest and went among passengers urging them to get into the boat and rigorously excluding all but women and children. Some would not go. Officer Lowe testified that he shouted, "Who's next for the boat?" and could get no replies. The boats even were sent away half-loaded—although the fear of their buckling in the middle was responsible as well for this—but the captain with the few boats at his disposal could hardly do more than persuade and advise in the terrible circumstances in which he was placed.

How appalling to think that with a few more boats—and the ship was provided with that particular kind of davit that would launch more boats—there would have been no decision of that kind to make! It could have been stated plainly: "This ship will sink in a few hours: there is room in the boats for all passengers, beginning with women and children."

Poor Captain Smith! I care not whether the responsibility for such speed in iceberg regions will rest on his shoulders or not: no man ever had to make such a choice as he had that night, and it seems difficult to see how he can be blamed for withholding from passengers such information as he had of the danger that was imminent.

When one reads in the Press that lifeboats arrived at the *Carpathia* half full, it seems at first sight a dreadful thing that this should have been allowed to happen; but it is so easy to make these criticisms afterwards, so easy to say that Captain Smith should have told everyone of the condition of the vessel. He was faced with many conditions that night which such criticism overlooks. Let any fair-minded person consider some few of the problems presented to him—the ship was bound to sink in a few hours; there was lifeboat accommodation for all women and children and some men; there was no way of getting some women to go except by telling them the ship was doomed, a course he deemed it best not to take; and he knew the danger of boats buckling when loaded full. His solution of these problems was apparently the following: to send the boats down half full, with such women as would go, and to tell the boats to stand by to pick up more passengers passed down from the cargo ports. There is good evidence that this was part of the plan: I heard an officer give the order to four boats and a lady in number 4 boat on the port side tells me the sailors were so long looking for the port where the captain personally had told them to wait, that they were in danger of being sucked under by the vessel. How far any systematic attempt was made to stand by the ports, I do not know: I never saw one open or any boat standing near on the starboard side; but then, boats 9 to 15 went down full, and on reaching the sea rowed away at once. There is good evidence, then, that Captain Smith fully intended to load the boats full in this way. The failure to carry out the intention is one of the things the whole world regrets, but consider again the great size of the ship and the short time to make decisions, and the omission is more easily understood. The fact is that such a contingency as lowering away boats was not even considered beforehand, and there is much cause for gratitude that as many as seven hundred and five people were rescued. The whole question of a captain's duties seems to require revision. It was totally impossible for any one man to attempt to control the ship that night, and the weather conditions could not well have been more favorable for doing so. One of the reforms that seem inevitable is that one man shall be responsible for the boats, their manning, loading and lowering, leaving the captain free to be on the bridge to the last moment.

But to return for a time to the means taken to attract the notice of other ships. The wireless operators were now in touch with several ships, and calling to them to come quickly for the water was pouring in and the *Titanic* beginning to go down by the head. Bride testified that the first reply received was from a German boat, the *Frankfurt*, which was: "All right: stand by," but not giving her position. From comparison of the strength of signals received from the *Frankfurt* and from other boats, the operators estimated the *Frankfurt* was the nearest; but subsequent events proved that this was not so. She was, in fact, one hundred and forty miles away and arrived at 10.50 a. m. next morning, when the *Carpathia* had left with the rescued. The next reply was from the *Carpathia*, fifty-eight miles away on the outbound route to the Mediterranean, and it was a prompt and welcome one—"Coming hard," followed by the position. Then followed the *Olympic*, and with her they talked for some time, but she was five hundred and sixty miles away on the southern route, too far to be of any immediate help. At the speed of 23 knots she would expect to be up about 1 p. m. next day, and this was about the time that those in boat 13 had calculated. We had always assumed in the boat that the stokers who gave this information had it from one of the officers before they left; but in the absence of any knowledge of the much nearer ship, the *Carpathia*, it is more probable that they knew in a general way where the sister ship, the *Olympic*, should be, and had made a rough calculation.

Other ships in touch by wireless were the *Mount Temple*, fifty miles; the *Birma*, one hundred miles; the *Parisian*, one hundred and fifty miles; the *Virginian*, one hundred and fifty miles; and the *Baltic*, three hundred miles. But closer than any of these—closer even than the *Carpathia*—were two ships: the *Californian*, less than twenty miles away, with the wireless operator off duty and unable to catch the "C. Q. D." signal which was now making the air for many miles around quiver in its appeal for help—immediate, urgent help—for the hundreds of people who stood on the *Titanic*'s deck.

The second vessel was a small steamer some few miles ahead on the port side, without any wireless apparatus, her name and destination still unknown; and yet the evidence for her presence that night seems too strong to be disregarded. Mr. Boxhall states that he and Captain Smith saw her quite plainly some five miles away, and could distinguish the masthead lights and a red port light. They at once hailed her with rockets and Morse electric signals, to which Boxhall saw no reply, but

Captain Smith and stewards affirmed they did. The second and third officers saw the signals sent and her lights, the latter from the lifeboat of which he was in charge. Seaman Hopkins testified that he was told by the captain to row for the light; and we in boat 13 certainly saw it in the same position and rowed towards it for some time. But notwithstanding all the efforts made to attract its attention, it drew slowly away and the lights sank below the horizon.

The pity of it! So near, and so many people waiting for the shelter its decks could have given so easily. It seems impossible to think that this ship ever replied to the signals: those who said so must have been mistaken. The United States Senate Committee in its report does not hesitate to say that this unknown steamer and the *Californian* are identical, and that the failure on the part of the latter to come to the help of the *Titanic* is culpable negligence. There is undoubted evidence that some of the crew on the *Californian* saw our rockets; but it seems impossible to believe that the captain and officers knew of our distress and deliberately ignored it. Judgment on the matter had better be suspended until further information is forthcoming. An engineer who has served in the trans-Atlantic service tells me that it is a common practise for small boats to leave the fishing smacks to which they belong and row away for miles; sometimes even being lost and wandering about among icebergs, and even not being found again. In these circumstances, rockets are part of a fishing smack's equipment, and are sent up to indicate to the small boats how to return. Is it conceivable that the *Californian* thought our rockets were such signals, and therefore paid no attention to them?

Incidentally, this engineer did not hesitate to add that it is doubtful if a big liner would stop to help a small fishing-boat sending off distress signals, or even would turn about to help one which she herself had cut down as it lay in her path without a light. He was strong in his affirmation that such things were commonly known to all officers in the trans-Atlantic service.

With regard to the other vessels in wireless communication, the *Mount Temple* was the only one near enough from the point of distance to have arrived in time to be of help, but between her and the *Titanic* lay the enormous ice-floe, and icebergs were near her in addition.

The seven ships which caught the message started at once to her help but were all stopped on the way (except the *Birma*) by the *Carpathia*'s wireless announcing the fate of the *Titanic* and the people aboard her. The message must have affected the captains of these ships very deeply: they would understand far better than the traveling public what is meant to lose such a beautiful ship on her first voyage.

The only thing now left to be done was to get the lifeboats away as quickly as possible, and to this task the other officers were in the meantime devoting all their endeavors. Mr. Lightoller sent away boat after boat: in one he had put twenty-four women and children, in another thirty, in another thirty-five; and then, running short of seamen to man the boats he sent Major Peuchen, an expert yachtsman, in the next, to help with its navigation. By the time these had been filled, he had difficulty in finding women for the fifth and sixth boats for the reasons already stated. All this time the passengers remained—to use his own expression—"as quiet as if in church." To man and supervise the loading of six boats must have taken him nearly up to the time of the *Titanic's* sinking, taking an average of some twenty minutes to a boat. Still at work to the end, he remained on the ship till she sank and went down with her. His evidence before the United States Committee was as follows: "Did you leave the ship?" "No, sir." "Did the ship leave you?" "Yes, sir."

It was a piece of work well and cleanly done, and his escape from the ship, one of the most wonderful of all, seems almost a reward for his devotion to duty.

Captain Smith, Officers Wilde and Murdock were similarly engaged in other parts of the ship, urging women to get in the boats, in some cases directing junior officers to go down in some of them—Officers Pitman, Boxhall, and Lowe were sent in this way—in others placing members of the crew in charge. As the boats were lowered, orders were shouted to them where to make for: some were told to stand by and wait for further instructions, others to row for the light of the disappearing steamer.

It is a pitiful thing to recall the effects of sending down the first boats half full. In some cases men in the company of their wives had actually taken seats in the boats—young men, married only a few weeks and on their wedding trip—and had done so only because no more women could then be found; but the strict interpretation by the particular officer in charge there of the rule of "Women and children only," compelled them to get out again. Some of these boats were lowered and reached the *Carpathia* with many vacant seats. The anguish of the young wives in such circumstances can only be imagined. In other parts of the ship, however, a different interpretation was placed on the rule, and men were allowed and even invited by officers to get in—not only to form part of the crew, but even as passengers. This, of course, in the first boats and when no more women could be found.

The varied understanding of this rule was a frequent subject of discussion on the *Carpathia*—in fact, the rule itself was debated with much heart-searching. There were not wanting many who doubted the justice of its rigid enforcement, who could not think it well that a husband should be separated from his wife and family, leaving them penniless, or a young bridegroom from his wife of a few short weeks, while ladies with few relatives, with no one dependent upon them, and few responsibilities of any kind, were saved. It was mostly these ladies who pressed this view, and even men seemed to think there was a good deal to be said for it. Perhaps there is, theoretically, but it would be impossible, I think, in practise. To quote Mr. Lightoller again in his evidence before the United States Senate Committee—when asked if it was a rule of the sea that women and children be saved first, he replied, "No, it is a rule of human nature." That is no doubt the real reason for its existence.

But the selective process of circumstances brought about results that were very bitter to some. It was heartrending for ladies who had lost all they held dearest in the world to hear that in one boat was a stoker picked up out of the sea so drunk that he stood up and brandished his arms about, and had to be thrown down by ladies and sat upon to keep him quiet. If comparisons can be drawn, it did seem better that an educated, refined man should be saved than one who had flown to drink as his refuge in time of danger.

These discussions turned sometimes to the old enquiry—"What is the purpose of all this? Why the disaster? Why this man saved and that man lost? Who has arranged that my husband should live a few short happy years in the world, and the happiest days in those years with me these last few weeks, and then be taken from me?" I heard no one attribute all this to a Divine Power who ordains and arranges the lives of men, and as part of a definite scheme sends such calamity and misery in order to purify, to teach, to spiritualize. I do not say there were not people who thought and said they saw Divine Wisdom in it all—so inscrutable that we in our ignorance saw it not; but I did not hear it expressed, and this book is intended to be no more than a partial chronicle of the many different experiences and convictions.

There were those, on the other hand, who did not fail to say emphatically that indifference to the rights and feelings of others, blindness to duty towards our fellow men and women, was in the last analysis the cause of most of the human misery in the world. And it should undoubtedly appeal more to our sense of justice to attribute these things to our own lack of consideration for others than to shift the responsibility on to a Power whom we first postulate as being All-wise and All-loving.

Some first-class suite bedrooms were decorated in the Georgian style (above); others were magnificent examples of Empire décor. (The illustration is of the *Olympic* which was completed earlier than the *Titanic* and was more extensively photographed.)

The social elite gathered in the first-class lounge. (The illustration is of the *Olympic*.)

All the boats were lowered and sent away by about 2 a. m., and by this time the ship was very low in the water, the forecastle deck completely submerged, and the sea creeping steadily up to the bridge and probably only a few yards away.

No one on the ship can have had any doubt now as to her ultimate fate, and yet the fifteen hundred passengers and crew on board made no demonstration, and not a sound came from them as they stood quietly on the decks or went about their duties below. It seems incredible, and yet if it was a continuation of the same feeling that existed on deck before the boats left—and I have no doubt it was—the explanation is straightforward and reasonable in its simplicity. An attempt is made in the last chapter to show why the attitude of the crowd was so quietly courageous. There are accounts which picture excited crowds running about the deck in terror, fighting and struggling, but two of the most accurate observers, Colonel Gracie and Mr. Lightoller, affirm that this was not so, that absolute order and quietness prevailed. The band still played to cheer the hearts of all near; the engineers and their crew—I have never heard any one speak of a single engineer being seen on deck—still worked at the electric light engines, far away below, keeping them going until no human being could do so a second longer, right until the ship tilted on end and the engines broke loose and fell down. The light failed then only because the engines were no longer there to produce light, not because the men who worked them were not standing by them to do their duty. To be down in the bowels of the ship, far away from the deck where at any rate there was a chance of a dive and a swim and a possible rescue; to know that when the ship went—as they knew it must soon—there could be no possible hope of climbing up in time to reach the sea; to know all these things and yet to keep the engines going that the decks might be lighted to the last moment, required sublime courage.

But this courage is required of every engineer and it is not called by that name: it is called "duty." To stand by his engines to the last possible moment is his duty. There could be no better example of the supremest courage being but duty well done than to remember the engineers of the *Titanic* still at work as she heeled over and flung them with their engines down the length of the ship. The simple statement that the lights kept on to the last is really their epitaph, but Lowell's words would seem to apply to them with peculiar force—

> The longer on this earth we live
> And weigh the various qualities of men—
> The more we feel the high, stern-featured beauty
> Of plain devotedness to duty.

> Steadfast and still, nor paid with mortal praise,
> But finding amplest recompense
> For life's ungarlanded expense
> In work done squarely and unwasted days.

For some time before she sank, the *Titanic* had a considerable list to port, so much so that one boat at any rate swung so far away from the side that difficulty was experienced in getting passengers in. This list was increased towards the end, and Colonel Gracie relates that Mr. Lightoller, who has a deep, powerful voice, ordered all passengers to the starboard side. This was close before the end. They crossed over, and as they did so a crowd of steerage passengers rushed up and filled the decks so full that there was barely room to move. Soon afterwards the great vessel swung slowly, stern in the air, the lights went out, and while some were flung into the water and others dived off, the great majority still clung to the rails, to the sides and roofs of deck-structures, lying prone on the deck. And in this position they were when, a few minutes later, the enormous vessel dived obliquely downwards. As she went, no doubt many still clung to the rails, but most would do their best to get away from her and jump as she slid forwards and downwards. Whatever they did, there can be little question that most of them would be taken down by suction, to come up again a few moments later and to fill the air with those heartrending cries which fell on the ears of those in the lifeboats with such amazement. Another survivor, on the other hand, relates that he had dived from the stern before she heeled over, and swam round under her enormous triple screws lifted by now high out of the water as she stood on end. Fascinated by the extraordinary sight, he watched them up above his head, but presently realizing the necessity of getting away as quickly as possible, he started to swim from the ship, but as he did she dived forward, the screws passing near his head. His experience is that not only was no suction present, but even a wave was created which washed him away from the place where she had gone down.

Of all those fifteen hundred people, flung into the sea as the *Titanic* went down, innocent victims of thoughtlessness and apathy of those responsible for their safety, only a very few found their way to the *Carpathia*. It will serve no good purpose to dwell any longer on the scene of helpless men and women struggling in the water. The heart of everyone who has read of their helplessness has gone out to them in deepest love and sympathy; and the knowledge that their struggle in the water was in most cases short and not physically painful because of the low temperature—the evidence seems to show that few lost their lives by drowning—is some consolation.

If everyone sees to it that his sympathy with them is so practical as to force him to follow up the question of reforms personally, not leaving it to experts alone, then he will have at any rate done something to atone for the loss of so many valuable lives.

We had now better follow the adventures of those who were rescued from the final event in the disaster. Two accounts—those of Colonel Gracie and Mr. Lightoller—agree very closely. The former went down clinging to a rail, the latter dived before the ship went right under, but was sucked down and held against one of the blowers. They were both carried down for what seemed a long distance, but Mr. Lightoller was finally blown up again by a "terrific gust" that came up the blower and forced him clear. Colonel Gracie came to the surface after holding his breath for what seemed an eternity, and they both swam about holding on to any wreckage they could find. Finally they saw an upturned collapsible boat and climbed on it in company with twenty other men, among them Bride, the Marconi operator. After remaining thus for some hours, with the sea washing them to the waist, they stood up as day broke, in two rows, back to back, balancing themselves as well as they could, and afraid to turn lest the boat should roll over. Finally a lifeboat saw them and took them off, an operation attended with the greatest difficulty, and they reached the *Carpathia* in the early dawn. Not many people have gone through such an experience as those men did, lying all night on an overturned, ill-balanced boat, and praying together, as they did all the time, for the day and a ship to take them off.

Some account must now be attempted of the journey of the fleet of boats to the *Carpathia*, but it must necessarily be very brief. Experiences differed considerably: some had no encounters at all with icebergs, no lack of men to row, discovered lights and food and water, were picked up after only a few hours' exposure, and suffered very little discomfort; others seemed to see icebergs round them all night long and to be always rowing round them; others had so few men aboard—in some cases only two or three—that ladies had to row and in one case to steer, found no lights, food or water, and were adrift many hours, in some cases nearly eight.

The first boat to be picked up by the *Carpathia* was one in charge of Mr. Boxhall. There was only one other man rowing and ladies worked at the oars. A green light burning in this boat all night was the greatest comfort to the rest of us who had nothing to steer by: although it meant little in the way of safety in itself, it was a point to which we could look. The green light was the first intimation Captain Rostron had of our position, and he steered for it and picked up its passengers first.

Mr. Pitman was sent by First Officer Murdock in charge of boat 5, with forty passengers and five of the crew. It would have held more, but no women could be found at the time it was lowered. Mr. Pitman says that after leaving the ship he felt confident she would float and they would all return. A passenger in this boat relates that men could not be induced to embark when she went down, and made appointments for the next morning with him. Tied to boat 5 was boat 7, one of those that contained few people: a few were transferred from number 5, but it would have held many more.

Fifth Officer Lowe was in charge of boat 14, with fifty-five women and children, and some of the crew. So full was the boat that as he went down Mr. Lowe had to fire his revolver along the ship's side to prevent any more climbing in and causing her to buckle. This boat, like boat 13, was difficult to release from the lowering tackle, and had to be cut away after reaching the sea. Mr. Lowe took in charge four other boats, tied them together with lines, found some of them not full, and transferred all his passengers to these, distributing them in the darkness as well as he could. Then returning to the place where the *Titanic* had sunk, he picked up some of those swimming in the water and went back to the four boats. On the way to the *Carpathia* he encountered one of the collapsible boats, and took aboard all those in her, as she seemed to be sinking.

Boat 12 was one of the four tied together, and the seaman in charge testified that he tried to row to the drowning, but with forty women and children and only one other man to row, it was not possible to pull such a heavy boat to the scene of the wreck.

Boat 2 was a small ship's boat and had four or five passengers and seven of the crew.

Boat 4 was one of the last to leave on the port side, and by this time there was such a list that deck chairs had to bridge the gap between the boat and the deck. When lowered, it remained for some time still attached to the ropes, and as the *Titanic* was rapidly sinking it seemed she would be pulled under. The boat was full of women, who besought the sailors to leave the ship, but in obedience to orders from the captain to stand by the cargo port, they remained near; so near, in fact, that they heard china falling and smashing as the ship went down by the head, and were nearly hit by wreckage thrown overboard by some of the officers and crew and intended to serve as rafts. They got clear finally, and were only a short distance away when the ship sank, so that they were able to pull some men aboard as they came to the surface.

This boat had an unpleasant experience in the night with icebergs; many were seen and avoided with difficulty.

Quartermaster Hickens was in charge of boat 6, and in the absence of sailors Major Peuchen was sent to help to man her. They were told to make for the light of the steamer seen on the port side, and followed it until it disappeared. There were forty women and children here.

Boat 8 had only one seaman, and as Captain Smith had enforced the rule of "Women and children only," ladies had to row. Later in the night, when little progress had been made, the seaman took an oar and put a lady in charge of the tiller. This boat again was in the midst of icebergs.

Of the four collapsible boats—although collapsible is not really the correct term, for only a small portion collapses, the canvas edge; "surf boats" is really their name— one was launched at the last moment by being pushed over as the sea rose to the edge of the deck, and was never righted. This is the one twenty men climbed on. Another was caught up by Mr. Lowe and the passengers transferred, with the exception of three men who had perished from the effects of immersion. The boat was allowed to drift away and was found more than a month later by the *Celtic* in just the same condition. It is interesting to note how long this boat had remained afloat after she was supposed to be no longer seaworthy. A curious coincidence arose from the fact that one of my brothers happened to be traveling on the *Celtic*, and looking over the side, saw adrift on the sea a boat belonging to the *Titanic* in which I had been wrecked.

The two other collapsible boats came to the *Carpathia* carrying full loads of passengers: in one, the forward starboard boat and one of the last to leave, was Mr. Ismay. Here four Chinamen were concealed under the feet of the passengers. How they got there no one knew—or indeed how they happened to be on the *Titanic*, for by the immigration laws of the United States they are not allowed to enter her ports.

It must be said, in conclusion, that there is the greatest cause for gratitude that all the boats launched carried their passengers safely to the rescue ship. It would not be right to accept this fact without calling attention to it: it would be easy to enumerate many things which might have been present as elements of danger.

# CHAPTER VII

# THE *CARPATHIA*'S RETURN TO NEW YORK

The journey of the *Carpathia* from the time she caught the "C. Q. D." from the *Titanic* at about 12.30 a. m. on Monday morning and turned swiftly about to her rescue, until she arrived at New York on the following Thursday at 8.30 p. m. was one that demanded of the captain, officers and crew of the vessel the most exact knowledge of navigation, the utmost vigilance in every department both before and after the rescue, and a capacity for organization that must sometimes have been taxed to the breaking point.

The extent to which all these qualities were found present and the manner in which they were exercised stands to the everlasting credit of the Cunard Line and those of its servants who were in charge of the *Carpathia*. Captain Rostron's part in all this is a great one, and wrapped up though his action is in a modesty that is conspicuous in its nobility, it stands out even in his own account as a piece of work well and courageously done.

As soon as the *Titanic* called for help and gave her position, the *Carpathia* was turned and headed north: all hands were called on duty, a new watch of stokers was put on, and the highest speed of which she was capable was demanded of the engineers, with the result that the distance of fifty-eight miles between the two ships was covered in three and a half hours, a speed well beyond her normal capacity. The three doctors on board each took charge of a saloon, in readiness to render help to any who needed their services, the stewards and catering staff were hard at work preparing hot drinks and meals, and the purser's staff ready with blankets and berths for the shipwrecked passengers as soon as they got on board. On deck the sailors got ready lifeboats, swung them out on the davits, and stood by, prepared to lower away their crews if necessary; fixed rope-ladders, cradle-chairs, nooses, and bags for the children at the hatches, to haul the rescued up the side. On the bridge was the captain with his officers, peering into the darkness eagerly to catch the first signs of the crippled *Titanic*, hoping, in spite of her last despairing message of "Sinking by the head," to find her still afloat when her position was reached. A double watch of lookout men was set, for there were other things as well as the *Titanic* to look for that night, and soon they found them. As Captain Rostron said in his evidence, they saw icebergs on either side of them between 2.45 and 4 a. m., passing twenty large ones, one hundred to two hundred feet high, and many smaller ones, and "frequently had to maneuver the ship to avoid them." It was a time when every faculty was called upon for the highest use of which it was capable. With the knowledge before them that the enormous *Titanic*, the supposedly unsinkable ship, had struck ice and was sinking rapidly; with the lookout constantly calling to the bridge, as he must have done, "Icebergs on the starboard," "Icebergs on the port," it required courage and judgment beyond the ordinary to drive the ship ahead through that lane of icebergs and "maneuver round them." As he himself said, he "took the risk of full speed in his desire to save life, and probably some people might blame him for taking such a risk." But the Senate Committee assured him that they, at any rate, would not, and we of the lifeboats have certainly no desire to do so.

The ship was finally stopped at 4 a. m., with an iceberg reported dead ahead (the same no doubt we had to row around in boat 13 as we approached the *Carpathia*), and about the same time the first lifeboat was sighted. Again she had to be maneuvered round the the iceberg to pick up the boat, which was the one in charge of Mr. Boxhall. From him the captain learned that the *Titanic* had gone down, and that he was too late to save any one but those in lifeboats, which he could now see drawing up from every part of the horizon. Meanwhile, the passengers of the *Carpathia*, some of them aroused by the unusual vibration of the screw, some by sailors tramping overhead as they swung away the lifeboats and got ropes and lowering tackle ready, were beginning to come on deck just as day broke; and here an extraordinary sight met their eyes. As far as the eye could reach to the north and west lay an unbroken stretch of field ice, with icebergs still attached to the floe and rearing aloft their mass as a hill might suddenly rise from a level plain. Ahead and to the south and east huge floating monsters were showing up through the waning darkness, their number added to moment by moment as the dawn broke and flushed the horizon pink. It is remarkable how "busy" all those icebergs made the sea look: to have gone to bed with nothing but sea and sky and to come on deck to find so many objects in sight made quite a change in the character of the sea: it looked quite crowded; and a lifeboat alongside and people clambering aboard, mostly women, in nightdresses and dressing-gowns, in cloaks and shawls, in anything but ordinary clothes! Out ahead and on all sides little torches glittered faintly for a few moments and then guttered out—and shouts and cheers floated across the quiet sea. It would be difficult to imagine a more unexpected sight than this that lay before the *Carpathia*'s passengers as they lined the sides that morning in the early dawn.

No novelist would dare to picture such an array of beautiful climatic conditions—the rosy dawn, the morning star, the moon on the horizon, the sea stretching in level beauty to the sky-line—and on this sea to place an ice-field like the Arctic regions and icebergs in numbers everywhere—white and turning pink and deadly cold—and near them, rowing round the icebergs to avoid them, little boats coming suddenly out of mid-ocean, with passengers rescued from the most wonderful ship the world has known. No artist would have conceived such a picture: it would have seemed so highly dramatic as to border on the impossible, and would not have been attempted. Such a combination of events would pass the limit permitted the imagination of both author and artist.

The passengers crowded the rails and looked down at us as we rowed up in the early morning; stood quietly aside while the crew at the gangways below took us aboard, and watched us as if the ship had been in dock and we had rowed up to join her in a somewhat unusual way. Some of them have related that we were very quiet as we came aboard: it is quite true, we were; but so were they. There was very little excitement on either side: just the quiet demeanor of people who are in the presence of something too big as yet to lie within their mental grasp, and which they cannot yet discuss. And so they asked us politely to have hot coffee, which we did; and food, which we generally declined—we were not hungry—and they said very little at first about the lost *Titanic* and our adventures in the night.

Much that is exaggerated and false has been written about the mental condition of passengers as they came aboard: we have been described as being too dazed to understand what was happening, as being too overwhelmed to speak, and as looking before us with "set, staring gaze," "dazed with the shadow of the dread event." That is, no doubt, what most people would expect in the circumstances, but I know it does not give a faithful record of how we did arrive: in fact it is simply not true. As remarked before, the one thing that matters in describing an event of this kind is the exact truth, as near as the fallible human mind can state it; and my own impression of our mental condition is that of supreme gratitude and relief at treading the firm decks of a ship again. I am aware that experiences differed considerably according to the boats occupied; that those who were uncertain of the fate of their relatives and friends had much to make them anxious and troubled; and that it is not possible to look into another person's consciousness and say what is written there; but dealing with mental conditions as far as they are delineated by facial and bodily expressions, I think joy, relief, gratitude were the dominant emotions written on the faces of those who climbed the rope-ladders and were hauled up in cradles.

It must not be forgotten that no one in any one boat knew who were saved in other boats: few knew even how many boats there were and how many passengers could be saved. It was at the time probable that friends would follow them to the *Carpathia*, or be found on other steamers, or even on the pier at which we landed. The hysterical scenes that have been described are imaginative; true, one woman did fill the saloon with hysterical cries immediately after coming aboard, but she could not have known for a certainty that any of her friends were lost: probably the sense of relief after some hours of journeying about the sea was too much for her for a time.

One of the first things we did was to crowd round a steward with a bundle of telegraph forms. He was the bearer of the welcome news that passengers might send Marconigrams to their relatives free of charge, and soon he bore away the first sheaf of hastily scribbled messages to the operator; by the time the last boatload was aboard, the pile must have risen high in the Marconi cabin. We learned afterwards that many of these never reached their destination; and this is not a matter for surprise. There was only one operator—Cottam—on board, and although he was assisted to some extent later, when Bride from the *Titanic* had recovered from his injuries sufficiently to work the apparatus, he had so much to do that he fell asleep over this work on Tuesday night after three days' continuous duty without rest. But we did not know the messages were held back, and imagined our friends were aware of our safety; then, too, a roll-call of the rescued was held in the *Carpathia's* saloon on the Monday, and this was Marconied to land in advance of all messages. It seemed certain, then, that friends at home would have all anxiety removed, but there were mistakes in the official list first telegraphed. The experience of my own friends illustrates this: the Marconigram I wrote never got through to England; nor was my name ever mentioned in any list of the saved (even a week after landing in New York, I saw it in a black-edged "final" list of the missing), and it seemed certain that I had never reached the *Carpathia*; so much so that, as I write, there are before me obituary notices from the English papers giving a short sketch of my life in England. After landing in New York and realizing from the lists of the saved which a reporter showed me that my friends had no news since the *Titanic* sank on Monday morning until that night (Thursday, 9 p. m.), I cabled to England at once (as I had but two shillings rescued from the *Titanic*, the White Star Line paid for the cables), but the messages were not delivered until 8.20 a. m. next morning. At 9 a. m. my friends read in the papers a short account of the disaster which I had supplied to the press, so that they knew of my safety and experiences in the wreck almost at the same time. I am grateful to remember that many of my friends in London refused to count me among the missing during the three days when I was so reported.

There is another side to this record of how the news came through, and a sad one, indeed. Again I wish it were not necessary to tell such things, but since they all bear on the equipment of the trans-Atlantic lines—powerful Marconi apparatus, relays of operators, etc.—it is best they should be told. The name of an American gentleman—the same who sat near me in the library on Sunday afternoon and whom I identified later from a photograph—was consistently reported in the lists as saved and aboard the *Carpathia:* his son journeyed to New York to meet him, rejoicing at his deliverance, and never found him there. When I met his family some days later and was able to give them some details of his life aboard ship, it seemed almost cruel to tell them of the opposite experience that had befallen my friends at home.

Returning to the journey of the *Carpathia*—the last boatload of passengers was taken aboard at 8.30 a. m., the lifeboats were hauled on deck while the collapsibles were abandoned, and the *Carpathia* proceeded to steam round the scene of the wreck in the hope of picking up anyone floating on wreckage. Before doing so the captain arranged in the saloon a service over the spot where the *Titanic* sank, as nearly as could be calculated—a service, as he said, of respect to those who were lost and of gratitude for those who were saved.

She cruised round and round the scene, but found nothing to indicate there was any hope of picking up more passengers; and as the *Californian* had now arrived, followed shortly afterwards by the *Birma*, a Russian tramp steamer, Captain Rostron decided to leave any further search to them and to make all speed with the rescued to land. As we moved round, there was surprisingly little wreckage to be seen: wooden deck-chairs and small pieces of other wood, but nothing of any size. But covering the sea in huge patches was a mass of reddish-yellow "seaweed," as we called it for want of a name. It was said to be cork, but I never heard definitely its correct description.

The problem of where to land us had next to be decided. The *Carpathia* was bound for Gibraltar, and the captain might continue his journey there, landing us at the Azores on the way; but he would require more linen and provisions, the passengers were mostly women and children, ill-clad, disheveled, and in need of many attentions he could not give them. Then, too, he would soon be out of the range of wireless communication, with the weak apparatus his ship had, and he soon decided against that course. Halifax was the nearest in point of distance, but this meant steaming north through the ice, and he thought his passengers did not want to see more ice. He headed back therefore to New York, which he had left the previous Thursday, working all afternoon along the edge of the ice-field which stretched away north as far as the unaided eye could reach. I have wondered since if we could possibly have landed our passengers on this ice-floe from the lifeboats and gone back to pick up those swimming, had we known it was there: I should think it quite feasible to have done so. It was certainly an extraordinary sight to stand on deck and see the sea covered with solid ice, white and dazzling in the sun and dotted here and there with icebergs. We ran close up, only two or three hundred yards away, and steamed parallel to the floe, until it ended towards night and we saw to our infinite satisfaction the last of the icebergs and the field fading away astern. Many of the rescued have no wish ever to see an iceberg again. We learnt afterwards the field was nearly seventy miles long and twelve miles wide, and had lain between us and the *Birma* on her way to the rescue. Mr. Boxhall testified that he had crossed the Grand Banks many times, but had never seen field-ice before. The testimony of the captains and officers of other steamers in the neighborhood is of the same kind: they had "never seen so many icebergs this time of the year," or "never seen such dangerous ice floes and threatening bergs." Undoubtedly the *Titanic* was faced that night with unusual and unexpected conditions of ice: the captain knew not the extent of these conditions, but he knew somewhat of their existence. Alas, that he heeded not their warning!

During the day, the bodies of eight of the crew were committed to the deep: four of them had been taken out of the boats dead and four died during the day. The engines were stopped and all passengers on deck bared their heads while a short service was read; when it was over the ship steamed on again to carry the living back to land.

The passengers on the *Carpathia* were by now hard at work finding clothing for the survivors: the barber's shop was raided for ties. collars, hair-pins, combs, etc., of which it happened there was a large stock in hand; one good Samaritan went round the ship with a box of tooth-brushes offering them indiscriminately to all. In some cases, clothing could not be found for the ladies and they spent the rest of the time on board in their dressing-gowns and cloaks in which they came away from the *Titanic*. They even slept in them, for, in the absence of berths, women had to sleep on the floor of the saloons and in the library each night on straw *paillasses*, and here it was not possible to undress properly. The men were given the smoking-room floor and a supply of blankets, but the room was small, and some elected to sleep out on deck. I found a pile of towels on the bathroom floor ready for next morning's baths, and made up a very comfortable bed on these. Later I was waked in the middle of the night by a man offering me a berth in his four-berth cabin: another occupant was unable to leave his berth for physical reasons, and so the cabin could not be given up to ladies.

On Tuesday the survivors met in the saloon and formed a committee among themselves to collect subscriptions for a general fund, out of which it was resolved by vote to provide as far as possible for the destitute among the steerage passengers, to present a loving cup to Captain Rostron and medals to the officers and crew of the *Carpathia*, and to divide any surplus among the crew of the *Titanic*. The work of this committee is not yet (June 1st) at an end, but all the resolutions except the last one have been acted upon, and that is now receiving the attention of the committee. The presentations to the captain and crew were made the day the *Carpathia* returned to New York from her Mediterranean trip, and it is a pleasure to all the survivors to know that the United States Senate has recognized the service rendered to humanity by the *Carpathia* and has voted Captain Rostron a gold medal commemorative of the rescue. On the afternoon of Tuesday, I visited the steerage in company with a fellow-passenger, to take down the names of all who were saved. We grouped them into nationalities—English, Irish, and Swedish mostly—and learnt from them their names and homes, the amount of money they possessed, and whether they had friends in America. The Irish girls almost universally had no money rescued from the wreck, and were going to friends in New York or places near, while the Swedish passengers, among whom were a considerable number of men, had saved the greater part of their money and in addition had railway tickets through to their destinations inland. The saving of their money marked a curious racial difference, for which I can offer no explanation: no doubt the Irish girls never had very much but they must have had the necessary amount fixed by the immigration laws. There were some pitiful cases of women with children and the husband lost; some with one or two children saved and the others lost; in one case, a whole family was missing, and only a friend left to tell of them. Among the Irish group was one girl of really remarkable beauty, black hair and deep violet eyes with long lashes, and perfectly shaped features, and quite young, not more than eighteen or twenty; I think she lost no relatives on the *Titanic*.

The following letter to the London *Times* is reproduced here to show something of what our feeling was on board the *Carpathia* towards the loss of the *Titanic*. It was written soon after we had the definite information on the Wednesday that ice warnings had been sent to the *Titanic*, and when we all felt that something must be done to awaken public opinion to safeguard ocean travel in the future. We were not aware, of course, how much the outside world knew, and it seemed well to do something to inform the English public of what had happened at as early an opportunity as possible. I have not had occasion to change any of the opinions expressed in this letter.

SIR:—

As one of few surviving Englishmen from the steamship *Titanic*, which sank in mid-Atlantic on Monday morning last, I am asking you to lay before your readers a few facts concerning the disaster, in the hope that something may be done in the near future to ensure the safety of that portion of the traveling public who use the Atlantic highway for business or pleasure.

I wish to dissociate myself entirely from any report that would seek to fix the responsibility on any person or persons or body of people, and by simply calling attention to matters of fact the authenticity of which is, I think, beyond question and can be established in any Court of Inquiry, to allow your readers to draw their own conclusions as to the responsibility for the collision.

First, that it was known to those in charge of the *Titanic* that we were in the iceberg region; that the atmospheric and temperature conditions suggested the near presence of icebergs; that a wireless message was received from a ship ahead of us warning us that they had been seen in the locality of which latitude and longitude were given.

Second, that at the time of the collision the *Titanic* was running at a high rate of speed.

Third, that the accommodation for saving passengers and crew was totally inadequate, being sufficient only for a total of about 950. This gave, with the highest possible complement of 3,400, a less than one in three chance of being saved in the case of accident.

Fourth, that the number landed in the *Carpathia*, approximately 700, is a high percentage of the possible 950, and bears excellent testimony to the courage, resource, and devotion to duty of the officers and crew of the vessel; many instances of their nobility and personal self-sacrifice are within our possession, and we know that they did all they could do with the means at their disposal.

Fifth, that the practise of running mail and passenger vessels through fog and iceberg regions at a high speed is a common one; they are timed to run almost as an express train is run, and they cannot, therefore, slow down more than a few knots in time of possible danger.

I have neither knowledge nor experience to say what remedies I consider should be applied; but, perhaps, the following suggestions may serve as a help:—

First, that no vessel should be allowed to leave a British port without sufficient boat and other accommodation to allow each passenger and member of the crew a seat; and that at the time of booking this fact should be pointed out to a passenger, and the number of the seat in the particular boat allotted to him then.

Second, that as soon as is practicable after sailing each passenger should go through boat drill in company with the crew assigned to his boat.

Third, that each passenger boat engaged in the Transatlantic service should be instructed to slow down to a few knots when in the iceberg region, and should be fitted with an efficient searchlight.

Yours faithfully,<br>LAWRENCE BEESLEY.

It seemed well, too, while on the *Carpathia* to prepare as accurate an account as possible of the disaster and to have this ready for the press, in order to calm public opinion and to forestall the incorrect and hysterical accounts which some American reporters are in the habit of preparing on occasions of this kind. The first impression is often the most permanent, and in a disaster of this magnitude, where exact and accurate information is so necessary, preparation of a report was essential. It was written in odd corners of the deck and saloon of the *Carpathia*, and fell, it seemed very happily, into the hands of the one reporter who could best deal with it, the Associated Press. I understand it was the first report that came through and had a good deal of the effect intended.

The *Carpathia* returned to New York in almost every kind of climatic conditions: icebergs, ice-fields and bitter cold to commence with; brilliant warm sun, thunder and lightning in the middle of one night (and so closely did the peal follow the flash that women in the saloon leaped up in alarm saying rockets were being sent up again); cold winds most of the time; fogs every morning and during a good part of one day, with the foghorn blowing constantly; rain; choppy sea with the spray blowing overboard and coming in through the saloon windows; we said we had almost everything but hot weather and stormy seas. So that when we were told that Nantucket Lightship had been sighted on Thursday morning from the bridge, a great sigh of relief went round to think New York and land would be reached before next morning.

There is no doubt that a good many felt the waiting period of those four days very trying: the ship crowded far beyond its limits of comfort, the want of necessities of clothing and toilet, and above all the anticipation of meeting with relatives on the pier, with, in many cases, the knowledge that other friends were left behind and would not return home again. A few looked forward to meeting on the pier their friends to whom they had said *au revoir* on the *Titanic*'s deck, brought there by a faster boat, they said, or at any rate to hear that they were following behind us in another boat: a very few, indeed, for the thought of the icy water and the many hours' immersion seemed to weigh against such a possibility; but we encouraged them to hope the *Californian* and the *Birma* had picked some up; stranger things have happened, and we had all been through strange experiences. But in the midst of this rather tense feeling, one fact stands out as remarkable—no one was ill. Captain Rostron testified that on Tuesday the doctor reported a clean bill of health, except for frost-bites and shaken nerves. There were none of the illnesses supposed to follow from exposure for hours in the cold night—and, it must be remembered, a considerable number swam about for some time when the *Titanic* sank, and then either sat for hours in their wet things or lay flat on an upturned boat with the sea water washing partly over them until they were taken off in a lifeboat; no scenes of women weeping and brooding over their losses hour by hour until they were driven mad with grief—yet all this has been reported to the press by people on board the *Carpathia*. These women met their sorrow with the sublimest courage, came on deck and talked with their fellow-men and women face to face, and in the midst of their loss did not forget to rejoice with those who had joined their friends on the *Carpathia*'s deck or come with them in a boat. There was no need for those ashore to call the *Carpathia* a "death-ship," or to send coroners and coffins to the pier to meet her: her passengers were generally in good health and they did not pretend they were not.

Presently land came in sight, and very good it was to see it again: it was eight days since we left Southampton, but the time seemed to have "stretched out to the crack of doom," and to have become eight weeks instead. So many dramatic incidents had been crowded into the last few days that the first four peaceful, uneventful days, marked by nothing that seared the memory, had faded almost out of recollection. It needed an effort to return to Southampton, Cherbourg and Queenstown, as though returning to some event of last year. I think we all realized that time may be measured more by events than by seconds and minutes: what the astronomer would call "2.20 a. m. April 15th, 1912," the survivors called "the sinking of the *Titanic*"; the "hours" that followed were designated "being adrift in an open sea," and "4.30 a. m." was "being rescued by the *Carpathia*." The clock was a mental one, and the hours, minutes and seconds marked deeply on its face were emotions, strong and silent.

Surrounded by tugs of every kind, from which (as well as from every available building near the river) magnesium bombs were shot off by photographers, while reporters shouted for news of the disaster and photographs of passengers, the *Carpathia* drew slowly to her station at the Cunard pier, the gangways were pushed across, and we set foot at last on American soil, very thankful, grateful people.

The mental and physical condition of the rescued as they came ashore has, here again, been greatly exaggerated—one description says we were "half-fainting, half-hysterical, bordering on hallucination, only now beginning to realize the horror." It is unfortunate such pictures should be presented to the world. There were some painful scenes of meeting between relatives of those who were lost, but once again women showed their self-control and went through the ordeal in most cases with extraordinary calm. It is well to record that the same account added: "A few, strangely enough, are calm and lucid"; if for "few" we read "a large majority," it will be much nearer the true description of the landing on the Cunard pier in New York. There seems to be no adequate reason why a report of such a scene should depict mainly the sorrow and grief, should seek for every detail to satisfy the horrible and the morbid in the human mind. The first questions the excited crowds of reporters asked as they crowded round were whether it was true that officers shot passengers, and then themselves; whether passengers shot each other; whether any scenes of horror had been noticed, and what they were.

It would have been well to have noticed the wonderful state of health of most of the rescued, their gratitude for their deliverance, the thousand and one things that gave cause for rejoicing. In the midst of so much description of the hysterical side of the scene, place should be found for the normal—and I venture to think the normal was the dominant feature in the landing that night. In the last chapter I shall try to record the persistence of the normal all through the disaster. Nothing has been a greater surprise than to find people that do not act in conditions of danger and grief as they would be generally supposed to act—and, I must add, as they are generally described as acting.

And so, with her work of rescue well done, the good ship *Carpathia* returned to New York. Everyone who came in her, everyone on the dock, and everyone who heard of her journey will agree with Captain Rostron when he says: "I thank God that I was within wireless hailing distance, and that I got there in time to pick up the survivors of the wreck."

CHAPTER VIII

# THE LESSONS TAUGHT BY THE
# LOSS OF THE *TITANIC*

One of the most pitiful things in the relations of human beings to each other—the action and reaction of events that is called concretely "human life"—is that every now and then some of them should be called upon to lay down their lives from no sense of imperative, calculated duty such as inspires the soldier or the sailor, but suddenly, without any previous knowledge or warning of danger, without any opportunity of escape, and without any desire to risk such conditions of danger of their own free will. It is a blot on our civilization that these things are necessary from time to time, to arouse those responsible for the safety of human life from the lethargic selfishness which has governed them. The *Titanic*'s two-thousand-odd passengers went aboard thinking they were on an absolutely safe ship, and all the time there were many people—designers, builders, experts, government officials—who knew there were insufficient boats on board, that the *Titanic* had no right to go fast in iceberg regions—who knew these things and took no steps and enacted no laws to prevent their happening. Not that they omitted to do these things deliberately, but were lulled into a state of selfish inaction from which it needed such a tragedy as this to arouse them. It was a cruel necessity which demanded that a few should die to arouse many millions to a sense of their own insecurity, to the fact that for years the possibility of such a disaster has been imminent. Passengers have known none of these things, and while no good end would have been served by relating to them needless tales of danger on the high seas, one thing is certain—that, had they known them, many would not have traveled in such conditions and thereby safeguards would soon have been forced on the builders, the companies, and the Government. But there were people who knew and did not fail to call attention to the dangers: in the House of Commons the matter has been frequently brought up privately, and an American naval officer, Captain E. K. Roden, in an article that has since been widely reproduced, called attention to the defects of this very ship, the *Titanic*—taking her as an example of all other liners—and pointed out that she was not unsinkable and had not proper boat accommodation.

The question, then, of responsibility for the loss of the *Titanic* must be considered: not from any idea that blame should be laid here or there and a scapegoat provided—that is a waste of time. But if a fixing of responsibility leads to quick and efficient remedy, then it should be done relentlessly: our simple duty to those whom the *Titanic* carried down with her demands no less. Dealing first with the precautions for the safety of the ship as apart from safety appliances, there can be no question, I suppose, that the direct responsibility for the loss of the *Titanic* and so many lives must be laid on her captain. He was responsible for setting the course, day by day and hour by hour, for the speed she was traveling; and he alone would have the power to decide whether or not speed must be slackened with icebergs ahead. No officer would have any right to interfere in the navigation, although they would no doubt be consulted. Nor would any official connected with the management of the line—Mr. Ismay, for example—be allowed to direct the captain in these matters, and there is no evidence that he ever tried to do so. The very fact that the captain of a ship has such absolute authority increases his responsibility enormously. Even supposing the White Star Line and Mr. Ismay had urged him before sailing to make a record, —again an assumption—they cannot be held directly responsible for the collision: he was in charge of the lives of everyone on board and no one but he was supposed to estimate the risk of traveling at the speed he did, when ice was reported ahead of him. His action cannot be justified on the ground of prudent seamanship.

But the question of indirect responsibility raises at once many issues and, I think, removes from Captain Smith a good deal of personal responsibility for the loss of his ship. Some of these issues it will be well to consider.

In the first place, disabusing our minds again of the knowledge that the *Titanic* struck an iceberg and sank, let us estimate the probabilities of such a thing happening. An iceberg is small and occupies little room by comparison with the broad ocean on which it floats; and the chances of another small object like a ship colliding with it and being sunk are very small: the chances are, as a matter of fact, one in a million. This is not a figure of speech: that is the actual risk for total loss by collision with an iceberg as accepted by insurance companies. The one-in-a-million accident was what sunk the *Titanic*.

Even so, had Captain Smith been alone in taking that risk, he would have had to bear all the blame for the resulting disaster. But it seems he is not alone: the same risk has been taken over and over again by fast mail-passenger liners, in fog and in iceberg regions. Their captains have taken the long—very long—chance many times and won every time; he took it as he had done many times before, and lost. Of course, the chances that night of striking an iceberg were much greater than one in a million: they had been enormously increased by the extreme southerly position of icebergs and field ice and by the unusual number of the former. Thinking over the scene that met our eyes from the deck of the *Carpathia* after we boarded her—the great number of icebergs wherever the eye could reach—the chances of *not* hitting one in the darkness of the night seemed small. Indeed, the more one thinks about the *Carpathia* coming at full speed through all those icebergs in the darkness, the more inexplicable does it seem. True, the captain had an extra lookout watch and every sense of every man on the bridge alert to detect the least sign of danger, and again he was not going so fast as the *Titanic* and would have his ship under more control; but granted all that, he appears to have taken a great risk as he dogged and twisted round the awful two-hundred-foot monsters in the dark night. Does it mean that the risk is not so great as we who have seen the abnormal and not the normal side of taking risks with icebergs might suppose? He had his own ship and passengers to consider, and he had no right to take too great a risk.

But Captain Smith could not know icebergs were there in such numbers: what warnings he had of them is not yet thoroughly established—there were probably three—but it is in the highest degree unlikely that he knew that any vessel had seen them in such quantities as we saw them Monday morning; in fact, it is unthinkable. He thought, no doubt, he was taking an ordinary risk, and it turned out to be an extraordinary one. To read some criticisms it would seem as if he deliberately ran his ship in defiance of all custom through a region infested with icebergs, and did a thing which no one has ever done before; that he outraged all precedent by not slowing down. But it is plain that he did not. Every captain who has run full speed through fog and iceberg regions is to blame for the disaster as much as he is: they got through and he did not. Other liners can go faster than the *Titanic* could possibly do; had they struck ice they would have been injured even more deeply than she was, for it must not be forgotten that the force of impact varies as the *square* of the velocity—i. e., it is four times as much at sixteen knots as at eight knots, nine times as much at twenty-four, and so on. And with not much margin of time left for these fast boats, they must go full speed ahead nearly all the time. Remember how they advertise to "Leave New York Wednesday, dine in London the following Monday "—and it is done regularly, much as an express train is run to time. Their officers, too, would have been less able to avoid a collision than Murdock of the *Titanic* was, for at the greater speed, they would be on the iceberg in shorter time. Many passengers can tell of crossing with fog a good deal of the way, sometimes almost all the way, and they have been only a few hours late at the end of the journey.

So that it is the custom that is at fault, not one particular captain. Custom is established largely by demand, and supply too is the answer to demand. What the public demanded the White Star Line supplied, and so both the public and the Line are concerned with the question of indirect responsibility.

The public has demanded, more and more every year, greater speed as well as greater comfort, and by ceasing to patronize the low-speed boats has gradually forced the pace to what it is at present. Not that speed in itself is a dangerous thing—it is sometimes much safer to go quickly than slowly—but that, given the facilities for speed and the stimulus exerted by the constant public demand for it, occasions arise when the judgment of those in command of a ship becomes swayed— largely unconsciously, no doubt—in favor of taking risks which the smaller liners would never take. The demand on the skipper of a boat like the *Californian*, for example, which lay hove-to nineteen miles away with her engines stopped, is infinitesimal compared with that on Captain Smith. An old traveler told me on the *Carpathia* that he has often grumbled to the officers for what he called absurd precautions in lying to and wasting his time, which he regarded as very valuable; but after hearing of the *Titanic*'s loss he recognized that he was to some extent responsible for the speed at which she had traveled, and would never be so again. He had been one of the traveling public who had constantly demanded to be taken to his journey's end in the shortest possible time, and had "made a row" about it if he was likely to be late. There are some business men to whom the five or six days on board are exceedingly irksome and represent a waste of time; even an hour saved at the journey's end is a consideration to them. And if the demand is not always a conscious one, it is there as an unconscious factor always urging the highest speed of which the ship is capable. The man who demands fast travel unreasonably must undoubtedly take his share in the responsibility. He asks to be taken over at a speed which will land him in something over four days; he forgets perhaps that Columbus took ninety days in a forty-ton boat, and that only fifty years ago paddle steamers took six weeks, and all the time the demand is greater and the strain is more: the public demand speed and luxury; the lines supply it, until presently the safety limit is reached, the undue risk is taken—and the *Titanic* goes down. All of us who have cried for greater speed must take our share in the responsibility. The expression of such a desire and the discontent with so-called slow travel are the seed sown in the minds of men, to bear fruit presently in an insistence on greater speed. We may not have done so directly, but we may perhaps have talked about it and thought about it, and we know no action begins without thought.

The White Star Line has received very rough handling from some of the press, but the greater part of this criticism seems to be unwarranted and to arise from the desire to find a scapegoat. After all they had made better provision for the passengers the *Titanic* carried than any other line has done, for they had built what they believed to be a huge life-boat, unsinkable in all ordinary conditions. Those who embarked in her were almost certainly in the safest ship (along with the *Olympic*) afloat: she was probably quite immune from the ordinary effects of wind, waves and collisions at sea, and needed to fear nothing but running on a rock or, what was worse, a floating iceberg; for the effects of collision were, so far as damage was concerned, the same as if it had been a rock, and the danger greater, for one is charted and the other is not. Then, too, while the theory of the unsinkable boat has been destroyed at the same time as the boat itself, we should not forget that it served a useful purpose on deck that night—it eliminated largely the possibility of panic, and those rushes for the boats which might have swamped some of them. I do not wish for a moment to suggest that such things would have happened, because the more information that comes to hand of the conduct of the people on board, the more wonderful seems the complete self-control of all, even when the last boats had gone and nothing but the rising waters met their eyes—only that the generally entertained theory rendered such things less probable. The theory, indeed, was really a safeguard, though built on a false premise.

There is no evidence that the White Star Line instructed the captain to push the boat or to make any records: the probabilities are that no such attempt would be made on the first trip. The general instructions to their commanders bear quite the other interpretation: it will be well to quote them in full as issued to the press during the sittings of the United States Senate Committee.

### Instructions to commanders

Commanders must distinctly understand that the issue of regulations does not in any way relieve them from responsibility for the safe and efficient navigation of their respective vessels, and they are also en-joined to remember that they must run no risks which might by any possibility result in accident to their ships. It is to be hoped that they will ever bear in mind that the safety of the lives and property entrusted to their care is the ruling principle that should govern them in the navigation of their vessels, and that no supposed gain in expedition or saving of time on the voyage is to be purchased at the risk of accident.

Commanders are reminded that the steamers are to a great extent uninsured, and that their own livelihood, as well as the company's success, depends upon immunity from accident; no precaution which ensures safe navigation is to be considered excessive.

Nothing could be plainer than these instructions, and had they been obeyed, the disaster would never have happened: they warn commanders against the only thing left as a menace to their unsinkable boat—the lack of "precaution which ensures safe navigation."

In addition, the White Star Line had complied to the full extent with the requirements of the British Government: their ship had been subjected to an inspection so rigid that, as one officer remarked in evidence, it became a nuisance. The Board of Trade employs the best experts, and knows the dangers that attend ocean travel and the precautions that should be taken by every commander. If these precautions are not taken, it will be necessary to legislate until they are. No motorist is allowed to career at full speed along a public highway in dangerous conditions, and it should be an offence for a captain to do the same on the high seas with a ship full of unsuspecting passengers. They have entrusted their lives to the government of their country—through its regulations—and they are entitled to the same protection in mid-Atlantic as they are in Oxford Street or Broadway. The open sea should no longer be regarded as a neutral zone where no country's police laws are operative.

Of course there are difficulties in the way of drafting international regulations: many governments would have to be consulted and many difficulties that seem insuperable overcome; but that is the purpose for which governments are employed, that is why experts and ministers of governments are appointed and paid—to overcome difficulties for the people who appoint them and who expect them, among other things, to protect their lives.

The American Government must share the same responsibility: it is useless to attempt to fix it on the British Board of Trade for the reason that the boats were built in England and inspected there by British officials. They carried American citizens largely, and entered American ports. It would have been the simplest matter for the United States Government to veto the entry of any ship which did not conform to its laws of regulating speed in conditions of fog and icebergs—had they provided such laws. The fact is that the American nation has practically no mercantile marine, and in time of a disaster such as this it forgets, perhaps, that it has exactly the same right—and therefore the same responsibility—as the British Government to inspect, and to legislate: the right that is easily enforced by refusal to allow entry. The regulation of speed in dangerous regions could well be undertaken by some fleet of international police patrol vessels, with power to stop if necessary any boat found guilty of reckless racing. The additional duty of warning ships of the exact locality of icebergs could be performed by these boats. It would not of course be possible or advisable to fix a "speed limit," because the region of icebergs varies in position as the icebergs float south, varies in point of danger as they melt and disappear, and the whole question has to be left largely to the judgment of the captain on the spot; but it would be possible to make it an offence against the law to go beyond a certain speed in known conditions of danger.

So much for the question of regulating speed on the high seas. The secondary question of safety appliances is governed by the same principle—that, in the last analysis, it is not the captain, not the passenger, not the builders and owners, but the governments through their experts, who are to be held responsible for the provision of life-saving devices. Morally, of course, the owners and builders are responsible, but at present moral responsibility is too weak an incentive in human affairs—that is the miserable part of the whole wretched business—to induce owners generally to make every possible provision for the lives of those in their charge; to place human safety so far above every other consideration that no plan shall be left unconsidered, no device left untested, by which passengers can escape from a sinking ship. But it is not correct to say, as has been said frequently, that it is greed and dividend-hunting that have characterized the policy of the steamship companies in their failure to provide safety appliances: these things in themselves are not expensive. They have vied with each other in making their lines attractive in point of speed, size and comfort, and they have been quite justified in doing so: such things are the product of ordinary competition between commercial houses.

Where they have all failed morally is to extend to their passengers the consideration that places their lives as of more interest to them than any other conceivable thing. They are not alone in this: thousands of other people have done the same thing and would do it to-day—in factories, in workshops, in mines, did not the government intervene and insist on safety precautions. The thing is a defect in human life of to-day— thoughtlessness for the well-being of our fellow-men; and we are all guilty of it in some degree. It is folly for the public to rise up now and condemn the steamship companies: their failing is the common failing of the immorality of indifference.

The remedy is the law, and it is the only remedy at present that will really accomplish anything. The British law on the subject dates from 1894, and requires only twenty boats for a ship the size of the *Titanic*: the owners and builders have obeyed this law and fulfilled their legal responsibility. Increase this responsibility and they will fulfil it again—and the matter is ended so far as appliances are concerned. It should perhaps be mentioned that in a period of ten years only nine passengers were lost on British ships: the law seemed to be sufficient in fact.

The position of the American Government, however, is worse than that of the British Government. Its regulations require more than double the boat accommodation which the British regulations do, and yet it has allowed hundreds of thousands of its subjects to enter its ports on boats that defied its own laws. Had their government not been guilty of the same indifference, passengers would not have been allowed aboard any British ship lacking in boat-accommodation—the simple expedient again of refusing entry. The reply of the British Government to the Senate Committee, accusing the Board of Trade of "insufficient requirements and lax inspection," might well be—" Ye have a law: see to it yourselves!"

It will be well now to consider briefly the various appliances that have been suggested to ensure the safety of passengers and crew, and in doing so it may be remembered that the average man and woman has the same right as the expert to consider and discuss these things: they are not so technical as to prevent anyone of ordinary intelligence from understanding their construction. Using the term in its widest sense, we come first to:—

### Bulkheads and water-tight compartments

It is impossible to attempt a discussion here of the exact constructional details of these parts of a ship; but in order to illustrate briefly what is the purpose of having bulkheads, we may take the *Titanic* as an example. She was divided into sixteen compartments by fifteen transverse steel walls called bulkheads.[1] If a hole is made in the side of the ship in any one compartment, steel water-tight doors seal off the only openings in that compartment and separate it as a damaged unit from the rest of the ship and the vessel is brought to land in safety. Ships have even put into the nearest port for inspection after collision, and finding only one compartment full of water and no other damage, have left again for their home port without troubling to disembark passengers and effect repairs.

The design of the *Titanic*'s bulkheads calls for some attention. The

[1] See Figs. 1 and 2, p. 47.

White Star Line publicity stressed the watertight compartments of the *Titanic,* which were sealed off by double-cylinder doors like the one above. According to company claims, the doors could be closed instantly from the Captain's bridge, or shut automatically if the deck below flooded.

Newly invented Welin davits were designed to handle three times as many lifeboats as the *Titanic* carried. After the collision, however, the crew did not know how to handle them, and much time was lost.

*Scientific American*, in an excellent article on the comparative safety of the *Titanic*'s and other types of water-tight compartments, draws attention to the following weaknesses in the former—from the point of view of possible collision with an iceberg. She had no longitudinal bulkheads, which would subdivide her into smaller compartments and prevent the water filling the whole of a large compartment. Probably, too, the length of a large compartment was in any case too great—fifty-three feet.

The *Mauretania*, on the other hand, in addition to transverse bulkheads, is fitted with longitudinal torpedo bulkheads, and the space between them and the side of the ship is utilized as a coal bunker. Then, too, in the *Mauretania* all bulkheads are carried up to the top deck, whereas in the case of the *Titanic* they reached in some parts only to the saloon deck and in others to a lower deck still—the weakness of this being that, when the water reached to the top of a bulkhead as the ship sank by the head, it flowed over and filled the next compartment. The British Admiralty, which subsidizes the *Mauretania* and *Lusitania* as fast cruisers in time of war, insisted on this type of construction, and it is considered vastly better than that used in the *Titanic*. The writer of the article thinks it possible that these ships might not have sunk as the result of a similar collision. But the ideal ship from the point of bulkhead construction, he considers to have been the *Great Eastern*, constructed many years ago by the famous engineer Brunel. So thorough was her system of compartments divided and subdivided by many transverse and longitudinal bulkheads that when she tore a hole eighty feet long in her side by striking a rock, she reached port in safety. Unfortunately the weight and cost of this method was so great that his plan was subsequently abandoned.

But it would not be just to say that the construction of the *Titanic* was a serious mistake on the part of the White Star Line or her builders, on the ground that her bulkheads were not so well constructed as those of the *Lusitania* and *Mauretania*, which were built to fulfil British Admiralty regulations for time of war—an extraordinary risk which no builder of a passenger steamer—as such—would be expected to take into consideration when designing the vessel. It should be constantly borne in mind that the *Titanic* met extraordinary conditions on the night of the collision: she was probably the safest ship afloat in all ordinary conditions. Collision with an iceberg is not an ordinary risk; but this disaster will probably result in altering the whole construction of bulkheads and compartments to the *Great Eastern* type, in order to include the one-in-a-million risk of iceberg collision and loss.

Here comes in the question of increased cost of construction, and in addition the great loss of cargo-carrying space with decreased earning capacity, both of which will mean an increase in the passenger rates. This the traveling public will have to face and undoubtedly will be willing to face for the satisfaction of knowing that what was so confidently affirmed by passengers on the *Titanic's* deck that night of the collision will then be really true—that "we are on an unsinkable boat"—so far as human forethought can devise. After all, this *must* be the solution to the problem how best to ensure safety at sea. Other safety appliances are useful and necessary, but not useable in certain conditions of weather. The ship itself must always be the "safety appliance" that is really trustworthy, and nothing must be left undone to ensure this.

### Wireless apparatus and operators

The range of the apparatus might well be extended, but the principal defect is the lack of an operator for night duty on some ships. The awful fact that the *Californian* lay a few miles away, able to save every soul on board, and could not catch the message because the operator was asleep, seems too cruel to dwell upon. Even on the *Carpathia*, the operator was on the point of retiring when the message arrived, and we should have been much longer afloat—and some boats possibly swamped—had he not caught the message when he did. It has been suggested that officers should have a working knowledge of wireless telegraphy, and this is no doubt a wise provision. It would enable them to supervise the work of the operators more closely and from all the evidence, this seems a necessity. The exchange of vitally important messages between a sinking ship and those rushing to her rescue should be under the control of an experienced officer. To take but one example— Bride testified that after giving the *Birma* the "C. Q. D." message and the position (incidentally Signor Marconi has stated that this has been abandoned in favour of "S. O. S.") and getting a reply, they got into touch with the *Carpathia*, and while talking with her were interrupted by the *Birma* asking what was the matter. No doubt it was the duty of the *Birma* to come at once without asking any questions, but the reply from the *Titanic*, telling the *Birma's* operator not to be a "fool" by interrupting, seems to have been a needless waste of precious moments: to reply, "We are sinking" would have taken no longer, especially when in their own estimation of the strength of the signals they thought the *Birma* was the nearer ship. It is well to notice that some large liners have already a staff of three operators.

### Submarine signaling apparatus

There are occasions when wireless apparatus is useless as a means of saving life at sea promptly.

One of its weaknesses is that when the ships' engines are stopped, messages can no longer be sent out, that is, with the system at present adopted. It will be remembered that the *Titanic*'s messages got gradually fainter and then ceased altogether as she came to rest with her engines shut down.

Again, in fogs—and most accidents occur in fogs—while wireless informs of the accident, it does not enable one ship to locate another closely enough to take off her passengers at once. There is as yet no method known by which wireless telegraphy will fix the direction of a message; and after a ship has been in fog for any considerable length of time it is more difficult to give the exact position to another vessel bringing help.

Nothing could illustrate these two points better than the story of how the *Baltic* found the *Republic* in the year 1909, in a dense fog off Nantucket Lightship, when the latter was drifting helplessly after collision with the *Florida*. The *Baltic* received a wireless message stating the *Republic*'s condition and the information that she was in touch with Nantucket through a submarine bell which she could hear ringing. The *Baltic* turned and went towards the position in the fog, picked up the submarine bell-signal from Nantucket, and then began searching near this position for the *Republic*. It took her twelve hours to find the damaged ship, zigzagging across a circle within which she thought the *Republic* might lie. In a rough sea it is doubtful whether the *Republic* would have remained afloat long enough for the *Baltic* to find her and take off all her passengers.

Now on these two occasions when wireless telegraphy was found to be unreliable, the usefulness of the submarine bell at once becomes apparent. The *Baltic* could have gone unerringly to the *Republic* in the dense fog had the latter been fitted with a submarine emergency bell. It will perhaps be well to spend a little time describing the submarine signaling apparatus to see how this result could have been obtained: twelve anxious hours in a dense fog on a ship which was injured so badly that she subsequently foundered, is an experience which every appliance known to human invention should be enlisted to prevent.

Submarine signaling has never received that public notice which wireless telegraphy has, for the reason that it does not appeal so readily to the popular mind. That it is an absolute necessity to every ship carrying passengers—or carrying anything, for that matter—is beyond question. It is an additional safeguard that no ship can afford to be without.

There are many occasions when the atmosphere fails lamentably as a medium for carrying messages. When fog falls down, as it does sometimes in a moment, on the hundreds of ships coasting down the traffic ways round our shores—ways which are defined so easily in clear weather and with such difficulty in fogs—the hundreds of lighthouses and lightships which serve as warning beacons, and on which many millions of money have been spent, are for all practical purposes as useless to the navigator as if they had never been built: he is just as helpless as if he were back in the years before 1514, when Trinity House was granted a charter by Henry VIII "for the relief . . . of the shipping of this realm of England," and began a system of lights on the shores, of which the present chain of lighthouses and lightships is the outcome.

Nor is the foghorn much better: the presence of different layers of fog and air, and their varying densities, which cause both reflection and refraction of sound, prevent the air from being a reliable medium for carrying it. Now, submarine signaling has none of these defects, for the medium is water, subject to no such variable conditions as the air. Its density is practically non variable, and sound travels through it at the rate of 4,400 feet per second, without deviation or reflection.

The apparatus consists of a bell designed to ring either pneumatically from a lightship, electrically from the shore (the bell itself being a tripod at the bottom of the sea), automatically from a floating bell-buoy, or by hand from a ship or boat. The sound travels from the bell in every direction, like waves in a pond, and falls, it may be, on the side of a ship. The receiving apparatus is fixed inside the skin of the ship and consists of a small iron tank, 16 inches square and 18 inches deep. The front of the tank facing the ship's iron skin is missing and the tank, being filled with water, is bolted to the framework and sealed firmly to the ship's side by rubber facing. In this way a portion of the ship's iron hull is washed by the sea on one side and water in the tank on the other. Vibrations from a bell ringing at a distance fall on the iron side, travel through, and strike on two microphones hanging in the tank. These microphones transmit the sound along wires to the chart room, where telephones convey the message to the officer on duty.

There are two of these tanks or "receivers" fitted against the ship's side, one on the port and one on the starboard side, near the bows, and as far down below the water level as is possible. The direction of sounds coming to the microphones hanging in these tanks can be estimated by switching alternately to the port and starboard tanks. If the sound is of greater intensity on the port side, then the bell signaling is off the port bows; and similarly on the starboard side.

The ship is turned towards the sound until the same volume of sound is heard from both receivers, when the bell is known to be dead ahead. So accurate is this in practise that a trained operator can steer his ship in the densest fog directly to a lightship or any other point where a sub-marine bell is sending its warning beneath the sea. It must be repeated that the medium in which these signals are transmitted is a constant one, not subject to any of the limitations and variations imposed on the atmosphere and the ether as media for the transmission of light, blasts of a foghorn, and wireless vibrations. At present the chief use of submarine signaling is from the shore or a lightship to ships at sea, and not from ship to ship or from ship to the shore: in other words ships carry only receiving apparatus, and lighthouses and lightships use only signaling apparatus. Some of the lighthouses and lightships on our coasts already have these submarine bells in addition to their lights, and in bad weather the bells send out their messages to warn ships of their proximity to a danger point. This invention enables ships to pick up the sound of bell after bell on a coast and run along it in the densest fog almost as well as in daylight; passenger steamers coming into port do not have to wander about in the fog, groping their way blindly into harbor. By having a code of rings, and judging by the intensity of the sound, it is possible to tell almost exactly where a ship is in relation to the coast or to some lightship. The British Admiralty report in 1906 said: "If the lightships round the coast were fitted with submarine bells, it would be possible for ships fitted with receiving apparatus to navigate in fog with almost as great certainty as in clear weather." And the following remark of a captain engaged in coast service is instructive. He had been asked to cut down expenses by omitting the submarine signaling apparatus, but replied: "I would rather take out the wireless. That only enables me to tell other people where I am. The submarine signal enables me to find out where I am myself."

The range of the apparatus is not so wide as that of wireless tele-graphy, varying from 10 to 15 miles for a large ship (although instances of 20 to 30 are on record), and from 3 to 8 miles for a small ship.

At present the receiving apparatus is fixed on only some 650 steamers of the merchant marine, these being mostly the first-class passenger liners. There is no question that it should be installed, along with wireless apparatus, on every ship of over 1,000 tons gross tonnage. Equally important is the provision of signaling apparatus on board ships: it is obviously just as necessary to transmit a signal as to receive one; but at present the sending of signals from ships has not been perfected. The invention of signal-transmitting apparatus to be used while the ship is under way is as yet in the experimental stage; but while she is at rest a bell similar to those used by lighthouses can be sunk over her side and rung by hand with exactly the same effect. But liners are not pro-vided with them (they cost only £60!). As mentioned before, with another £60 spent on the *Republic*'s equipment, the *Baltic* could have picked up her bell and steered direct to her—just as they both heard the bell of Nantucket Lightship. Again, if the *Titanic* had been provided with a bell and the *Californian* with receiving apparatus—neither of them was—the officer on the bridge could have heard the signals from the telephones near.

A smaller size for use in lifeboats is provided, and would be heard by receiving apparatus for approximately five miles. If we had hung one of these bells over the side of the lifeboats afloat that night we should have been free from the anxiety of being run down as we lay across the *Carpathia*'s path, without a light. Or if we had gone adrift in a dense fog and wandered miles apart from each other on the sea (as we inevitably should have done), the *Carpathia* could still have picked up each boat individually by means of the bell signal.

In those ships fitted with receiving apparatus, at least one officer is obliged to understand the working of the apparatus: a very wise precaution, and, as suggested above, one that should be taken with respect to wireless apparatus also.

It was a very great pleasure to me to see all this apparatus in manufacture and in use at one of the principal submarine signaling works in America and to hear some of the remarkable stories of its value in actual practise. I was struck by the aptness of the motto adopted by them—"De profundis clamavi"—in relation to the *Titanic*'s end and the calls of our passengers from the sea when she sank. "Out of the deep have I called unto Thee" is indeed a suitable motto for those who are doing all they can to prevent such calls arising from their fellow men and women "out of the deep."

### *Fixing of steamship routes*

The "lanes" along which the liners travel are fixed by agreement among the steamship companies in consultation with the Hydrographic departments of the different countries. These routes are arranged so that east-bound steamers are always a number of miles away from those going west, and thus the danger of collision between east- and west-bound vessels is entirely eliminated. The "lanes" can be moved farther south if icebergs threaten, and north again when the danger is removed. Of course the farther south they are placed, the longer the journey to be made, and the longer the time spent on board, with consequent grumbling by some passengers. For example, the lanes since the disaster to the *Titanic* have been moved one hundred miles farther south, which means one hundred and eighty miles longer journey, taking eight hours.

The only real precaution against colliding with icebergs is to go south of the place where they are likely to be: there is no other way.

### Lifeboats

The provision was of course woefully inadequate. The only humane plan is to have a numbered seat in a boat assigned to each passenger and member of the crew. It would seem well to have this number pointed out at the time of booking a berth, and to have a plan in each cabin showing where the boat is and how to get to it the most direct way—a most important consideration with a ship like the *Titanic* with over two miles of deck space. Boat-drills of the passengers and crew of each boat should be held, under compulsion, as soon as possible after leaving port. I asked an officer as to the possibility of having such a drill immediately after the gangways are withdrawn and before the tugs are allowed to haul the ship out of dock, but he says the difficulties are almost insuperable at such a time. If so, the drill should be conducted in sections as soon as possible after sailing, and should be conducted in a thorough manner. Children in school are called upon suddenly to go through fire-drill, and there is no reason why passengers on board ship should not be similarly trained. So much depends on order and readiness in time of danger. Undoubtedly, the whole subject of manning, provisioning, loading and lowering of lifeboats should be in the hands of an expert officer, who should have no other duties. The modern liner has become far too big to permit the captain to exercise control over the whole ship, and all vitally important subdivisions should be controlled by a separate authority. It seems a piece of bitter irony to remember that on the *Titanic* a special chef was engaged at a large salary—larger perhaps than that of any officer—and no boat-master (or some such officer) was considered necessary. The general system again—not criminal neglect, as some hasty criticisms would say, but lack of consideration for our fellow-man, the placing of luxurious attractions above that kindly forethought that allows no precaution to be neglected for even the humblest passenger. But it must not be overlooked that the provision of sufficient lifeboats on deck is not evidence they will all be launched easily or all the passengers taken off safely. It must be remembered that ideal conditions prevailed that night for launching boats from the decks of the *Titanic*: there was no list that prevented the boats getting away, they could be launched on both sides, and when they were lowered the sea was so calm that they pulled away without any of the smashing against the side that is possible in rough seas. Sometimes it would mean that only those boats on the side sheltered from a heavy sea could ever get away, and this would at once halve the boat accommodation. And when launched, there would be the danger of swamping in such a heavy sea. All things considered, lifeboats might be the poorest sort of safeguard in certain conditions.

Life-rafts are said to be much inferior to lifeboats in a rough sea, and collapsible boats made of canvas and thin wood soon decay under exposure to weather and are danger-traps at a critical moment.

Some of the lifeboats should be provided with motors, to keep the boats together and to tow if necessary. The launching is an important matter: the *Titanic*'s davits worked excellently and no doubt were largely responsible for all the boats getting away safely: they were far superior to those on most liners.

### Pontoons

After the sinking of the *Bourgogne*, when two Americans lost their lives, a prize of £4,000 was offered by their heirs for the best life-saving device applicable to ships at sea. A board sat to consider the various appliances sent in by competitors, and finally awarded the prize to an Englishman, whose design provided for a flat structure the width of the ship, which could be floated off when required and would accommodate several hundred passengers. It has never been adopted by any steamship line. Other similar designs are known, by which the whole of the after-deck can be pushed over from the stern by a ratchet arrangement, with air-tanks below to buoy it up: it seems to be a practical suggestion.

One point where the *Titanic* management failed lamentably was to provide a properly trained crew to each lifeboat. The rowing was in most cases execrable. There is no more reason why a steward should be able to row than a passenger—less so than some of the passengers who were lost; men of leisure accustomed to all kinds of sport (including rowing), and in addition probably more fit physically than a steward to row for hours on the open sea. And if a steward cannot row, he has no right to be at an oar; so that, under the unwritten rule that passengers take precedence of the crew when there is not sufficient accommodation for all (a situation that should never be allowed to arise again, for a member of the crew should have an equal opportunity with a passenger to save his life), the majority of stewards and cooks should have stayed behind and passengers have come instead: they could not have been of less use, and they might have been of more. It will be remembered that the proportion of crew saved to passengers was 210 to 495, a high proportion.

Another point arises out of these figures—deduct 21 members of the crew who were stewardesses, and 189 men of the crew are left as against the 495 passengers. Of these some got on the overturned collapsible boat after the *Titanic* sank, and a few were picked up by the lifeboats, but these were not many in all. Now with the 17 boats brought to the *Carpathia* and an average of six of the crew to man each boat—probably a higher average than was realized—we get a total of 102 who should have been saved as against 189 who actually were. There were, as is known, stokers and stewards in the boats who were not members of the lifeboats' crews. It may seem heartless to analyze figures in this way, and suggest that some of the crew who got to the *Carpathia* never should have done so; but, after all, passengers took their passage under certain rules—written and unwritten—and one is that in times of danger the servants of the company in whose boats they sail shall first of all see to the safety of the passengers before thinking of their own. There were only 126 men passengers saved as against 189 of the crew, and 661 men lost as against 686 of the crew, so that actually the crew had a greater percentage saved than the men passengers—22 per cent against 16.

But steamship companies are faced with real difficulties in this matter. The crews are never the same for two voyages together: they sign on for the one trip, then perhaps take a berth on shore as waiters, stokers in hotel furnace-rooms, etc.—to resume life on board any other ship that is handy when the desire comes to go to sea again. They can in no sense be regarded as part of a homogeneous crew, subject to regular discipline and educated to appreciate the morale of a particular liner, as a man of war's crew is.

## Searchlights

These seem an absolute necessity, and the wonder is that they have not been fitted before to all ocean liners. Not only are they of use in lighting up the sea a long distance ahead, but as flashlight signals they permit of communication with other ships. As I write, through the window can be seen the flashes from river steamers plying up the Hudson in New York, each with its searchlight, examining the river, lighting up the bank for hundreds of yards ahead, and bringing every object within its reach into prominence. They are regularly used too in the Suez Canal.

I suppose there is no question that the collision would have been avoided had a searchlight been fitted to the *Titanic*'s masthead: the climatic conditions for its use must have been ideal that night. There are other things besides icebergs: derelicts are reported from time to time, and fishermen lie in the lanes without lights. They would not always be of practical use, however. They would be of no service in heavy rain, in fog, in snow, or in flying spray, and the effect is sometimes to dazzle the eyes of the lookout.

While writing of the lookout, much has been made of the omission to provide the lookout on the *Titanic* with glasses. The general opinion of officers seems to be that it is better not to provide them, but to rely on good eyesight and wide-awake men. After all, in a question of actual practise, the opinion of officers should be accepted as final, even if it seems to the landsman the better thing to provide glasses.

## Cruising lightships

One or two internationally owned and controlled lightships, fitted with every known device for signaling and communication, would rob those regions of most of their terrors. They could watch and chart the icebergs, report their exact position, the amount and direction of daily drift in the changing currents that are found there. To them, too, might be entrusted the duty of police patrol.

# CHAPTER IX

# SOME IMPRESSIONS

No one can pass through an event like the wreck of the *Titanic* without recording mentally many impressions, deep and vivid, of what has been seen and felt. In so far as such impressions are of benefit to mankind they should not be allowed to pass unnoticed, and this chapter is an attempt to picture how people thought and felt from the time they first heard of the disaster to the landing in New York, when there was opportunity to judge of events somewhat from a distance. While it is to some extent a personal record, the mental impressions of other survivors have been compared and found to be in many cases closely in agreement. Naturally it is very imperfect, and pretends to be no more than a sketch of the way people act under the influence of strong emotions produced by imminent danger.

In the first place, the principal fact that stands out is the almost entire absence of any expressions of fear or alarm on the part of passengers, and the conformity to the normal on the part of almost everyone. I think it is no exaggeration to say that those who read of the disaster quietly at home, and pictured to themselves the scene as the *Titanic* was sinking, had more of the sense of horror than those who stood on the deck and watched her go down inch by inch. The fact is that the sense of fear came to the passengers very slowly—a result of the absence of any signs of danger and the peaceful night—and as it became evident gradually that there was serious damage to the ship, the fear that came with the knowledge was largely destroyed as it came. There was no sudden overwhelming sense of danger that passed through thought so quickly that it was difficult to catch up and grapple with it—no need for the warning to " be not afraid of sudden fear," such as might have been present had we collided head-on with a crash and a shock that flung everyone out of his bunk to the floor. Everyone had time to give each condition of danger attention as it came along, and the result of their judgment was as if they had said: " Well, here is this thing to be faced, and we must see it through as quietly as we can." Quietness and self-control were undoubtedly the two qualities most expressed. There were times when danger loomed more nearly and there was temporarily some excitement—for example when the first rocket went up—but after the first realization of what it meant, the crowd took hold of the situation and soon gained the same quiet control that was evident at first. As the sense of fear ebbed and flowed, it was so obviously a thing within one's own power to control, that, quite unconsciously realizing the absolute necessity of keeping cool, every one for his own safety put away the thought of danger as far as was possible. Then, too, the curious sense of the whole thing being a dream was very prominent: that all were looking on at the scene from a near-by vantage point in a position of perfect safety, and that those who walked the decks or tied one another's lifebelts on were the actors in a scene of which we were but spectators: that the dream would end soon and we should wake up to find the scene had vanished. Many people have had a similar experience in times of danger, but it was very noticeable standing on the *Titanic*'s deck. I remember observing it particularly while tying on a lifebelt for a man on the deck. It is fortunate that it should be so: to be able to survey such a scene dispassionately is a wonderful aid in the destruction of the fears that go with it. One thing that helped considerably to establish this orderly condition of affairs was the quietness of the surroundings. It may seem weariness to refer again to this, but I am convinced it had much to do with keeping everyone calm. The ship was motionless; there was not a breath of wind; the sky was clear; the sea like a mill-pond—the general "atmosphere" was peaceful, and all on board responded unconsciously to it. But what controlled the situation principally was the quality of obedience and respect for authority which is a dominant characteristic of the Teutonic race. Passengers did as they were told by the officers in charge: women went to the decks below, men remained where they were told and waited in silence for the next order, knowing instinctively that this was the only way to bring about the best result for all on board. The officers, in their turn, carried out the work assigned to them by their superior officers as quickly and orderly as circumstances permitted, the senior ones being in control of the manning, filling and lowering of the lifeboats, while the junior officers were lowered in individual boats to take command of the fleet adrift on the sea. Similarly, the engineers below, the band, the gymnasium instructor, were all performing their tasks as they came along: orderly, quietly, without question or stopping to consider what was their chance of safety. This correlation on the part of passengers, officers and crew was simply obedience to duty, and it was innate rather than the product of reasoned judgment.

I hope it will not seem to detract in any way from the heroism of those who faced the last plunge of the *Titanic* so courageously when all the boats had gone—if it does, it is the difficulty of expressing an idea in adequate words—to say that their quiet heroism was largely unconscious, temperamental, not a definite choice between two ways of acting. All that was visible on deck before the boats left tended to this conclusion and the testimony of those who went down with the ship and were afterwards rescued is of the same kind.

Certainly it seems to express much more general nobility of character in a race of people—consisting of different nationalities—to find heroism an unconscious quality of the race than to have it arising as an effort of will, to have to bring it out consciously.

It is unfortunate that some sections of the press should seek to chronicle mainly the individual acts of heroism: the collective behavior of a crowd is of so much more importance to the world and so much more a test—if a test be wanted—of how a race of people behaves. The attempt to record the acts of individuals leads apparently to such false reports as that of Major Butt holding at bay with a revolver a crowd of passengers and shooting them down as they tried to rush the boats, or of Captain Smith shouting, "Be British," through a megaphone, and subsequently committing suicide along with First Officer Murdock. It is only a morbid sense of things that would describe such incidents as heroic. Everyone knows that Major Butt was a brave man, but his record of heroism would not be enhanced if he, a trained army officer, were compelled under orders from the captain to shoot down unarmed passengers. It might in other conditions have been necessary, but it would not be heroic. Similarly there could be nothing heroic in Captain Smith or Murdock putting an end to their lives. It is conceivable men might be so overwhelmed by the sense of disaster that they knew not how they were acting; but to be really heroic would have been to stop with the ship—as of course they did—with the hope of being picked up along with passengers and crew and returning to face an enquiry and to give evidence that would be of supreme value to the whole world for the prevention of similar disasters. It was not possible; but if heroism consists in doing the greatest good to the greatest number, it would have been heroic for both officers to *expect* to be saved. We do not know what they thought, but I, for one, like to imagine that they did so. Second Officer Lightoller worked steadily at the boats until the last possible moment, went down with the ship, was saved in what seemed a miraculous manner, and returned to give valuable evidence before the commissions of two countries.

The second thing that stands out prominently in the emotions produced by the disaster is that in moments of urgent need men and women turn for help to something entirely outside themselves. I remember reading some years ago a story of an atheist who was the guest at dinner of a regimental mess in India. The colonel listened to his remarks on atheism in silence, and invited him for a drive the following morning. He took his guest up a rough mountain road in a light carriage drawn by two ponies, and when some distance from the plain below, turned the carriage round and allowed the ponies to run away—as it seemed—downhill. In the terror of approaching disaster, the atheist was lifted out of his reasoned convictions and prayed aloud for help, when the colonel reined in his ponies, and with the remark that the whole drive had been planned with the intention of proving to his guest that there was a power outside his own reason, descended quietly to level ground.

The story may or may not be true, and in any case is not introduced as an attack on atheism, but it illustrates in a striking way the frailty of dependence on a man's own power and resource in imminent danger. To those men standing on the top deck with the boats all lowered, and still more so when the boats had all left, there came the realization that human resources were exhausted and human avenues of escape closed. With it came the appeal to whatever consciousness each had of a Power that had created the universe. After all, some Power had made the brilliant stars above, countless millions of miles away, moving in definite order, formed on a definite plan and obeying a definite law: had made each one of the passengers with ability to think and act; with the best proof, after all, of being created—the knowledge of their own existence; and now, if at any time, was the time to appeal to that Power. When the boats had left and it was seen the ship was going down rapidly, men stood in groups on the deck engaged in prayer, and later, as some of them lay on the overturned collapsible boat, they repeated together over and over again the Lord's Prayer—irrespective of religious beliefs, some, perhaps, without religious beliefs, united in a common appeal for deliverance from their surroundings. And this was not because it was a habit, because they had learned this prayer "at their mother's knee": men do not do such things through habit. It must have been because each one saw removed the thousand-and-one ways in which he had relied on human, material things to help him—including even dependence on the overturned boat with its bubble of air inside, which any moment a rising swell might remove as it tilted the boat too far sideways, and sink the boat below the surface—saw laid bare his utter dependence on something that had made him and given him power to think—whether he named it God or Divine Power or First Cause or Creator, or named it not at all but recognized it unconsciously—saw these things and expressed them in the form of words he was best acquainted with in common with his fellow-men. He did so, not through a sense of duty to his particular religion, not because he had learned the words, but because he recognized that it was the most practical thing to do— the thing best fitted to help him. Men do practical things in times like that: they would not waste a moment on mere words if those words were not an expression of the most intensely real conviction of which they were capable. Again, like the feeling of heroism, this appeal is innate and intuitive, and it certainly has its foundation on a knowledge—largely concealed, no doubt—of immortality. I think this must be obvious: there could be no other explanation of such a general sinking of all the emotions of the human mind expressed in a thousand different ways by a thousand different people in favor of this single appeal.

The behavior of people during the hours in the lifeboats, the landing on the *Carpathia*, the life there and the landing in New York, can all be summarized by saying that people did not act at all as they were expected to act—or rather as most people expected they would act, and in some cases have erroneously said they did act. Events were there to be faced, and not to crush people down. Situations arose which demanded courage, resource, and in the cases of those who had lost friends most dear to them, enormous self-control; but very wonderfully they responded. There was the same quiet demeanor and poise, the same inborn dominion over circumstances, the same conformity to a normal standard which characterized the crowd of passengers on the deck of the *Titanic*—and for the same reasons.

The first two or three days ashore were undoubtedly rather trying to some of the survivors. It seemed as if coming into the world again— the four days shut off from any news seemed a long time—and finding what a shock the disaster had produced, the flags half-mast, the staring head-lines, the sense of gloom noticeable everywhere, made things worse than they had been on the *Carpathia*. The difference in "atmosphere" was very marked, and people gave way to some extent under it and felt the reaction. Gratitude for their deliverance and a desire to "make the best of things" must have helped soon, however, to restore them to normal conditions. It is not at all surprising that some survivors felt quieter on the *Carpathia* with its lack of news from the outside world, if the following extract from a leading New York evening paper was some of the material of which the "atmosphere" on shore was composed:—

"Stunned by the terrific impact, the dazed passengers rushed from their staterooms into the main saloon amid the crash of splintering steel, rending of plates and shattering of girders, while the boom of falling pinnacles of ice upon the broken deck of the great vessel added to the horror. . . . In a wild ungovernable mob they poured out of the saloons to witness one of the most appalling scenes possible to conceive. . . . For a hundred feet the bow was a shapeless mass of bent, broken and splintered steel and iron."

And so on, horror piled on horror, and not a word of it true, or remotely approaching the truth.

This paper was selling in the streets of New York while the *Carpathia* was coming into dock, while relatives of those on board were at the docks to meet them and anxiously buying any paper that might contain news. No one on the *Carpathia* could have supplied such information; there was no one else in the world at that moment who knew any details of the *Titanic* disaster, and the only possible conclusion is that the whole thing was a deliberate fabrication to sell the paper.

This is a repetition of the same defect in human nature noticed in the provision of safety appliances on board ship—the lack of consideration for the other man. The remedy is the same—the law: it should be a criminal offence for anyone to disseminate deliberate falsehoods that cause fear and grief. The moral responsibility of the press is very great, and its duty of supplying the public with only clean, correct news is correspondingly heavy. If the general public is not yet prepared to go so far as to stop the publication of such news by refusing to buy those papers that publish it, then the law should be enlarged to include such cases. Libel is an offence, and this is very much worse than any libel could ever be.

It is only right to add that the majority of the New York papers were careful only to report such news as had been obtained legitimately from survivors or from *Carpathia* passengers. It was sometimes exaggerated and sometimes not true at all, but from the point of reporting what was heard, most of it was quite correct.

One more thing must be referred to—the prevalence of superstitious beliefs concerning the *Titanic*. I suppose no ship ever left port with so much miserable nonsense showered on her. In the first place, there is no doubt many people refused to sail on her because it was her maiden voyage, and this apparently is a common superstition: even the clerk of the White Star Office where I purchased my ticket admitted it was a reason that prevented people from sailing. A number of people have written to the press to say they had thought of sailing on her, or had decided to sail on her, but because of "omens" canceled the passage. Many referred to the sister ship, the *Olympic*, pointed to the "ill luck" that they say has dogged her—her collision with the *Hawke*, and a second mishap necessitating repairs and a wait in harbor, where passengers deserted her; they prophesied even greater disaster for the *Titanic*, saying they would not dream of traveling on the boat. Even some aboard were very nervous, in an undefined way. One lady said she had never wished to take this boat, but her friends had insisted and bought her ticket and she had not had a happy moment since. A friend told me of the voyage of the *Olympic* from Southampton after the wait in harbor, and said there was a sense of gloom pervading the whole ship: the stewards and stewardesses even going so far as to say it was a "death-ship." This crew, by the way, was largely transferred to the *Titanic*.

The incident with the *New York* at Southampton, the appearance of the stoker at Queenstown in the funnel, combine with all this to make a mass of nonsense in which apparently sensible people believe, or which at any rate they discuss. Correspondence is published with an official of the White Star Line from some one imploring them not to name the new ship "Gigantic," because it seems like "tempting fate" when the *Titanic* has been sunk. It would seem almost as if we were back in the Middle Ages when witches were burned because they kept black cats. There seems no more reason why a black stoker should be an ill omen for the *Titanic* than a black cat should be for an old woman.

The only reason for referring to these foolish details is that a surprisingly large number of people think there may be "something in it." The effect is this: that if a ship's company and a number of passengers get imbued with that undefined dread of the unknown—the relics no doubt of the savage's fear of what he does not understand—it has an unpleasant effect on the harmonious working of the ship: the officers and crew feel the depressing influence, and it may even spread so far as to prevent them being as alert and keen as they otherwise would; may even result in some duty not being as well done as usual. Just as the unconscious demand for speed and haste to get across the Atlantic may have tempted captains to take a risk they might otherwise not have done, so these gloomy forebodings may have more effect sometimes than we imagine. Only a little thing is required sometimes to weigh down the balance for and against a certain course of action.

At the end of this chapter of mental impressions it must be recorded that one impression remains constant with us all to-day—that of the deepest gratitude that we came safely through the wreck of the *Titanic*; and its corollary—that our legacy from the wreck, our debt to those who were lost with her, is to see, as far as in us lies, that such things are impossible ever again. Meanwhile we can say of them, as Shelley, himself the victim of a similar disaster, says of his friend Keats in "Adonais":—

> Peace, peace! he is not dead, he doth not sleep—
> He hath awakened from the dream of life—
> He lives, he wakes—'T is Death is dead, not he;
> Mourn not for Adonais.

# The Titanic

# THE TRUTH ABOUT THE
# TITANIC

*By*

Colonel Archibald Gracie

# CONTENTS

CHAPTER I

# THE LAST DAY ABOARD SHIP

*There is that Leviathan.*—Ps. 104 : 26

As the sole survivor of all the men passengers of the *Titanic* stationed during the loading of six or more lifeboats with women and children on the port side of the ship, forward on the glass-sheltered Deck A, and later on the Boat Deck above, it is my duty to bear testimony to the heroism on the part of all concerned. First, to my men companions who calmly stood by until the lifeboats had departed loaded with women and the available complement of crew, and who, fifteen to twenty minutes later, sank with the ship, conscious of giving up their lives to save the weak and the helpless.

Second, to Second Officer Lightoller and his ship's crew, who did their duty as if similar occurrences were matters of daily routine; and thirdly, to the women, who showed no signs of fear or panic whatsoever under conditions more appalling than were ever recorded before in the history of disasters at sea.

I think those of my readers who are accustomed to tales of thrilling adventure will be glad to learn first-hand of the heroism displayed on the *Titanic* by those to whom it is my privilege and sad duty to pay this tribute. I will confine the details of my narrative for the most part to what I personally saw, and did, and heard during that never-to-be-forgotten maiden trip of the *Titanic*, which ended with shipwreck and her foundering about 2.22 a. m., Monday, April 15, 1912, after striking an iceberg "in or near latitude 41 degrees, 46 minutes N., longitude 50 degrees, 14 minutes W., North Atlantic Ocean," whereby the loss of 1,490 lives ensued.

On Sunday morning, April 14th, this marvelous ship, the perfection of all vessels hitherto conceived by the brain of man, had, for three and one-half days, proceeded on her way from Southampton to New York over a sea of glass, so level it appeared, without encountering a ripple brought on the surface of the water by a storm.

The Captain had each day improved upon the previous day's speed, and prophesied that, with continued fair weather, we should make an early arrival record for this maiden trip. But his reckoning never took into consideration that Protean monster of the Northern seas which, even before this, had been so fatal to the navigator's calculations and so formidable a weapon of destruction.

Our explorers have pierced to the furthest north and south of the icebergs' retreat, but the knowledge of their habitat, insuring our great ocean liners in their successful efforts to elude them, has not reached the detail of time and place where they become detached and obstruct their path.

In the twenty-four hours' run ending the 14th, according to the posted reckoning, the ship had covered 546 miles, and we were told that the next twenty-four hours would see even a better record made.

Towards evening the report, which I heard, was spread that wireless messages from passing steamers had been received advising the officers of our ship of the presence of icebergs and ice-floes. The increasing cold and the necessity of being more warmly clad when appearing on deck were outward and visible signs in corroboration of these warnings. But despite them all no diminution of speed was indicated and the engines kept up their steady running.

Not for fifty years, the old sailors tell us, had so great a mass of ice and icebergs at this time of the year been seen so far south.

The pleasure and comfort which all of us enjoyed upon this floating palace, with its extraordinary provisions for such purposes, seemed an ominous feature to many of us, including myself, who felt it almost too good to last without some terrible retribution inflicted by the hand of an angry omnipotence. Our sentiment in this respect was voiced by one of the most able and distinguished of our fellow passengers, Mr. Charles M. Hays, President of the Canadian Grand Trunk Railroad. Engaged as he then was in studying and providing the hotel equipment along the line of new extensions to his own great railroad system, the consideration of the subject and of the magnificence of the *Titanic*'s accommodations was thus brought home to him. This was the prophetic utterance with which, alas, he sealed his fate a few hours thereafter: "The White Star, the Cunard and the Hamburg-American lines," said he, "are now devoting their attention to a struggle for supremacy in obtaining the most luxurious appointments for their ships, but the time will soon come when the greatest and most appalling of all disasters at sea will be the result."

In the various trips which I have made across the Atlantic, it has been my custom aboard ship, whenever the weather permitted, to take as much exercise every day as might be needful to put myself in prime physical condition, but on board the *Titanic*, during the first days of the voyage, from Wednesday to Saturday, I had departed from this, my usual self-imposed regimen, for during this interval I had devoted my time to social enjoyment and to the reading of books taken from the ship's well-supplied library. I enjoyed myself as if I were in a summer palace on the seashore, surrounded with every comfort—there was nothing to indicate or suggest that we were on the stormy Atlantic Ocean. The motion of the ship and the noise of its machinery were scarcely discernible on deck or in the saloons, either day or night. But when Sunday morning came, I considered it high time to begin my customary exercises, and determined for the rest of the voyage to patronize the squash racquet court, the gymnasium, the swimming pool, etc. I was up early before breakfast and met the professional racquet player in a half hour's warming up, preparatory for a swim in the six-foot deep tank of salt water, heated to a refreshing temperature. In no swimming bath had I ever enjoyed such pleasure before. How curtailed that enjoyment would have been had the presentiment come to me telling how near it was to being my last plunge, and that before dawn of another day I would be swimming for my life in mid-ocean, under water and on the surface, in a temperature of 28 degrees Fahrenheit!

Impressed on my memory as if it were but yesterday, my mind pictures the personal appearance and recalls the conversation which I had with each of these employees of the ship. The racquet professional, F. Wright, was a clean-cut typical young Englishman, similar to hundreds I have seen and with whom I have played, in bygone years, my favorite game of cricket, which has done more than any other sport for my physical development. I have not seen his name mentioned in any account of the disaster, and therefore take this opportunity of speaking of him, for I am perhaps the only survivor able to relate anything about his last days on earth.

Hundreds of letters have been written to us survivors, many containing photographs for identification of some lost loved one, whom perchance we may have seen or talked to before he met his fate. To these numerous inquiries I have been able to reply satisfactorily only in rare instances. The next and last time I saw Wright was on the stairway of Deck C within three-quarters of an hour after the collision. I was going to my cabin when I met him on the stairs going up. "Hadn't we better cancel that appointment for to-morrow morning?" I said rather jocosely to him. "Yes," he replied, but did not stop to tell what he then must have known of the conditions in the racquet court on G Deck, which, according to other witnesses, had at that time become flooded. His voice was calm, without enthusiasm, and perhaps his face was a little whiter than usual.

To the swimming pool attendant I also made promise to be on hand earlier the next morning, but I never saw him again.

One of the characters of the ship, best known to us all, was the gymnasium instructor, T. W. McCawley. He, also, expected me to make my first appearance for real good exercise on the morrow, but alas, he, too, was swallowed up by the sea. How well we survivors all remember this sturdy little man in white flannels and with his broad English accent! With what tireless enthusiasm he showed us the many mechanical devices under his charge and urged us to take advantage of the opportunity of using them, going through the motions of bicycle racing, rowing, boxing, camel and horseback riding, etc.

Such was my morning's preparation for the unforeseen physical exertions I was compelled to put forth for dear life at midnight, a few hours later. Could any better training for the terrible ordeal have been planned?

The exercise and the swim gave me an appetite for a hearty breakfast. Then followed the church service in the dining saloon, and I remember how much I was impressed with the "Prayer for those at Sea," also the words of the hymn, which we sang, No. 418 of the Hymnal. About a fortnight later, when I next heard it sung, I was in the little church at Smithtown, Long Island, attending the memorial service in honor of my old friend and fellow member of the Union Club, James Clinch Smith. To his sister, who sat next to me in the pew, I called attention to the fact that it was the last hymn we sang on this Sunday morning on board the *Titanic*. She was much affected, and gave the reason for its selection for the memorial service to her brother because it was known as Jim's favorite hymn, being the first piece set to music ever played by him as a child and for which he was rewarded with a promised prize, donated by his father.

What a remarkable coincidence that at the first and last ship's service on board the *Titanic*, the hymn we sang began with these impressive lines:

> O God our help in ages past,
>   Our hope for years to come,
> Our shelter from the stormy blast
>   And our eternal home.

One day was so like another that it is difficult to differentiate in our description all the details of this last day's incidents aboard ship.

The book that I finished and returned to the ship's library was Mary Johnston's *Old Dominion*. While peacefully reading the tales of adventure and accounts of extraordinary escapes therein, how little I

Ladies and gentlemen in riding habit exercised on mechanical horses and camels in the ship's gymnasium. (The illustration is of the *Olympic*.)

The first-class smoking room reflects the dignity of a private club. (The illustration is of the *Olympic*.)

thought that in the next few hours I should be a witness and a party to a scene to which this book could furnish no counterpart, and that my own preservation from a watery grave would afford a remarkable illustration of how ofttimes "truth is stranger than fiction."

During this day I saw much of Mr. and Mrs. Isidor Straus. In fact, from the very beginning to the end of our trip on the *Titanic*, we had been together several times each day. I was with them on the deck the day we left Southampton and witnessed that ominous accident to the American liner, *New York*, lying at her pier, when the displacement of water by the movement of our gigantic ship caused a suction which pulled the smaller ship from her moorings and nearly caused a collision. At the time of this, Mr. Straus was telling me that it seemed only a few years back that he had taken passage on this same ship, the *New York*, on her maiden trip and when she was spoken of as the "last word in shipbuilding." He then called the attention of his wife and myself to the progress that had since been made, by comparison of the two ships then lying side by side. During our daily talks thereafter, he related much of special interest concerning incidents in his remarkable career, beginning with his early manhood in Georgia when, with the Confederate Government Commissioners, as an agent for the purchase of supplies, he ran the blockade of Europe. His friendship with President Cleveland, and how the latter had honored him, were among the topics of daily conversation that interested me most.

On this Sunday, our last day aboard ship, he finished the reading of a book I had loaned him, in which he expressed intense interest. This book was *The Truth About Chickamauga*, of which I am the author, and it was to gain a much-needed rest after seven years of work thereon, and in order to get it off my mind, that I had taken this trip across the ocean and back. As a counter-irritant, my experience was a dose which was highly efficacious.

I recall how Mr. and Mrs. Straus were particularly happy about noon time on this same day in anticipation of communicating by wireless telegraphy with their son and his wife on their way to Europe on board the passing ship *Amerika*. Some time before six o'clock, full of contentment, they told me of the message of greeting received in reply. This last good-bye to their loved ones must have been a consoling thought when the end came a few hours thereafter.

That night after dinner, with my table companions, Messrs. James Clinch Smith and Edward A. Kent, according to usual custom, we adjourned to the palm room, with many others, for the usual coffee at individual tables where we listened to the always delightful music of the *Titanic*'s band. On these occasions, full dress was always *en règle*; and it was a subject both of observation and admiration, that there were so many beautiful women—then especially in evidence—aboard the ship.

I invariably circulated around during these delightful evenings, chatting with those I knew, and with those whose acquaintance I had made during the voyage. I might specify names and particularize subjects of conversation, but the details, while interesting to those concerned, might not be so to all my readers. The recollections of those with whom I was thus closely associated in this disaster, including those who suffered the death from which I escaped and those who survived with me, will be a treasured memory and bond of union until my dying day. From the palm room, the men of my coterie would always go to the smoking-room, and almost every evening join in conversation with some of the well-known men whom we met there, including within my own recollections Major Archie Butt, President Taft's Military Aid, discussing politics; Clarence Moore, of Washington, D. C., relating his venturesome trip some years ago through the West Virginia woods and mountains, helping a newspaper reporter in obtaining an interview with the outlaw, Captain Anse Hatfield; Frank D. Millet, the well-known artist, planning a journey west; Arthur Ryerson and others.

During these evenings I also conversed with Mr. John B. Thayer, Second Vice-President of the Pennsylvania Railroad, and with Mr. George D. Widener, a son of the Philadelphia street-car magnate, Mr. P. A. B. Widener.

My stay in the smoking-room on this particular evening for the first time was short, and I retired early with my cabin steward Cullen's promise to awaken me betimes next morning to get ready for the engagements I had made before breakfast for the game of racquets, work in the gymnasium and the swim that was to follow.

I cannot regard it as a mere coincidence that on this particular Sunday night I was thus prompted to retire early for nearly three hours of invigorating sleep, whereas an accident occurring at midnight of any of the four preceding days would have found me mentally and physically tired. That I was thus strengthened for the terrible ordeal, better even than had I been forewarned of it, I regard on the contrary as the first provision for my safety (answering the constant prayers of those at home), made by the guardian angel to whose care I was entrusted during the series of miraculous escapes presently to be recorded.

# CHAPTER II

# STRUCK BY AN ICEBERG

*Watchman, what of the night?*—Isaiah 21 : 11

My stateroom was an outside one on Deck C on the starboard quarter, somewhat abaft amidships. It was No. C, 51. I was enjoying a good night's rest when I was aroused by a sudden shock and noise forward on the starboard side, which I at once concluded was caused by a collision, with some other ship perhaps. I jumped from my bed, turned on the electric light, glanced at my watch nearby on the dresser, which I had changed to agree with ship's time on the day before and which now registered twelve o'clock. Correct ship's time would make it about 11.45. I opened the door of my cabin, looked out into the corridor, but could not see or hear anyone—there was no commotion whatever; but immediately following the collision came a great noise of escaping steam. I listened intently, but could hear no machinery. There was no mistaking that something wrong had happened, because of the ship stopping and the blowing off of steam.

Removing my night clothing I dressed myself hurriedly in underclothing, shoes and stockings, trousers and a Norfolk coat. I give these details in order that some idea of the lapse of time may be formed by an account of what I did during the interval. From my cabin, through the corridor to the stairway was but a short distance, and I ascended to the third deck above, that is, to the Boat Deck. I found here only one young lad, seemingly bent on the same quest as myself.

From the first cabin quarter, forward on the port side, we strained our eyes to discover what had struck us. From vantage points where the view was not obstructed by the lifeboats on this deck I sought the object, but in vain, though I swept the horizon near and far and discovered nothing.

It was a beautiful night, cloudless, and the stars shining brightly. The atmosphere was quite cold, but no ice or iceberg was in sight. If another ship had struck us there was no trace of it, and it did not yet occur to me that it was an iceberg with which we had collided. Not satisfied with a partial investigation, I made a complete tour of the deck, searching every point of the compass with my eyes. Going toward the stern, I vaulted over the iron gate and fence that divide the first and second cabin passengers. I disregarded the "not allowed" notice. I looked about me towards the officers' quarters in expectation of being challenged for non-observance of rules. In view of the collision I had expected to see some of the ship's officers on the Boat Deck, but there was no sign of an officer anywhere, and no one from whom to obtain any information about what had happened. Making my tour of the Boat Deck, the only other beings I saw were a middle-aged couple of the second cabin promenading unconcernedly, arm in arm, forward on the starboard quarter, against the wind, the man in a gray overcoat and outing cap.

Having gained no satisfaction whatever, I descended to the glass-enclosed Deck A, port side, and looked over the rail to see whether the ship was on an even keel, but I still could see nothing wrong. Entering the companionway, I passed Mr. Ismay with a member of the crew hurrying up the stairway. He wore a day suit, and, as usual, was hatless. He seemed too much preoccupied to notice anyone. Therefore I did not speak to him, but regarded his face very closely, perchance to learn from his manner how serious the accident might be. It occurred to me then that he was putting on as brave a face as possible so as to cause no alarm among the passengers.

At the foot of the stairway were a number of men passengers, and I now for the first time discovered that others were aroused as well as myself, among them my friend, Clinch Smith, from whom I first learned that an iceberg had struck us. He opened his hand and showed me some ice, flat like my watch, coolly suggesting that I might take it home for a souvenir. All of us will remember the way he had of cracking a joke without a smile. While we stood there, the story of the collision came to us—how someone in the smoking-room, when the ship struck, rushed out to see what it was, and returning, told them that he had a glimpse of an iceberg towering fifty feet above Deck A, which, if true, would indicate a height of over one hundred feet. Here, too, I learned that the mail room was flooded and that the plucky postal clerks, in two feet of water, were at their posts. They were engaged in transferring to the upper deck, from the ship's post-office, the two hundred bags of registered mail containing four hundred thousand letters. The names of these men, who all sank with the ship, deserve to be recorded. They were: John S. Marsh, William L. Gwynn, Oscar S. Woody, Iago Smith and E. D. Williamson. The first three were Americans, the others Englishmen, and the families of the former were provided for by their Government.

And now Clinch Smith and myself noticed a list on the floor of the companionway. We kept our own counsel about it, not wishing to frighten anyone or cause any unnecessary alarm, especially among the ladies, who then appeared upon the scene. We did not consider it our duty to express our individual opinion upon the serious character of the accident which now appealed to us with the greatest force. He and I resolved to stick together in the final emergency, united in the silent bond of friendship, and lend a helping hand to each other whenever required. I recall having in my mind's eye at this moment all that I had read and heard in days gone by about shipwrecks, and pictured Smith and myself clinging to an overloaded raft in an open sea with a scarcity of food and water. We agreed to visit our respective staterooms and join each other later. All possessions in my stateroom were hastily packed into three large traveling bags so that the luggage might be ready in the event of a hasty transfer to another ship.

Fortunately I put on my long Newmarket overcoat that reached below my knees, and as I passed from the corridor into the companion-way my worst fears were confirmed. Men and women were slipping on life-preservers, the stewards assisting in adjusting them. Steward Cullen insisted upon my returning to my stateroom for mine. I did so and he fastened one on me while I brought out the other for use by someone else.

Out on Deck A, port side, towards the stern, many men and women had already collected. I sought and found the unprotected ladies to whom I had proffered my services during the voyage when they boarded the ship at Southampton, Mrs. E. D. Appleton, wife of my St. Paul's School friend and schoolmate; Mrs. R. C. Cornell, wife of the well-known New York Justice, and Mrs. J. Murray Brown, wife of the Boston publisher, all old friends of my wife. These three sisters were returning home from a sad mission abroad, where they had laid to rest the remains of a fourth sister, Lady Victor Drummond, of whose death I had read accounts in the London papers, and all the sad details connected therewith were told me by the sisters themselves. That they would have to pass through a still greater ordeal seemed impossible, and how little did I know of the responsibility I took upon myself for their safety! Accompanying them, also unprotected, was their friend, Miss Edith Evans, to whom they introduced me. Mr. and Mrs. Straus, Colonel and Mrs. Astor and others well known to me were among those here congregated on the port side of Deck A, including, besides Clinch Smith, two of our coterie of after-dinner companions, Hugh Woolner, son of the English sculptor, whose works are to be seen in Westminster Abbey, and H. Björnström Steffanson, the young lieutenant of the

Swedish army, who, during the voyage, had told me of his acquaintance with Mrs. Gracie's relatives in Sweden.

It was now that the band began to play, and continued while the boats were being lowered. We considered this a wise provision tending to allay excitement. I did not recognize any of the tunes, but I know they were cheerful and were not hymns. If, as has been reported, "Nearer My God to Thee" was one of the selections, I assuredly should have noticed it and regarded it as a tactless warning of immediate death to us all and one likely to create a panic that our special efforts were directed towards avoiding, and which we accomplished to the fullest extent. I know of only two survivors whose names are cited by the newspapers as authority for the statement that this hymn was one of those played. On the other hand, all whom I have questioned or corresponded with, including the best qualified, testified emphatically to the contrary.

Our hopes were buoyed with the information, imparted through the ship's officers, that there had been an interchange of wireless messages with passing ships, one of which was certainly coming to our rescue. To reassure the ladies of whom I had assumed special charge, I showed them a bright white light of what I took to be a ship about five miles off and which I felt sure was coming to our rescue. Colonel Astor heard me telling this to them and he asked me to show it and I pointed the light out to him. In so doing we both had now to lean over the rail of the ship and look close in towards the bow, avoiding a lifeboat even then made ready with its gunwale lowered to the level of the floor of the Boat Deck above us and obstructing our view; but instead of growing brighter the light grew dim and less and less distinct and passed away altogether. The light, as I have since learned, with tearful regret for the lost who might have been saved, belonged to the steamer *Californian* of the Leyland line, Captain Stanley Lord, bound from London to Boston. She belonged to the International Mercantile Marine Company, the owners of the *Titanic*.

This was the ship from which two of the six "ice messages" were sent. The first one received and acknowledged by the *Titanic* was one at 7.30 p. m., an intercepted message to another ship. The next was about 11 p. m., when the Captain of the *Californian* saw a ship approaching from the eastward, which he was advised to be the *Titanic*, and under his orders this message was sent: "We are stopped and surrounded by ice." To this the *Titanic*'s wireless operator brusquely replied, "Shut up, I am busy. I am working Cape Race." The business here referred to was the sending of wireless messages for passengers on the *Titanic*; and the stronger current of the *Californian* eastward interfered therewith. Though the navigation of the ship and the issues of life and death were at stake, the right of way was given to communication with Cape Race until within a few minutes of the *Titanic*'s collision with the iceberg.

Nearly all this time, until 11.30 p. m., the wireless operator of the *Californian* was listening with 'phones on his head, but at 11.30 p. m., while the *Titanic* was still talking to Cape Race, the former ship's operator "put the 'phones down, took off his clothes and turned in."

The fate of thousands of lives hung in the balance many times that ill-omened night, but *the circumstances in connection with the S. S. Californian* (Br. Rep. pp. 43–46), furnish the evidence corroborating that of the American Investigation, viz., that it was not chance, but the grossest negligence alone which sealed the fate of all the noble lives, men and women, that were lost.

It appears from the evidence referred to, information in regard to which we learned after our arrival in New York, that the Captain of the *Californian* and his crew were watching our lights from the deck of their ship, which remained approximately stationary until 5.15 a. m. on the following morning. During this interval it is shown that they were never distant more than six or seven miles. In fact, at 12 o'clock, the *Californian* was only four or five miles off at the point and in the general direction where she was seen by myself and at least a dozen others, who bore testimony before the American Committee, from the decks of the *Titanic*. The white rockets which we sent up, referred to presently, were also plainly seen at the time. Captain Lord was completely in possession of the knowledge that he was in proximity to a ship in distress. He could have put himself into immediate communication with us by wireless had he desired confirmation of the name of the ship and the disaster which had befallen it. His indifference is made apparent by his orders to "go on Morseing," instead of utilizing the more modern method of the inventive genius and gentleman, Mr. Marconi, which eventually saved us all. "The night was clear and the sea was smooth. The ice by which the *Californian* was surrounded," says the British Report, "was loose ice extending for a distance of not more than two or three miles in the direction of the *Titanic*." When she first saw the rockets, the *Californian* could have pushed through the ice to the open water without any serious risk and so have come to the assistance of the *Titanic*. A discussion of this subject is the most painful of all others for those who lost their loved ones aboard our ship.

When we realized that the ship whose lights we saw was not coming towards us, our hopes of rescue were correspondingly depressed, but the men's counsel to preserve calmness prevailed; and to reassure the ladies they repeated the much advertised fiction of "the unsinkable ship" on the supposed highest qualified authority. It was at this point that Miss Evans related to me the story that years ago in London she had been told by a fortune-teller to "beware of water," and now "she knew she would be drowned." My efforts to persuade her to the contrary were futile. Though she gave voice to her story, she presented no evidence whatever of fear, and when I saw and conversed with her an hour later when conditions appeared especially desperate, and the last lifeboat was supposed to have departed, she was perfectly calm and did not revert again to the superstitious tale.

From my own conclusions, and those of others, it appears that about forty-five minutes had now elapsed since the collision when Captain Smith's orders were transmitted to the crew to lower the lifeboats, loaded with women and children first. The self-abnegation of Mr. and Mrs. Isidor Straus here shone forth heroically when she promptly and emphatically exclaimed: "No! I will not be separated from my husband; as we have lived, so will we die together;" and when he, too, declined the assistance proffered on my earnest solicitation that, because of his age and helplessness, exception should be made and he be allowed to accompany his wife in the boat. "No!" he said, "I do not wish any distinction in my favor which is not granted to others." As near as I can recall them these were the words which they addressed to me. They expressed themselves as fully prepared to die, and calmly sat down in steamer chairs on the glass-enclosed Deck A, prepared to meet their fate. Further entreaties to make them change their decision were of no avail. Later they moved to the Boat Deck above, accompanying Mrs. Straus's maid, who entered a lifeboat.

When the order to load the boats was received I had promptly moved forward with the ladies in my charge toward the boats then being lowered from the Boat Deck above to Deck A on the port side of the ship, where we then were. A tall, slim young Englishman, Sixth Officer J. P. Moody, whose name I learned later, with other members of the ship's crew, barred the progress of us men passengers any nearer to the boats. All that was left me was then to consign these ladies in my charge to the protection of the ship's officer, and I thereby was relieved of their responsibility and felt sure that they would be safely loaded in the boats at this point. I remember a steward rolling a small barrel out of the door of the companionway. "What have you there?" said I. "Bread for the lifeboats," was his quick and cheery reply, as I passed inside the ship for the last time, searching for two of my table companions, Mrs. Churchill Candee of Washington and Mr. Edward A. Kent. It was then that I met Wright, the racquet player, and exchanged the few words on the stairway already related.

Considering it well to have a supply of blankets for use in the open boats exposed to the cold, I concluded, while passing, to make another, and my last, descent to my stateroom for this purpose, only to find it locked, and on asking the reason why was told by some other steward than Cullen that it was done "to prevent looting." Advising him of what was wanted, I went with him to the cabin stewards' quarters nearby, where extra blankets were stored, and where I obtained them. I then went the length of the ship inside on this glass-enclosed Deck A from aft, forwards, looking in every room and corner for my missing table companions, but no passengers whatever were to be seen except in the smoking-room, and there all alone by themselves, seated around a table, were four men, three of whom were personally well known to me, Major Butt, Clarence Moore and Frank Millet, but the fourth was a stranger, whom I therefore cannot identify. All four seemed perfectly oblivious of what was going on on the decks outside. It is impossible to suppose that they did not know of the collision with an iceberg and that the room they were in had been deserted by all others, who had hastened away. It occurred to me at the time that these men desired to show their entire indifference to the danger and that if I advised them as to how seriously I regarded it, they would laugh at me. This was the last I ever saw of any of them, and I know of no one who testifies to seeing them later, except a lady who mentions having seen Major Butt on the bridge five minutes before the last boat left the ship. There is no authentic story of what they did when the water reached this deck, and their ultimate fate is only a matter of conjecture. That they went down in the ship on this Deck A, when the steerage passengers (as described later) blocked the way to the deck above, is my personal belief, founded on the following facts, to wit: First, that neither I nor anyone else, so far as I know, ever saw any of them on the Boat Deck, and second, that the bodies of none of them were ever recovered, indicating the possibility that all went down inside the ship or the enclosed deck.

I next find myself forward on the port side, part of the time on the Boat Deck, and part on the deck below it, called Deck A, where I rejoined Clinch Smith, who reported that Mrs. Candee had departed on one of the boats. We remained together until the ship went down. I was on the Boat Deck when I saw and heard the first rocket, and then successive ones sent up at intervals thereafter. These were followed by the Morse red and blue lights, which were signaled near by us on the deck where we were; but we looked in vain for any response. These signals of distress indicated to every one of us that the ship's fate was sealed, and that she might sink before the lifeboats could be lowered.

And now I am on Deck A again, where I helped in the loading of two boats lowered from the deck above. There were twenty boats in all on the ship: 14 wooden lifeboats, each thirty feet long by nine feet one inch broad, constructed to carry sixty-five persons each: 2 wooden cutters, emergency boats, twenty-five feet two inches long by seven feet two inches broad, constructed to carry forty persons each; and 4 Engelhardt "surf-boats" with canvas collapsible sides extending above the gunwales, twenty-five feet five inches long by eight feet broad, constructed to carry forty-seven persons each. The lifeboats were ranged along the ship's rail, or its prolongation forward and aft on the Boat Deck, the odd numbered on the starboard and the even numbered on the port side. Two of the Engelhardt boats were on the Boat Deck forward beneath the Emergency boats suspended on davits above. The other Engelhardt boats were on the roof of the officers' house forward of the first funnel. They are designated respectively by the letters, A, B, C, D; A and C on the starboard, B and D on the port sides. They have a rounded bottom like a canoe. The name "collapsible boat" generally applied has given rise to mistaken impressions in regard to them, because of the adjustable canvas sides above-mentioned.

At this quarter I was no longer held back from approaching near the boats, but my assistance and work as one of the crew in the loading of boats and getting them away as quickly as possible were accepted, for there was now no time to spare. The Second Officer, Lightoller, was in command on the port side forward, where I was. One of his feet was planted in the lifeboat, and the other on the rail of Deck A, while we, through the wood frames of the lowered glass windows on this deck, passed women, children, and babies in rapid succession without any confusion whatsoever. Among this number was Mrs. Astor, whom I lifted over the four-feet high rail of the ship through the frame. Her husband held her left arm as we carefully passed her to Lightoller, who seated her in the boat. A dialogue now ensued between Colonel Astor and the officer, every word of which I listened to with intense interest. Astor was close to me in the adjoining window-frame, to the left of mine. Leaning out over the rail he asked permission of Lightoller to enter the boat to protect his wife, which, in view of her delicate condition, seems to have been a reasonable request, but the officer, intent upon his duty, and obeying orders, and not knowing the millionaire from the rest of us, replied: "No, sir, no men are allowed in these boats until women are loaded first." Colonel Astor did not demur, but bore the refusal bravely and resignedly, simply asking the number of the boat to help find his wife later in case he also was rescued. "Number 4," was Lightoller's reply. Nothing more was said. Colonel Astor moved away from this point and I never saw him again. I do not for a moment believe the report that he attempted to enter, or did enter, a boat and it is evident that if any such thought occurred to him at all it must have been at this present time and in this boat with his wife. Second Officer Lightoller recalled the incident perfectly when I reminded him of it. It was only through me that Colonel Astor's identity was established in his mind. "I assumed," said he, "that I was asked to give the number of the lifeboat as the passenger intended, for some unknown cause, to make complaint about me." From the fact that I never saw Colonel Astor on the Boat Deck later, and also because his body, when found, was crushed (according to the statement of one who saw it at Halifax, Mr. Harry K. White, of Boston, Mr. Edward A. Kent's brother-in-law, my schoolmate and friend from boyhood), I am of the opinion that he met his fate on the ship when the boilers tore through it, as described later.

One of the incidents I recall when loading the boats at this point was my seeing a young woman clinging tightly to a baby in her arms as she approached near the ship's high rail, but unwilling even for a moment to allow anyone else to hold the little one while assisting her to board the lifeboat. As she drew back sorrowfully to the outer edge of the crowd on the deck, I followed and persuaded her to accompany me to the rail again, promising if she would entrust the baby to me I would see that the officer passed it to her after she got aboard. I remember her trepidation as she acceded to my suggestion and the happy expression of relief when the mother was safely seated with the baby restored to her. "Where is my baby?" was her anxious wail. "I have your baby," I cried, as it was tenderly handed along. I remember this incident well because of my feeling at the time, when I had the babe in my care; though the interval was short, I wondered how I should manage with it in my arms if the lifeboats got away and I should be plunged into the water with it as the ship sank.

According to Lightoller's testimony before the Senate Committee he put twenty to twenty-five women, with two seamen to row, in the first boat and thirty, with two seamen in the second.

Our labors in loading the boats were now shifted to the Boat Deck above, where Clinch Smith and I, with others, followed Lightoller and the crew. On this deck some difficulty was experienced in getting the boats ready to lower. Several causes may have contributed to this, viz., lack of drill and insufficient number of seamen for such emergency, or because of the new tackle not working smoothly. We had the hardest time with the Engelhardt boat, lifting and pushing it towards and over the rail. My shoulders and the whole weight of my body were used in assisting the crew at this work. Lightoller's testimony tells us that as the situation grew more serious he began to take chances and in loading the third boat he filled it up as full as he dared to, with about thirty-five persons. By this time he was short of seamen, and in the fourth boat he put the first man passenger. "Are you a sailor?" Lightoller asked, and received the reply from the gentleman addressed that he was "a yachtsman." Lightoller told him if he was "sailor enough to get out over the bulwarks to the lifeboats, to go ahead." This passenger was Major Arthur Peuchen, of Toronto, who acquitted himself as a brave man should. My energies were so concentrated upon this work of loading the boats at this quarter that lapse of time, sense of sight and sense of hearing recorded no impressions during this interval until the last boat was loaded; but there is one fact of which I am positive, and that is that every man, woman, officer and member of the crew did their full duty without a sign of fear or confusion. Lightoller's strong and steady voice rang out his orders in clear firm tones, inspiring confidence and obedience. There was not one woman who shed tears or gave any sign of fear or distress. There was not a man at this quarter of the ship who indicated a desire to get into the boats and escape with the women. There was not a member of the crew who shirked, or left his post. The coolness, courage, and sense of duty that I here witnessed made me thankful to God and proud of my Anglo-Saxon race that gave this perfect and superb exhibition of self-control at this hour of severest trial. "The boat's deck was only ten feet from the water when I lowered the sixth boat," testified Lightoller, "and when we lowered the first, the distance to the water was seventy feet. We had now loaded all the women who were in sight at that quarter of the ship, and I ran along the deck with Clinch Smith on the port side some distance aft shouting, "Are there any more women?" "Are there any more women?" On my return there was a very palpable list to port as if the ship was about to topple over. The deck was on a corresponding slant. "All passengers to the starboard side," was Lightoller's loud command, heard by all of us. Here I thought the final crisis had come, with the boats all gone, and when we were to be precipitated into the sea.

Prayerful thoughts now began to rise in me that my life might be pre-served and I be restored to my loved ones at home. I weighed myself in the balance, doubtful whether I was thus deserving of God's mercy and protection. I questioned myself as to the performance of my religious duties according to the instructions of my earliest Preceptor, the Rev. Henry A. Coit, whose St. Paul's School at Concord, N. H., I had attended. My West Point training in the matter of recognition of con-stituted authority and maintenance of composure stood me in good stead.

My friend, Clinch Smith, urged immediate obedience to Lightoller's orders, and, with other men passengers, we crossed over to the starboard quarter of the ship, forward on the same Boat Deck where, as I afterwards learned, the officer in command was First Officer Murdoch, who had also done noble work, and was soon thereafter to lose his life. Though the deck here was not so noticeably aslant as on the port side, the conditions appeared fully as desperate. All the lifeboats had been lowered and had departed. There was somewhat of a crowd congregated along the rail. The light was sufficient for me to recognize distinctly many of those with whom I was well acquainted. Here, pale and determined, was Mr. John B. Thayer, Second Vice-President of the Pennsylvania Railroad, and Mr. George D. Widener. They were looking over the ship's gunwale, talking earnestly as if debating what to do. Next to them it pained me to discover Mrs. J. M.. Brown and Miss Evans, the two ladies whom more than an hour previous I had, as related, consigned to the care of Sixth Officer Moody on Deck A, where he, as previously described, blocked my purpose of accompanying these ladies and personally assisting them into the boat. They showed no signs of perturbation whatever as they conversed quietly with me. Mrs. Brown quickly related how they became separated, in the crowd, from her sisters, Mrs. Appleton and Mrs. Cornell. Alas! that they had not remained on the same port side of the ship, or moved forward on Deck A, or the Boat Deck! Instead, they had wandered in some unexplained way to the very furthest point diagonally from where they were at first. At the time of introduction I had not caught Miss Evans' name, and when we were here together at this critical moment I thought it important to ask, and she gave me her name. Meantime the crew were working on the roof of the officers' quarters to cut loose one of the Engelhardt boats. All this took place more quickly than it takes to write it.

Meantime, I will describe what was going on at the quarter where I left Lightoller loading the last boat on the port side. The information was obtained personally from him, in answer to my careful questioning during the next few days on board the *Carpathia*, when I made notes thereof, which were confirmed again the next week in Washington, where we were both summoned before the Senate Investigating Committee. "Men from the steerage," he said, "rushed the boat." "Rush" is the word he used, meaning they got in without his permission. He drew his pistol and ordered them out, threatening to shoot if they attempted to enter the boat again. I presume it was in consequence of this incident that the crew established the line which I encountered, presently referred to, which blocked the men passengers from approaching the last boat loaded on the port side forward, where we had been, and the last one that was safely loaded from the ship.

During this very short interval I was on the starboard side, as described, next to the rail, with Mrs. Brown and Miss Evans, when I heard a member of the crew, coming from the quarter where the last boat was loaded, say that there was room for more ladies in it. I immediately seized each lady by the arm, and, with Miss Evans on my right and Mrs. Brown on my left, hurried, with three other ladies following us, toward the port side; but I had not proceeded half-way, and near amidship, when I was stopped by the aforesaid line of the crew barring my progress, and one of the officers told me that only the women could pass.

The story of what now happened to Mrs. Brown and Miss Evans after they left me must be told by Mrs. Brown, as related to me by herself when I rejoined her next on board the *Carpathia*. Miss Evans led the way, she said, as they neared the rail where what proved to be the last lifeboat was being loaded, but in a spirit of most heroic self-sacrifice Miss Evans insisted upon Mrs. Brown's taking precedence in being assisted aboard the boat. "You go first," she said. "You are married and have children." But when Miss Evans attempted to follow after, she was unable to do so for some unknown cause. The women in the boat were not able, it would appear, to pull Miss Evans in. It was necessary for her first to clear the four feet high ship's gunwale, and no man or member of the crew was at this particular point to lift her over. I have questioned Mr. Lightoller several times about this, but he has not been able to give any satisfactory explanation and cannot understand it, for when he gave orders to lower away, there was no woman in sight. I have further questioned him as to whether there was an interval between the ship's rail and the lifeboat he was loading, but he says, "No," for until the very last boat he stood, as has already been described, with one foot planted on the ship's gunwale and the other in the lifeboat. I had thought that the list of the ship might have caused too much of an interval for him to have done this. Perhaps what I have read in a letter of Mrs. Brown may furnish some reason why Miss Evans' efforts to board the lifeboat, in which there was plenty of room for her, were unavailing. "Never mind," she is said to have called out, "I will go on a later boat." She then ran away and was not seen again; but there was no later boat, and it would seem that after a momentary impulse, being disappointed and being unable to get into the boat, she went aft on the port side, and no one saw her again. Neither the second officer nor I saw any women on the deck during the interval thereafter of fifteen or twenty minutes before the great ship sank.

An inspection of the American and British Reports shows that all women and children of the first cabin were saved except five. Out of the one hundred and fifty these were the five lost: (1) Miss Evans; (2) Mrs. Straus; (3) Mrs. H. J. Allison, of Montreal; (4) her daughter, Miss Allison, and (5) Miss A. E. Isham, of New York. The first two have already been accounted for. Mrs. Allison and Miss Allison could have been saved had they not chosen to remain on the ship. They refused to enter the lifeboat unless Mr. Allison was allowed to go with them. This statement was made in my presence by Mrs. H. A. Cassobeer, of New York, who related it to Mrs. Allison's brother, Mr. G. F. Johnston, and myself. Those of us who survived among the first cabin passengers will remember this beautiful Mrs. Allison, and will be glad to know of the heroic mould in which she was cast, as exemplified by her fate, which was similar to that of another, Mrs. Straus, who has been memorialized the world over. The fifth lady lost was Miss A. E. Isham, and she is the only one of whom no survivor, so far as I can learn, is able to give any information whatever as to where she was or what she did on that fateful Sunday night. Her relatives, learning that her stateroom, No. C, 49, adjoined mine, wrote me in the hope that I might be able to furnish some information to their sorrowing hearts about her last hours on the shipwrecked *Titanic*. It was with much regret that I replied that I had not seen my neighbor at any time, and, not having the pleasure of her acquaintance, identification was impossible. I was, however, glad to be able to assure her family of one point, viz., that she did not meet with the horrible fate which they feared, in being locked in her stateroom and drowned. I had revisited my stateroom twice after being aroused by the collision, and am sure that she was fully warned of what had happened, and after she left her stateroom it was locked behind her, as was mine.

The simple statement of fact that all of the first cabin women were sent off in the lifeboats and saved, except five—three of whom met heroic death through choice and two by some mischance—is in itself the most sublime tribute that could be paid to the self-sacrifice and the gallantry of the first cabin men, including all the grand heroes who sank with the ship and those of us who survived their fate. All authentic testimony of both first and second cabin passengers is also in evidence that the Captain's order for women and children to be loaded first met with the unanimous approval of us all, and in every instance was carried out both in letter and in spirit. In Second Officer Lightoller's testimony before the Senate Committee, when asked whether the Captain's order was a rule of the sea, he answered that it was "the rule of human nature." There is no doubt in my mind that the men at that quarter where we were would have adopted the same rule spontaneously whether ordered by the Captain, or not. Speaking from my own personal observation, which by comparison with that of the second officer I find in accord with his, all six boat loads, including the last, departed with women and children only, with not a man passenger except Major Peuchen, whose services were enlisted to replace the lack of crew. I may say further that with the single exception of Colonel Astor's plea for the protection of his wife, in delicate condition, there was not one who made a move or a suggestion to enter a boat.

While the light was dim on the decks it was always sufficient for me to recognize anyone with whom I was acquainted, and I am happy in being able to record the names of those I know beyond any doubt whatever, as with me in these last terrible scenes when Lightoller's boats were being lowered and after the last lifeboat had left the ship. The names of these were: James Clinch Smith, Colonel John Jacob Astor, Mr. John B. Thayer and Mr. George D. Widener. So far as I know, and my research has been exhaustive, I am the sole surviving passenger who was with or assisted Lightoller in the loading of the last boats. When I first saw and realized that every lifeboat had left the ship, the sensation felt was not an agreeable one. No thought of fear entered my head, but I experienced a feeling which others may recall when holding the breath in the face of some frightful emergency and when "vox faucibus hæsit," as frequently happened to the old Trojan hero of our school days. This was the nearest approach to fear, if it can be so characterized, that is discernible in an analysis of my actions or feelings while in the midst of the many dangers which beset me during that night of terror. Though still worse and seemingly many hopeless conditions soon prevailed, and unexpected ones, too, when I felt that "any moment might be my last," I had no time to contemplate danger when there was continuous need of quick thought, action and composure withal. Had I become rattled for a moment, or in the slightest degree been undecided during the several emergencies presently cited, I am certain that I never should have lived to tell the tale of my miraculous escape. For it is eminently fitting, in gratitude to my Maker, that I should make the acknowledgment that I know of no recorded instance of Providential deliverance more directly attributable to cause and effect, illustrating the efficacy of prayer and how "God helps those who help themselves." I should have only courted the fate of many hundreds of others had I supinely made no effort to supplement my prayers with all the strength and power which He has granted to me. While I said to myself, "Good-bye to all at home," I hoped and prayed for escape. My mind was nerved to do the duty of the moment, and my muscles seemed to be hardened in preparation for any struggle that might come. When I learned that there was still another boat, the Engelhardt, on the roof of the officers' quarters, I felt encouraged with the thought that here was a chance of getting away before the ship sank; but what was one boat among so many eager to board her?

During my short absence in conducting the ladies to a position of safety, Mr. Thayer and Mr. Widener had disappeared, but I know not whither. Mr. Widener's son, Harry, was probably with them, but Mr. Thayer supposed that his young son, Jack, had left the ship in the same boat with his mother. Messrs. Thayer and Widener must have gone toward the stern during the short interval of my absence. No one at this point had jumped into the sea. If there had been any, both Clinch Smith and I would have known it. After the water struck the bridge forward there were many who rushed aft, climbed over the rail and jumped, but I never saw one of them.

I was now working with the crew at the davits on the starboard side forward, adjusting them, ready for lowering the Engelhardt boat from the roof of the officers' house to the Boat Deck below. Some one of the crew on the roof, where it was, sang out, " Has any passenger a knife ? " I took mine out of my pocket and tossed it to him, saying, " Here is a small penknife, if that will do any good." It appeared to me then that there was more trouble than there ought to have been in removing the canvas cover and cutting the boat loose, and that some means should have been available for doing this without any delay. Meantime, four or five long oars were placed aslant against the walls of the officers' house to break the fall of the boat, which was pushed from the roof and slipped with a crash down on the Boat Deck, smashing several of the oars. Clinch Smith and I scurried out of the way and stood leaning with our backs against the rail, watching this procedure and feeling anxious lest the boat might have been stove in, or otherwise injured so as to cause her to leak in the water. The account of the junior Marconi operator, Harold S. Bride, supplements mine. " I saw a collapsible boat," he said, " near a funnel, and went over to it. Twelve men were trying to boost it down to the Boat Deck. They were having an awful time. It was the last boat left. I looked at it longingly a few minutes; then I gave a hand and over she went."

About this time I recall that an officer on the roof of the house called down to the crew at this quarter, "Are there any seamen down there among you?" "Aye, aye, sir," was the response, and quite a number left the Boat Deck to assist in what I supposed to have been the cutting loose of the other Engelhardt boat up there on the roof. Again I heard an inquiry for another knife. I thought I recognized the voice of the second officer working up there with the crew. Lightoller has told me, and has written me as well, that "boat A on the starboard side did not leave the ship," [1] while "B was thrown down to the Boat Deck," and was the one on which he and I eventually climbed. The crew had thrown the Engelhardt boat to the deck, but I did not understand why they were so long about launching it, unless they were waiting to cut the other one loose and launch them both at the same time. Two young men of the crew, nice looking, dressed in white, one tall and the other smaller, were coolly debating as to whether the compartments would hold the ship afloat. They were standing with their backs to the rail looking on at the rest of the crew, and I recall asking one of them why he did not assist.

At this time there were other passengers around, but Clinch Smith was the only one associated with me here to the last. It was about this time, fifteen minutes after the launching of the last lifeboat on the port side, that I heard a noise that spread consternation among us all. This was no less than the water striking the bridge and gurgling up the hatchway forward. It seemed momentarily as if it would reach the Boat Deck. It appeared as if it would take the crew a long time to turn the Engelhardt boat right side up and lift it over the rail, and there were so many ready to board her that she would have been swamped. Probably taking these points into consideration, Clinch Smith made the proposition that we should leave and go toward the stern, still on the starboard side, so he started and I followed immediately after him. We had taken but a few steps in the direction indicated when there arose before us from the decks below, a mass of humanity several lines deep, covering the Boat Deck, facing us, and completely blocking our passage toward the stern.

There were women in the crowd, as well as men, and they seemed to be steerage passengers who had just come up from the decks below. Instantly, when they saw us and the water on the deck chasing us from behind, they turned in the opposite direction towards the stern. This brought them at that point plumb against the iron fence and railing which divide the first and second cabin passengers. Even among these people there was no hysterical cry, or evidence of panic, but oh, the agony of it! Clinch Smith and I instantly saw that we could make no progress ahead, and with the water following us behind over the deck, we were in a desperate place. I can never forget the exact point on the ship where he and I were located, viz., at the opening of the angle made by the walls of the officers' house and only a short distance abaft the *Titanic*'s forward "expansion joint." Clinch Smith was immediately on

[1] With the evidence on the subject presented later he recognizes that Boat A floated away and was afterwards utilized.

my left, nearer the apex of the angle, and our backs were turned toward the ship's rail and the sea. Looking up toward the roof of the officers' house I saw a man to the right of me and above lying on his stomach on the roof, with his legs dangling over. Clinch Smith jumped to reach this roof, and I promptly followed. The efforts of both of us failed. I was loaded down with heavy long-skirted overcoat and Norfolk coat beneath, with clumsy life-preserver over all, which made my jump fall short. As I came down, the water struck my right side. I crouched down into it preparatory to jumping with it, and rose as if on the crest of a wave on the seashore. This expedient brought the attainment of the object I had in view. I was able to reach the roof and the iron railing that is along the edge of it, and pulled myself over on top of the officers' house on my stomach near the base of the second funnel. The feat which I instinctively accomplished was the simple one, familiar to all bathers in the surf at the seashore. I had no time to advise Clinch Smith to adopt it. To my utter dismay, a hasty glance to my left and right showed that he had not followed my example, and that the wave, if I may call it such, which had mounted me to the roof, had completely covered him, as well as all people on both sides of me, including the man I had first seen athwart the roof.

I was thus parted forever from my friend, Clinch Smith, with whom I had agreed to remain to the last struggle. I felt almost a pang of responsibility for our separation; but he was not in sight and there was no chance of rendering assistance. His ultimate fate is a matter of conjecture. Hemmed in by the mass of people toward the stern, and cornered in the locality previously described, it seems certain that as the ship keeled over and sank, his body was caught in the angle or in the coils of rope and other appurtenances on the deck and borne down to the depths below. There could not be a braver man than James Clinch Smith. He was the embodiment of coolness and courage during the whole period of the disaster. While in constant touch and communication with him at the various points on the ship when we were together on this tragic night, he never showed the slightest sign of fear, but manifested the same quiet imperturbable manner so well known to all of his friends, who join with his family in mourning his loss. His conduct should be an inspiration to us all, and an appropriate epitaph to his memory taken from the words of Christ would be: "Greater love hath no man than this, that a man lay down his life for his friend."

# CHAPTER III

# THE FOUNDERING OF THE
# *TITANIC*

*There is sorrow on the sea; it cannot be quiet.*—Jeremiah 49 : 23

**B**efore I resume the story of my personal escape it is pertinent that I should, at this juncture, discuss certain points wherein the statements of survivors are strangely at variance.

*First:* Was there an explosion of the ship's boilers?

I am of opinion that there was none, because I should have been conscious of it. When aboard ship I should have heard it and felt it, but I did not. As my senses were on the lookout for every danger, I cannot conceive it possible that an explosion occurred without my being made aware of it. When I went down holding on to the ship and was under water, I heard no sound indicating anything of the sort, and when I came to the surface there was no ship in sight. Furthermore, there was no perceptible wave which such a disturbance would have created.

The two ranking surviving officers of the *Titanic*, viz., Second Officer Lightoller and Third Officer Pitman, with whom I had a discussion on this and other points in almost daily conversation in my cabin on the *Carpathia*, agreed with me that there was no explosion of the boilers. The second officer and myself had various similar experiences, and, as will be noticed in the course of this narrative, we were very near together during all the perils of that awful night. The only material difference worth noting was the manner in which each parted company with the ship, and finally reached the bottom-up Engelhardt boat on top of which we made our escape. According to his testimony before the Senate Committee, he stood on the roof of the officers' quarters in front of the first funnel, facing forward, and as the ship dived, he dived also, while I held on to the iron railing on the same roof, near the second funnel, as has been described, and as the ship sank I was pulled down with it. The distance between us on the ship was then about fifteen yards.

THE TRUTH ABOUT THE "TITANIC"

There are so many newspaper and other published reports citing the statements of certain survivors as authority for this story of an explosion of the boilers that the reading world generally has been made to believe it. Among the names of passengers whose alleged statements (I have received letters repudiating some of these interviews) are thus given credence, I have read those of Miss Cornelia Andrews, of Hudson, N. Y.; Mrs. W. E. Carter, of Philadelphia, Pa.; Mr. John Pillsbury Snyder, of Minneapolis, Minn.; Miss Minahan, of Fond du Lac, Wis., and Lady Duff Gordon, of England, all of whom, according to the newspaper reports, describe their position in the lifeboats around the ship and how they heard, or saw, the "ship blow up," or "the boilers explode" with one or two explosions just before the ship sank out of their sight. On the other hand, Mr. Hugh Woolner told me on the *Carpathia* that from his position in the lifeboat, which he claims was the nearest one to the *Titanic* when she sank some seventy-five yards away, there was a terrific noise on the ship, as she slanted towards the head before the final plunge, which sounded like the crashing of millions of dishes of crockery. Woolner and I when on board the *Carpathia*, as presently described, had our cabin together, where we were visited by Officers Lightoller and Pitman. This was one of the points we discussed together, and the conclusion was at once reached as to the cause of this tremendous crash. Since then, Lightoller has been subjected to rigid examination before this country's and England's Investigating Committees, and has been a party to discussions with experts, including the designers and builders of the *Titanic*. His conclusion expressed on the *Carpathia* is now strengthened, and he says that there was no explosion of the boilers and that the great noise which was mistaken for it was due to "the boilers leaving their beds" on E Deck when the ship was aslant and, with their great weight, sliding along the deck, crushing and tearing through the doomed vessel forward toward the bow. Third Officer Pitman also gave his testimony on this, as well as the next point considered. Before the Senate Committee he said: "Then she turned right on end and made a big plunge forward. The *Titanic* did not break asunder. I heard reports like big guns in the distance. I assumed the great bulkheads had gone to pieces." Cabin-steward Samuel Rule said: "I think the noise we heard was that of the boilers and engines breaking away from their seatings and falling down through the forward bulkhead. At the time it occurred, the ship was standing nearly upright in the water."

The peculiar way in which the *Titanic* is described as hesitating and assuming a vertical position before her final dive to the depths below can be accounted for only on this hypothesis of the sliding of the boilers from their beds. A second-cabin passenger, Mr. Lawrence Beesley, a Cambridge University man, has written an excellent book about the *Titanic* disaster, dwelling especially upon the lessons to be learned from it. His account given to the newspapers also contains the most graphic description from the viewpoint of those in the lifeboats, telling how the great ship looked before her final plunge. He "was a mile or two miles away," he writes, "when the oarsmen lay on their oars and all in the lifeboat were motionless as we watched the ship in absolute silence—save some who would not look and buried their heads on each other's shoulders. . . . As we gazed awe-struck, she tilted slightly up, revolving apparently about a centre of gravity just astern of amidships until she attained a vertical upright position, and there she remained—motionless! As she swung up, her lights, which had shown without a flicker all night, went out suddenly, then came on again for a single flash and then went out altogether; and as they did so there came a noise which many people, wrongly, I think, have described as an explosion. It has always seemed to me that it was nothing but the engines and machinery coming loose from their place and bearings and falling through the compartments, smashing everything in their way. It was partly a roar, partly a groan, partly a rattle and partly a smash, and it was not a sudden roar as an explosion would be; it went on successively for some seconds, possibly fifteen or twenty, as the heavy machinery dropped down to the bottom (now the bows) of the ship; I suppose it fell through the end and sank first before the ship. (For evidence of shattered timbers, see Hagan's testimony, p. 156.) But it was a noise no one had heard before and no one wishes to hear again. It was stupefying, stupendous, as it came to us along the water. It was as if all the heavy things one could think of had been thrown downstairs from the top of a house, smashing each other, and the stairs and everything in the way.

"Several apparently authentic accounts have been given in which definite stories of explosions have been related—in some cases even with wreckage blown up and the ship broken in two; but I think such accounts will not stand close analysis. In the first place, the fires had been withdrawn and the steam allowed to escape some time before she sank, and the possibility from explosion from this cause seems very remote."

*Second:* Did the ship break in two?

I was on the *Carpathia* when I first heard any one make reference to this point. The seventeen-year-old son of Mr. John B. Thayer, "Jack" Thayer, Jr., and his young friend from Philadelphia, R. N. Williams, Jr., the tennis expert, in describing their experiences to me were positive that they saw the ship split in two. This was from their position in

The 29 enormous boilers for the *Titanic* dwarf an attendant in the aisle. These boilers crashed through the ship as it sank.

Steerage passengers ate in a relatively simple dining room, similar to this one on the *Olympic*.

the water on the starboard quarter. "Jack" Thayer gave this same description to an artist, who reproduced it in an illustration in the New York *Herald*, which many of us have seen. Some of the passengers, whose names I have just mentioned, are also cited by the newspapers as authority for the statements that the ship "broke in two," that she "buckled amidships," that she "was literally torn to pieces," etc. On the other hand, there is much testimony available which is at variance with this much-advertised sensational newspaper account. Summing up its investigation of this point the Senate Committee's Report reads: "There have been many conflicting statements as to whether the ship broke in two, but the preponderance of evidence is to the effect that she assumed an almost end-on position and sank intact." This was as Lightoller testified before the Committee, that the *Titanic*'s decks were "absolutely intact" when she went down. On this point, too, Beesley is in accord, from his viewpoint in the lifeboat some distance away out of danger, whence, more composedly than others, he could see the last of the ill-fated ship as the men lay on their oars watching until she disappeared. "No phenomenon," he continues, "like that pictured in some American and English papers occurred—that of the ship breaking in two, and the two ends being raised above the surface. When the noise was over, the *Titanic* was still upright like a column; we could see her now only as the stern and some 150 feet of her stood outlined against the star-specked sky, looming black in the darkness, and in this position she continued for some minutes—I think as much as five minutes—but it may have been less. Then, as sinking back a little at the stern, I thought she slid slowly forwards through the water and dived slantingly down."

From my personal viewpoint I also know that the *Titanic*'s decks were intact at the time she sank, and when I sank with her, there was over seven-sixteenths of the ship already under water, and there was no indication then of any impending break of the deck or ship. I recently visited the sister ship of the *Titanic*, viz., the *Olympic*, at her dock in New York harbor. This was for the purpose of still further familiarizing myself with the corresponding localities which were the scene of my personal experiences on the *Titanic*, and which are referred to in this narrative. The only difference in the deck plan of the sister ship which I noted, and which the courteous officers of the *Olympic* mentioned, is that the latter ship's Deck A is not glass-enclosed like the *Titanic*'s; but one of the principal points of discovery that I made during my investigation concerns this matter of the alleged breaking in two of this magnificent ship. The White Star Line officers pointed out to me what they called the ship's "forward expansion joint," and they claimed the *Titanic* was so constructed that she must have split in two at this point, if she did so at all. I was interested in observing that this "expansion joint" was less than twelve feet forward from that point on the Boat Deck whence I jumped, as described (to the iron railing on the roof of the officers' quarters). It is indicated by a black streak of leather-covering running transversely across the deck and then up the vertical white wall of the officers' house. This "joint" extends, however, only through the Boat Deck and Decks A and B, which are super-imposed on Deck C. If there was any splitting in two, it seems to me also that this superstructure, weakly joined, would have been the part to split; but it certainly did not. It was only a few seconds before the time of the alleged break that I stepped across this dividing line of the two sections and went down with the after section about twelve feet from this "expansion joint."

One explanation which I offer of what must be a delusion on the part of the advocates of the "break-in-two" theory is that when the forward funnel fell, as hereafter described, it may have looked as if the ship itself was splitting in two, particularly to the young men who are cited as authority.

*Third:* Did either the Captain or the First Officer shoot himself?

Notwithstanding all the current rumors and newspaper statements answering this question affirmatively, I have been unable to find any passenger or member of the crew cited as authority for the statement that either Captain Smith or First Officer Murdoch did anything of the sort. On the contrary, so far as relates to Captain Smith, there are several witnesses, including Harold S. Bride, the junior Marconi operator, who saw him at the last on the bridge of his ship, and later, when sinking and struggling in the water. Neither can I discover any authentic testi-mony about First Officer Murdoch's shooting himself. On the contrary, I find fully sufficient evidence that he did not. He was a brave and effic-ient officer and no sufficient motive for self-destruction can be ad-vanced. He performed his full duty under difficult circumstances, and was entitled to praise and honor. During the last fifteen minutes before the ship sank, I was located at that quarter forward on the Boat Deck, starboard side, where Murdoch was in command and where the crew under him were engaged in the vain attempt of launching the Engel-hardt boat. The report of a pistol shot during this interval ringing in my ears within a few feet of me would certainly have attracted my attention, and later, when I moved astern, the distance between us was not so great as to prevent my hearing it. The "big wave" or "giant wave," described by Harold Bride, swept away Murdoch and the crew from the Boat Deck first before it struck me, and when I rose with it to the roof of the officers' house, Bride's reported testimony fits in with mine so far as relates to time, place, and circumstance, and I quote his words as follows: "About ten minutes before the ship sank, Captain Smith gave word for every man to look to his own safety. I sprang to aid the men struggling to launch the life raft (Engelhardt boat), and we had succeeded in getting it to the edge of the ship when a giant wave carried it away." Lightoller also told me on board the *Carpathia* that he saw Murdoch when he was engulfed by the water and that if before this a pistol had been fired within the short distance that separated them, he also is confident that he would have heard it.

*Fourth:* On which side did the ship list?

The testimony on this point, which at first blush appears conflicting, proves on investigation not at all so, but just what was to be expected from the mechanical construction of the ship. We find the most authoritative testimony in evidence that the *Titanic* listed on the starboard side, and again, on equally authoritative testimony, that she listed on the port side. Quartermaster Hitchens, who was at the wheel when the iceberg struck the ship, testified on this point before the Senate Committee as follows: "The Captain came back to the wheel house and looked at the commutator (clinometer) in front of the compass, which is a little instrument like a clock to tell you how the ship is listing. The ship had a list of five degrees to the starboard about five or ten minutes after the impact." Mr. Karl Behr, the well-known tennis player, interviewed by the New York *Tribune* is quoted as saying: "We had just retired when the collision came. I pulled on my clothes and went down the deck to the Beckwith cabin and, after I had roused them, I noted that the ship listed to the starboard, and that was the first thing that made me think that we were in for serious trouble." On the other hand, the first time I noticed this list was, as already described in my narrative, when I met Clinch Smith in the companionway and we saw a slight list to port, which gave us the first warning of how serious the accident was. The next and last time, as has also been described, was when Second Officer Lightoller ordered all passengers to the starboard side because of the very palpable list to port, when the great ship suddenly appeared to be about to topple over. Lightoller also corroborates the statement as to this list on the port side. Other witnesses might be quoted, some of whom testify to the starboard list, and others to the one to port. The conclusion, therefore, is reached that the *Titanic* listed at one time to starboard and at another time to port. This is as it should be because of the transverse water-tight compartments which made the water, immediately after the compact, rush from the starboard quarter to the port, and then back again, keeping the ship balancing on her keel until she finally sank. If she had been constructed otherwise, with longitudinal compartments only, it is evident that after the impact on the starboard side, the *Titanic* would have listed only to the starboard side, and after a very much shorter interval would have careened over on that quarter, and a much smaller proportion of lives would have been saved.

CHAPTER IV

# STRUGGLING IN THE WATER
# FOR LIFE

*Out of the deep have I called unto Thee, O Lord.*—Ps. 130 : 1

I now resume the narrative description of my miraculous escape, and it is with considerable diffidence that I do so, for the personal equation monopolizes more attention than may be pleasing to my readers who are not relatives or intimate friends.

As may be noticed in Chapter II, it was Clinch Smith's suggestion and on his initiative that we left that point on the starboard side of the Boat Deck where the crew, under Chief Officer Wilde and First Officer Murdoch, were in vain trying to launch the Engelhardt boat B which had been thrown down from the roof of the officers' quarters forward of the first funnel. I say "Boat B" because I have the information to that effect in a letter from Second Officer Lightoller. Confirmation of this statement I also find in the reported interview of a Saloon Steward, Thomas Whitely, in the New York *Tribune* the day after the *Carpathia's* arrival. An analysis of his statement shows that Boat A became entangled and was abandoned, while he saw the other, bottom up and filled with people. It was on this boat that he also eventually climbed and was saved with the rest of us. Clinch Smith and I got away from this point just before the water reached it and drowned Chief Officer Wilde and First Officer Murdoch, and others who were not successful in effecting a lodgment on the boat as it was swept off the deck. This moment was the first fateful crisis of the many that immediately followed. As bearing upon it I quote the reported statement of Harold S. Bride, the junior Marconi operator. His account also helps to determine the fate of Captain Smith. He says: "Then came the Captain's voice [from the bridge to the Marconi operators], 'Men, you have done your full duty. You can do no more. Abandon your cabin. Now, it is every man for himself.'" "Phillips continued to work," he says, "for about ten minutes or about fifteen minutes after the Captain had released him. The water was then coming into our cabin. . . . I went to the place

147

where I had seen the collapsible boat on the Boat Deck and to my surprise I saw the boat, and the men still trying to push it off. They could
not do it. I went up to them and was just lending a hand when a large
wave came awash of the deck. The big wave carried the boat off. I had
hold of an oarlock and I went off with it. The next I knew I was in the
boat. But that was not all. I was in the boat and the boat was upside
down and I was under it. . . . How I got out from under the boat I do
not know, but I felt a breath at last."

From this it appears evident that, so far as Clinch Smith is concerned,
it would have been better to have stayed by this Engelhardt boat to the
last, for here he had a chance of escape like Bride and others of the
crew who clung to it, but which I only reached again after an incredibly
long swim under water. The next crisis, which was the fatal one to
Clinch Smith and to the great mass of people that suddenly arose
before us as I followed him astern, has already been described. The
simple expedient of jumping with the "big wave" as demonstrated
above carried me to safety, away from a dangerous position to the
highest part of the ship; but I was the only one who adopted it successfully. The force of the wave that struck Clinch Smith and the others
undoubtedly knocked most of them there unconscious against the
walls of the officers' quarters and other appurtenances of the ship on the
Boat Deck. As the ship keeled over forward, I believe that their bodies
were caught in the angles of this deck, or entangled in the ropes, and in
these other appurtenances thereon, and sank with the ship.

My holding on to the iron railing just when I did prevented my being
knocked unconscious. I pulled myself over on the roof on my stomach,
but before I could get to my feet I was in a whirlpool of water, swirling
round and round, as I still tried to cling to the railing as the ship
plunged to the depths below. Down, down, I went: it seemed a great
distance. There was a very noticeable pressure upon my ears, though
there must have been plenty of air that the ship carried down with it.
When under water I retained, as it appears, a sense of general direction,
and, as soon as I could do so, swam away from the starboard side of the
ship, as I knew my life depended upon it. I swam with all my strength,
and I seemed endowed with an extra supply for the occasion. I was
incited to desperate effort by the thought of boiling water, or steam,
from the expected explosion of the ship's boilers, and that I would be
scalded to death, like the sailors of whom I had read in the account of
the British battle-ship *Victoria* sunk in collision with the *Camperdown*
in the Mediterranean in 1893. Second Officer Lightoller told me he
also had the same idea, and that if the fires had not been drawn the
boilers would explode and the water become boiling hot. As a conse-

quence, the plunge in the icy water produced no sense of coldness whatever, and I had no thought of cold until later on when I climbed on the bottom of the upturned boat. My being drawn down by suction to a greater depth was undoubtedly checked to some degree by the life-preserver which I wore, but it is to the buoyancy of the water, caused by the volume of air rising from the sinking ship, that I attributed the assistance which enabled me to strike out and swim faster and further under water than I ever did before. I held my breath for what seemed an interminable time until I could scarcely stand it any longer, but I congratulated myself then and there that not one drop of sea-water was allowed to enter my mouth. With renewed determination and set jaws, I swam on. Just at the moment I thought that for lack of breath I would have to give in, I seemed to have been provided with a second wind, and it was just then that the thought that this was my last moment came upon me. I wanted to convey the news of how I died to my loved ones at home. As I swam beneath the surface of the ocean, I prayed that my spirit could go to them and say, "Good-bye, until we meet again in heaven." In this connection, the thought was in my mind of a well authenticated experience of mental telepathy that occurred to a member of my wife's family. Here in my case was a similar experience of a ship-wrecked loved one, and I thought if I prayed hard enough that this, my last wish to communicate with my wife and daughter, might be granted.

To what extent my prayer was answered let Mrs. Gracie describe in her own written words, as follows: "I was in my room at my sister's house, where I was visiting, in New York. After retiring, being unable to rest I questioned myself several times over, wondering what it was that prevented the customary long and peaceful slumber, lately enjoyed. 'What is the matter?' I uttered. A voice in reply seemed to say, 'On your knees and pray.' Instantly, I literally obeyed with my prayer book in my hand, which by chance opened at the prayer 'For those at Sea.' The thought then flashed through my mind, 'Archie is praying for me.' I continued wide awake until a little before five o'clock a. m., by the watch that lay beside me. About 7 a. m. I dozed a while and then got up to dress for breakfast. At 8 o'clock my sister, Mrs. Dalliba Dutton, came softly to the door, newspaper in hand, to gently break the tragic news that the *Titanic* had sunk, and showed me the list of only twenty names saved, headed with '*Colonel* Archibald Butt'; but my husband's name was not included. My head sank in her protecting arms as I murmured helplessly, 'He is all I have in the whole world.' I could only pray for strength, and later in the day, believing myself a widow, I wrote to my daughter, who was in the care of our housekeeper and servants in our Washington home, 'Cannot you see your father in his tenderness for women and children, helping them all, and then going down with the ship? If he has gone, I will not live long, but I would not have him take a boat.'"

But let me now resume my personal narrative. With this second wind under water there came to me a new lease of life and strength, until finally I noticed by the increase of light that I was drawing near to the surface. Though it was not daylight, the clear star-lit night made a noticeable difference in the degree of light immediately below the surface of the water. As I was rising, I came in contact with ascending wreckage, but the only thing I struck of material size was a small plank, which I tucked under my right arm. This circumstance brought with it the reflection that it was advisable for me to secure what best I could to keep me afloat on the surface until succor arrived. When my head at last rose above the water, I detected a piece of wreckage like a wooden crate, and I eagerly seized it as a nucleus of the projected raft to be constructed from what flotsam and jetsam I might collect. Looking about me, I could see no *Titanic* in sight. She had entirely disappeared beneath the calm surface of the ocean and without a sign of any wave. That the sea had swallowed her up with all her precious belongings was indicated by the slight sound of a gulp behind me as the water closed over her. The length of time that I was under water can be estimated by the fact that I sank with her, and when I came up there was no ship in sight. The accounts of others as to the length of time it took the *Titanic* to sink afford the best measure of the interval I was below the surface.

What impressed me at the time that my eyes beheld the horrible scene was a thin light-gray smoky vapor that hung like a pall a few feet above the broad expanse of sea that was covered with a mass of tangled wreckage. That it was a tangible vapor, and not a product of imagination, I feel well assured. It may have been caused by smoke or steam rising to the surface around the area where the ship had sunk. At any rate it produced a supernatural effect, and the pictures I had seen by Dante and the description I had read in my Virgil of the infernal regions, of Charon, and the River Lethe, were then uppermost in my thoughts. Add to this, within the area described, which was as far as my eyes could reach, there arose to the sky the most horrible sounds ever heard by mortal man except by those of us who survived this terrible tragedy. The agonizing cries of death from over a thousand throats, the wails and groans of the suffering, the shrieks of the terror-stricken and the awful gaspings for breath of those in the last throes of drowning, none of us will ever forget to our dying day. "Help! Help! Boat ahoy! Boat ahoy!" and "My God! My God!" were the heartrending cries and shrieks of men, which floated to us over the surface of the dark waters continuously for the next hour, but as time went on, growing weaker and weaker until they died out entirely.

As I clung to my wreckage, I noticed just in front of me, a few yards away, a group of three bodies with heads in the water, face downwards, and just behind me to my right another body, all giving unmistakable evidence of being drowned. Possibly these had gone down to the depths as I had done, but did not have the lung power that I had to hold the breath and swim under water, an accomplishment which I had practised from my school days. There was no one alive or struggling in the water or calling for aid within the immediate vicinity of where I arose to the surface. I threw my right leg over the wooden crate in an attempt to straddle and balance myself on top of it, but I turned over in a somersault with it under water, and up to the surface again. What may be of interest is the thought that then occurred to me of the accounts and pictures of a wreck, indelibly impressed upon my memory when a boy, because of my acquaintance with some of the victims, of a frightful disaster of that day, namely the wreck of the *Ville de Havre* in the English Channel in 1873, and I had in mind Mrs. Bulkley's description, and the picture of her clinging to some wreckage as a rescue boat caught sight of her, bringing the comforting words over the water, "We are English sailors coming to save you." I looked around, praying for a similar interposition of Fate, but I knew the thought of a rescuing boat was a vain one—for had not all the lifeboats, loaded with women and children, departed from the ship fifteen or twenty minutes before I sank with it? And had I not seen the procession of them on the port side fading away from our sight?

But my prayerful thought and hope were answered in an unexpected direction. I espied to my left, a considerable distance away, a better vehicle of escape than the wooden crate on which my attempt to ride had resulted in a second ducking. What I saw was no less than the same Engelhardt, or "surf-boat," to whose launching I had lent my efforts, until the water broke upon the ship's Boat Deck where we were. On top of this upturned boat, half reclining on her bottom, were now more than a dozen men, whom, by their dress, I took to be all members of the crew of the ship. Thank God, I did not hesitate a moment in discarding the friendly crate that had been my first aid. I struck out through the wreckage and after a considerable swim reached the port side amidships of this Engelhardt boat, which with her companions, wherever utilized, did good service in saving the lives of many others. All honor to the Dane, Captain Engelhardt of Copenhagen, who built them. I say "port side" because this boat as it was propelled through the water had Lightoller in the bow and Bride at the stern, and I believe an analysis of the testimony shows that the actual bow of the boat was turned about by the wave that struck it on the Boat Deck and the splash of the funnel thereafter, so that its bow pointed in an opposite direction to that of the ship. There was one member of the crew on this craft at the bow and another at the stern who had "pieces of boarding," improvised paddles, which were used effectually for propulsion.

When I reached the side of the boat I met with a doubtful reception, and, as no extending hand was held out to me, I grabbed, by the muscle of the left arm, a young member of the crew nearest and facing me. At the same time I threw my right leg over the boat astraddle, pulling myself aboard, with a friendly lift to my foot given by someone astern as I assumed a reclining position with them on the bottom of the capsized boat. Then after me came a dozen other swimmers who clambered around and whom we helped aboard. Among them was one completely exhausted, who came on the same port side as myself. I pulled him in and he lay face downward in front of me for several hours, until just before dawn he was able to stand up with the rest of us. The journey of our craft from the scene of the disaster will be described in the following chapter. The moment of getting aboard this upturned boat was one of supreme mental relief, more so than any other until I reached the deck of the hospitable *Carpathia* on the next morning. I now felt for the first time after the lifeboats left us aboard ship that I had some chance of escape from the horrible fate of drowning in the icy waters of the middle Atlantic. Every moment of time during the many experiences of that night, it seemed as if I had all the God-given physical strength and courage needed for each emergency, and never suffered an instant from any exhaustion, or required the need of a helping hand. The only time of any stress whatever was during the swim, just described, under water, at the moment when I gained my second wind which brought me to the surface gasping somewhat, but full of vigor. I was all the time on the lookout for the next danger that was to be overcome. I kept my presence of mind and courage throughout it all. Had I lost either for one moment, I never could have escaped to tell the tale. This is in answer to many questions as to my personal sensations during these scenes and the successive dangers which I encountered. From a psychological viewpoint also, it may be a study of interest illustrating the power of mind over matter. The sensation of fear has a visible effect upon one. It palsies one's thoughts and actions. One becomes thereby short of breath; the heart actually beats quicker and as one loses one's head one grows desperate and is gone. I have questioned those who have been near drowning and who know this statement to be a fact. It is the same in other emergencies, and the lesson to be learned is that we should—

> Let courage rise with danger,
> And strength to strength oppose.

To attain this courage in the hour of danger is very much a matter of physical, mental and religious training. But courage and strength would have availed me little had I not providentially escaped from being knocked senseless, or maimed, as so many other strong swimmers undoubtedly were. The narrow escapes that I had from being thus knocked unconscious could be recapitulated, and I still bear the scars on my body of wounds received at the moment, or moments, when I was struck by some undefined object. I received a blow on the top of my head, but I did not notice it or the other wounds until I arrived on board the *Carpathia*, when I found inflamed cuts on both my legs and bruises on my knees, which soon became black and blue, and I was sore to the touch all over my body for several days.

It is necessary for me to turn to the accounts of others for a description of what happened during the interval that I was under water. My information about it is derived from many sources and includes various points of general interest, showing how the *Titanic* looked when she foundered, the undisputed facts that there was very little suction and that the forward funnel broke from the ship, falling on the starboard side into the sea. Various points of personal interest are also derived from the same source which the reader can analyze, for estimating the interval that I was below the surface of the ocean and the distance covered in my swim under water; for after I rose to the surface it appears that I had passed under both the falling funnel and then under the upturned boat, and a considerable distance beyond. Had I gone but a short distance under water and arisen straight up, I should have met the horrible fate of being struck by the falling funnel which, according to the evidence submitted, must have killed or drowned a number of unfortunates struggling in the water. I select these accounts of my shipwrecked companions, which supplement my personal experience, particularly the accounts of the same reliable and authoritative witnesses already cited, and from those who were rescued, as I was, on the bottom of the upset Engelhardt boat.

The following is from the account of Mr. Beesley: "The water was by now up to the last row of portholes. We were about two miles from her, and the crew insisted that such a tremendous wave would be formed by suction as she went down, that we ought to get as far as possible away. The 'Captain' (as he calls Stoker Fred Barrett), and all, lay on their oars. Presently, about 2 a. m. (2.15 a. m. per book account), as near as I can remember, we observed her settling very rapidly, with the bow and bridge completely under water, and concluded it was now only a question of minutes before she went; and so it proved. She slowly tilted, straight on end, with the stern vertically upward. . . . To our amazement, she remained in that upright position for a time which I estimate as five minutes." On a previous page of my narrative, I have already quoted from his book account how "the stern and some 150 feet of the ship stood outlined against the star-specked sky, looming black in the darkness, and in this position she continued for some minutes—I think as much as five minutes, but it may have been less." Now, when I disappeared under the sea, sinking with the ship, there is nothing more surely established in my testimony than that about nine-sixteenths of the *Titanic* was still out of the water, and when my head reached the surface she had entirely disappeared.

The New York *Times*, of April 19, 1912, contained the story of Mr. and Mrs. D. H. Bishop, first cabin passengers from Dowagiac, Michigan. Their short account is one of the best I have read. As they wrote it independently of Beesley's account, and from a different point of view, being in another lifeboat (No. 7, the first to leave the ship), the following corroborative testimony, taken from their story, helps to establish the truth:

"We did not begin to understand the situation till we were perhaps a mile away from the *Titanic*. Then we could see the row of lights along the deck begin to slant gradually upward from the bow. Very slowly the lines of light began to point downward at a greater and greater angle. The sinking was so slow that you could not perceive the lights of the deck changing their position. The slant seemed to be greater about every quarter of an hour. That was the only difference.

"In a couple of hours she began to go down more rapidly. . . . Suddenly the ship seemed to shoot up out of the water and stand there perpendicularly. It seemed to us that it stood *upright in the water for four full minutes*.[1] Then it began to slide gently downwards. Its speed increased as it went down head first, so that the stern shot down with a rush."

Harold Bride, who was swept from the Boat Deck, held on to an oar-lock of the Engelhardt boat (which Clinch Smith and I had left a few moments before, as has already been described). I have cited his account of coming up under the boat and then clambering upon it. He testifies to there being no suction and adds the following: "I suppose I was 150 feet away when the *Titanic*, on her nose with her after-quarter sticking

[1] Italics are mine.—AUTHOR.

straight up into the air, began to settle—slowly. When at last the waves washed over her rudder, there was not the least bit of suction I could feel. She must have kept going just so slowly as she had been." Second Officer Lightoller too, in his conversation with me, verified his testimony before the Senate Committee that, "The last boat, a flat collapsible (the Engelhardt), to put off was the one on top of the officers' quarters. Men jumped upon it on deck and waited for the water to float it off. The forward funnel fell into the water, just missing the raft (as he calls our upset boat). The funnel probably killed persons in the water. This was the boat I eventually got on. About thirty men clambered out of the water on to it."

Seventeen-year-old "Jack" Thayer was also on the starboard side of the ship, and jumped from the rail before the Engelhardt boat was swept from the Boat Deck by the "giant wave." Young Thayer's reported description of this is as follows:

"I jumped out, feet first, went down, and as I came up I was pushed away from the ship by some force. I was sucked down again, and as I came up I was pushed out again and twisted around by a large wave, coming up in the midst of a great deal of small wreckage. My hand touched the canvas fender of an overturned lifeboat. I looked up and saw some men on the top. One of them helped me up. In a short time the bottom was covered with twenty-five or thirty men. The assistant wireless operator (Bride) was right next to me holding on to me and kneeling in the water."

In my conversations with Thayer, Lightoller and others, it appears that the funnel fell in the water between the Engelhardt boat and the ship, washing the former further away from the *Titanic*'s starboard side.

Since the foregoing was written, the testimony before the United States Senate Committee has been printed in pamphlet form, from which I have been able to obtain other evidence, and particularly that of Second Officer Lightoller in regard to the last quarter of an hour or so on board the ship and up to the time we reached the upset boat. I have also obtained and substantiated other evidence bearing upon the same period. Mr. Lightoller testified as follows: "Half an hour, or three-quarters of an hour before I left the ship, when it was taking a heavy list—not a heavy list—a list over to port, the order was called, I think by the chief officer, 'Everyone on the starboard side to straighten her up,' which I repeated. When I left the ship I saw no women or children aboard whatever. All the boats on the port side were lowered with the exception of one—the last boat, which was stowed on top of the officers' quarters. We had not time to launch it, nor yet to open it. When all the other boats were away, I called for men to go up there;

told them to cut her adrift and throw her down. It floated off the ship, and I understand the men standing on top, who assisted to launch it down, jumped on to it as it was on the deck and floated off with it. It was the collapsible type of boat, and the bottom-up boat we eventually got on. When this lifeboat floated off the ship, we were thrown off a couple of times. When I came to it, it was bottom-up and there was no one on it. Immediately after finding that overturned lifeboat, and when I came alongside of it, there were quite a lot of us in the water around it preparatory to getting up on it. Then the forward funnel fell down. It fell alongside of the lifeboat about four inches clear of it on all the people there alongside of the boat. Eventually, about thirty of us got on it: Mr. Thayer, Bride, the second Marconi operator, and Col. Gracie. I think all the rest were firemen taken out of the water."

Compare this with the description given by J. Hagan in correspondence which he began with me last May. J. Hagan is a poor chap, who described himself in this correspondence as one who "was working my passage to get to America for the first time," and I am convinced that he certainly earned it, and, moreover, was one of us on that upset boat that night. His name does not appear on the list of the crew and must not be confounded with "John Hagan, booked as fireman on the steamer, who sailed for England April 20th on the *Lapland*," whereas our John Hagan was admitted to St. Vincent's hospital on April 22nd. In describing this period John Hagan says it was by the Captain's orders, when the ship was listing to port, that passengers were sent to the starboard side to straighten the ship. He went half-way and returned to where Lightoller was loading the last boat lowered. Lightoller told him there was another boat on the roof of the officers' house if he cared to get it down. This was the Engelhardt Boat B which, with three others, he could not open until assisted by three more, and then they pushed it, upside down, on the Boat Deck below. Hagan cut the string of the oars and was passing the first oar down to the others, who had left him, when the boat floated into the water, upside down. He jumped to the Boat Deck and into the water after the boat and "clung to the tail end of the keel." The ship was shaking very much, part of it being under water. "On looking up at it, I could see death in a minute for us as the forward funnel was falling and it looked a certainty it would strike our boat and smash it to pieces; but the funnel missed us about a yard, splashing our boat thirty yards outward from the ship, and washing off several who had got on when the boat first floated." Hagan managed to cling to it but got a severe soaking. The cries of distress that he heard near by were an experience he can never forget. It appeared to him that the flooring of the ship forward had broken away and was floating all around. Some of the men on the upset boat made use of some pieces of boarding for paddles with which to help keep clear of the ship.

John Collins, assistant cook on the *Titanic*, also gave his interesting testimony before the Senate Committee. He appears to have come on deck at the last moment on the starboard side and witnessed the Engelhardt boat when it floated off into the sea, he being carried off by the same wave when he was amidships on the bow as the ship sank, and kept down under water for at least two or three minutes. When he came up, he saw this boat again—the same boat on which he had seen men working when the waves washed it off the deck, and the men clinging to it. He was only about four or five yards off and swam over to it and got on to it. He says he is sure there were probably fifteen thereon at the time he got on. Those who were on the boat did not help him to get on. They were watching the ship. After he got on the boat, he did not see any lights on the *Titanic*, though the stern of the ship was still afloat when he first reached the surface. He accounts for the wave that washed him off amidships as due to the suction which took place when the bow went down in the water and the waves washed the decks clear. He saw a mass of people in the wreckage, hundreds in number, and heard their awful cries.

CHAPTER V

# ALL NIGHT ON BOTTOM OF HALF-
# SUBMERGED UPTURNED BOAT

*O God of our salvation, Thou who art the hope of them that remain in the
broad sea . . .—Ps. 65 : 5, 7*

All my companions in shipwreck who made their escape with me
on top of the bottom-side-up Engelhardt boat, must recall the
anxious moment after the limit was reached when "about 30 men had
clambered out of the water on to the boat." The weight of each additional body submerged our lifecraft more and more beneath the
surface. There were men swimming in the water all about us. One more
clambering aboard would have swamped our already crowded craft.
The situation was a desperate one, and was only saved by the refusal of
the crew, especially those at the stern of the boat, to take aboard another passenger. After pulling aboard the man who lay exhausted, face
downward in front of me, I turned my head away from the sights in the
water lest I should be called upon to refuse the pleading cries of those who
were struggling for their lives. What happened at this juncture, therefore,
my fellow companions in shipwreck can better describe. Steward
Thomas Whiteley, interviewed by the New York *Tribune*, said: "I
drifted near a boat wrong-side-up. About 30 men were clinging to it.
They refused to let me get on. Somebody tried to hit me with an oar,
but I scrambled on to her." Harry Senior, a fireman on the *Titanic*, as
interviewed in the London *Illustrated News* of May 4th, and in the New
York *Times* of April 19th, is reported as follows: "On the overturned
boat in question were, amongst others, Charles Lightoller, Second
Officer of the *Titanic*; Col. Archibald Gracie, and Mr. J. B. Thayer, Jr.,
all of whom had gone down with the liner and had come to the surface
again"; and "I tried to get aboard of her, but some chap hit me over
the head with an oar. There were too many on her. I got around to the
other side of the boat and climbed on. There were thirty-five of us,
including the second officer, and no women. I saw any amount of
drowning and dead around us." Bride's story in the same issue of the

New York *Times* says: "It was a terrible sight all around—men swimming and sinking. Others came near. Nobody gave them a hand. The bottom-up boat already had more men than it would hold and was sinking. At first the large waves splashed over my clothing; then they began to splash over my head and I had to breathe when I could."

Though I did not see, I could not avoid hearing what took place at this most tragic crisis in all my life. The men with the paddles, forward and aft, so steered the boat as to avoid contact with the unfortunate swimmers pointed out struggling in the water. I heard the constant explanation made as we passed men swimming in the wreckage, "Hold on to what you have, old boy; one more of you aboard would sink us all." In no instance, I am happy to say, did I hear any word of rebuke uttered by a swimmer because of refusal to grant assistance. There was no case of cruel violence. But there was one transcendent piece of heroism that will remain fixed in my memory as the most sublime and coolest exhibition of courage and cheerful resignation to fate and fearlessness of death. This was when a reluctant refusal of assistance met with the ringing response in the deep manly voice of a powerful man, who, in his extremity, replied: "All right, boys; good luck and God bless you." I have often wished that the identity of this hero might be established and an individual tribute to his memory preserved. He was not an acquaintance of mine, for the tones of his voice would have enabled me to recognize him.

Collins in his testimony and Hagan in his letter to me refer to the same incident, the former before the Senate Committee, saying: "All those who wanted to get on and tried to get on got on with the exception of only one. This man was not pushed off by anyone, but those on the boat asked him not to try to get on. We were all on the boat running [shifting our weight] from one side to the other to keep her steady. If this man had caught hold of her he would have tumbled the whole lot of us off. He acquiesced and said, 'that is all right, boys; keep cool; God bless you,' and he bade us good-bye."

Hagan refers to the same man who "swam close to us saying, 'Hello boys, keep calm, boys,' asking to be helped up, and was told he could not get on as it might turn the boat over. He asked for a plank and was told to cling to what he had. It was very hard to see so brave a man swim away saying, 'God bless you.'"

All this time our nearly submerged boat was amidst the wreckage and fast being paddled out of the danger zone whence arose the heart-rending cries already described of the struggling swimmers. It was at this juncture that expressions were used by some of the uncouth members of the ship's crew, which grated upon my sensibilities. The hearts of these men, as I presently discovered, were all right and they were far from meaning any offence when they adopted their usual slang, sounding harsh to my ears, and referred to our less fortunate ship-wreçked companions as "the blokes swimming in the water." What I thus heard made me feel like an alien among my fellow boatmates, and I did them the injustice of believing that I, as the only passenger aboard, would, in case of diversity of interest, receive short shrift at their hands and for this reason I thought it best to have as little to say as possible. During all these struggles I had been uttering silent prayers for deliverance, and it occurred to me that this was the occasion of all others when we should join in an appeal to the Almighty as our last and only hope in life, and so it remained for one of these men, whom I had regarded as uncouth, a Roman Catholic seaman, to take precedence in suggesting the thought in the heart of everyone of us. He was astern and in arm's length of me. He first made inquiry as to the religion of each of us and found Episcopalians, Roman Catholics and Presbyterians. The suggestion that we should say the Lord's Prayer together met with instant approval, and our voices with one accord burst forth in repeating that great appeal to the Creator and Preserver of all mankind, and the only prayer that everyone of us knew and could unite in, thereby manifesting that we were all sons of God and brothers to each other whatever our sphere in life or creed might be. Recollections of this incident are embodied in my account as well as those of Bride and Thayer, independently reported in the New York papers on the morning after our arrival. This is what Bride recalls: "Somebody said 'don't the rest of you think we ought to pray?' The man who made the suggestion asked what the religion of the others was. Each man called out his religion. One was a Catholic, one a Methodist, one a Presbyterian. It was decided the most appropriate prayer for all of us was the Lord's Prayer. We spoke it over in chorus, with the man who first suggested that we pray as the leader."

Referring to this incident in his sermon on "The Lessons of the Great Disaster," the Rev. Dr. Newell Dwight Hillis, of Plymouth Church, says: "When Col. Gracie came up, after the sinking of the *Titanic*, he says that he made his way to a sunken raft. The submerged little raft was under water often, but every man, without regard to nationality, broke into instant prayer. There were many voices, but they all had one signification—their sole hope was in God. There were no millionaires, for millions fell away like leaves; there were no poor; men were neither wise nor ignorant; they were simply human souls on the sinking raft; the night was black and the waves yeasty with foam, and the grave where the *Titanic* lay was silent under them, and the stars were silent over them! But as they prayed, each man by that inner light saw an invisible Friend walking across the waves. Henceforth, these need no books on Apologetics to prove there is a God. This man who has written his story tells us that God heard the prayers of some by giving them death, and heard the prayers of others equally by keeping them in life; but God alone is great!"

The lesson thus drawn from the incident described must be well appreciated by all my boatmates who realized the utter helplessness of our position, and that the only hope we then had in life was in our God, and as the Rev. Dr. Hillis says: "In that moment the evanescent, transient, temporary things dissolved like smoke, and the big, permanent things stood out—God, Truth, Purity, Love, and Oh! how happy those who were good friends with God, their conscience and their record."

We all recognize the fact that our escape from a watery grave was due to the conditions of wind and weather. All night long we prayed that the calm might last. Towards morning the sea became rougher, and it was for the two-fold purpose of avoiding the ice-cold water,[1] and also to attract attention, that we all stood up in column, two abreast, facing the bow. The waves at this time broke over the keel, and we maintained a balance to prevent the escape of the small volume of air confined between sea and upset boat by shifting the weight of our bodies first to port and then to starboard. I believe that the life of everyone of us depended upon the preservation of this confined air-bubble, and our anxious thought was lest some of this air might escape and deeper down our overloaded boat would sink. Had the boat been completely turned over, compelling us to cling to the submerged gunwale, it could not have supported our weight, and we should have been frozen to death in the ice-cold water before rescue could reach us. My exertions had been so continuous and so strenuous before I got aboard this capsized boat that I had taken no notice of the icy temperature of the water. We all suffered severely from cold and exposure. The boat was so loaded down with the heavy weight it carried that it became partly submerged, and the water washed up to our waists as we lay in our reclining position. Several of our companions near the stern of the boat, unable to stand the exposure and strain, gave up the struggle and fell off.

After we had left the danger zone in the vicinity of the wreck, conversation between us first developed, and I heard the men aft of me discussing the fate of the Captain. At least two of them, according to their statements made at the time, had seen him on this craft of ours shortly

[1] Temperature of water 28 degrees, of air 27 degrees Fahrenheit, at midnight, April 14th (American Inquiry, p. 1142).

after it was floated from the ship. In the interviews already referred to, Harry Senior the fireman, referring to the same overturned boat, said: "The Captain had been able to reach this boat. They had pulled him on, but he slipped off again." Still another witness, the entrée cook of the *Titanic*, J. Maynard, who was on our boat, corroborates what I heard said at the time about the inability of the Captain to keep his hold on the boat. From several sources I have the information about the falling of the funnel, the splash of which swept from the upturned boat several who were first clinging thereto, and among the number possibly was the Captain. From the following account of Bride, it would appear he was swept off himself and regained his hold later. "I saw a boat of some kind near me and put all my strength into an effort to swim to it. It was hard work. I was all done when a hand reached out from the boat and pulled me aboard. It was our same collapsible. The same crew was on it. There was just room for me to roll on the edge. I lay there, not caring what happened." Fortunately for us all, the majority of us were not thus exhausted or desperate. On the contrary, these men on this upset boat had plenty of strength and the purpose to battle for their lives. There were no beacon torches on crag and cliff; no shouts in the pauses of the storm to tell them there was hope; nor deep-toned bell with its loudest peal sending cheerily, o'er the deep, comfort to these wretched souls in their extremity. There were, however, lights forward, and on the port side to be seen all the time until the *Carpathia* appeared. These lights were only those of the *Titanic*'s other lifeboats, and thus it was, as they gazed with eager anxious eyes that

"Fresh hope did give them strength and strength deliverance." [1]

The suffering on the boat from cold was intense. My neighbor in front, whom I had pulled aboard, must also have been suffering from exhaustion, but it was astern of us whence came later the reports about fellow boatmates who gave up the struggle and fell off from exhaustion, or died, unable to stand the exposure and strain. Among the number, we are told by Bride and Whiteley, was the senior Marconi operator, Phillips, but their statement that it was Phillips' lifeless body which we transferred first to a lifeboat and thence to the *Carpathia* is a mistake, for the body referred to both Lightoller and myself know to have been that of a member of the crew, as described later. Bride himself suffered severely. "Somebody sat on my legs," he says. "They were wedged in between slats and were being wrenched." When he reached the *Carpathia* he was taken to the hospital and on our arrival in New York was carried ashore with his "feet badly crushed and frostbitten."

[1] Maturin's *Bertram*.

The combination of cold and the awful scenes of suffering and death which he witnessed from our upturned boat deeply affected another first cabin survivor, an Englishman, Mr. R. H. Barkworth, whose tender heart is creditable to his character.

Another survivor of our upturned boat, James McGann, a fireman, interviewed by the New York *Tribune* on April 20th, says that he was one of the thirty of us, mostly firemen, clinging to it as she left the ship. As to the suffering endured that night he says: "All our legs were frost-bitten and we were all in the hospital for a day at least."

"Hagan" also adds his testimony as to the sufferings endured by our boatmates. He says: "One man on the upturned boat rolled off, into the water, at the stern, dead with fright and cold. Another died in the lifeboat." Here he refers to the lifeless body which we transferred, and finally put aboard the *Carpathia*, but which was not Phillips'.

Lightoller testified: "I think there were three or four who died during the night aboard our boat. The Marconi junior operator told me that the senior operator was on this boat and died, presumably from cold."

But the uncommunicative little member of the crew beside me did not seem to suffer much. He was like a number of others who were possessed of hats or caps—his was an outing cap; while those who sank under water had lost them. The upper part of his body appeared to be comparatively dry; so I believe he and some others escaped being drawn under with the *Titanic* by clinging to the Engelhardt boat from the outset when it parted company with the ship and was washed from the deck by the "giant wave." He seemed so dry and comfortable while I felt so damp in my waterlogged clothing, my teeth chattering and my hair wet with the icy water, that I ventured to request the loan of his dry cap to warm my head for a short while. "And what wad oi do?" was his curt reply, "Ah, never mind," said I, as I thought it would make no difference a hundred years hence. Poor chap, it would seem that all his possessions were lost when his kit went down with the ship. Not far from me and on the starboard side was a more loquacious member of the crew. I was not near enough, however, to him to indulge in any imaginary warmth from the fumes of the O-be-joyful spirits which he gave unmistakable evidence of having indulged in before leaving the ship. Most of the conversation, as well as excitement, came from behind me, astern. The names of other survivors who, besides those mentioned, escaped on the same nearly submerged life craft with me are recorded in the history of Boat B in Chapter V, which contains the results of my research work in regard thereto.

After we paddled away free from the wreckage and swimmers in the water that surrounded us, our undivided attention until the dawn of the next day was concentrated upon scanning the horizon in every direction for the lights of a ship that might rescue us before the sea grew rougher, for the abnormal conditions of wind and weather that prevailed that night were the causes of the salvation, as well as the destruction, of those aboard this ill-fated vessel. The absolute calm of the sea, while it militated against the detection of the iceberg in our path, at the same time made it possible for all of the lifeboats lowered from the davits to make their long and dangerous descent to the water without being smashed against the sides of the ship, or swamped by the waves breaking against them, for, notwithstanding newspaper reports to the contrary, there appears no authentic testimony of any survivor showing that any loaded boat in the act of being lowered was capsized or suffered injury. On the other hand, we have the positive statements accounting for each individual boatload, showing that every one of them was thus lowered in safety. But it was this very calm of the sea, as has been said, which encompassed the destruction of the ship. The beatings of the waves against the iceberg's sides usually give audible warning miles away to the approaching vessel, while the white foam at the base, due to the same cause, is also discernible. But in our case the beautiful star-lit night and cloudless sky, combined with the glassy sea, further facilitated the iceberg's approach without detection, for no background was afforded against which to silhouette the deadly outline of this black appearing Protean monster which only looks white when the sun is shining upon it.

All experienced navigators of the northern seas, as I am informed on the highest authority, knowing the dangers attending such conditions, invariably take extra precautions to avoid disaster. The *Titanic*'s officers were no novices, and were well trained in the knowledge of this and all other dangers of the sea. From the Captain down, they were the pick of the best that the White Star Line had in its employ. Our Captain, Edward J. Smith, was the one always selected to "try out" each new ship of the Line, and was regarded, with his thirty-eight years of service in the company, as both safe and competent. Did he take any precautions for safety, in view of the existing dangerous conditions? Alas! no! as appears from the testimony in regard thereto, taken before the Investigating Committee and Board in America and in England which we review in another chapter. And yet, warnings had been received on the *Titanic*'s bridge from six different neighboring ships, one in fact definitely locating the latitude and longitude where the iceberg was encountered, and that too at a point of time calculated by one of the *Titanic*'s officers. Who can satisfactorily explain this heedlessness of danger?

It was shortly after we had emerged from the horrible scene of men swimming in the water that I was glad to notice the presence among us on the upturned boat of the same officer with whom all my work that night and all my experience was connected in helping to load and lower the boats on the *Titanic*'s Boat Deck and Deck "A". I identified him at once by his voice and his appearance, but his name was not learned until I met him again later in my cabin on board the *Carpathia*—Charles H. Lightoller. For what he did on the ship that night whereby six or more boatloads of women and children were saved and discipline maintained aboard ship, as well as on the Engelhardt upturned boat, he is entitled to honor and the thanks of his own countrymen and of us Americans as well. As soon as he was recognized, the loquacious member of the crew astern, already referred to, volunteered in our behalf and called out to him "We will all obey what the officer orders." The result was at once noticeable. The presence of a leader among us was now felt, and lent us purpose and courage. The excitement at the stern was demonstrated by the frequent suggestion of, "Now boys, all together"; and then in unison we shouted, "Boat ahoy! Boat ahoy!" This was kept up for some time until it was seen to be a mere waste of strength. So it seemed to me, and I decided to husband mine and make provision for what the future, or the morrow, might require. After a while Lightoller, myself and others managed with success to discourage these continuous shouts regarded as a vain hope of attracting attention.

When the presence of the Marconi boy at the stern was made known, Lightoller called out, from his position in the bow, questions which all of us heard, as to the names of the steamships with which he had been in communication for assistance. We on the boat recall the names mentioned by Bride—the *Baltic*, *Olympic* and *Carpathia*. It was then that the *Carpathia*'s name was heard by us for the first time, and it was to catch sight of this sturdy little Cunarder that we strained our eyes in the direction whence she finally appeared.

We had correctly judged that most of the lights seen by us belonged to our own *Titanic*'s lifeboats, but Lightoller and all of us were badly fooled by the green-colored lights and rockets directly ahead of us, which loomed up especially bright at intervals. This, as will be noticed in a future chapter, was Third Officer Boxhall's Emergency Boat No. 2. We were assured that these were the lights of a ship and were all glad to believe it. There could be no mistake about it and our craft was navigated toward it as fast as its propelling conditions made possible; but it did not take long for us to realize that this light, whatever it was, was receding instead of approaching us.

Some of our boatmates on the *Titanic*'s decks had seen the same white light to which I have already made reference in Chapter II, and the argument was now advanced that it must have been a sailing ship, for a steamer would have soon come to our rescue; but a sailing ship would be prevented by wind, or lack of facilities in coming to our aid. I imagined that it was the lights of such a ship that we again saw on our port side astern in the direction where, when dawn broke, we saw the icebergs far away on the horizon.

Some time before dawn a call came from the stern of the boat, "There is a steamer coming behind us." At the same time a warning cry was given that we should not all look back at once lest the equilibrium of our precarious craft might be disturbed. Lightoller took in the situation and called out, "All you men stand steady and I will be the one to look astern." He looked, but there was no responsive chord that tickled our ears with hope.

The incident just described happened when we were all standing up, facing forward in column, two abreast. Some time before this, for some undefined reason, Lightoller had asked the question, "How many are there of us on this boat?" and someone answered "thirty, sir." All testimony on the subject establishes this number. I may cite Lightoller, who testified: "I should roughly estimate about thirty. She was packed standing from stem to stern at daylight. We took all on board that we could. I did not see any effort made by others to get aboard. There were a great number of people in the water but not near us. They were some distance away from us."

Personally, I could not look around to count, but I know that forward of me there were eight and counting myself and the man abreast would make two more. As every bit of room on the Engelhardt bottom was occupied and as the weight aboard nearly submerged it, I believe that more than half our boatload was behind me. There is a circumstance that I recall which further establishes how closely packed we were. When standing up I held on once or twice to the life-preserver on the back of my boatmate in front in order to balance myself. At the same time and in the same way the man in my rear held on to me. This procedure, being objectionable to those concerned, was promptly discontinued.

It was at quite an early stage that I had seen far in the distance the unmistakable mast lights of a steamer about four or five points away on the port side, as our course was directed toward the green-colored lights of the imaginary ship which we hoped was coming to our rescue, but which, in fact, was the already-mentioned *Titanic* lifeboat of Officer Boxhall. I recall our anxiety, as we had no lights, that this imaginary ship might not see us and might run over our craft and swamp us. But my eyes were fixed for hours that night on the lights of that steamer, far away in the distance, which afterwards proved to be those of the *Carpathia*. To my great disappointment, they seemed to make no progress towards us to our rescue. This we were told later was due to meeting an iceberg as she was proceeding full speed toward the scene of the *Titanic*'s wreck. She had come to a stop in sight of the lights of our lifeboats (or such as had them). The first boat to come to her sides was Boxhall's with its green lights. Finally dawn appeared and there on the port side of our upset boat where we had been looking with anxious eyes, glory be to God, we saw the steamer *Carpathia* about four or five miles away, with other *Titanic* lifeboats rowing towards her. But on our starboard side, much to our surprise, for we had seen no lights on that quarter, were four of the *Titanic*'s lifeboats strung together in line. These were respectively Numbers 14, 10, 12 and 4, according to testimony submitted in our next chapter.

Meantime, the water had grown rougher, and, as previously described, was washing over the keel and we had to make shift to preserve the equilibrium. Right glad were all of us on our upturned boat when in that awful hour the break of day brought this glorious sight to our eyes. Lightoller put his whistle to his cold lips and blew a shrill blast, attracting the attention of the boats about half a mile away. "Come over and take us off," he cried. "Aye, aye, sir," was the ready response as two of the boats cast off from the others and rowed directly towards us. Just before the bows of the two boats reached us, Lightoller ordered us not to scramble, but each to take his turn, so that the transfer might be made in safety. When my turn came, in order not to endanger the lives of the others, or plunge them into the sea, I went carefully, hands first, into the rescuing lifeboat. Lightoller remained to the last, lifting a lifeless body into the boat beside me. I worked over the body for some time, rubbing the temples and the wrists, but when I turned the neck it was perfectly stiff. Recognizing that *rigor mortis* had set in, I knew the man was dead. He was dressed like a member of the crew, and I recall that he wore gray woolen socks. His hair was dark. Our lifeboat was so crowded that I had to rest on this dead body until we reached the *Carpathia*, where he was taken aboard and buried. My efforts to obtain his name have been exhaustive, but futile. Lightoller was uncertain as to which one he was of two men he had in mind; but we both know that it was not the body of Phillips, the senior Marconi operator. In the lifeboat to which we were transferred were said to be sixty-five or seventy of us. The number was beyond the limit of safety. The boat sank low in the water, and the sea now became rougher. Lightoller assumed the command and steered at the stern. I was glad to recognize young Thayer amidships. There was a French woman in the bow near us actively ill but brave and considerate. She was very kind in loaning an extra steamer rug to Barkworth, by my side, who shared it with a member of the crew (a fireman perhaps) and myself. That steamer rug was a great comfort as we drew it over our heads and huddled close together to obtain some warmth. For a short time another *Titanic* lifeboat was towed by ours. My lifebelt was wet and uncomfortable and I threw it overboard. Fortunately there was no further need of it for the use intended. I regret I did not preserve it as a relic. When we were first transferred and only two of the lifeboats came to our rescue, some took it hard that the other two did not also come to our relief, when we saw how few these others had aboard; but the officer in command of them, whom we afterwards knew as Fifth Officer Lowe, had cleverly rigged up a sail on his boat and, towing another astern, made his way to the *Carpathia* a long time ahead of us, but picked up on his way other unfortunates in another Engelhardt boat, Boat A, which had shipped considerable water.

My research, particularly the testimony taken before the Senate Committee, establishes the identity of the *Titanic* lifeboats to which, at daydawn, we of the upset boat were transferred. There were Boats No. 12 and No. 4. The former was the one that Lightoller, Barkworth, Thayer, Jr., and myself were in. Frederick Clench, able seaman, was in charge of this boat, and his testimony, as follows, is interesting:

"I looked along the water's edge and saw some men on a raft. Then I heard two whistles blown. I sang out, 'Aye, aye, I am coming over,' and we pulled over and found it was not a raft exactly, but an overturned boat, and Mr. Lightoller was there on that boat and I thought the wireless operator, too. We took them on board our boat and shared the amount of room. They were all standing on the bottom, wet through apparently. Mr. Lightoller took charge of us. Then we started ahead for the *Carpathia*. We had to row a tidy distance to the *Carpathia* because there were boats ahead of us and we had a boat in tow, with others besides all the people we had aboard. We were pretty well full up before, but the additional ones taken on made about seventy in our boat."

This corresponds with Lightoller's testimony on the same point. He says:

"I counted sixty-five heads, not including myself, and none that were in the bottom of the boat. I roughly estimated about seventy-five in the boat, which was dangerously full, and it was all I could do to nurse her up to the sea."

From Steward Cunningham's testimony I found a corroboration of

Thirty men sought refuge on this overturned, partly submerged lifeboat for over two hours.

The devotion and courage of Mr. and Mrs. Isidor Straus became a legend in the *Titanic's* last minutes.

my estimate of our distance, at daydawn, from the *Carpathia*. This he says "was about four or five miles."

Another seaman, Samuel S. Hemming, who was in Boat No. 4, commanded by Quartermaster Perkis, also gave his testimony as follows:

"As day broke we heard some hollering going on and we saw some men standing on what we thought was ice about half a mile away, but we found them on the bottom of an upturned boat. Two boats cast off and we pulled to them and took them in our two boats. There were no women or children on this boat, and I heard there was one dead body. Second Officer Lightoller was on the overturned boat. He did not get into our boat. Only about four or five got into ours and the balance of them went into the other boat."

It seemed to me an interminable time before we reached the *Carpathia*. Ranged along her sides were others of the *Titanic*'s lifeboats which had been rowed to the Cunarder and had been emptied of their loads of survivors. In one of these boats on the port side, standing up, I noticed my friend, Third Officer H. J. Pitman, with whom I had made my trip eastward on the Atlantic on board the *Oceanic*. All along the sides of the *Carpathia* were strung rope ladders. There were no persons about me needing my assistance, so I mounted the ladder, and, for the purpose of testing my strength, I ran up as fast as I could and experienced no difficulty or feeling of exhaustion. I entered the first hatchway I came to and felt like falling down on my knees and kissing the deck in gratitude for the preservation of my life. I made my way to the second-cabin dispensary, where I was handed a hot drink. I then went to the deck above and was met with a warm reception in the dining saloon. Nothing could exceed the kindness of the ladies, who did everything possible for my comfort. All my wet clothing, overcoat and shoes, were sent down to the bake-oven to be dried. Being thus in lack of clothing, I lay down on the lounge in the dining saloon corner to the right of the entrance under rugs and blankets, waiting for a complete outfit of dry clothing.

I am particularly grateful to a number of kind people on the *Carpathia* who helped replenish my wardrobe, but especially to Mr. Louis M. Ogden, a family connection and old friend. To Mrs. Ogden and to Mr. and Mrs. Spedden, who were on the *Titanic*, and to their boy's trained nurse, I am also most grateful. They gave me hot cordials and hot coffee which soon warmed me up and dispersed the cold. Among the *Carpathia*'s passengers, bound for the Mediterranean, I discovered a number of friends of Mrs. Gracie's and mine—Miss K. Steele, sister of Charles Steele, of New York, Mr. and Mrs. Charles H. Marshall and

Miss Marshall, of New York. Leaning over the rail of the port side I saw anxiously gazing down upon us many familiar faces of fellow survivors, and, among them, friends and acquaintances to whom I waved my hand as I stood up in the bow of my boat. This boat No. 12 was the last to reach the *Carpathia* and her passengers transferred about 8.30 a. m.

# CHAPTER VI

# THE PORT SIDE: WOMEN AND CHILDREN FIRST

## *Foreword*

The previous chapters, describing my personal experience on board the *Titanic* and remarkable escape from death in the icy waters of the middle Atlantic, were written some months ago. In the interim I have received the pamphlets, printed in convenient form, containing the hearings of both the American and British Courts of Inquiry, and have given them considerable study.

These official sources of information have added materially to my store of knowledge concerning the shipwreck, and corroborate to a marked degree the description from my personal viewpoint, all the salient points of which were written before our arrival in New York, and on the S. S. *Carpathia*, under circumstances which will be related in a future chapter.

During the same interval, by correspondence with survivors and by reading all available printed matter in books, magazine articles and news-papers, I have become still more conversant with the story of this, the greatest of maritime disasters, which caused more excitement in our country than any other single event that has occurred in its history within a generation.

The adopted standard by which I propose to measure the truth of all statements in this book is the evidence obtained from these Courts of Inquiry, after it has been subjected to careful and impartial analysis. All accounts of the disaster, from newspapers and individual sources, for which no basis can be found after submission to this refining process, will find no place or mention herein. In the discussion of points of historical interest or of individual conduct, where such are matters of public record, I shall endeavor to present them fairly before the reader, who can pass thereon his or her own opinion after a study of the testimony bearing on both sides of any controversy. In connection with such discussion where the reflections cast upon individuals in the sworn testimony of witnesses have already gained publicity, I claim immunity from any real or imaginary animadversions which may be provoked by my impartial reference thereto.

I have already recorded my personal observation of how strictly the rule of human nature, "Women and Children First," was enforced on the port side of the great steamship, whence no man escaped alive who made his station on this quarter and bade good-bye to wife, mother or sister.

I have done my best, during the limited time allowed, to exhaust all the above-defined sources of information, in an effort to preserve as complete a list as possible of those comrades of mine who, from first to last, on this port side of the ship, helped to preserve order and discipline, upholding the courage of women and children, until all the boats had left the *Titanic*, and who then sank with the ship when she went down.

I shall now present the record and story of each lifeboat, on both port and starboard sides of the ship, giving so far as I have been able to obtain them the names of persons loaded aboard each boat, passengers and crew; those picked up out of the water; the stowaways found concealed beneath the thwarts, and those men who, without orders, jumped from the deck into boats being lowered, injuring the occupants and endangering the lives of women and children. At the same time will be described the conditions existing when each boat was loaded and lowered, and whatever incidents occurred in the transfer of passengers to the rescuing steamer *Carpathia*.

The general testimony of record, covering the conduct which was exhibited on the port side of the ship, is contained in the careful statements of that splendid officer, Charles H. Lightoller, before the United States Senate Committee (Am. Inq., p. 88):

Senator Smith: From what you have said, you discriminated entirely in the interest of the passengers—first women and children—in filling these lifeboats?

Mr. Lightoller: Yes, sir.

Senator Smith: Why did you do that? Because of the captain's orders, or because of the rule of the sea?

Mr. Lightoller: The rule of human nature.

And also in his testimony before the British Inquiry (p. 71):

"I asked the captain on the Boat Deck, 'Shall I get women and children in the boats?' The captain replied, 'Yes, and lower away.' I was carrying out his orders. I am speaking of the port side of the ship. I was running the port side only. All the boats on this side were lowered except the last, which was stowed on top of the officers' quarters. This was the surf boat—the Engelhardt boat (A). We had not time to launch it nor yet to open it."

(Br. Inq.) "I had no difficulty in filling the boat. The people were perfectly ready and quiet. There was no jostling or pushing or crowding whatever. The men all refrained from asserting their strength and from crowding back the women and children. They could not have stood quieter if they had been in church."

And referring to the last boats that left the ship (Br. Inq., p. 83):

"When we were lowering the women, there were any amount of Americans standing near who gave me every assistance they could."

The crow's nest on the foremast was just about level with the water when the bridge was submerged. The people left on the ship, or that part which was not submerged, did not make any demonstration. There was not a sign of any lamentation.

On the port side on deck I can say, as far as my own observations went, from my own endeavor and that of others to obtain women, there were none left on the deck.

My testimony on the same point before the United States Senate Committee (Am. Inq., p. 992) was as follows:

"I want to say that there was nothing but the most heroic conduct on the part of all men and women at that time where I was at the bow on the port side. There was no man who asked to get in a boat with the single exception that I have already mentioned. (Referring to Col. Astor's request to go aboard to protect his wife. Am. Inq., p. 991.) No women even sobbed or wrung their hands, and everything appeared perfectly orderly. Lightoller was splendid in his conduct with the crew, and the crew did their duty. It seemed to me it was a little bit more difficult than it should have been to launch the boats alongside the ship. I do not know the cause of that. I know I had to use my muscle as best I could in trying to push those boats so as to get them over the gunwale. I refer to these in a general way as to its being difficult in trying to lift them and push them over. (As was the case with the Engelhardt "D.") The crew, at first, sort of resented my working with them, but they were very glad when I worked with them later on. Every opportunity I got to help, I helped."

How these statements are corroborated by the testimony of others is recorded in the detailed description of each boat that left the ship on the port side as follows:

## BOAT NO. 6 [1]

### No male passengers

*Passengers:* Miss Bowerman, Mrs. J. J. Brown, Mrs. Candee, Mrs. Cavendish and her maid (Miss Barber), Mrs. Meyer, Miss Norton,

---

[1] British Report (p. 38) puts this boat first to leave port side at 12.55. Lightoller's testimony shows it could not have been the first.

Mrs. Rothschild, Mrs. L. P. Smith, Mrs. Stone and her maid (Miss Icard).

*Ordered in to supply lack of crew:* Major A. G. Peuchen.

*Said good-bye to wives and sank with ship:* Messrs. Cavendish, Meyer, Rothschild and L. P. Smith.

*Crew:* Hitchins, Q. M. (in charge). Seaman Fleet. (One fireman transferred from No. 16 to row.) Also a boy with injured arm whom Captain Smith had ordered in.

*Total:* 28. (Br. Inq.)

### INCIDENTS

Lightoller's testimony (Am. Inq., p. 79):

I was calling for seamen and one of the seamen jumped out of the boat and started to lower away. The boat was half way down when a woman called out that there was only one man in it. I had only two seamen and could not part with them, and was in rather a fix to know what to do when a passenger called out: "If you like, I will go." This was a first-class passenger, Major Peuchen, of Toronto. I said: "Are you a seaman?" and he said: "I am a yachtsman." I said: "If you are sailor enough to get out on that fall—that is a difficult thing to get to over the ship's side, eight feet away, and means a long swing, on a dark night—if you are sailor enough to get out there, you can go down"; and he proved he was, by going down.

F. Fleet, L. O. (Am. Inq., 363) and (Br. Inq.):

Witness says there were twenty-three women, Major Peuchen and Seamen Hitchens and himself. As he left the deck he heard Mr. Lightoller shouting: "Any more women?" No. 6 and one other cut adrift after reaching the *Carpathia*.

Major Arthur Godfrey Peuchen, Manufacturing Chemist, Toronto, Canada, and Major of Toronto's crack regiment, The Queen's Own Rifles (Am. Inq., p. 334), testified:

I was standing on the Boat Deck, port side, near the second officer and the captain. One of them said: "We must get these masts and sails out of these boats; you might give us a hand." I jumped in, and with a knife cut the lashings of the mast and sail and moved the mast out of the boat. Only women were allowed in, and the men had to stand back. This was the order, and the second officer stood there and carried it out to the limit. He allowed no men, except sailors who were manning the boat. I did not see one single male passenger get in or attempt to get in. I never saw such perfect order. The discipline was perfect. I did not see a cowardly act by any man.

When I first came on this upper deck there were about 100 stokers coming up with their dunnage bags and they seemed to crowd this whole deck in front of the boats. One of the officers, I don't know which one, a very powerful man, came along and drove these men right off this deck like a lot of sheep. They did not put up any resistance. I admired him for it. Later, there were counted 20 women, one quartermaster, one sailor and one stowaway, before I was ordered in.

In getting into the boat I went aft and said to the quartermaster: "What do you want me to do?" "Get down and put that plug in," he answered. I made a dive down for the plug. The ladies were all sitting pretty well aft and I could not see at all. It was dark down there. I felt with my hands and then said it would be better for him to do it and me do his work. I said, "Now, you get down and put in the plug and I will undo the shackles," that is, take the blocks off, so he dropped the blocks and got down to fix the plug, and then he came back to assist me saying, "Hurry up." He said: "This boat is going to founder." I thought he meant our lifeboat was going to founder, but he meant the large boat, and that we were to hurry up and get away from it, so we got the rudder in and he told me to go forward and take an oar. I did so, and got an oar on the port side. Sailor Fleet was on my left on the starboard side. The quartermaster told us to row as hard as we could to get away from the suction. We got a short distance away when an Italian, a stowaway, made his appearance. He had a broken wrist or arm, and was of no use to row. He was stowed away under the boat where we could not see him.

Toward morning we tied up to another boat (No. 16) for fifteen minutes. We said to those in the other boat: "Surely you can spare us one man if you have so many." One man, a fireman, was accordingly transferred, who assisted in rowing on the starboard side. The women helped with the oars, and very pluckily too.[1]

We were to the weather of the *Carpathia*, and so she stayed there until we all came down on her. I looked at my watch and it was something after eight o'clock.

Mrs. Candee's account of her experience is as follows:
She last saw Mr. Kent in the companionway between Decks A and B.

---

1 "An English girl (Miss Norton) and I rowed for four hours and a half."—Mrs. Meyer in New York *Times*, April 14th, 1912.

He took charge of an ivory miniature of her mother, etc., which afterwards were found on his body when brought into Halifax. He appeared at the time to hesitate accepting her valuables, seeming to have a premonition of his fate.

She witnessed the same incident described by Major Peuchen, when a group of firemen came up on deck and were ordered by the officer to return below. She, however, gives praise to these men. They obeyed like soldiers, and without a murmur or a protest, though they knew better than anyone else on the ship that they were going straight to their death. No boats had been lowered when these firemen first appeared upon the Boat Deck, and it would have been an easy matter for them to have "rushed" the boats.

Her stateroom steward also gave an exhibition of courage. After he had tied on her life-preserver and had locked her room as a precaution against looters, which she believed was done all through the deck, she said to this brave man: "It is time for you to look out for yourself," to which the steward replied, "Oh, plenty of time for that, Madam, plenty of time for that." He was lost.

As she got into boat No. 6, it being dark and not seeing where she stepped, her foot encountered the oars lying lengthwise in the boat and her ankle was thus twisted and broken.

Just before her boat was lowered away a man's voice said: "Captain, we have no seaman." Captain Smith then seized a boy by the arm and said: "Here's one." The boy went into the boat as ordered by the captain, but afterwards he was found to be disabled. She does not think he was an Italian.

Her impression is that there were other boats in the water which had been lowered before hers. There was a French woman about fifty years of age in the boat who was constantly calling for her son. Mrs. Candee sat near her. After arrival on the *Carpathia* this French woman became hysterical.

Notwithstanding Hitchens' statements, she says that there was absolutely no upset feeling on the woman's part at any time, even when the boat, as it was being lowered, on several occasions hung at a dangerous angle—sometimes bow up and sometimes stern up. The lowering process seemed to be done by jerks. She herself called out to the men lowering the boat and gave instructions: otherwise they would have been swamped.

The Italian boy who was in the boat was not a stowaway, he was ordered in by the captain as already related. Neither did he refuse to row. When he tried to do so, it was futile, because of an injury to his arm or wrist.

Through the courtesy of another fellow passenger, Mrs. J. J. Brown, of Denver, Colorado, I am able to give her experiences in boat No. 6, told in a delightful, graphic manner; so much so that I would like to insert it all did not space prevent:

In telling of the people she conversed with, that Sunday evening, she refers to an exceedingly intellectual and much-traveled acquaintance, Mrs. Bucknell, whose husband had founded the Bucknell University of Philadelphia; also to another passenger from the same city, Dr. Brewe, who had done much in scientific research. During her conversation with Mrs. Bucknell, the latter reiterated a statement previously made on the tender at Cherbourg while waiting for the *Titanic*. She said she feared boarding the ship because she had evil forebodings that something might happen. Mrs. Brown laughed at her premonitions and shortly afterwards sought her quarters.

Instead of retiring to slumber, Mrs. Brown was absorbed in reading and gave little thought to the crash at her window overhead which threw her to the floor. Picking herself up she proceeded to see what the steamer had struck; but thinking nothing serious had occurred, though realizing that the engines had stopped immediately after the crash and the boat was at a standstill, she picked up her book and began reading again. Finally she saw her curtains moving while she was reading, but no one was visible. She again looked out and saw a man whose face was blanched, his eyes protruding, wearing the look of a haunted creature. He was gasping for breath and in an undertone gasped, "Get your life-preserver." He was one of the buyers for Gimbel Bros., of Paris and New York.

She got down her life-preserver, snatched up her furs and hurriedly mounted the stairs to A Deck, where she found passengers putting on lifebelts like hers. Mrs. Bucknell approached and whispered, "Didn't I tell you something was going to happen?" She found the lifeboats lowered from the falls and made flush with the deck. Madame de Villiers appeared from below in a nightdress and evening slippers, with no stockings. She wore a long woolen motorcoat. Touching Mrs. Brown's arm, in a terrified voice she said she was going below for her money and valuables. After much persuasion Mrs. Brown prevailed upon her not to do so, but to get into the boat. She hesitated and became very much excited, but was finally prevailed upon to enter the lifeboat. Mrs. Brown was walking away, eager to see what was being done elsewhere. Suddenly she saw a shadow and a few seconds later someone seized her, saying: "You are going, too," and she was dropped fully four feet into the lowering lifeboat. There was but one man in charge of the boat. As it was lowered by jerks by an officer above, she discovered that a great gush of water was spouting through the porthole from D Deck, and the lifeboat was in grave danger of being submerged. She immediately grasped an oar and held the lifeboat away from the ship.

When the sea was reached, smooth as glass, she looked up and saw the benign, resigned countenance, the venerable white hair and the Chesterfieldian bearing of the beloved Captain Smith with whom she had crossed twice before, and only three months previous on the *Olympic*. He peered down upon those in the boat, like a solicitous father, and directed them to row to the light in the distance—all boats keeping together.

Because of the fewness of men in the boat she found it necessary for someone to bend to the oars. She placed her oar in an oarlock and asked a young woman nearby to hold one while she placed the other on the further side. To Mrs. Brown's surprise the young lady (who must have been Miss Norton, spoken of elsewhere), immediately began to row like a galley slave, every stroke counting. Together they managed to pull away from the steamer.

By this time E and C Decks were completely submerged. Those ladies who had husbands, sons or fathers on the doomed steamer buried their heads on the shoulders of those near them and moaned and groaned. Mrs. Brown's eyes were glued on the fast-disappearing ship. Suddenly there was a rift in the water, the sea opened up and the surface foamed like giant arms and spread around the ship and the vessel disappeared from sight, and not a sound was heard.

Then follows Mrs. Brown's account of the conduct of the quarter-master in the boat which will be found under the heading presently given, and it will be noticed that her statements correspond with those of all others in the boat.

The dawn disclosed the awful situation. There were fields of ice on which, like points on the landscape, rested innumerable pyramids of ice. Seemingly a half hour later, the sun, like a ball of molten lead, appeared in the background. The hand of nature portrayed a scenic effect beyond the ken of the human mind. The heretofore smooth sea became choppy and retarded their progress. All the while the people in boat No. 6 saw the other small lifeboats being hauled aboard the *Carpathia*. By the time their boat reached the *Carpathia* a heavy sea was running, and, No. 6 boat being among the last to approach, it was found difficult to get close to the ship. Three or four unsuccessful attempts were made. Each time they were dashed against the keel, and bounded off like a rubber ball. A rope was then thrown down, which was spliced in four at the bottom, and a Jacob's ladder was made. Catching hold, they were hoisted up, where a dozen of the crew and officers and doctors were waiting. They were caught and handled as tenderly as though they were children.

### HITCHENS' CONDUCT

Major Peuchen (Am. Inq., p. 334) continued:

There was an officers' call, sort of a whistle, calling us to come back to the boat. The quartermaster told us to stop rowing. We all thought we ought to go back to the ship, but the quartermaster said "No, we are not going back to the boat; it is our lives now, not theirs." It was the women who rebelled against this action. I asked him to assist us in rowing and let some of the women steer the boat, as it was a perfectly calm night and no skill was required. He refused, and told me he was in command of that boat and that I was to row.

He imagined he saw a light. I have done a great deal of yachting in my life. I have owned a yacht for six years. I saw a reflection. He thought it was a boat of some kind: probably it might be a buoy, and he called out to the next boat asking them if they knew any buoys were around there. This struck me as being perfectly absurd.

I heard what seemed to be one, two, three rumbling sounds; then the lights of the ship went out. Then the terrible cries and calls for help— moaning and crying. It affected all the women in our boat whose husbands were among those in the water. This went on for some time, gradually getting fainter and fainter. At first it was horrible to listen to. We must have been five-eighths of a mile away when this took place. There were only two of us rowing a very heavy boat with a good many people in it, and I do not think we covered very much ground. Some of the women in the boat urged the quartermaster to return. He said there was no use going back—that there were only a "lot of stiffs there." The women resented it very much.

Seaman Fleet (Am. Inq., p. 363):

All the women asked us to pull to the place where the *Titanic* went down, but the quartermaster, who was at the tiller all the time, would not allow it. They asked him, but he would not hear of it.

Mrs. Candee continues:

Hitchens was cowardly and almost crazed with fear all the time. After we left the ship he thought he heard the captain say: "Come along-side," and was for turning back until reminded by the passengers that the Captain's final orders were: "Keep boats together and row away from the ship." She heard this order given.

After that he constantly reminded us who were at the oars that if we did not make better speed with our rowing we would all be sucked under the water by the foundering of the ship. This he repeated whenever our muscles flagged.

Directly the *Titanic* had foundered a discussion arose as to whether we should return. Hitchens said our boat would immediately be swamped if we went into the confusion. The reason for this was that our boat was not manned with enough oars.

Then after the sinking of the *Titanic* Hitchens reminded us frequently that we were hundreds of miles from land, without water, without food, without protection against cold, and if a storm should come up that we would be helpless. Therefore, we faced death by starvation or by drowning. He said we did not even know the direction in which we were rowing. I corrected him by pointing to the north star immediately over our bow.

When our boat came alongside No. 16, Hitchens immediately ordered the boats lashed together. He resigned the helm and settled down to rest. When the *Carpathia* hove in sight he ordered that we drift. Addressing the people in both boats Mrs. Candee said: "Where those lights are lies our salvation; shall we not go towards them?" The reply was a murmur of approval and immediate recourse to the oars.

Hitchens was requested to assist in the toilsome rowing. Women tried to taunt and provoke him into activity. When it was suggested that he permit the injured boy to take the tiller and that Hitchens should row, he declined, and in every case he refused labor. He spoke with such uncivility to one of the ladies that a man's voice was heard in rebuke: "You are speaking to a lady," to which he replied: "I know whom I am speaking to, and I am commanding this boat."

When asked if the *Carpathia* would come and pick us up he replied: "No, she is not going to pick us up; she is to pick up bodies." This when said to wives and mothers of the dead men was needlessly brutal.

When we neared the *Carpathia* he refused to go round on the smooth side because it necessitated keeping longer in the rough sea, so we made a difficult landing.

In Mrs. Brown's account of her experience she relates the following about the conduct of the quartermaster in charge of the boat in which she was:

He, Quartermaster Hitchens, was at the rudder and standing much higher than we were, shivering like an aspen. As they rowed away from the ship he burst out in a frightened voice and warned them of the fate that awaited them, saying that the task in rowing away from the sinking ship was futile, as she was so large that in sinking she would draw everything for miles around down with her suction, and, if they escaped that, the boilers would burst and rip up the bottom of the sea, tearing the icebergs asunder and completely submerging them. They were truly doomed either way. He dwelt upon the dire fate awaiting them, describing the accident that happened to the S. S. *New York* when the *Titanic* left the docks at Southampton.

After the ship had sunk and none of the calamities that were predicted by the terrified quartermaster were experienced, he was asked to return and pick up those in the water. Again the people in the boat were admonished and told how the frantic drowning victims would grapple the side of the boat and capsize it. He not yielding to the entreaties, those at the oars pulled away vigorously towards a faintly glimmering light on the horizon. After three hours of pulling the light grew fainter, and then completely disappeared. Then this quartermaster, who stood on his pinnacle trembling, with an attitude like some one preaching to the multitude, fanning the air with his hands, recommenced his tirade of awful forebodings, telling those in the boat that they were likely to drift for days, all the while reminding them that they were surrounded by icebergs, as he pointed to a pyramid of ice looming up in the distance, possibly seventy feet high. He forcibly impressed upon them that there was no water in the casks in the lifeboats, and no bread, no compass and no chart. No one answered him. All seemed to be stricken dumb. One of the ladies in the boat had had the presence of mind to procure her silver brandy flask. As she held it in her hand the silver glittered and he being attracted to it implored her to give it to him, saying that he was frozen. She refused the brandy, but removed her steamer blanket and placed it around his shoulders, while another lady wrapped a second blanket around his waist and limbs, he looking "as snug as a bug in a rug."

The quartermaster was then asked to relieve one or the other of those struggling at the oars, as someone else could manage the rudder while he rowed. He flatly refused and continued to lampoon them, shouting: "Here, you fellow on the starboard side, your oar is not being put in the water at the right angle." No one made any protest to his outbursts, as he broke the monotony, but they continued to pull at the oars with no goal in sight. Presently he raised his voice and shouted to another lifeboat to pull near and lash alongside, commanding some of the other ladies to take the light and signal to the other lifeboats. His command was immediately obeyed. He also gave another command to drop the oars and lay to. Some time later, after more shouts, a lifeboat hove to and obeyed his orders to throw a rope, and was tied alongside. On the cross-seat of that boat stood a man in white pajamas, looking like a snow man in that icy region. His teeth were chattering and he appeared quite numb. Seeing his predicament, Mrs. Brown told him he had better get to rowing and keep his blood in circulation. But the suggestion met with a forcible protest from the quartermaster in charge. Mrs. Brown and her companions at the oars, after their exercise, felt the blasts from the ice-fields and demanded that they should be allowed to row to keep warm.

Over into their boat jumped a half-frozen stoker, black and covered with dust. As he was dressed in thin jumpers, she picked up a large sable stole which she had dropped into the boat and wrapped it around his limbs from his waist down and tied the tails around his ankles. She handed him an oar and told the pajama man to cut loose. A howl arose from the quartermaster in charge. He moved to prevent it, and Mrs. Brown told him if he did he would be thrown overboard. Someone laid a hand on her shoulder to stay her threats, but she knew it would not be necessary to push him over, for had she only moved in the quarter-master's direction, he would have tumbled into the sea, so paralyzed was he with fright. By this time he had worked himself up to a pitch of sheer despair, fearing that a scramble of any kind would remove the plug from the bottom of the boat. He then became very impertinent, and our fur-enveloped stoker in as broad a cockney as one hears in the Haymarket shouted: "Oi sy, don't you know you are talkin' to a lidy?" For the time being the seaman was silenced and we resumed our task at the oars. Two other ladies came to the rescue.

While glancing around watching the edge of the horizon, the beautifully modulated voice of the young Englishwoman at the oar (Miss Norton) exclaimed, "There is a flash of lightning." "It is a falling star," replied our pessimistic seaman. As it became bright he was then convinced that it was a ship. However, the distance, as we rowed, seemed interminable. We saw the ship was anchored. Again the declaration was made that we, regardless of what our quartermaster said, would row toward her, and the young Englishwoman from the Thames got to work, accompanying her strokes with cheerful words to the wilted occupants of the boat.

Mrs. Brown finishes the quartermaster in her final account of him. On entering the dining-room on the *Carpathia*, she saw him in one corner—this brave and heroic seaman! A cluster of people were around him as he wildly gesticulated, trying to impress upon them what difficulty he had in maintaining discipline among the occupants of his boat, but on seeing Mrs. Brown and a few others of the boat nearby he did not tarry long, but made a hasty retreat.

R. Hitchens, Q. M. (Am. Inq., p. 451. Br. Inq.) explains his conduct:
I was put in charge of No. 6 by the Second Officer, Mr. Lightoller.
We lowered away from the ship. I told them in the boat somebody
would have to pull. There was no use stopping alongside the ship, which
was gradually going by the head. We were in a dangerous place, so I
told them to man the oars—ladies and all. "All of you do your best."
I relieved one of the young ladies with an oar and told her to take the
tiller. She immediately let the boat come athwart, and the ladies in the
boat got very nervous; so I took the tiller back again and told them to
manage the best way they could. The lady I refer to, Mrs. Meyer, was
rather vexed with me in the boat and I spoke rather straight to her. She
accused me of wrapping myself up in the blankets in the boat, using bad
language and drinking all the whisky, which I deny, sir. I was standing
to attention, exposed, steering the boat all night, which is a very cold
billet. I would rather be pulling the boat than be steering, but I saw
no one there to steer, so I thought, being in charge of the boat, it was
the best way to steer myself, especially when I saw the ladies get very
nervous.

I do not remember that the women urged me to go toward the *Titanic*.
I did not row toward the scene of the *Titanic* because the suction of the
ship would draw the boat, with all its occupants, under water. I did not
know which way to go back to the *Titanic*. I was looking at all the other
boats. We were looking at each other's lights. After the lights disappeared and went out, we did hear cries of distress—a lot of crying,
moaning and screaming, for two or three minutes. We made fast to
another boat—that of the master-at-arms. It was No. 16. I had thirty-
eight women in my boat. I counted them, sir. One seaman, Fleet; the
Canadian Major, who testified here yesterday, myself and the Italian
boy.

We got down to the *Carpathia* and I saw every lady and everybody
out of the boat, and I saw them carefully hoisted on board the *Carpathia*,
and I was the last man to leave the boat.

## BOAT NO. 8 [1]

### *No male passengers in this boat*

*Passengers:* Mrs. Bucknell and her maid (Albina Bazzani); Miss
Cherry, Mrs. Kenyon, Miss Leader, Mrs. Pears, Mrs. Penasco and her
maid (Mlle. Olivia); Countess Rothes and her maid (Miss Maloney);
Mrs. Swift, Mrs. Taussig, Miss Taussig, Mrs. White and her maid

---

[1] British Report (p. 38) puts this boat second on port side at 1.10. Notwithstanding
Seaman Fleet's testimony (Am. Inq., p. 363), I think she must have preceded No. 6.

(Amelia Bessetti); Mrs. Wick, Miss Wick, Miss Young and Mrs. Straus' maid (Ellen Bird).

*Women:* 24.

*Said good-bye to wives and sank with the ship:* Messrs. Kenyon, Pears, Penasco, Taussig and Wick.

*Crew:* Seaman T. Jones, Stewards Crawford and Hart, and a cook. *Total:* 28.

### INCIDENTS

T. Jones, seaman (Am. Inq., p. 570):

The captain asked me if the plug was in the boat and I answered, "Yes, sir." "All right," he said, "any more ladies?" He shouted twice again, "Any more ladies?"

I pulled for the light, but I found that I could not get to it; so I stood by for a while. I wanted to return to the ship, but the ladies were frightened. In all, I had thirty-five ladies and three stewards, Crawford, Hart and another. There were no men who offered to get in the boat. I did not see any children, and very few women when we left the ship. There was one old lady there and an old gentleman, her husband. She wanted him to enter the boat with her but he backed away. She never said anything; if she did, we could not hear it, because the steam was blowing so and making such a noise.[1]

Senator Newlands: Can you give me the names of any passengers on this boat?

Witness: One lady—she had a lot to say and I put her to steering the boat.

Senator Newlands: What was her name?

Witness: Lady Rothes; she was a countess, or something.

A. Crawford, steward (Am. Inq., pp. 111, 827, 842):

After we struck I went out and saw the iceberg, a large black object, much higher than B Deck, passing along the starboard side. We filled No. 8 with women. Captain Smith and a steward lowered the forward falls. Captain Smith told me to get in. He gave orders to row for the light and to land the people there and come back to the ship. The Countess Rothes was at the tiller all night. There were two lights not further than ten miles—stationary masthead lights. Everybody saw them—all the ladies in the boat. They asked if we were drawing nearer to the steamer, but we could not seem to make any headway, and near

---

[1] By the testimony of the witness and Steward Crawford it appears that Mr. and Mrs. Straus approached this boat and their maid got in, but Mr. Straus would not follow his wife and she refused to leave him.

daybreak we saw another steamer coming up, which proved to be the *Carpathia*, and then we turned around and came back. We were the furthest boat away. I am sure it was a steamer, because a sailing vessel would not have had two masthead lights.

Mrs. J. Stuart White (Am. Inq., p. 1008):

Senator Smith: Did you see anything after the accident bearing on the discipline of the officers or crew, or their conduct which you desire to speak of?

Mrs. White: Before we cut loose from the ship these stewards took out cigarettes and lighted them. On an occasion like that! That is one thing I saw. All of these men escaped under the pretense of being oarsmen. The man who rowed near me took his oar and rowed all over the boat in every direction. I said to him: "Why don't you put the oar in the oarlock?" He said: "Do you put it in that hole?" I said: "Certainly." He said: "I never had an oar in my hand before." I spoke to the other man and he said: "I have never had an oar in my hand before, but I think I can row." These were the men we were put to sea with, that night—with all those magnificent fellows left on board who would have been such a protection to us—those were the kind of men with whom we were put to sea that night! There were twenty-two women and four men in my boat. None of the men seemed to understand the management of a boat except one who was at the end of our boat and gave the orders. The officer who put us in the boat gave strict orders to make for the light opposite, land passengers and then get back just as soon as possible. That was the light everybody saw in the distance. I saw it distinctly. It was ten miles away, but we rowed, and rowed, and rowed, and then we all decided that it was impossible for us to get to it, and the thing to do was to go back and see what we could do for the others. We had only twenty-two in our boat. We turned and went back and lingered around for a long time. We could not locate the other boats except by hearing them. The only way to look was by my electric light. I had an electric cane with an electric light in it. The lamp in the boat was worth absolutely nothing. There was no excitement whatever on the ship. Nobody seemed frightened. Nobody was panic-stricken. There was a lot of pathos when husbands and wives kissed each other good-bye.

We were the second boat (No. 8) that got away from the ship and we saw nothing that happened after that. We were not near enough. We heard the yells of the passengers as they went down, but we saw none of the harrowing part of it. The women in our boat all rowed—every one of them. Miss Young rowed every minute. The men (the stewards) did not know the first thing about it and could not row. Mrs Swift rowed all the way to the *Carpathia*. Countess Rothes stood at the tiller. Where would we have been if it had not been for the women, with such men as were put in charge of the boat? Our head seaman was giving orders and these men knew nothing about a boat. They would say: "If you don't stop talking through that hole in your face there will be one less in the boat." We were in the hands of men of that kind. I settled two or three fights between them and quieted them down. Imagine getting right out there and taking out a pipe and smoking it, which was most dangerous. We had woolen rugs all around us. There was another thing which I thought a disgraceful point. The men were asked when they got in if they could row. Imagine asking men who are supposed to be at the head of lifeboats if they can row!

Senator Smith: There were no male passengers in your boat?

Mrs. White: Not one. I never saw a finer body of men in my life than the men passengers on this ship—athletes and men of sense—and if they had been permitted to enter these lifeboats with their families, the boats would have been properly manned and many more lives saved, instead of allowing stewards to get in the boats and save their lives under the pretense that they could row when they knew nothing about it.

## BOAT NO. 10 [1]

### *No male passengers in this boat*

*Passengers:* First cabin, Miss Andrews, Miss Longley, Mrs. Hogeboom. Second cabin, Mrs. Parrish, Mrs. Shelley. 41 women, 7 children.

*Crew:* Seamen: Buley (in charge), Evans; Fireman Rice; Stewards Burke and one other.

*Stowaway:* 1 Japanese.

*Jumped from A Deck into boat being lowered:* 1 Armenian.

*Total:* 55.

#### INCIDENTS

Edward J. Buley, A. B. (Am. Inq., p. 604):

Chief Officer Wilde said: "See if you can find another seaman to give you a hand, and jump in." I found Evans, my mate, the able-bodied seaman, and we both got in the boat.

Much of Seaman Buley's and of Steward Burke's testimony is a repetition of that of Seaman Evans, so I cite the latter only:

F. O. Evans, A. B. (Am. Inq., p. 675):

I went up (on the Boat Deck) with the remainder of the crew and

---

[1] British Report (p. 38) says third at 1.20. I think No. 6 went later, though Buley (Am. Inq., p. 604) claims No. 10 as the last lifeboat lowered.

uncovered all of the port boats. Then to the starboard side and lowered the boats there with the assistance of the Boatswain of the ship, A. Nichol. I went next (after No. 12) to No. 10. Mr. Murdoch was standing there. I lowered the boat with the assistance of a steward. The chief officer said: "Get into that boat." I got into the bows. A young ship's baker (J. Joughin) was getting the children and chucking them into the boat. Mr. Murdoch and the baker made the women jump across into the boat about two feet and a half. "He threw them on to the women and he was catching children by their dresses and chucking them in." One woman in a black dress slipped and fell. She seemed nervous and did not like to jump at first. When she did jump she did not go far enough, but fell between the ship and the boat. She was pulled in by some men on the deck below, went up to the Boat Deck again, took another jump, and landed safely in the boat. There were none of the children hurt. The only accident was with this woman. The only man passenger was a foreigner, up forward. He, as the boat was being lowered, jumped from A Deck into the boat—deliberately jumped across and saved himself.

When we got to the water it was impossible to get to the tripper underneath the thwart on account of women being packed so tight. We had to lift the fall up off the hook by hand to release the spring to get the block and fall away from it. We pushed off from the ship and rowed away about 200 yards. We tied up to three other boats. We gave the man our painter and made fast to No. 12. We stopped there about an hour, and Officer Lowe came over with his boat No. 14 and said: "You seamen will have to distribute these passengers among these boats. Tie them together and come into my boat to go over to the wreckage and pick up anyone that is alive there."

Witness testified that the larger lifeboats would hold sixty people.

Senator Smith: Do you wish to be understood that each lifeboat like Nos. 12 and 14 and 10 could be filled to its fullest capacity and lowered to the water with safety?

Mr. Evans: Yes, because we did it then, sir.

Senator Smith: That is a pretty good answer.

Mr. Evans: It was my first experience in seeing a boat loaded like that, sir.

The stern of the ship, after plunging forward, remained floating in a perpendicular position about four or five minutes.

W. Burke, dining-room steward (Am. Inq., p. 822):

I went to my station and found that my boat, No. 1, had gone. Then to the port side and assisted with No. 8 boat and saw her lowered.

Then I passed to No. 10. The officer said, " Get right in there," and pushed me toward the boat, and I got in. When there were no women to be had around the deck the officer gave the order for the boat to be lowered.

After the two seamen (Buley and Evans) were transferred to boat No. 14, some of the women forward said to me: "There are two men down here in the bottom of the boat." I got hold of them and pulled one out. He apparently was a Japanese and could not speak English. I put him at an oar. The other appeared to be an Italian. I tried to speak to him but he said: "Armenian." I also put him at an oar. I afterwards made fast to an officer's boat—I think it was Mr. Lightoller's (i. e., No. 12).

Mrs. Imanita Shelley's affidavit (Am. Inq., p. 1146):
Mrs. Shelley with her mother, Mrs. L. D. Parrish, were second-cabin passengers. Mrs. Shelley had been sick and it was with difficulty that she reached the deck, where she was assisted to a chair. After some time a sailor ran to her and implored her to get in the lifeboat that was then being launched—one of the last on the ship. Pushing her mother toward the sailor, Mrs. Shelley made for the davits where the boat hung.

There was a space of between four or five feet between the edge of the deck and the suspended boat. The sailor picked up Mrs. Parrish and threw her bodily into the boat. Mrs. Shelley jumped and landed safely. There were a fireman and a ship's baker among the crew at the time of launching. The boat was filled with women and children, as many as could get in without overcrowding. There was trouble with the tackle and the ropes had to be cut.

Just as they reached the water, a crazed Italian jumped from the deck into the lifeboat, landing on Mrs. Parrish, severely bruising her right side and leg.

Orders had been given to keep in sight of the ship's boat which had been sent out ahead to look for help. Throughout the entire period, from the time of the collision and taking to the boats, the ship's crew behaved in an ideal manner. Not a man tried to get into a boat unless ordered to, and many were seen to strip off their clothing and wrap it around the women and children, who came up half-clad from their beds. Mrs. Shelley says that no crew could have behaved in a more perfect manner.

J. Joughin, head baker (Br. Inq.):
Chief Officer Wilde shouted to the stewards to keep the men passengers back, but there was no necessity for the order as they were keeping

back. The order was splendid. The stewards, firemen and sailors got in line and passed the ladies in; and then we had difficulty to find ladies to go into the boat. No distinction at all as to class was made. I saw a number of third-class women with their bags, which they would not let go.

The boat was let down and the women were forcibly drawn into it. The boat was a yard and a half from the ship's side. There was a slight list and we had to drop them in. The officer ordered two sailors and a steward to get in.

## BOAT NO. 12 [1]

### *No male passenger in this boat*

*Passengers:* Miss Phillips.
*Bade good-bye to his daughter and sank with the ship:* Mr. Phillips.
*Women and children:* 40.
*Crew:* Seamen Poigndestre (in charge), F. Clench. Later, Lucas and two firemen were transferred from boat "D".
*Jumped from deck below as boat was lowered:* 1 Frenchman.
*Total:* 43.

Transfers were made to this boat *first* from Engelhardt "D" and *second*, from Engelhardt upset boat "B," so that it reached the *Carpathia*'s side with seventy, or more.

#### INCIDENTS

F. Clench, A. B. (Am. Inq., p. 636):

The second officer and myself stood on the gunwale and helped load women and children. The chief officer passed them along to us and we filled three boats, No. 12 first. In each there were about forty or fifty people. After finishing No. 16 boat, I went back to No. 12. "How many men (crew) have you in this boat?" the chief officer said, and I said, "Only one, sir." He looked up and said: "Jump into that boat," and that made a complement of two seamen. An able seaman was in charge of this boat. (Poigndestre.) We had instructions to keep our eye on No. 14 and keep together.

There was only one male passenger in our boat, and that was a Frenchman who jumped in and we could not find him. He got under the thwart, mixed up with the women, just as we dropped into the water before the boat was lowered and without our knowledge. Officer Lowe

---

[1] British Report (p. 38) says this was the fourth boat lowered on port side at 1.25 a. m.

transferred some of his people into our boat and others, making close on to sixty, and pretty full up. When Mr. Lowe was gone I heard shouts. I looked around and saw a boat in the way that appeared to be like a funnel; we thought it was the top of a funnel. (It was Engelhardt overturned boat "B.") There were about twenty on this, and we took off approximately ten, making seventy in my boat.

John Poigndestre, A. B. (Br. Inq., p. 82):

Lightoller ordered us to lay off and stand by close to the ship. Boat "D" and three lifeboats made fast to No. 12. Stood off about 100 yards after ship sank. Not enough sailors to help pick up swimmers. No light. Transfer of about a dozen woman passengers from No. 14 to No. 12. About 150 yards off when *Titanic* sank. No compass.

## BOAT NO. 14 [1]

### *No male passenger in this boat*

*Passengers:* Mrs. Compton, Miss Compton, Mrs. Minahan, Miss Minahan, Mrs. Collyer, Miss Collyer.

*Picked up out of sea:* W. F. Hoyt (who died), Steward J. Stewart, and a plucky Japanese.

*Women:* 50.

*Volunteer when crew was short:* C. Williams.

*Crew:* Fifth Officer Lowe, Seaman Scarrot, 2 firemen, Stewards Crowe and Morris.

*Stowaway:* 1 Italian.

*Bade good-bye and sank with ship:* Dr. Minahan, Mr. Compton, Mr. Collyer.

*Total:* 60.

#### INCIDENTS

H. G. Lowe, Fifth Officer (Am. Inq., 116):

Nos. 12, 14 and 16 were down about the same time. I told Mr. Moody that three boats had gone away and that an officer ought to go with them. He said: "You go." There was difficulty in lowering when I got near the water. I dropped her about five feet, because I was not going to take the chance of being dropped down upon by somebody. While I was on the Boat Deck, two men tried to jump into the boat. I chased them out.

[1] British Report (p. 38) says this was the fifth boat on the port side, lowered at 1.30.

We filled boats 14 and 16 with women and children. Moody filled No. 16 and I filled No. 14. Lightoller was there part of the time. They were all women and children, barring one passenger, who was an Italian, and he sneaked in dressed like a woman. He had a shawl over his head. There was another passenger, a chap by the name of C. Williams, whom I took for rowing. He gave me his name and address (referring to book), "C. Williams, Racket Champion of the World, 2 Drury Road, Harrow-on-the-Hill, Middlesex, England."

As I was being lowered, I expected every moment that my boat would be doubled up under my feet. I had overcrowded her, but I knew that I had to take a certain amount of risk. I thought if one additional body was to fall into that boat, that slight additional weight might part the hooks, or carry away something; so as we were coming down past the open decks, I saw a lot of Latin people all along the ship's rails. They were glaring more or less like wild beasts, ready to spring. That is why I yelled out to "look out," and let go, bang! right along the ship's side. There was a space I should say of about three feet between the side of the boat and the ship's side, and as I went down I fired these shots without any intention of hurting anybody and with the positive knowledge that I did not hurt anybody. I fired, I think, three times.

Later, 150 yards away, I herded five boats together. I was in No. 14; then I had 10, 12, collapsible "D" and one other boat (No. 4), and made them tie up. I waited until the yells and shrieks had subsided for the people to thin out, and then I deemed it safe for me to go amongst the wreckage; so I transferred all my passengers, somewhere about fifty-three, from my boat and equally distributed them among my other four boats. Then I asked for volunteers to go with me to the wreck, and it was at this time that I found the Italian. He came aft and had a shawl over his head, and I suppose he had skirts. Anyhow, I pulled the shawl off his face and saw he was a man. He was in a great hurry to get into the other boat and I got hold of him and pitched him in.

Senator Smith: Pitched him in?

Mr. Lowe: Yes; because he was not worth being handled better.

Senator Smith: You pitched him in among the women?

Mr. Lowe: No, sir; in the forepart of the lifeboat in which I transferred my passengers.

Senator Smith: Did you use some pretty emphatic language when you did this?

Mr. Lowe: No, sir: I did not say a word to him.

Then I went off and rowed to the wreckage and around the wreckage and picked up four people alive. I do not know who these live persons were. They never came near me afterwards either to say this or that or the other. But one died, Mr. W. F. Hoyt, of New York. After we got him in the boat we took his collar off so as to give him more chance to breathe, but unfortunately, he died. He was too far gone when we picked him up. I then left the wreck. I went right around, and, strange to say, I did not see a single female body around the wreckage. I did not have a light in my boat. Then I could see the *Carpathia* coming up and I thought: "Well, I am the fastest boat of the lot," as I was sailing, you see. I was going through the water four or five knots, bowling along very nicely.

By and by, I noticed a collapsible boat, Engelhardt "D." It looked rather sorry, so I thought: "Well, I will go down and pick her up and make sure of her." This was Quartermaster Bright's boat. Mrs. H. B. Harris, of New York, was in it. She had a broken arm. I had taken this first collapsible ("D") in tow and I noticed that there was another collapsible ("A") in a worse plight than this one that I had in tow. I got to her just in time and took off, I suppose, about twenty men and one lady. I left three male bodies in it. I may have been a bit hard-hearted in doing this. I thought: "I am not here to worry about bodies; I am here to save life and not bother about bodies." The people on the raft told me these had been dead for some time. I do not know whether any one endeavored to find anything on their persons that would identify them, because they were all up to their ankles in water when I took them off.

Joseph Scarrot, A. B. (Br. Inq., pp. 29, 30): I myself took charge of No. 14 as the only sailorman there. The Chief Officer ordered women and children to be taken in. Some men came and tried to rush the boat. They were foreigners and could not understand the orders I gave them, but I managed to keep them away. I had to use some persuasion with a boat tiller. One man jumped in twice and I had to throw him out the third time. I got all the women and children into the boat. There were fifty-four women and four children—one of them a baby in arms. There were myself, two firemen, three or four stewards and Mr. Lowe, who got into the boat. I told him the trouble I had with the men and he brought out his revolver and fired two shots and said: "If there is any more trouble I will fire at them." The shots fired were fired between the boat and the ship's side. The after fall got twisted and we dropped the boat by the releasing gear and got clear of the ship. There were four men rowing. There was a man in the boat who we thought was a sailor, but he was not. He was a window cleaner. The *Titanic* was then about fifty yards off, and we lay there with the other boats. Mr. Lowe was at the helm. We went in the direction of the cries and came among hundreds of dead bodies and lifebelts. We got one man, who died shortly after he

THE LAST PHOTOGRAPH OF THE TITANIC'S COM-
MANDER AND THREE OFFICERS

(Reading from left to right:—Captain E. J. Smith, Dr. W. F. O'Loughlin, First
Officer W. M. Murdoch, and Purser H. W. McElroy)

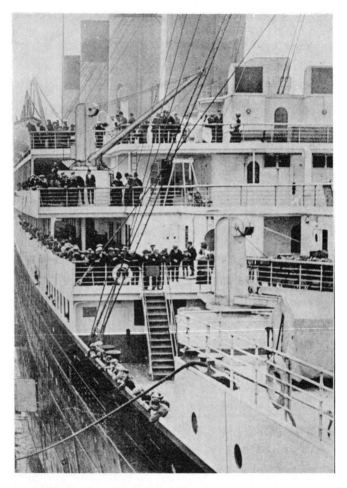

Passengers line four decks of the *Olympic*, nearly identical sister ship of the *Titanic*.

got into the boat. One of the stewards tried to restore him, but without avail. There was another man who was calling for help, but among the bodies and wreckage it was too late for us to reach him. It took half an hour to get to that man. Cannot say exactly, but think we got about twenty off of the Engelhardt boat ("A").

E. J. Buley, A. B. (Am. Inq., p. 605):
(After his transfer from No. 10 to No. 14.) Then, with Lowe in his boat No. 14, I went back to where the *Titanic* sank and picked up the remaining live bodies. We got four; all the others were dead. We turned over several to see if they were alive. It looked as if none of them were drowned. They looked as if frozen. The lifebelts they had on were that much (indicating) out of the water, and their heads lay back with their faces on the water. They were head and shoulders out of water, with their heads thrown back. In the morning, after we had picked up all that were alive, there was a collapsible boat ("A") swamped, which we saw with a lot of people up to their knees in water. We sailed over to them. We then picked up another boat ("D") and took her in tow. I think we were about the seventh or eighth boat alongside the *Carpathia*.

F. O. Evans, A. B. (Am. Inq., p. 677):
So from No. 10 we got into his (Lowe's) boat, No. 14, and went straight over towards the wreckage with eight or nine men and picked up four persons alive, one of whom died on the way to the *Carpathia*. Another picked up was named J. Stewart, a steward. You could not hardly count the number of dead bodies. I was afraid to look over the sides because it might break my nerves down. We saw no other people in the water or heard their cries, other than these four picked up. The officer said: "Hoist a sail forward." I did so and made sail in the direction of the collapsible boat "A" about a mile and a half away, which had been swamped. There were in it one woman and about ten or eleven men. Then we picked up another collapsible boat ("D") and took her in tow to the *Carpathia*. There were then about twenty-five people in our boat No. 14, including the one who died.

One of the ladies there passed over a flask of whisky to the people who were all wet through. She asked if anybody needed the spirits, and these people were all soaking wet and nearly perished and they passed it around among these men and women. It took about twenty minutes after we sighted the *Carpathia* to get alongside of her. We saw five or six icebergs—some of them tremendous, about the height of the *Titanic*

—and field ice. After we got on the *Carpathia* we saw, at a rough estimate, a twenty-five mile floe, sir, flat like the floor.

F. Crowe, steward (Am. Inq., p. 615):
I assisted in handing the women and children into boat No. 12, and
was asked if I could take an oar. I said: "Yes," and was told to man the
boat, I believe, by Mr. Murdoch. After getting the women and children
in we lowered down to within four or five feet of the water, and then the
block and tackle got twisted in some way, causing us to have to cut the
ropes to allow the boat to get into the water. This officer, Lowe, told
us to do this. He was in the boat with us. I stood by the lever—the lever
releasing the blocks from the hooks in the boat. He told me to wait, to
get away and cut the line to raise the lever, thereby causing the hooks to
open and allow the boat to drop in the water.

There was some shooting that occurred at the time the boat was
lowered. There were various men passengers, probably Italians or some
foreign nationality other than English or American, who attempted to
"rush" the boats. The officers threatened to shoot any man who put
his foot into the boat. An officer fired a revolver, but either downward
or upward, not shooting at any one of the passengers at all and not
injuring anybody. He fired perfectly clear upward and downward and
stopped the rush. There was no disorder after that. One woman cried,
but that was all. There was no panic or anything in the boat.

After getting into the water I pushed out to the other boats. In No.
14 there were fifty-seven women and children and about six men, including one officer, and I may have been seven. I am not quite sure. I
know how many, because when we got out a distance the officer asked
me how many people were in the boat.

When the boat was released and fell I think she must have sprung a
leak. A lady stated that there was some water coming up over her ankles.
Two men and this lady assisted in bailing it out with bails that were
kept in the boat for that purpose. We transferred our people to other
boats so as to return to the wreck and see if we could pick up anybody
else. Returning to the wreck, we heard various cries and endeavored
to get among them, and we were successful in doing so, and picked up
one body that was floating around in the water. It was that of a man and
he expired shortly afterwards. Going further into the wreckage we came
across a steward (J. Stewart) and got him into the boat. He was very
cold and his hands were kind of stiff. He recovered by the time that we
got back to the *Carpathia*.

A Japanese or Chinese young fellow that we picked up on top of
some wreckage, which may have been a sideboard or table that was

floating around, also survived.[1] We stopped (in the wreckage) until daybreak, and we saw in the distance an Engelhardt collapsible boat ("A") with a crew of men in it. We went over to the boat and found twenty men and one woman; also three dead bodies, which we left. Returning under sail we took another collapsible boat in tow (boat "D") containing fully sixty people, women and children.

I did not see the iceberg that struck the ship. When it came daylight and we could see, there were two or three bergs around, and one man pointed out that that must have been the berg, and another man pointed out another berg. Really, I do not think anybody knew which one struck the ship.

Mrs. Charlotte Collyer, third-class passenger, in *The Semi-Monthly Magazine*, May, 1912:

A little further on we saw a floating door that must have been torn loose when the ship went down. Lying upon it, face downward, was a small Japanese. He had lashed himself with a rope to his frail raft, using the broken hinges to make the knots secure. As far as we could see, he was dead. The sea washed over him every time the door bobbed up and down, and he was frozen stiff. He did not answer when he was hailed, and the officer hesitated about trying to save him.

"What's the use?" said Mr. Lowe. "He's dead, likely, and if he isn't there's others better worth saving than a Jap!"

He had actually turned our boat around, but he changed his mind and went back. The Japanese was hauled on board, and one of the women rubbed his chest, while others chafed his hands and feet. In less time than it takes to tell, he opened his eyes. He spoke to us in his own tongue; then, seeing that we did not understand, he struggled to his feet, stretched his arms above his head, stamped his feet and in five minutes or so had almost recovered his strength. One of the sailors near to him was so tired that he could hardly pull his oar. The Japanese bustled over, pushed him from his seat, took his oar and worked like a hero until we were finally picked up. I saw Mr. Lowe watching him in open-mouthed surprise.

"By Jove!" muttered the officer, "I'm ashamed of what I said about the little blighter. I'd save the likes o' him six times over if I got the chance."

Miss Minahan's affidavit (Am. Inq., p. 1109):

After the *Titanic* went down the cries were horrible. Some of the

[1] Undoubtedly reference is here made to the same Japanese described in an account attributed to a second-class passenger, Mrs. Collyer, and which follows Crowe's testimony.

women implored Officer Lowe of No. 10 to divide his passengers among
the three other boats and go back to rescue them. His first answer to
these requests was: "You ought to be d—— glad you are here and have
got your own life." After some time he was persuaded to do as he was
asked. As I came up to him to be transferred to the other boat, he said:
"Jump, G—d d—n you, jump." I had shown no hesitancy and was
waiting until my turn. He had been so blasphemous during the hours we
were in his boat that the women in my end of the boat all thought he
was under the influence of liquor. (Testimony elsewhere shows that
Officer Lowe is a teetotaler.) Then he took all the men who had rowed
No. 14, together with the men from other boats, and went back to the
scene of the wreck. We were left with a steward and a stoker to row our
boat, which was crowded. The steward did his best, but the stoker
refused at first to row, but finally helped two men who were the only
ones pulling on that side. It was just four o'clock when we sighted the
*Carpathia*, and we were three hours getting to her. On the *Carpathia* we
were treated with every kindness and given every comfort possible.

The above affidavit being of record shows Officer Lowe in an unfortunate, bad light. There is no doubt of it that he was intemperate in
his language only. In all other respects he was a first-class officer, as
proven by what he accomplished. But I am glad that I have the account
of another lady passenger in the same boat, which is a tribute to what
he did. I met Officer Lowe in Washington the time that both of us were
summoned before the U. S. Court of Inquiry, and I am quite sure that
the only point against him is that he was a little hasty in speech in the
accomplishment of his work.

Miss Compton, who lost her brother, I had the pleasure of meeting
on the *Carpathia*. She is still a sufferer from injuries received in the
wreck, and yet has been very kind in sending me an account of her
experience, from which I cite the following:

As she stood on the rail to step into boat No. 14 it was impossible to
see whether she would step into the boat or into the water. She was
pushed into the boat with such violence that she found herself on her
hands and knees, but fortunately landed on a coil of rope. This seemed
to be the general experience of the women. All the passengers entered
the lifeboat at the same point and were told to move along to make
place for those who followed. This was difficult, as the thwarts were
so high that it was difficult to climb over them, encumbered as the ladies
were with lifebelts. It was a case of throwing one's self over rather than
climbing over.

Miss Compton from her place in the stern of the lifeboat overheard the conversation between Officer Lowe and another officer, which the former gave in his testimony.

Just before the boat was lowered a man jumped in. He was immediately hauled out. Mr. Lowe then pulled his revolver and said: "If anyone else tries that this is what he will get." He then fired his revolver in the air.

She mentions the same difficulties, elsewhere recorded, about the difficulties in lowering the boat, first the stern very high, and then the bow; also how the ropes were cut and No. 14 struck the water hard. At this time the count showed 58 in the boat, and a later one made the number 60. A child near her answered in neither of the counts.

"Mr. Lowe's manly bearing," she says, "gave us all confidence. As I look back now he seems to me to personify the best traditions of the British sailor. He asked us all to try and find a lantern, but none was to be found. Mr. Lowe had with him, however, an electric light which he flashed from time to time. Almost at once the boat began to leak and in a few moments the women in the forward part of the boat were standing in water. There was nothing to bail with and I believe the men used their hats.

"Officer Lowe insisted on having the mast put up. He crawled forward and in a few moments the mast was raised and ready. He said this was necessary as no doubt with dawn there would be a breeze. He returned to his place and asked the stewards and firemen, who were acting as crew, if they had any matches, and insisted on having them passed to him. He then asked if they had any tobacco and said: 'Keep it in your pockets, for tobacco makes you thirsty.' Mr. Lowe wished to remain near the ship that he might have a chance to help someone after she sank. Some of the women protested and he replied: 'I don't like to leave her, but if you feel that way about it we will pull away a little distance.'"

Miss Compton's account corroborates other information about boat No. 14, which we have elsewhere. She was among the number transferred to Engelhardt boat "D." "I now found myself," she said, "in the stern of a collapsible boat. In spite of Mr. Lowe's warning the four small boats began to separate, each going its own way. Soon it seemed as though our boat was the only one on the sea. We went through a great deal of wreckage. The men who were supposed to be rowing—one was a fireman—made no effort to keep away from it. They were all the time looking towards the horizon. With daylight we saw the *Carpathia*, and not so very long afterwards Officer Lowe, sailing towards us, for, as he had predicted, quite a strong breeze had sprung up. We caught the rope which he threw us from the stern of his boat. Someone in ours succeeded in catching it and we were taken in tow to the *Carpathia*."

## BOAT NO. 16 [1]

*No male passenger*

*Passengers:* Fifty women and children—second and third-class.

*Crew:* Master-at-arms Bailey in charge. Seaman Archer, Steward Andrews, Stewardess Leather, and two others.

*Total:* 56.

### INCIDENTS

E. Archer, A. B. (Am. Inq., p. 645):

I assisted in getting Nos. 12, 14 and 16 out—getting the falls and everything ready and passengers into No. 14. Then I went to No. 16. I saw that the plug was in tight. I never saw any man get in, only my mate. I heard the officer give orders to lower the boat and to allow nobody in it, having fifty passengers and only my mate and myself. The master-at-arms came down after us; he was the coxswain and took charge. When we were loading the boat there was no effort on the part of others to crowd into it; no confusion at all. No individual men, or others were repelled from getting in; everything was quiet and steady. One of the lady passengers suggested going back to see if there were any people in the water we could get, but I never heard any more of it after that. There was one lady in the boat, a stewardess (Mrs. Leather) who tried to assist in rowing. I told her it was not necessary, but she said she would like to do it to keep herself warm. There was one fireman found in the boat after we got clear. I do not know how he came there. He was transferred to another boat (No. 6) to help row.

C. E. Andrews, steward (Am. Inq., p. 623):

Besides these six men I should think there were about fifty passengers.

There was no effort on the part of the steerage men to get into our boat. I was told by the officer to allow none in it. When the officer started to fill the boat with passengers and the men to man it, there were no individuals who tried to get in, or that he permitted to get in. There was no confusion whatever. The officer asked me if I could take an oar. I said I could.

## BOAT NO. 2 [2]

Only one old man, third-class, a foreigner in this boat.

*Passengers:* Miss Allen (now Mrs. J. B. Mennell), Mrs. Appleton,

[1] British Report (p. 38) gives this as the sixth boat lowered from the port side at 1.35 a. m.

[2] British Report (p. 38) gives this as the seventh boat lowered on the port side at 1.45 a. m.

Mrs. Cornell, Mrs. Douglas and maid (Miss Le Roy), Miss Madill, Mrs. Robert and maid (Amelia Kenchen). One old man, third-class, foreigner, and family: Brahim Youssef, Hanne Youssef, and children Marian and Georges. The rest second and third-class.

*Bade good-bye to wife and sank with ship:* Mr. Douglas.

*Crew:* Fourth Officer Boxhall, Seamen Osman and Steward Johnston, cook.

*Total:* 25.

### INCIDENTS

J. G. Boxhall, Fourth Officer (Am. Inq., p. 240, and Br. Inq.):

I was sent away in Emergency boat 2, the last boat but one on the port side. There was one of the lifeboats (No. 4) lowered away a few minutes after I left. That was the next lifeboat to me aft. Engelhardt boat "D" was being got ready. There was no anxiety of people to get into these boats. There were four men in this boat—a sailorman (Osman), a steward (Johnston), a cook and myself, and one male passenger who did not speak English—a middle-aged man with a black beard. He had his wife there and some children. When the order was given to lower the boat, which seemed to be pretty full, it was about twenty minutes to half an hour before the ship sank. Someone shouted through a megaphone: "Some of the boats come back and come around to the starboard side." All rowed except this male passenger. I handled one oar and a lady assisted me. She asked to do it. I got around to the starboard side intending to go alongside. I reckoned I could take about three more people off the ship with safety; and when about 22 yards off there was a little suction, as the boat seemed to be drawn closer, and I thought it would be dangerous to go nearer the ship. I suggested going back (after ship sank) to the sailorman in the boat, but decided it was unwise to do so. There was a lady there, Mrs. Douglas, whom I asked to steer the boat according to my orders. She assisted me greatly in it. They told me on board the *Carpathia* afterwards that it was about ten minutes after four when we went alongside.

After we left the *Titanic* I showed green lights most of the time. When within two or three ship lengths of the *Carpathia*, it was just breaking daylight, and I saw her engines were stopped. She had stopped within half a mile or a quarter of a mile of an iceberg. There were several other bergs, and I could see field ice as far as I could see. The bergs looked white in the sun, though when I first saw them at daylight they looked black. This was the first time I had seen field ice on the Grand Banks. I estimate about 25 in my boat.

F. Osman, A. B. (Am. Inq., p. 538):

All of us went up and cleared away the boats. After that we loaded all the boats there were. I went away in No. 2, the fourth from the last to leave the ship. Boxhall was in command. Murdoch directed the loading. All passengers were women and children, except one man, a third-class passenger, his wife and two children. After I got in the boat the officer found a bunch of rockets which was put in the boat by mistake for a box of biscuits. The officer fired some off, and the *Carpathia* came to us first and picked us up half an hour before anybody else. Not until morning did we see an iceberg about 100 feet out of the water with one big point sticking on one side of it, apparently dark, like dirty ice, 100 yards away. I knew that was the one we struck. It looked as if there was a piece broken off.

There was no panic at all. There was no suction whatever. When we were in the boat I shoved off from the ship and I said to the officer: "See if you can get alongside to see if you can get some more hands—squeeze some more hands in"; so the women started to get nervous after I said that, and the officer said: "All right." The women disagreed to that. We pulled around to the starboard side of the ship and found that we could not get to the starboard side because it was listing too far. We pulled astern again that way, and after we lay astern we lay on our oars and saw the ship go down. It seemed to me as if all the engines and everything that was in the after part slid down into the forward part. We did not go back to the place where the ship had sunk because the women were all nervous, and we pulled around as far as we could get from it so that the women would not see and cause a panic. We got as close as we would dare to. We could not have taken any more hands into the boat. It was impossible. We might have gotten one in; that is all. There was no panic amongst the steerage pasengers when we started manning the boats. I saw several people come up from the steerage and go straight up to the Boat Deck, and the men stood back while the women and children got into the boats—steerage passengers as well as others.

Senator Burton: So in your judgment it was safer to have gone on the boat than to have stayed on the *Titanic*?

Witness: Oh, yes, sir.

Senator Burton: That was when you left?

Witness: Yes, sir.

Senator Burton: What did you think when the first boat was launched?

Witness: I did not think she was going down then.

J. Johnston, steward (Br. Inq.):

*Crew:* Boxhall and four men, including perhaps McCullough. (None such on list.) Boxhall said: "Shall we go back in the direction of cries of distress?" which were a half or three-quarters of a mile off. Ladies said: "No." Officer Boxhall signaled the *Carpathia* with lamp. Soon after launching the swish of the water was heard against the icebergs. In the morning *Carpathia* on the edge of ice-field about 200 yards off.

Mrs. Walter D. Douglas's affidavit (Am. Inq., p. 1100):

Mr. Boxhall had difficulty in getting the boat loose and called for a knife. We finally were launched. Mrs. Appleton and a man from the steerage faced me. Mrs. Appleton's sister, Mrs. Cornell, was back of me and on the side of her the officer. I think there were eighteen or twenty in the boat. There were many who did not speak English. The rowing was very difficult, for no one knew how. We tried to steer under Mr. Boxhall's orders, and he put an old lantern, with very little oil in it, on a pole, which I held up for some time. Mrs. Appleton and some other women had been rowing, and did row all the time. Mr. Boxhall had put into the Emergency boat a tin box of green lights like rockets. These he sent off at intervals, and very quickly we saw the lights of the *Carpathia*, whose captain said he saw our green lights ten miles away and steered directly towards us, so we were the first boat to arrive at the *Carpathia*. When we pulled alongside, Mr. Boxhall called out: "Slow down your engines and take us aboard. I have only one seaman."

Mrs. J. B. Mennell (*née* Allen):

My aunt, Mrs. Roberts' maid, came to the door and asked if she could speak to me. I went into the corridor and she said: "Miss Allen, the baggage room is full of water." I replied she needn't worry, that the water-tight compartments would be shut and it would be all right for her to go back to her cabin. She went back and returned to us immediately to say her cabin, which was forward on Deck E, was flooded.

We were on the Boat Deck some minutes before being ordered into the lifeboat. Neither my aunt, Mrs. Roberts, my cousin, Miss Madill, nor myself ever saw or heard the band. As we stood there we saw a line of men file by and get into the boat—some sixteen or eighteen stokers. An officer [1] came along and shouted to them: "Get out, you damned cowards; I'd like to see everyone of you overboard." They all got out and the officer said: "Women and children into this boat," and we got in and were lowered.

With the exception of two very harrowing leave-takings, we saw nothing but perfect order and quiet on board the *Titanic*. We were

[1] Probably the same officer, Murdoch, described by Major Peuchen, p. 175, this chapter.

rowed round the stern to the starboard side and away from the ship, as our boat was a small one and Boxhall feared the suction. Mrs. Cornell helped to row all the time.

As the *Titanic* plunged deeper and deeper we could see her stern rising higher and higher until her lights began to go out. As the last lights on the stern went out we saw her plunge distinctively, bow first and intact. Then the screams began and seemed to last eternally. We rowed back, after the *Titanic* was under water, toward the place where she had gone down, but we saw no one in the water, nor were we near enough to any other lifeboats to see them. When Boxhall lit his first light the screams grew louder and then died down.

We could hear the lapping of the water on the icebergs, but saw none, even when Boxhall lit his green lights, which he did at regular intervals, till we sighted the *Carpathia*. Our boat was the first one picked up by the *Carpathia*. I happened to be the first one up the ladder, as the others seemed afraid to start up, and when the officer who received me asked where the *Titanic* was, I told him she had gone down.

Capt. A. H. Rostron, of the *Carpathia* (Am. Inq., p. 22):

We picked up the first boat, which was in charge of an officer who I saw was not under full control of his boat. He sang out that he had only one seaman in the boat, so I had to maneuver the ship to get as close to the boat as possible, as I knew well it would be difficult to do the pulling. By the time we had the first boat's people it was breaking day, and then I could see the remaining boats all around within an area of about four miles. I also saw icebergs all around me. There were about twenty icebergs that would be anywhere from about 150 to 200 feet high, and numerous smaller bergs; also numerous ones we call "growlers" anywhere from 10 to 12 feet high and 10 to 15 feet long, above the water.

## BOAT NO. 4 [1]

### *No man passenger in this boat*

*Passengers:* Mrs. Astor and maid (Miss Bidois), Miss Bowen, Mrs. Carter and maid (Miss Serepeca), Mrs. Clark, Mrs. Cummings, Miss Eustis, Mrs. Ryerson and children, Miss S. R., Miss E. and Master J. B. and maid (Chandowson), Mrs. Stephenson, Mrs. Thayer and maid, Mrs. Widener and maid.

*Women and children:* 36. (Br. Rpt.)

[1] British Report (p. 38) says this was the eighth and last *lifeboat* that left the ship and lowered at 1.55 a. m.

*Crew:* Perkis, Q. M., in charge. Seamen: McCarthy, Hemmings,[1] Lyons [2]; Storekeeper Foley and Assistant Storekeeper Prentice [1]; Firemen: Smith and Dillon [1]; Greasers: Granger and Scott [1]; Stewards: Cunningham,[1] Siebert.[2]

*Bade good-bye to wives and sank with ship:* Messrs. Astor, Clark, Cummings, Ryerson, Thayer, Widener and his son Harry.

*Stowaway:* 1 Frenchman.

*Total:* 40. (Br. Rpt.)

### INCIDENTS

C. H. Lightoller, Second Officer (Am. Inq., p. 81):

Previous to putting out Engelhardt Boat "D," Lightoller says, referring to boat No. 4: "We had previously lowered a boat from A Deck, one deck down below. That was through my fault. It was the first boat I had lowered. I was intending to put the passengers in from A Deck. On lowering the boat I found that the windows were closed; so I sent someone down to open the windows and carried on with the other boats, but decided it was not worth while lowering them down—that I could manage just as well from the Boat Deck. When I came forward from the other boats I loaded that boat from A Deck by getting the women out through the windows. My idea in filling the boats there was because there was a wire hawser running along the side of the ship for coaling purposes and it was handy to tie the boat in to hold it so that nobody could drop between the side of the boat and the ship. No. 4 was the fifth boat or the sixth lowered on the port side." [3]

W. J. Perkis, Quartermaster (Am. Inq., p. 581):

I lowered No. 4 into the water and left that boat and walked aft; and I came back and a man that was in the boat, one of the seamen, sang out to me: "We need another hand down here," so I slid down the lifeline there from the davit into the boat. I took charge of the boat after I got in, with two sailormen besides myself. There were forty-two, including all hands. We picked up eight people afterwards swimming with lifepreservers when about a ship's length away from the ship. No. 4 was the last big boat on the port side to leave the ship. Two that were picked up died in the boat—a seaman (Lyons) and a steward (Siebert). All the others were passengers. After we picked up the men I could not hear

[1] Picked up from sea.

[2] Picked up from sea but died in boat.

[3] I agree with this statement though other testimony and the British Report decide against us. The difference may be reconciled by the fact that the loading of this boat began early, but the final lowering was delayed.

any more cries anywhere. The discipline on board the ship was excellent. Every man knew his station and took it. There was no excitement whatever among the officers or crew, the firemen or stewards. They conducted themselves the same as they would if it were a minor, everyday occurrence.

Senator Perkins (addressing Perkis, Symon and Hogg):

All three of you seem to be pretty capable young men and have had a great deal of experience at sea, and yet you have never been wrecked?

Mr. Perkis: Yes, sir.

Senator Perkins: Is there any other one of you who has been in a shipwreck?

Mr. Hogg: I have been in a collision, Senator, but with no loss of life.

Senator Perkins: Unless you have something more to state that you think will throw light on this subject, that will be all, and we thank you for what you have said.

Mr. Hogg: That is all I have to say except this: I think the women ought to have a gold medal on their breasts. God bless them. I will always raise my hat to a woman after what I saw.

Senator Perkins: What countrywomen were they?

Mr. Hogg: They were American women I had in mind. They were all Americans.

Senator Perkins: Did they man the oars? Did they take the oars and pull?

Mr. Hogg: Yes, sir; I took an oar all the time myself and also steered. Then I got one lady to steer; then another to assist me with an oar. She rowed to keep herself warm.

Senator Perkins: One of you stated that his boat picked up eight people, and the other that he did not pick up any. Could you not have picked up just as well as this other man?

Mr. Hogg: I wanted to assist in picking up people, but I had an order from somebody in the boat (No. 7)—I do not know who it was—not to take in any more; that we had done our best.

Senator Perkins: I merely ask the question because of the natural thought that if one boat picked up eight persons the other boat may have been able to do so.—You did not get any orders, Mr. Symon (boat No. 1), not to pick up any more people?

Mr. Symon: No, sir; there were no more around about where I was.

Senator Perkins: As I understand, one of the boats had more packed into it than the other. As I understand it, Mr. Symon pulled away from the ship and then when he came back there they picked up all the people that were around?

Mr. Symon made no reply.

S. S. Hemming, A. B. (Am. Inq.):

Everything was black over the starboard side. I could not see any boats. I went over to the port side and saw a boat off the port quarter and I went along the port side and got up the after boat davits and slid down the fall and swam to the boat about 200 yards. When I reached the boat I tried to get hold of the grab-line on the bows. I pulled my head above the gunwale, and I said: "Give us a hand, Jack." Foley was in the boat; I saw him standing up. He said: "Is that you, Sam?" I said: "Yes" to him and the women and children pulled me in the boat.

After the ship sank we pulled back and picked up seven of the crew including a seaman, Lyons, a fireman, Dillon, and two stewards, Cunningham and Siebert. We made for the light of another lifeboat and kept in company with her. Then day broke and we saw two more lifeboats. We pulled toward them and we all made fast by the painter. Then we helped with boat No. 12 to take off the people on an overturned boat ("B"). From this boat ("B") we took about four or five, and the balance went into the other boat. There were about twenty altogether on this boat ("B").

A. Cunningham, steward (Am. Inq., p. 794):

I first learned of the very serious character of the collision from my own knowledge when I saw the water on the post-office deck. I waited on the ship until all the boats had gone, and then threw myself into the water. This was about 2 o'clock. I was in the water about half an hour before the ship sank. I swam clear of the ship about three-quarters of a mile. I was afraid of the suction. My mate, Siebert, left the ship with me. I heard a lifeboat and called to it and went toward it. I found Quartermaster Perkis in charge. Hemmings, the sailor, Foley (storekeeper) and a fireman (Dillon) were in this boat. I never saw any male passengers in the boat. We picked up Prentice, assistant storekeeper. I think No. 4 was the nearest to the scene of the accident because it picked up more persons in the water. About 7.30 we got aboard the *Carpathia*. When we sighted her she might have been four or five miles away.

R. P. Dillon, trimmer (Br. Inq.):

I went down with the ship and sank about two fathoms. Swam about twenty minutes in the water and was picked up by No. 4. About 1,000 others in the water in my estimation. Saw no women. Recovered consciousness and found Sailor Lyons and another lying on top of me dead.

Thomas Granger, greaser (Br. Inq.):

I went to the port side of the Boat Deck aft, climbed down a rope and got into a boat near the ship's side, No. 4, which had come back because there were not enough men to pull her. She was full of women and children. F. Scott, greaser, also went down the falls and got into this boat. Perkis, quartermaster, and Hemmings then in it. Afterwards picked up Dillon and another man (Prentice) out of the water.

F. Scott, greaser (Br. Inq.):

We went on deck on starboard side first as she had listed over to the port side, but we saw no boats. When I came up the engineers came up just after me on the Boat Deck. I saw only eight of them out of thirty-six on the deck. Then we went to the port side and saw boats. An officer fired a shot and I heard him say that if any man tried to get in that boat he would shoot him like a dog. At this time all the boats had gone from the starboard side. I saw one of the boats, No. 4, returning to the ship's side and I climbed on the davits and tried to get down the falls but fell in the water and was picked up. It was nearly two o'clock when I got on the davits and down the fall.

Mrs. E. B. Ryerson's affidavit (Am. Inq., p. 1107):

We were ordered down to A Deck, which was partly enclosed. We saw people getting into boats, but waited our turn. My boy, Jack, was with me. An officer at the window said: "That boy cannot go." My husband said: "Of course that boy goes with his mother; he is only thirteen"; so they let him pass. I turned and kissed my husband and as we left he and the other men I knew, Mr. Thayer, Mr. Widener and others, were standing together very quietly. There were two men and an officer inside and a sailor outside to help us. I fell on top of the women who were already in the boat and scrambled to the bow with my eldest daughter. Miss Bowen and my boy were in the stern, and my second daughter was in the middle of the boat with my maid. Mrs. Thayer, Mrs. Widener, Mrs. Astor and Miss Eustis were the only ones I knew in our boat.

Presently an officer called out from the upper deck: "How many women are there in that boat?" Someone answered: "Twenty-four." "That's enough; lower away."

The ropes seemed to stick at one end. Someone called for a knife, but it was not needed until we got into the water as it was but a short distance; and then I realized for the first time how far the ship had sunk. The deck we left was only about twenty feet from the sea. I could see all the portholes open and the water washing in, and the decks still lighted. Then they called out: "How many seamen have you?" and they answered: "One." "That is not enough," said the officer, "I will send you another"; and he sent a sailor down the rope. In a few minutes several other men, not sailors, came down the ropes over the davits and dropped into our boat. The order was given to pull away, and then they rowed off. Someone shouted something about a gangway, and no one seemed to know what to do. Barrels and chairs were being thrown overboard. As the bow of the ship went down the lights went out. The stern stood up for several minutes black against the stars and then the boat plunged down. Then began the cries for help of people drowning all around us, which seemed to go on forever. Someone called out: "Pull for your lives or you will be sucked under," and everyone that could rowed like mad. I could see my younger daughter and Mrs. Thayer and Mrs. Astor rowing, but there seemed to be no suction. Then we turned and picked up some of those in the water. Some of the women protested, but others persisted, and we dragged in six or seven men. The men rescued were stewards, stokers, sailors, etc., and were so chilled and frozen already that they could hardly move. Two of them died in the stern later and many of them were raving and moaning and delirious most of the time. We had no lights or compass. There were several babies in the boat.

Officer Lowe called out to tie together, and as soon as we could make out the other boats in the dark five were tied together. We could dimly see an overturned boat with about twenty men standing on it, back to back. As the sailors in our boat said we could still carry from eight to ten people, we called for another boat to volunteer and go and rescue them, so we cut loose our painters and between us got all the men off. Then when the sun rose we saw the *Carpathia* standing up about five miles away, and for the first time saw the icebergs all around us. We got on board about 8 o'clock.

Mrs. Thayer's affidavit:

The after part of the ship then reared in the air, with the stern upwards, until it assumed an almost vertical position. It seemed to remain stationary in this position for many seconds (perhaps twenty), then suddenly dove straight down out of sight. It was 2.20 a. m. when the *Titanic* disappeared, according to a wrist watch worn by one of the passengers in my boat.

We pulled back to where the vessel had sunk and on our way picked up six men who were swimming—two of whom were drunk and gave us much trouble all the time. The six men we picked up were hauled into the boat by the women. Two of these men died in the boat.

The boat we were in started to take in water; I do not know how. We had to bail. I was standing in ice cold water up to the top of my boots all the time, and rowing continuously for nearly five hours. We took off about fifteen more people who were standing on a capsized boat. In all, our boat had by that time sixty-five or sixty-six people. There was no room to sit down in our boat, so we all stood, except some sitting along the side.

I think the steerage passengers had as good a chance as any of the rest to be saved.

The boat I was in was picked up by the *Carpathia* at 7 a. m. on Monday, we having rowed three miles to her, as we could not wait for her to come up on account of our boat taking in so much water that we would not have stayed afloat much longer.

I never saw greater courage or efficiency than was displayed by the officers of the ship. They were calm, polite and perfectly splendid. They also worked hard. The bedroom stewards also behaved extremely well.

Mrs. Stephenson's and Miss Eustis's story kindly handed me for publication in my book contains the following:

"We were in the companionway of A Deck when order came for *women and children to Boat Deck and men to starboard side.* Miss Eustis and I took each other's hands, not to be separated in the crowd, and all went on deck, we following close to Mrs. Thayer and her maid and going up narrow iron stairs to the forward Boat Deck which, on the *Titanic*, was the captain's bridge.

"At the top of the stairs we found Captain Smith looking much worried and anxiously waiting to get down after we got up. The ship listed heavily to port just then. As we leaned against the walls of the officers' quarters rockets were being fired over our heads, which was most alarming, as we fully realized if the *Titanic* had used her wireless to ill effect and was sending rockets it must be serious. Shortly after that the order came from the head dining room steward (Dodd) to go down to A Deck, when Mrs. Thayer remarked, 'Tell us where to go and we will follow. You ordered us up here and now you are taking us back,' and he said, 'Follow me.'

"On reaching the A Deck we could see, for the decks were lighted by electricity, that a boat was lowered parallel to the windows; these were opened and a steamer chair put under the rail for us to step on. The ship had listed badly by that time and the boat hung far out from the side, so that some of the men said, 'No woman could step across that space.' A call was made for a ladder on one of the lower decks, but before it ever got there we were all in the boat. Whether they had drawn the boat over with boathooks nearer the side I do not know, but the space was easily jumped with the help of two men in the boat.

"I remember seeing Colonel Astor, who called 'Good-bye' and said he would follow in another boat, asking the number of our boat, which they said was 'No. 4.' In going through the window I was obliged to throw back the steamer rug, for, with my fur coat and huge cork life-preserver, I was very clumsy. Later we found the stewards or crew had thrown the steamer rugs into the boat, and they did good service, Miss Eustis' around a baby thinly clad, and mine for a poor member of the crew pulled in from the sea.

"Our boat I think took off every woman on the deck at that time and was the last on the port side to be lowered.

"When we reached the sea we found the ship badly listed, her nose well in so that there was water on the D Deck, which we could plainly see as the boat was lighted and the ports on D Deck were square instead of round. No lights could be found in our boat and the men had great difficulty in casting off the blocks as they did not know how they worked. My fear here was great, as she seemed to be going faster and faster and I dreaded lest we should be drawn in before we could cast off.

"When we finally were ready to move the order was called from the deck to go to the stern hatch and take off some men. There was no hatch open and we could see no men, but our crew obeyed orders, much to our alarm, for they were throwing wreckage over and we could hear a cracking noise resembling china breaking. We implored the men to pull away from the ship, but they refused, and we pulled three men into the boat who had dropped off the ship and were swimming towards us. One man was drunk and had a bottle of brandy in his pocket which the quartermaster promptly threw overboard and the drunken man was thrown into the bottom of the boat and a blanket thrown over him. After these three men were hauled in, they told how fast the ship was sinking and we all implored them to pull for our lives to get out from the suction when she should go down. The lights on the ship burned till just before she went. When the call came that she was going I covered my face and heard some one call, 'She's broken.' After what seemed a long time I turned my head only to see the stern almost perpendicular in the air so that the full outline of the blades of the propeller showed above the water. She then gave her final plunge and the air was filled with cries. We rowed back and pulled in five more men from the sea. Their suffering from the icy water was intense and two men who had been pulled into the stern afterwards died, but we kept their bodies with us until we reached the *Carpathia*, where they were taken aboard and Monday afternoon given a decent burial with three others.

"After rescuing our men we found several lifeboats near us and an order was given to tie together, which we obeyed. It did not seem as if we were together long when one boat said they could rescue more could they get rid of some of the women and children aboard and some of them were put into our boat. Soon after cries of 'Ship ahoy' and a long low moan came to us and an officer in command of one of the boats ordered us to follow him. We felt that we were already too crowded to go, but our men, with quartermaster and boatswain in command, followed the officer and we pulled over to what proved to be an over-turned boat crowded with men. We had to approach it very cautiously, fearing our wash would sweep them off. We could take only a few and they had to come very cautiously. The other boat (No. 12) took most of them and we then rowed away."

This rescue, which Mrs. Stephenson so well describes, occurred at dawn. Her story now returns to the prior period of night time.

"The sea was smooth and the night brilliant with more stars than I had ever seen.

"Occasionally a green light showed which proved to be on the Emergency boat, and our men all recognized it as such. We all prayed for dawn, and there was no conversation, everyone being so awed by the disaster and bitterly cold.

"With the dawn came the wind, and before long quite a sea was running. Just before daylight on the horizon we saw what we felt sure must be the lights of a ship. The quartermaster was a long time in admitting that we were right, urging that it was the moon, but we insisted and they then said it might be the *Carpathia* as they had been told before leaving the *Titanic* that she was coming to us. For a long time after daylight we were in great wreckage from the *Titanic*, principally steamer chairs and a few white pilasters.

"We felt we could never reach the *Carpathia* when we found she had stopped, and afterwards when we asked why she didn't come closer we were told that some of the early boats which put off from the starboard side reached her a little after four, while it was after six when we drew under the side of the open hatch.

"It had been a long trying row in the heavy sea and impossible to keep bow on to reach the ship. We stood in great danger of being swamped many times and Captain Rostron, who watched us come up, said he doubted if we could have lived an hour longer in that high sea. Our boat had considerable water in the centre, due to the leakage and also the water brought in by the eight men from their clothing. They had bailed her constantly in order to relieve the weight. Two of the women near us were dying seasick, but the babies slept most of the night in their mothers' arms. The boatswain's chair was slung down the side and there were also rope ladders. Only few, however, of the men were able to go up the ladders. Mail bags were dropped down in which the babies and little children were placed and hoisted up. We were told to throw off our life-preservers and then placed in a boatswain's chair and hoisted to the open hatch where ready arms pulled us in; warm blankets waited those in need and brandy was offered to everybody. We were shown at once to the saloon, where hot coffee and sandwiches were being served."

## ENGELHARDT BOAT "D" [1]

*No male passenger in this boat*

*Passengers:* Mrs. J. M. Brown, Mrs. Harris, Mrs. Frederick Hoyt, the Navratil children.

*Picked up from the sea:* Frederick Hoyt.

*Bade good-bye to wife and sank with ship:* Mr. Harris.

*Crew:* Bright, Q. M., in charge; Seaman Lucas; Steward Hardy.

*Stowaway:* One steerage foreigner, Joseph Dugemin.

*Jumped from deck below as boat was lowered:* H. B. Steffanson (Swede), and H. Woolner (Englishman).

*Total:* 44. British Report (p. 38): Crew 2, men passengers 2, women and children 40.

### INCIDENTS

C. H. Lightoller, Second Officer (Am. Inq., p. 81):

In the case of the last boat I got out, the very last of all to leave the ship, I had the utmost difficulty in finding women. After all the other boats were put out we came forward to put out the Engelhardt collapsible boats. In the meantime the forward Emergency boat (No. 2) had been put out by one of the other officers, so we rounded up the tackles and got the collapsible boat to put that over. Then I called for women and could not get any. Somebody said: "There are no women." This was on the Boat Deck where all the women were supposed to be because the boats were there. There were between fifteen and twenty people put into this boat—one seaman and another seaman, or steward. This was the very last boat lowered in the tackles. I noticed plenty of Americans standing near me, who gave me every assistance they could, regardless of nationality.

[1] British Report (p. 38) puts this as the last boat lowered at 2.05.

And before the British Court of Inquiry the same officer testified:

Someone shouted: "There are no more women." Some of the men began climbing in. Then someone said: "There are some more women," and when they came forward the men got out of the boat again. I saw no men in her, but I believe a couple of Chinese stowed away in her.

When that boat went away there were no women whatever. I did not consider it advisable to wait, but to try to get at once away from the ship. I did not want the boat to be "rushed." Splendid order was maintained. No attempt was made to "rush" that boat by the men. When this boat was being loaded I could see the water coming up the stairway. There was splendid order on the boat until the last. As far as I know there were no male passengers in the boats I saw off except the one man I ordered in, Major Peuchen.

A. J. Bright, Q. M. (Am. Inq., p. 831):

Quartermaster Rowe, Mr. Boxhall and myself fired the distress signals, six rockets I think in all, at intervals. After we had finished firing the distress signals, there were two boats left (Engelhardt collapsibles "C" and "D"). All the lifeboats were away before the collapsible boats were lowered. They had to be, because the collapsible boats were on the deck and the other boats had to be lowered before they could be used. The same tackle with which the lifeboats and the Emergency boats were lowered was employed after they had gone in lowering the collapsible boats.

Witness says that both he and Rowe assisted in getting out the starboard collapsible boat "C" and then he went to the port side and filled up the other boat "D" with passengers, about twenty-five in all. There was a third-class passenger, a man, in the boat, who was on his way to Albion, N. Y. (The passenger list shows this man to have been Joseph Dugemin.)

We were told to pull clear and get out of the suction. When boat "D" was lowered the forecastle head was just going under water; that would be about twenty feet lower than the bridge, and the ship had then sunk about fifty feet—all of that, because when boat "D" was lowered the foremost fall was lower down and the after one seemed to hang and he called out to hang on to the foremost fall and to see what was the matter and let go the after fall. Boat "D" was fifty to a hundred yards away when the ship sank.[1] They had a lantern in the boat but no oil to light it. After leaving the boat, witness heard something but not an explosion. It was like a rattling of chains more than anything else.

[1] The interval of time can then be approximated as nearly a half hour, that we remained on the ship after the lifeboats left.

After "D" got away Mr. Lowe came alongside in another boat, No. 14, and told them to stick together and asked for the number in "D" boat. Steward Hardy counted and told him. Lowe then put about ten or a dozen men from some other boat into witness's boat because it was not filled up. One seaman was taken out. This would make thirty-seven in "D" boat. Just at daylight they saw one of the collapsible boats, "A," that was awash—just flush with the water. Officer Lowe came and took boat "D" in tow, because it had very few men to pull, and towed it to boat "A" and took twelve men and one woman off and put them into his boat No. 14. They were standing in water just about to their ankles when No. 14 and "D" came up to them. They turned the swamped boat adrift with two (three) dead bodies. They were then towed under sail by Mr. Lowe's boat to the *Carpathia*, about four miles away.

William Lucas, A. B. (Br. Inq.):
Got into Engelhardt "D." The water was then right up under the bridge. Had not gone more than 100 yards when there was an explosion and 150 yards when the *Titanic* sank. Had to get some of the women to take oars. There was no rudder in the boat. Changed oars from one side to the other to get her away. Saw a faint red light abaft the *Titanic*'s beam about nine miles away—the headlight also. The witness was transferred to No. 12.

J. Hardy, Chief Steward, second-class (Am. Inq., p. 587):
We launched this boat filled with passengers. Mr. Lightoller and myself loaded it. I went away in it with the quartermaster (Bright) and two firemen. There were Syrians in the bottom of the boat, third-class passengers, chattering the whole night in their strange language. There were about twenty-five women and children. We lowered away and got to the water; the ship then had a heavy list to port. We got clear of the ship and rowed out some distance from her. Mr. Lowe told us to tie up with other boats, that we would be better seen and could keep better together. He, having a full complement of passengers in his boat, transferred about ten to ours, making thirty-five in our boat. When we left the ship, where we were lowered, there were no women and children there in sight at all. There was nobody to lower the boat. No men passengers when we were ready to lower it. They had gone; where, I could not say. We were not more than forty feet from the water when we were lowered. We picked up the husband (Frederick W. Hoyt) of a wife that we had loaded in the boat. The gentleman took to the water and climbed in the boat after we had lowered it. He sat there wringing wet alongside me, helping to row.

I had great respect and great regret for Officer Murdoch. I was walking along the deck forward with him and he said: "I believe she is gone, Hardy." This was a good half hour before my boat was lowered.

Senator Fletcher: Where were all these passengers; these 1,600 people?

Mr. Hardy: They must have been between decks or on the deck below or on the other side of the ship. I cannot conceive where they were.

In his letter to me, Mr. Frederick M. Hoyt relates his experience as follows:

"I knew Captain Smith for over fifteen years. Our conversation that night amounted to little or nothing. I simply sympathized with him on the accident; but at that time, as I then never expected to be saved, I did not want to bother him with questions, as I knew he had all he wanted to think of. He did suggest that I go down to A Deck and see if there were not a boat alongside. This I did, and to my surprise saw the boat "D" still hanging on the davits (there having been some delay in lowering her), and it occurred to me that if I swam out and waited for her to shove off they would pick me up, which was what happened."

Hugh Woolner, first-class passenger (Am. Inq., p. 887):

Then I said to Steffanson, "Let us go down on to A Deck." And we went down again, but there was nobody there. I looked on both sides of the deck and saw no people. It was absolutely deserted, and the electric lights along the ceiling of A Deck were beginning to turn red, just a glow, a red sort of glow. So I said to Steffanson, "This is getting to be rather a tight corner; let us go out through the door at the end." And as we went out *the sea came in onto the deck at our feet*. Then we hopped up onto the gunwale, preparing to jump into the sea, because if we had waited a minute longer we should have been boxed in against the ceiling. And as we looked out we saw this collapsible boat, the last boat on the port side, being lowered right in front of our faces.

Senator Smith: How far out?

Mr. Woolner: It was about nine feet out.

Senator Smith: Nine feet away from the side of A Deck?

Mr. Woolner: Yes.

Senator Smith: You saw a collapsible boat being lowered?

Mr. Woolner: Being lowered; yes.

Senator Smith: Was it filled with people?

Mr. Woolner: It was full up to the bow, and I said to Steffanson, "There is nobody in the bows. Let us make a jump for it. You go first." And he jumped out and tumbled in head over heels into the boat, and I jumped too and hit the gunwale with my chest, which had on the life-preserver, of course, and I sort of tumbled off the gunwale and caught the gunwale with my fingers and slipped off backwards.

Senator Smith: Into the water?

Mr. Woolner: As my legs dropped down I felt that they were in the sea.

Senator Smith: You are quite sure you jumped nine feet to get that boat?

Mr. Woolner: That is my estimate. By that time you see we were jumping slightly downward.

Senator Smith: Did you jump out or down?

Mr. Woolner: Both.

Senator Smith: Both out and down?

Mr. Woolner: Slightly down and out.

Senator Smith: It could not have been very far down if the water was on A Deck; it must have been out.

Mr. Woolner: Chiefly out; but it was sufficiently down for us to see just over the edge of the gunwale of the boat.

Senator Smith: You pulled yourself up out of the water?

Mr. Woolner: Yes; and then I hooked my right heel over the gunwale, and by this time Steffanson was standing up and he caught hold of me and lifted me in.

One lady (Mrs. Harris) had a broken elbow bone. She was in a white woolen jacket. At dawn Officer Lowe transferred five or six from his boat No. 14 to ours, which brought us down very close to the water. At daylight we saw a great many icebergs of different colors, as the sun struck them. Some looked white, some looked blue, some looked mauve and others were dark gray. There was one double-toothed one that looked to be of good size; it must have been about one hundred feet high.

The *Carpathia* seemed to come up slowly, and then she stopped. We looked out and saw there was a boat alongside and then we realized she was waiting for us to come up to her instead of her coming to us, as we hoped. Then Mr. Lowe towed us with his boat, No. 14, under sail. After taking a group of people off of boat "A"—a dozen of them—including one woman, we sailed to the *Carpathia*. There was a child in the boat —one of those little children whose parents everybody was looking for (the Navatil children).

The last of the *Titanic*'s boats which were never launched, but floated off, were the two Engelhardt collapsibles "A" and "B" on the roof of the officer's house. In my personal account I have already given the story of boat "B", the upset one on which Second Officer Lightoller, Jack Thayer, myself and others escaped. Since I wrote the account of my personal experience I have had access to other sources of information, including some already referred to; and though at the expense of some repetition, I think it may be of interest to include the record of this boat in the present chapter, as follows:

## ENGELHARDT BOAT "B"

### [*The Upset Boat*]

*Passengers:* A. H. Barkworth, Archibald Gracie, John B. Thayer, Jr., first cabin.

*Crew:* Second Officer Lightoller, Junior Marconi Operator Bride, Firemen: McGann, Senior; Chief Baker Joughin; Cooks: Collins, Maynard; Steward Whiteley, "J. Hagan." Seaman J. McGough (possibly). Two men died on boat. Body of one transferred to No. 12 and finally to *Carpathia*. He was a fireman probably, but Cunard Co. preserved no record of him or his burial.

#### INCIDENTS

C. H. Lightoller, Second Officer (Am. Inq., pp. 87, 91, 786):

I was on top of the officers' quarters and there was nothing more to be done. The ship then took a dive and I turned face forward and also took a dive from on top, practically amidships a little to the starboard, where I had got to. I was driven back against the blower, which is a large thing that shape (indicating) which faces forward to the wind and which then goes down to the stoke hole; but there is a grating there and it was against this grating that I was sucked by the water, and held there under water. There was a terrific blast of air and water and I was blown out clear. I came up above the water, which barely threw me away at all, because I went down again against these fiddley gratings immediately abreast of the funnel over the stoke hole to which this fiddley leads. Colonel Gracie, I believe, was sucked down in identically the same manner on the fiddley gratings, caused by the water rushing down below as the ship was going down.

I next found myself alongside of that overturned boat. This was before the *Titanic* sank. The funnel then fell down and if there was anybody on that side of the Engelhardt boat it fell on them. The ship was not then submerged by considerable. The stern was completely out of the water. I have heard some controversy as to the boilers exploding owing to coming in contact with salt water, by men who are capable of giving

Colonel Archibald Gracie.

FIFTH OFFICER LOWE TOWING THE CANVAS COLLAPSIBLE

THE CANVAS COLLAPSIBLE

an opinion, but there seems to be an open question as to whether cold water actually does cause boilers to explode.

I hardly had any opportunity to swim. It was the action of the funnel falling that threw us out a considerable distance away from the ship. We had no oars or other effective means for propelling the overturned boat. We had little bits of wood, but they were practically ineffective.

On our boat, as I have said before, were Colonel Gracie and young Thayer. I think they were the only two passengers. There were no women on our overturned boat. These were all taken out of the water and they were firemen and others of the crew—roughly about thirty. I take that from my own estimate and from the estimate of someone who was looking down from the bridge of the *Carpathia*.

And from the same officer's testimony before the British Court as follows:

An order was given to cut the lashings of the other Engelhardt boats. It was then too late as the water was rushing up to the Boat Deck and there was not time to get them to the falls. He then went across to the officers' quarters on the starboard side to see what he could do. Then the vessel seemed to take a bit of a dive. He swam off and cleared the ship. The water was so intensely cold that he first tried to get out of it into the crow's nest, close at hand. Next he was pushed up against the blower on the forepart of the funnel, the water rushing down this blower, holding him against the grating for a while. Then there seemed to be a rush of air and he was blown away from the grating. He was dragged below the surface, but not for many moments. He came up near the Engelhardt boat "B" which was not launched, but had been thrown into the water. The forward funnel then fell down. Some little time after this he saw half a dozen men standing on the collapsible boat, and got on to it. The whole of the third funnel was still visible, the vessel gradually raising her stern out of the water. The ship did not break in two, and could not be broken in two. She actually attained the perpendicular before sinking. His impression was that no lights were then burning in the after part not submerged. It is true that the after part of the vessel settled level with the water. He watched the ship keenly all the time. After she reached an angle of 60 degrees there was a rumbling sound which he attributed to the boilers leaving their beds and crashing down. Finally she attained an absolute perpendicular position and then went slowly down. He heard no explosion whatever, but noticed about that time that the water became much warmer. There were about those on the Engelhardt boat "B," several people struggling in the water who came on it. Nearly twenty-eight or thirty were taken off in the morning at daybreak. In this rescuing boat (No. 12), after the transfer, there were seventy-five. It was the last boat to the *Carpathia*. The next morning (Monday) he saw some icebergs from fifty to sixty to two hundred feet high, but the nearest was about ten miles away.

After the boats had left the side of the ship he heard orders given by the commander through the megaphone. He heard him say: "Bring that boat alongside." Witness presumed allusion was made to bringing of boats to the gangway doors. Witness could not gather whether the orders were being obeyed. Said he had not been on the Engelhardt boat more than half an hour before a swell was distinctly visible. In the morning there was quite a breeze. It was when he was at No. 6 boat that he noticed the list. Though the ship struck on the starboard side, it was not an extraordinary thing that there should be a list to port. It does not necessarily follow that there should be a list to the side where the water was coming in.

Harold Bride, junior Marconi operator in his Report of April 27th to W. B. Cross, Traffic Manager, Marconi Co. (Am. Inq., p. 1053), says:

Just at this moment the captain said: "You cannot do any more; save yourselves." Leaving the captain we climbed on top of the house comprising the officers' quarters and our own. Here I saw the last of Mr. Phillips, for he disappeared, walking aft. I now assisted in pushing off the collapsible boat on to the Boat Deck. Just as the boat fell, I noticed Captain Smith dive from the bridge into the sea. Then followed a general scramble out on to the Boat Deck, but no sooner had we got there than the sea washed over. I managed to catch hold of the boat we had previously fixed up and was swept overboard with her. I then experienced the most exciting three or four hours anyone can reasonably wish for, and was, in due course with the rest of the survivors, picked up by the *Carpathia*. As you probably heard, I got on the collapsible boat the second time, which was, as I had left it, upturned. I called Phillips but got no response. I learned later from several sources that he was on this boat and expired even before we were picked up by the *Titanic*'s lifeboat (No. 12). I am told that fright and exposure were the causes of his death. So far as I can find out, he was taken on board the *Carpathia* and buried at sea from her, though for some reason the bodies of those who died were not identified before burial from the *Carpathia*, and so I cannot vouch for the truth of this.

He also gave testimony before the American Inquiry (pp. 110, 161):

This boat was over the officers' cabin at the side of the forward funnel. It was pushed over on to the Boat Deck. It went over the starboard side and I went over with it. It was washed off and over the side of the ship by a wave into the water bottom side upward. I was inside the boat and under it, as it fell bottom side upward. I could not tell how long. It seemed a lifetime to me really. I got on top of the boat eventually. There was a big crowd on top when I got on. I should say that I remained under the boat three-quarters of an hour, or a half hour. I then got away from it as quickly as I could. I freed myself from it and cleared out of it but I do not know why, but swam back to it about three-quarters of an hour to an hour afterwards. I was upside down myself—I mean I was on my back.

It is estimated that there were between thirty and forty on the boat; no women. When it was pushed over on the Boat Deck we all scrambled down on to the Boat Deck again and were going to launch it properly when it was washed over before we had time to launch it. I happened to be nearest to it and I grabbed it and went down with it. There was a passenger on this boat; I could not see whether he was first, second or third class. I heard him say at the time that he was a passenger. I could not say whether it was Colonel Gracie. There were others who struggled to get on; dozens of them in the water. I should judge they were all part of the boat's crew.

I am twenty-two years old. Phillips was about twenty-four or twenty-five. My salary from the Marconi Co. is four pounds a month.

As to the attack made upon Mr. Phillips to take away his lifebelt I should say the man was dressed like a stoker. We forced him away. I held him and Mr. Phillips hit him.

J. Collins, cook (Am. Inq., p. 628):
This was my first voyage. I ran back to the upper deck to the port side with another steward and a woman and two children. The steward had one of the children in his arms and the woman was crying. I took the child from the woman and made for one of the boats. Then the word came around from the starboard side that there was a collapsible boat getting launched on that side and that all women and children were to make for it, so the other steward and I and the two children and the woman came around to the starboard side. We saw the collapsible boat taken off the saloon deck, and then the sailors and the firemen who were forward saw the ship's bow in the water and that she was sinking by her bow. They shouted out for us to go aft. We were just turning round to make for the stern when a wave washed us off the deck—washed us clear of it, and the child was washed out of my arms. I was kept down for at least two or three minutes under water.

Senator Bourne: Two or three minutes?

Mr. Collins: Yes; I am sure.

Senator Bourne: Were you unconscious?

Mr. Collins: No; not at all. It did not affect me much—the salt water.

Senator Bourne: But you were under water? You cannot stay under water two or three minutes.

Mr. Collins: Well, it seemed so to me. I could not exactly state how long. When I came to the surface I saw this boat that had been taken off. I saw a man on it. They had been working on it taking it off the saloon deck, and when the wave washed it off the deck, they clung to it. Then I made for it when I came to the surface, swimming for it. I was only four or five yards off of it. I am sure there were more than fifteen or sixteen who were then on it. They did not help me to get on. They were all watching the ship. All I had to do was to give a spring and I got on to it. We were drifting about for two hours in the water.

Senator Bourne: When you came up from the water on this collapsible boat, did you see any evidence of the ship as she sank then?

Mr. Collins: I did, sir; I saw her stern end.

Senator Bourne: Where were you on the boat at the time you were washed off the ship?

Mr. Collins: Amidships, sir.

Senator Bourne: You say you saw the stern end after you got on the collapsible boat?

Mr. Collins: Yes, sir.

Senator Bourne: Did you see the bow?

Mr. Collins: No, sir.

Senator Bourne: How far were you from the stern end of the ship when you came up and got on to the collapsible boat?

Mr. Collins: I could not just exactly state how far I was away from the *Titanic* when I came up. I was not far, because her lights were out then. Her lights went out when the water got almost to amidships on her.

Senator Bourne: As I understand it, you were amidships of the bow as the ship sank?

Mr. Collins: Yes, sir.

Senator Bourne: You were washed off by a wave? You were under water as you think for two or three minutes and then swam five or six yards to the collapsible boat and got aboard the boat? The stern (of ship) was still afloat?

Mr. Collins: The stern was still afloat.

Senator Bourne: The lights were burning?

Mr. Collins: I came to the surface, sir, and I happened to look around and I saw the lights and nothing more, and looked in front of me and saw the collapsible boat and I made for it.

Senator Bourne: How do you account for this wave that washed you off amidships?

Mr. Collins: By the suction which took place when the bow went down in the water. There were probably fifteen on the boat when I got on. There was some lifeboat that had a green light on it and we thought it was a ship, after the *Titanic* had sunk, and we commenced to shout. All we saw was the green light. We were drifting about two hours, and then we saw the topmast lights of the *Carpathia*. Then came daylight and we saw our own lifeboats and we were very close to them. When we spied them we shouted to them and they came over to us and they lifted a whole lot of us that were on the collapsible boat.

J. Joughin, head baker (Br. Inq.):

I got on to the starboard side of the poop; found myself in the water. I do not believe my head went under the water at all. I thought I saw some wreckage. Swam towards it and found collapsible boat ("B") with Lightoller and about twenty-five men on it. There was no room for me. I tried to get on, but was pushed off, but I hung around. I got around to the opposite side and cook Maynard, who recognized me, helped me and held on to me.

The experience of my fellow passenger on this boat, John B. Thayer, Jr., is embodied in accounts written by him on April 20th and 23rd, just after landing from the *Carpathia*: the first given to the press as the only statement he had made, the second in a very pathetic letter written to Judge Charles L. Long, of Springfield, Mass., whose son, Milton C. Long, was a companion of young Thayer all that evening, April 14th, until at the very last both jumped into the sea and Long was lost, as described:

"Thinking that father and mother had managed to get off in a boat we, Long and myself, went to the starboard side of the Boat Deck where the boats were getting away quickly. Some were already off in the distance. We thought of getting into one of them, the last boat on the forward part of the starboard side, but there seemed to be such a crowd around that I thought it unwise to make any attempt to get into it. I thought it would never reach the water right side up, but it did.

"Here I noticed nobody that I knew except Mr. Lingrey, whom I had met for the first time that evening. I lost sight of him in a few minutes. Long and I then stood by the rail just a little aft of the captain's bridge. There was such a big list to port that it seemed as if the ship would turn on her side.

"About this time the people began jumping from the stern. I thought of jumping myself, but was afraid of being stunned on hitting the water. Three times I made up my mind to jump out and slide down the davit ropes and try to swim to the boats that were lying off from the ship, but each time Long got hold of me and told me to wait a while. I got a sight on a rope between the davits and a star and noticed that the ship was gradually sinking. About this time she straightened up on an even keel again, and started to go down fairly fast at an angle of about thirty degrees. As she started to sink we left the davits and went back and stood by the rail aft, even with the second funnel. Long and myself stood by each other and jumped on the rail. We did not give each other any messages for home because neither of us thought we would ever get back. Long put his legs over the rail, while I straddled it. Hanging over the side and holding on to the rail with his hands he looked up at me and said: 'You are coming, boy, aren't you?' I replied: 'Go ahead, I'll be with you in a minute.' He let go and slid down the side and I never saw him again. Almost immediately after he jumped I jumped. All this last part took a very short time, and when we jumped we were about ten yards above the water. Long was perfectly calm all the time and kept his nerve to the very end."

How he sank and finally reached the upset boat is quoted accurately from the newspaper report from this same source given in my personal narrative. He continues as follows:

"As often as we saw other boats in the distance we would yell, 'Ship ahoy!' but they could not distinguish our cries from any of the others, so we all gave it up, thinking it useless. It was very cold, and the water washed over the upset boat almost all the time. Towards dawn the wind sprung up, roughening the water and making it difficult to keep the boat balanced. The wireless man raised our hopes a great deal by telling us that the *Carpathia* would be up in about three hours. About 3.30 or 4 o'clock some men at the bow of our boat sighted her mast lights. I could not see them as I was sitting down with a man kneeling on my leg. He finally got up, and I stood up. We had the Second Officer, Mr. Lightoller, on board. He had an officer's whistle and whistled for the boats in the distance to come up and take us off. Two of them came up. The first took half and the other took the balance, including myself. In the transfer we had difficulty in balancing our boat as the men would lean too far over, but we were all taken aboard the already crowded boats and taken to the *Carpathia* in safety."

One of these boats was No. 4, in which his mother was.

# CHAPTER VII

# STARBOARD SIDE: WOMEN FIRST, BUT MEN WHEN THERE WERE NO WOMEN

I know of the conditions existing on the port side of the ship from personal knowledge, as set forth in the first five chapters describing my personal experience, while the previous Chapter VI is derived from an exhaustive study of official and of other authoritative information relating to the same side from experiences of others. I have devoted an equal amount of study to the history of what happened on the starboard side of the ship, and the tabulated statements in this chapter are the outcome of my research into the experiences of my fellow passengers on this side of the ship where I was located only during the last half hour before the ship foundered, after all passengers on the port side had been ordered to the starboard in consequence of the great list to port, and after the departure of the last boat "D," that left the ship on the port side. During this last half hour, though it seemed shorter, my attention was confined to the work of the crew, assisting them in their vain efforts to launch the Engelhardt boat "B" thrown down from the roof of the officers' house. All the starboard boats had left the ship before I came there.

Many misunderstandings arose in the public mind because of ignorance of the size of the ship and inability to understand that the same conditions did not prevail at every point and that the same scenes were not witnessed by every one of us. Consider the great length of the ship, 852 feet; its breadth of beam, 92.6 feet; and its many decks, eleven in number; counting the roof of the officers' house as the top deck, then the Boat Deck, and Decks A, B, C, D, E, F, G, and, in the hold, two more. Bearing this in mind I illustrated to my New York friends, in answer to their questions, how impossible it would be for a person standing at the corner of 50th Street and Fifth Avenue to know just what was going on at 52nd Street on the same Avenue, or what was going on at the corner of 52nd Street and Madison Avenue. Therefore,

223

when one survivor's viewpoint differs from that of another, the explanation is easily found.

Consideration must also be taken of the fact that the accident occurred near midnight, and though it was a bright, starlit night, and the ship's electric lights shone almost to the last, it was possible to recognize only one's intimates at close quarters.

My research shows that there was no general order from the ship's officers on the starboard side for "Women and children first." On the other hand, I have the statements of Dr. Washington Dodge, John B. Thayer, Jr., and Mrs. Stephenson, also the same of a member of the crew testifying before the British Court of Inquiry, from which it appears that some sort of a command was issued ordering the women to the port side and the men to the starboard, indicating that no men would be allowed in the port boats, and only in the starboard side boats after the women had entered them first. If such were the orders, they were carried out to the letter. Another point of difference, especially conspicuous to myself, is the fact that on the starboard side there appears to have been an absence of women at the points where the boats were loaded, while on the port side all the boats loaded, from the first up to the last, found women at hand and ready to enter them. It was only at the time of the loading of the last boat "D," that my friend, Clinch Smith, and I ran up and down the port side shouting: "Are there any more women?" This too is the testimony of Officer Lightoller, in charge of loading boats on the port side.

## BOAT NO. 7 [1]

No disorder in loading or lowering this boat.

*Passengers:* Mesdames Bishop, Earnshaw, Gibson, Greenfield, Potter, Snyder and Misses Gibson and Hays, Messrs. Bishop, Chevré, Daniel, Greenfield, McGough, Maréchal, Seward, Sloper, Snyder, Tucker.

*Transferred from Boat No. 5:* Mrs. Dodge and her boy; Messrs. Calderhead and Flynn.

*Crew:* Seamen: Hogg (in charge), Jewell, Weller.

*Total:* 28.

### INCIDENTS

Archie Jewell, L. O. (Br. Inq.):

Was awakened by the crash and ran at once on deck where he saw a lot of ice. All went below again to get clothes on. The boatswain called all hands on deck. Went to No. 7 boat. The ship had stopped. All hands

[1] First to leave ship starboard side at 12.45 (Br. Rpt., p. 38).

cleared the boats, cleared away the falls and got them all right. Mr. Murdoch gave the order to lower boat No. 7 to the rail with women and children in the boat. Three or four Frenchmen, passengers, got into the boat. No. 7 was lowered from the Boat Deck. The orders were to stand by the gangway. This boat was the first on the starboard side lowered into the water. All the boats were down by the time it was pulled away from the ship because it was thought she was settling down.

Witness saw the ship go down by the head very slowly. The other lifeboats were further off, his being the nearest. No. 7 was then pulled further off and about half an hour later, or about an hour and a half after this boat was lowered, and when it was about 200 yards away, the ship took the final dip. He saw the stern straight up in the air with the lights still burning. After a few moments she then sank very quickly and he heard two or three explosions just as the stern went up in the air. No. 7 picked up no dead bodies. At daylight they saw a lot of icebergs all around, and reached the *Carpathia* about 9 o'clock. This boat had no compass and no light. (The above, given in detail, represents the general testimony of the next witness.)

G. A. Hogg, A. B. (Am. Inq., p. 577):
He had forty-two when the boat was shoved from the ship's side. He asked a lady if she could steer who said she could. He pulled around in search of other people. One man said: "We have done our best; there are no more people around." He said: "Very good, we will get away now." There was not a ripple on the water; it was as smooth as glass.

Mrs. H. W. Bishop, first-class passenger (Am. Inq., p. 998):
The Captain told Colonel Astor something in an undertone. He came back and told six of us who were standing with his wife that we had better put on our lifebelts. I had gotten down two flights of stairs to tell my husband, who had returned to the stateroom for the moment, before I heard the Captain announce that the lifebelts should be put on. We came back upstairs and found very few people on deck. There was very little confusion—only the older women were a little frightened. On the starboard side of the Boat Deck there were only two people—a young French bride and groom. By that time an old man had come upstairs and found Mr. and Mrs. Harder, of New York. He brought us all together and told us to be sure and stay together—that he would be back in a moment. We never saw him again.

About five minutes later the boats were lowered and we were pushed in. This was No. 7 lifeboat. My husband was pushed in with me and we were lowered with twenty-eight people in the boat. We counted off after we reached the water. There were only about twelve women and the rest were men—three crew and thirteen male passengers; several unmarried men—three or four of them foreigners. Somewhat later five people were put into our boat from another one, making thirty-three in ours. Then we rowed still further away as the women were nervous about suction. We had no compass and no light. We arrived at the *Carpathia* five or ten minutes after five. The conduct of the crew, as far as I could see, was absolutely beyond criticism. One of the crew in the boat was Jack Edmonds,(?) and there was another man, a Lookout (Hogg), of whom we all thought a great deal. He lost his brother.

D. H. Bishop, first-class passenger (Am. Inq., p. 1000):
There was an officer stationed at the side of the lifeboat. As witness's wife got in, he fell into the boat. The French aviator Maréchal was in the boat; also Mr. Greenfield and his mother. There was little confusion on the deck while the boat was being loaded; no rush to boats at all. Witness agrees with his wife in the matter of the counting of twenty-eight, but he knows that there were some who were missed. There was a woman with her baby transferred from another lifeboat. Witness knows of his own knowledge that No. 7 was the first boat lowered from the starboard side. They heard no order from any one for the men to stand back or "women first," or "women and children first." Witness also says that at the time his lifeboat was lowered that that order had not been given on the starboard side.

J. R. McGough's affidavit (Am. Inq., p. 1143):
After procuring life-preservers we went back to the top deck and discovered that orders had been given to launch the lifeboats, which were already being launched. Women and children were called for to board the boats first. Both women and men hesitated and did not feel inclined to get into the small boats. He had his back turned, looking in an opposite direction, and was caught by the shoulder by one of the officers who gave him a push saying: "Here, you are a big fellow; get into that boat."

Our boat was launched with twenty-eight people in all. Five were transferred from one of the others. There were several of us who wanted drinking water. It was unknown to us that there was a tank of water and crackers also in our boat until we reached the *Carpathia*. There was no light in our boat.

Mrs. Thomas Potter, Jr. Letter:
There was no panic. Everyone seemed more stunned than anything else . . . . We watched for upwards of two hours the gradual sinking of

the ship—first one row of light and then another disappearing at shorter and shorter intervals, with the bow well bent in the water, as though ready for a dive. After the lights went out, some ten minutes before the end, she was like some great living thing who made a last superhuman effort to right herself and then, failing, dove bow forward to the unfathomable depths below.

We did not row except to get away from the suction of the sinking ship, but remained lashed to another boat until the *Carpathia* came in sight just before dawn.

## BOAT NO. 5 [1]

No disorder in loading or lowering this boat.

*Passengers:* Mesdames Cassebeer, Chambers, Crosby, Dodge and her boy, Frauenthal, Goldenberg, Harder, Kimball, Stehli, Stengel, Taylor, Warren, and Misses Crosby, Newson, Ostby and Frolicher Stehli.

Messrs. Beckwith, Behr, Calderhead, Chambers, Flynn, Goldenberg, Harder, Kimball, Stehli, Taylor.

*Bade good-bye to wives and daughters and sank with ship:* Captain Crosby, Mr. Ostby and Mr. Warren.

*Jumped from deck into boat being lowered:* German Doctor Frauenthal and brother Isaac, P. Maugé.

*Crew:* Third Officer Pitman. Seaman: Olliver, Q. M.; Fireman Shiers; Stewards, Etches, Guy. Stewardess ——

*Total:* 41.

### INCIDENTS

H. J. Pitman, Third Officer (Am. Inq., p. 277, and Br. Inq.):

I lowered No. 5 boat to the level with the rail of the Boat Deck. A man in a dressing gown said that we had better get her loaded with women and children. I said: "I wait the commander's orders," to which he replied: "Very well," or something like that. It then dawned on me that it might be Mr. Ismay, judging by the description I had had given me. I went to the bridge and saw Captain Smith and told him that I thought it was Mr. Ismay that wanted me to get the boat away with women and children in it and he said: "Go ahead; carry on." I came along and brought in my boat. I stood in it and said: "Come along, ladies." There was a big crowd. Mr. Ismay helped get them along. We got the boat nearly full and I shouted out for any more ladies. None were to be seen so I allowed a few men to get into it. Then I jumped on the ship again. Mr. Murdoch said: "You go in charge of this boat and hang around the after gangway." About thirty (Br. Inq.) to forty women

[1] Second boat lowered on the starboard side at 12.55 (Br. Rpt., p. 38).

were in the boat, two children, half a dozen male passengers, myself and four of the crew. There would not have been so many men had there been any women around, but there were none. Murdoch shook hands with me and said "Good-bye; good luck," and I said: "Lower away." This boat was the second one lowered on the starboard side. No light in the boat.

The ship turned right on end and went down perpendicularly. She did not break in two. I heard a lot of people say that they heard boiler explosions, but I have my doubts about that. I do not see why the boilers would burst, because there was no steam there. They should have been stopped about two hours and a half. The fires had not been fed so there was very little steam there. From the distance I was from the ship, if it had occurred, I think I would have known it. As soon as the ship disappeared I said: "Now, men, we will pull toward the wreck." Everyone in my boat said it was a mad idea because we had far better save what few I had in my boat than go back to the scene of the wreck and be swamped by the crowds that were there. My boat would have accommodated a few more—about sixty in all. I turned No. 5 boat around to go in the direction from which these cries came but was dissuaded from my purpose by the passengers. My idea of lashing Nos. 5 and 7 together was to keep together so that if anything hove in sight before daylight we could steady ourselves and cause a far bigger show than one boat only. I transferred two men and a woman and a child from my boat to No. 7 to even them up a bit.

H. S. Etches, steward (Am. Inq., p. 810):

Witness assisted Mr. Murdoch, Mr. Ismay, Mr. Pitman and Quartermaster Olliver and two stewards in the loading and launching of No. 7, the gentlemen being asked to keep back and the ladies in first. There were more ladies to go in No. 7 because No. 5 boat, which we went to next, took in over thirty-six ladies. In No. 7 boat I saw one child, a baby boy, with a small woolen cap. After getting all the women that were there they called out three times—Mr. Ismay twice—in a loud voice: "Are there any more women before this boat goes?" and there was no answer. Mr. Murdoch called out, and at that moment a female came up whom he did not recognize. Mr. Ismay said: "Come along; jump in." She said: "I am only a stewardess." He said: "Never mind—you are a woman; take your place." That was the last woman I saw get into boat No. 5. There were two firemen in the bow; Olliver, the sailor, and myself; and Officer Pitman ordered us into the boat and lowered under Murdoch's order.

Senator Smith: What other men got into that boat?

Mr. Etches: There was a stout gentleman, sir, stepped forward then. He had assisted to put his wife in the boat. He leaned forward and she stood up in the boat and put her arms around his neck and kissed him, and I heard her say: "I cannot leave you," and with that I turned my head. The next moment I saw him sitting beside her in the bottom of the boat, and some voice said: "Throw that man out of the boat," but at that moment they started lowering away and the man remained.

Senator Smith: Who was he?

Mr Etches: I do not know his name, sir, but he was a very stout gentleman. (Dr. H. W. Frauenthal.)

We laid off about 100 yards from the ship and waited. She seemed to be going down at the head and we pulled away about a quarter of a mile and laid on our oars until the *Titanic* sank. She seemed to rise once as though she was going to take a final dive, but sort of checked as though she had scooped the water up and had levelled herself. She then seemed to settle very, very quiet, until the last when she rose and seemed to stand twenty seconds, stern in that position (indicating) and then she went down with an awful grating, like a small boat running off a shingley beach. There was no inrush of water, or anything. Mr. Pitman then said to pull back to the scene of the wreck. The ladies started calling out. Two ladies sitting in front where I was pulling said: "Appeal to the officer not to go back. Why should we lose all of our lives in a useless attempt to save others from the ship?" We did not go back. When we left the ship No. 5 had forty-two, including the children and six crew and the officer. Two were transferred with a lady and a child into boat No. 7.

Senator Smith: Of your own knowledge do you know whether any general call was made for passengers to rouse themselves from their berths; and when it was, or whether there was any other signal given?

Mr. Etches: The second steward (Dodd), sir, was calling all around the ship. He was directing some men to storerooms for provisions for the lifeboats, and others he was telling to arouse all the passengers and to tell them to be sure to take their life-preservers with them.

There was no lamp in No. 5. On Monday morning we saw a very large floe of flat ice and three or four bergs between in different places, and on the other bow there were two large bergs in the distance. The field ice was about three quarters of a mile at least from us between four and five o'clock in the morning. It was well over on the port side of the *Titanic* in the position she was going.

A. Olliver, Q. M. (Am. Inq., p. 526):

There were so many people in the boat when I got into it that I could not get near the plug to put the plug in. I implored the passengers to move so I could do it. When the boat was put in the water I let the tripper go and water came into the boat. I then forced my way to the plug and put it in; otherwise it would have been swamped. There was no rush when I got into the boat. I heard Mr. Pitman give an order to go back to the ship, but the women passengers implored him not to go. We were then about 300 yards away. Nearly all objected.

A. Shiers, fireman (Br. Inq., p. 48):
He saw no women left. There were about forty men and women in the boat. There was no confusion among the officers and crew. We did not go back when the *Titanic* went down. The women in the boat said: "Don't go back." They said: "If we go back the boat will be swamped." No compass in boat.

Paul Maugé, Ritz kitchen clerk (Br. Inq.):
Witness was berthed in the third-class corridor. Was awakened and went up on deck. Went down again and woke up the chef. Going through the second-class cabin he noticed that the assistants of the restaurant were there and not allowed to go on the Boat Deck. He saw the second or third boat on the starboard side let down into the water, and when it was about ten feet down from the Boat Deck he jumped into it. Before this he asked the chef to jump, but he was too fat and would not do so. (Laughter.) I asked him again when I got in the boat, but he refused. When his boat was passing one of the lower decks one of the crew of the *Titanic* tried to pull him out of the boat. He saw no passengers prevented from going up on deck. He thinks he was allowed to pass because he was dressed like a passenger.

Mrs. Catherine E. Crosby's affidavit (Am. Inq., p. 1144):
Deponent is the widow of Captain Edward Gifford Crosby and took passage with him and their daughter, Harriette R. Crosby.
At the time of the collision, Captain Crosby got up, dressed, went out, came back and said to her: "You will lie there and drown," and went out again. He said to their daughter: "The boat is badly damaged, but I think the water-tight compartments will hold her up."
Mrs. Crosby then got up and dressed, as did her daughter, and followed her husband on deck. She got into the first or second boat. About thirty-six persons got in with them.
There was no discrimination between men and women. Her husband became separated from her. She was suffering from cold while drifting around and one of the officers (Pitman) put a sail around her and over her head to keep her warm.

George A. Harder, first-class passenger (Am. Inq., p. 1028):

As we were being lowered, they lowered one side quicker than the other, but reached the water safely after a few scares. Someone said the plug was not in, and they could not get the boat detached from the tackle. Finally, a knife was found and the rope cut. We had about forty-two people in the boat—about thirty women, Officer Pitman, a sailor and three men of the crew. We rowed some distance from the ship—it may have been a quarter or an eighth of a mile. We were afraid of the suction. Passengers said: "Let us row a little further." They did so. Then this other boat, No. 7, came along. We tied alongside. They had twenty-nine in their boat, and we counted at the time thirty-six in ours, so we gave them four or five of our people in order to make it even.

After the ship went down we heard a lot of cries and a continuous yelling and moaning. I counted about ten icebergs in the morning. Our boat managed very well. It is true that the officer did want to go back to the ship, but all the passengers held out and said: "Do not do that; it would only be foolish; there would be so many around that it would only swamp the boat." There was no light in our boat.

C. E. H. Stengel, first-cabin passenger (Am. Inq., p. 975):

Senator Smith: Did you see any man attempt to enter these lifeboats who was forbidden to do so?

Mr. Stengel: I saw two. A certain physician [1] in New York, and his brother, jumped into the same boat my wife was in. Then the officer, or the man who was loading the boat said: "I will stop that. I will go down and get my gun." He left the deck momentarily and came right back again. I saw no attempt of anyone else to get into the lifeboats except these two gentlemen that jumped into the boat after it was started to lower.

Senator Bourne: When you were refused admission into the boat in which your wife was, were there a number of ladies and children there at the time?

Mr. Stengel: No, sir, there were not. These two gentlemen had put their wives in and were standing on the edge of the deck and when they started lowering away, they jumped in. I saw only two.

N. C. Chambers, first-class passenger (Am. Inq., 1041):

Witness referring to boat No. 5 as appearing sufficiently loaded says: "However, my wife said she was going in that boat and proceeded to jump in, calling to me to come. As I knew she would get out again

[1] Dr. H. W. Frauenthal.

had I not come, I finally jumped into the boat, although I did not consider it, from the looks of things, safe to put many more in. As I remember it, there were two more men, both called by their wives, who jumped in after I did. One of them, a German I believe, told me as I recollect it on the *Carpathia* that he had looked around and had seen no one else, and no one to ask whether he could get in, or not, and had jumped in. Witness describes the difficulty in finding whether the plug was in, or not, and recalls someone calling from above: "It's your own blooming business to see that the plug is in anyhow."

Mrs. C. E. H. Stengel, first-class passenger, writes as follows:
"As I stepped into the lifeboat an officer in charge said: 'No more; the boat is full.' My husband stepped back, obeying the order. As the boat was being lowered, four men deliberately jumped into it. One of them was a Hebrew doctor—another was his brother. This was done at the risk of the lives of all of us in the boat. The two companions of this man who did this were the ones who were later transferred to boat No. 7, to which we were tied. He weighed about 250 pounds and wore two life-preservers. These men who jumped in struck me and a little child. I was rendered unconscious and two of my ribs were very badly dislocated. With this exception there was absolutely no confusion and no disorder in the loading of our boat."

Mrs. F. M. Warren, first-class passenger's account:
. . . Following this we then went to our rooms, put on all our heavy wraps and went to the foot of the grand staircase on Deck D, again interviewing passengers and crew as to the danger. While standing there Mr. Andrews, one of the designers of the vessel, rushed by, going up the stairs. He was asked if there was any danger but made no reply. But a passenger who was afterwards saved told me that his face had on it a look of terror. Immediately after this the report became general that water was in the squash courts, which were on the deck below where we were standing, and that the baggage had already been submerged.

At the time we reached the Boat Deck, starboard side, there were very few passengers there, apparently, but it was dark and we could not estimate the number. There was a deafening roar of escaping steam, of which we had not been conscious while inside.

The only people we remembered seeing, except a young woman by the name of Miss Ostby, who had become separated from her father and was with us, were Mr. Astor, his wife and servants, who were standing near one of the boats which was being cleared preparatory to being lowered. The Astors did not get into this boat. They all went back inside and I saw nothing of them again until Mrs. Astor was taken onto the *Carpathia*.

We discovered that the boat next to the one the Astors had been near had been lowered to the level of the deck, so went towards it and were told by the officers in charge to get in. At this moment both men and women came crowding toward the spot. I was the second person assisted in. I supposed that Mr. Warren had followed, but saw when I turned that he was standing back and assisting the women. People came in so rapidly in the darkness that it was impossible to distinguish them, and I did not see him again.

The boat was commanded by Officer Pitman and manned by four of the *Titanic*'s men. The lowering of the craft was accomplished with great difficulty. First one end and then the other was dropped at apparently dangerous angles, and we feared that we would swamp as soon as we struck the water.

Mr. Pitman's orders were to pull far enough away to avoid suction if the ship sank. The sea was like glass, so smooth that the stars were clearly reflected. We were pulled quite a distance away and then rested, watching the rockets in terrible anxiety and realizing that the vessel was rapidly sinking, bow first. She went lower and lower, until the lower lights were extinguished, and then suddenly rose by the stern and slipped from sight. We had no light on our boat and were left in intense darkness save from an occasional glimmer of light from other lifeboats and one steady green light on one of the ship's boats which the officers of the *Carpathia* afterwards said was of material assistance in aiding them to come direct to the spot.

With daylight the wind increased and the sea became choppy, and we saw icebergs in every direction; some lying low in the water and others tall, like ships, and some of us thought they were ships. I was on the second boat picked up.

From the time of the accident until I left the ship there was nothing which in any way resembled a panic. There seemed to be a sort of aimless confusion and an utter lack of organized effort.


## BOAT NO. 3 [1]

No disorder in loading or lowering this boat.

*Passengers:* Mesdames Cardeza and maid (Anna Hard), Davidson, Dick, Graham, Harper, Hays and maid (Miss Pericault), Spedden and maid (Helen Wilson) and son Douglas and his trained nurse, Miss Burns, and Misses Graham and Shutes.

[1] Third boat lowered on starboard side, 1.00 (Br. Rpt., p. 38).

*Men:* Messrs. Cardeza and man-servant (Lesneur), Dick, Harper and man-servant (Hamad Hassah) and Spedden.

*Men who helped load women and children in this boat and sank with the ship:* Messrs. Case, Davidson, Hays and Roebling.

*Crew:* Seamen: Moore (in charge), Forward Pascoe, Steward: McKay; Firemen: "5 or 6"; or "10 or 12."

*Total:* 40.[1]

### INCIDENTS

G. Moore, A. B. (Am. Inq., 559):

When we swung boat No. 3 out I was told by the first officer to jump in the boat and pass the ladies in, and when there were no more about we took in men passengers. We had thirty-two in the boat, all told, and then lowered away. Two seamen were in the boat. There were a few men passengers and some five or six firemen. They got in after all the women and children. I took charge of the boat at the tiller.

Mrs. Frederick O. Spedden, first-class passenger's account:

... Number 3 and Number 5 were both marked on our boat. Our seaman told me that it was an old one taken from some other ship,[2] and he didn't seem sure at the time which was the correct number, which apparently was 3.

We tied up to a boat filled with women once, but the rope broke and we got pretty well separated from all the other lifeboats for some time. We had in all about forty in our boat, including ten or twelve stokers in the bow with us who seemed to exercise complete control over our coxswain, and urged him to order the men to row away from the sinking *Titanic*, as they were in mortal terror of the suction. Two oars were lost soon after we started and they didn't want to take the time to go back after them, in spite of some of the passengers telling them that there was absolutely no danger from suction. All this accounts for the fact of our being some distance off when the ship went down. We couldn't persuade the coxswain to turn around till we saw the lights of the *Carpathia* on the horizon. It was then that we burned some paper, as we couldn't find our lantern. When the dawn appeared and my small boy Douglas saw the bergs around us and remarked: "Oh, Muddie, look at the beautiful North Pole with no Santa Claus on it," we all couldn't refrain from smiling in spite of the tragedy of the situation.

[1] British Report (p. 38) says 15 crew, 10 men passengers, 25 women and children. Total 50.

[2] "All boats were new and none transferred from another ship," President Ismay's testimony.

No more accurately written or interesting account (one which I freely confess moves me to tears whenever re-read) has come to my notice than the following, which I have the consent of the author to insert in its entirety:

## WHEN THE *TITANIC* WENT DOWN
### By
### Miss Elizabeth W. Shutes

Such a biting cold air poured into my stateroom that I could not sleep, and the air had so strange an odor,[1] as if it came from a clammy cave. I had noticed that same odor in the ice cave on the Eiger glacier. It all came back to me so vividly that I could not sleep, but lay in my berth until the cabin grew so very cold that I got up and turned on my electric stove. It threw a cheerful red glow around, and the room was soon comfortable; but I lay waiting. I have always loved both day and night on shipboard, and am never fearful of anything, but now I was nervous about the icy air.

Suddenly a queer quivering ran under me, apparently the whole length of the ship. Startled by the very strangeness of the shivering motion, I sprang to the floor. With too perfect a trust in that mighty vessel I again lay down. Some one knocked at my door, and the voice of a friend said: "Come quickly to my cabin; an iceberg has just passed our window; I know we have just struck one."

No confusion, no noise of any kind, one could believe no danger imminent. Our stewardess came and said she could learn nothing. Looking out into the companionway I saw heads appearing asking questions from half-closed doors. All sepulchrally still, no excitement. I sat down again. My friend was by this time dressed; still her daughter and I talked on, Margaret pretending to eat a sandwich. Her hand shook so that the bread kept parting company from the chicken. Then I saw she was frightened, and for the first time I was too, but why get dressed, as no one had given the slightest hint of any possible danger? An officer's cap passed the door. I asked: "Is there an accident or danger of any kind?" "None, so far as I know," was his courteous answer, spoken quietly and most kindly. This same officer then entered a cabin a little distance down the companionway and, by this time distrustful of everything, I listened intently, and distinctly heard, "We can keep the water out for a while." Then, and not until then, did I realize the horror of an accident at sea. Now it was too late to dress; no time for a waist, but a coat and skirt were soon on; slippers were quicker than shoes;

1 Seaman Lee testifies to this odor.

the stewardess put on our life-preservers, and we were just ready when Mr. Roebling came to tell us he would take us to our friend's mother, who was waiting above.

We passed by the palm room, where two short hours before we had listened to a beautiful concert, just as one might sit in one's own home. With never a realizing sense of being on the ocean, why should not one forget?—no motion, no noise of machinery, nothing suggestive of a ship. Happy, laughing men and women constantly passing up and down those broad, strong staircases, and the music went on and the ship went on—nearer and nearer to its end. So short a life, so horrible a death for that great, great ship. What is a more stupendous work than a ship! The almost human pieces of machinery, yet a helpless child, powerless in its struggle with an almighty sea, and the great boat sank, fragile as a rowboat.

How different are these staircases now! No laughing throng, but on either side stand quietly, bravely, the stewards, all equipped with the white, ghostly life-preservers. Always the thing one tries not to see even crossing a ferry. Now only pale faces, each form strapped about with those white bars. So gruesome a scene. We passed on. The awful good-byes. The quiet look of hope in the brave men's eyes as the wives were put into the lifeboats. Nothing escaped one at this fearful moment. We left from the Sun Deck, seventy-five feet above the water. Mr. Case and Mr. Roebling, brave American men, saw us to the lifeboat, made no effort to save themselves, but stepped back on deck. Later they wertt to an honored grave.

Our lifeboat, with thirty-six in it, began lowering to the sea. This was done amid the greatest confusion. Rough seamen all giving different orders. No officer aboard. As only one side of the ropes worked, the lifeboat at one time was in such a position that it seemed we must capsize in mid-air. At last the ropes worked together, and we drew nearer and nearer the black, oily water. The first touch of our lifeboat on that black sea came to me as a last good-bye to life, and so we put off —a tiny boat on a great sea—rowed away from what had been a safe home for five days. The first wish on the part of all was to stay near the *Titanic*. We all felt so much safer near the ship. Surely such a vessel could not sink. I thought the danger must be exaggerated, and we could all be taken aboard again. But surely the outline of that great, good ship was growing less. The bow of the boat was getting black. Light after light was disappearing, and now those rough seamen put to their oars and we were told to hunt under seats, any place, anywhere, for a lantern, a light of any kind. Every place was empty. There was no water—no stimulant of any kind. Not a biscuit—nothing to keep us alive had we drifted long. Had no good *Carpathia*, with its splendid Captain Rostron, its orderly crew, come to our rescue we must have all perished. Our men knew nothing about the position of the stars, hardly how to pull together. Two oars were soon overboard. The men's hands were too cold to hold on. We stopped while they beat their hands and arms, then started on again. A sea, calm as a pond, kept our boat steady, and now that mammoth ship is fast, fast disappearing. Only one tiny light is left —a powerless little spark, a lantern fastened to the mast. Fascinated, I watched that black outline until the end. Then across the water swept that awful wail, the cry of those drowning people. In my ears I heard: "She's gone, lads; row like hell or we'll get the devil of a swell." And the horror, the helpless horror, the worst of all—need it have been?

To-day the question is being asked, "Would the *Titanic* disaster be so discussed had it not been for the great wealth gathered there?" It surely would be, for at a time like this wealth counts for nothing, but man's philanthropy, man's brains, man's heroism, count forever. So many men that stood for the making of a great nation, morally and politically, were swept away by the sinking of that big ship. That is why, day after day, the world goes on asking the why of it all. Had a kind Providence a guiding hand in this? Did our nation need so mighty a stroke to prove that man had grown too self-reliant, too sure of his own power over God's sea? God's part was the saving of the few souls on that calmest of oceans on that fearful night. Man's part was the pushing of the good ship, pushing against all reason, to save what?— a few hours and lose a thousand souls—to have the largest of ships arrive in port even a few hours sooner than anticipated. Risk all, but push, push on, on. The icebergs could be avoided. Surely man's experience ought to have lent aid, but just so surely it did not.

In years past a tendency to live more simply away from pomp and display led to the founding of our American nation. Now what are we demanding to-day? Those same needless luxuries. If they were not demanded they would not be supplied. Gymnasiums, swimming pools, tea rooms, had better give way to make space for the necessary number of lifeboats; lifeboats for the crew, also, who help pilot the good ship across the sea.

Sitting by me in the lifeboat were a mother and daughter (Mrs. Hays and Mrs. Davidson). The mother had left a husband on the *Titanic*, and the daughter a father and husband, and while we were near the other boats those two stricken women would call out a name and ask, "Are you there?" "No," would come back the awful answer, but these brave women never lost courage, forgot their own sorrow, telling me to sit close to them to keep warm. Now I began to wish for the warm velvet suit I left hanging in my cabin. I had thought of it for a minute, and then had quickly thrown on a lighter weight skirt. I knew the heavier one would make the life-preserver less useful. Had I only known how calm the ocean was that night, I would have felt that death was not so sure, and would have dressed for life rather than for the end. The life-preservers helped to keep us warm, but the night was bitter cold, and it grew colder and colder, and just before dawn, the coldest, darkest hour of all, no help seemed possible. As we put off from the *Titanic* never was a sky more brilliant, never have I seen so many falling stars. All tended to make those distress rockets that were sent up from the sinking ship look so small, so dull and futile. The brilliancy of the sky only intensified the blackness of the water, our utter loneliness on the sea. The other boats had drifted away from us; we must wait now for dawn and what the day was to bring us we dare not even hope. To see if I could not make the night seem shorter, I tried to imagine myself again in Japan. We had made two strange night departures there, and I was unafraid, and this Atlantic now was calmer than the Inland sea had been at that time. This helped a while, but my hands were freezing cold, and I had to give up pretending and think of the dawn that must soon come.

Two rough looking men had jumped into our boat as we were about to lower, and they kept striking matches, lighting cigars, until I feared we would have no matches left and might need them, so I asked them not to use any more, but they kept on. I do not know what they looked like. It was too dark to really distinguish features clearly, and when the dawn brought the light it brought something so wonderful with it no one looked at anything else or anyone else. Some one asked: "What time is it?" Matches were still left; one was struck. Four o'clock! Where had the hours of the night gone? Yes, dawn would soon be here; and it came, so surely, so strong with cheer. The stars slowly disappeared, and in their place came the faint pink glow of another day. Then I heard, "A light, a ship." I could not, would not, look while there was a bit of doubt, but kept my eyes away. All night long I had heard, "A light!" Each time it proved to be one of our other lifeboats, someone lighting a piece of paper, anything they could find to burn, and now I could not believe. Someone found a newspaper; it was lighted and held up. Then I looked and saw a ship. A ship bright with lights; strong and steady she waited, and we were to be saved. A straw hat was offered (Mrs. Davidson's); it would burn longer. That same ship that had come to save us might run us down. But no; she is still. The two, the ship and the dawn, came together, a living painting. White was the vessel, but whiter still were those horribly beautiful icebergs, and as we drew nearer and nearer that good ship we drew nearer to those mountains of ice. As far as the eye could reach they rose. Each one more fantastically chiselled than its neighbor. The floe glistened like an ever-ending meadow covered with new-fallen snow. Those same white mountains, marvellous in their purity, had made of the just ended night one of the blackest the sea has ever known. And near them stood the ship which had come in such quick response to the *Titanic*'s call for help. The man who works over hours is always the worth-while kind, and the Marconi operator awaiting a belated message had heard the poor ship's call for help, and we few out of so many were saved.

From the *Carpathia* a rope forming a tiny swing was lowered into our lifeboat, and one by one we were drawn into safety. The lady pulled up just ahead of me was very large, and I felt myself being jerked fearfully, when I heard some one say: "Careful, fellers; she's a lightweight." I bumped and bumped against the side of the ship until I felt like a bag of meal. My hands were so cold I could hardly hold on to the rope, and I was fearful of letting go. Again I heard: "Steady, fellers; not so fast!" I felt I should let go and bounce out of the ropes; I hardly think that would have been possible, but I felt so at the time. At last I found myself at an opening of some kind and there a kind doctor wrapped me in a warm rug and led me to the dining room, where warm stimulants were given us immediately and everything possible was done for us all. Lifeboats kept coming in, and heart-rending was the sight as widow after widow was brought aboard. Each hoped some lifeboat ahead of hers might have brought her husband safely to this waiting vessel. But always no.

I was still so cold that I had to get a towel and tie it around my waist. Then I went back to the dining-room and found dear little Louis,[1] the French baby, lying alone; his cold, bare feet had become unwrapped. I put a hot water bottle against this very beautiful boy. He smiled his thanks.

Knowing how much better I felt after taking the hot stimulant, I tried to get others to take something; but often they just shook their heads and said, "Oh, I can't."

Towards night we remembered we had nothing—no comb, brush, nothing of any kind—so we went to the barber-shop. The barber always has everything, but now he had only a few toothbrushes left. I bought a cloth cap of doubtful style; and felt like a walking orphan asylum, but very glad to have anything to cover my head. There were also a few showy silk handkerchiefs left. On the corner of each was embroidered

[1] One of the Navratil children whose pathetic story has been fully related in the newspapers.

in scarlet, "From a friend." These we bought and we were now fitted out for our three remaining days at sea.

Patiently through the dismal, foggy days we lived, waiting for land and possible news of the lost. For the brave American man, a heart full of gratitude, too deep for words, sends out a thanksgiving. That such men are born, live and die for others is a cause for deep gratitude. What country could have shown such men as belong to our American manhood? Thank God for them and for their noble death.

## EMERGENCY BOAT NO. 1 [1]

No disorder in loading or lowering this boat.

*Passengers:* Lady Duff Gordon and maid (Miss Francatelli).

*Men:* Lord Duff Gordon and Messrs. Solomon and Stengel.

*Total:* 5.

*Crew:* Seamen: Symons (in charge), Horswell. Firemen: Collins, Hendrickson, Pusey, Shee, Taylor.

*Total:* 7.

*Grand Total:* 12.

### INCIDENTS

G. Symons, A. B. (Br. Inq.):

Witness assisted in putting passengers in Nos. 5 and 3 under Mr. Murdoch's orders, women and children first. He saw 5 and 3 lowered away and went to No. 1. Mr. Murdoch ordered another sailor and five firemen in. Witness saw two ladies running out of the Saloon Deck who asked if they could get in the boat. Murdoch said: "Jump in." The officer looked around for more, but none were in sight and he ordered to lower away, with the witness in charge. Before leaving the Boat Deck witness saw a white light a point and a half on the port bow about five miles away.

Just after boat No. 1 got away, the water was up to C Deck just under where the ship's name is. Witness got about 200 yards away and ordered the crew to lay on their oars. The ship's stern was well up in the air. The foremost lights had disappeared and the only light left was the mast light. The stern was up out of the water at an angle of forty-five degrees; the propeller could just be seen. The boat was pulled away a little further to escape suction; then he stopped and watched.

After the *Titanic* went down he heard the people shrieking for help, but was afraid to go back for fear of their swarming upon him, though there was plenty of room in the boat for eight or a dozen more. He

[1] This was the fourth boat to leave the starboard side.

determined on this course himself as "*master of the situation.*" [1] About a day before landing in New York a present of five pounds came as a surprise to the witness from Sir Cosmo Duff Gordon.

The President: You state that you were surprised that no one in the boat suggested that you should go back to the assistance of the drowning people?

Witness: Yes.

The President: Why were you surprised?

Witness: I fully expected someone to do so.

The President: It seemed reasonable that such a suggestion should be made?

Witness: Yes: I should say it would have been reasonable.

The President: You said in America to Senator Perkins that you had fourteen to twenty passengers in the boat?

Witness: I thought I had; I was in the dark.

The President: You were not in the dark when you gave that evidence.

Witness said he thought he was asked how many people there were in the boat, all told.

The Attorney-General: You meant that the 14 to 20 meant everybody?

Witness: Yes.

The Attorney-General: But you know you only had twelve all told?

Witness: Yes.

The President: You must have known perfectly well when you gave this evidence that the number in your boat was twelve. Why did you tell them in America that there were fourteen to twenty in the boat?

Witness: I do not know; it was a mistake I made then and the way they muddled us up.

The Attorney-General: It was a very plain question. Did you know the names of any passengers?

Witness: I knew Sir Cosmo Duff Gordon's name when we arrived in America.

The Attorney-General: Did you say anything in America about having received the five pounds?

Witness: No, sir; and I was not asked.

The Attorney-General: You were asked these very questions in America which we have been putting to you to-day about going back?

Witness: Yes, sir.

The Attorney-General: Why did you not say that you heard the cries, but in the exercise of your discretion as "master of the situation" you did not go back?

[1] Italics are mine.—AUTHOR.

Witness: They took us in three at a time in America and they hurried us through the questions.

The Attorney-General: They asked you: "Did you make any effort to get there," and you said: "Yes; we went back and could not see anything." But you said nothing about your discretion. Why did you not tell them that part of the story? You realized that if you had gone back you might have rescued a good many people?

Witness: Yes.

The Attorney-General: The sea was calm, the night was calm and there could not have been a more favorable night for rescuing people?

Witness: Yes.

The testimony at the American Inquiry above referred to, because of which this witness was called to account, follows:

G. Symons, L. O. (Am. Inq., p. 573):

I was in command of boat No. 1.

Senator Perkins: How many passengers did you have on her?

Mr. Symons: From fourteen to twenty.

Senator Perkins: Were they passengers or crew?

Mr. Symons: There were seven men ordered in; two seamen and five firemen. They were ordered in by Mr. Murdoch.

Senator Perkins: How many did you have all told?

Mr. Symons: I would not say for certain; it was fourteen or twenty. Then we were ordered away.

Senator Perkins: You did not return to the ship again?

Mr. Symons: Yes; we came back after the ship was gone and saw nothing.

Senator Perkins: Did you rescue anyone that was in the water?

Mr. Symons: No, sir; we saw nothing when we came back.

Witness then testified that there was no confusion or excitement among the passengers. It was just the same as if it was an everyday affair. He never saw any rush whatever to get into either of the two boats. He heard the cries of the people in the water.

Senator Perkins: Did you say your boat could take more? Did you make any effort to get them?

Mr. Symons: Yes. We came back, but when we came back we did not see anybody or hear anybody.

He says that his boat could have accommodated easily ten more. He was in charge of her and was ordered away by Officer Murdoch. Did not pull back to the ship again until she went down.

Senator Perkins: And so you made no attempt to save any other people after you were ordered to pull away from the ship by someone?

Mr. Symons: I pulled off and came back after the ship had gone down.

Senator Perkins: And then there were no people there?

Mr. Symons: No, sir; I never saw any.

C. E. H. Stengel, first-class passenger (Am. Inq., p. 971):

There was a small boat they called an Emergency boat in which were three people, Sir Duff Gordon, his wife and Miss Francatelli. I asked to get into the boat. There was no one else around that I could see except the people working at the boats. The officer said: "Jump in." The railing was rather high. I jumped onto it and rolled into the boat. The officer said: "That's the funniest thing I have seen to-night," and laughed heartily. After getting down part of the way the boat began to tip and somebody "hollered" to stop lowering. A man named A. L. Soloman also asked to get in with us. There were five passengers, three stokers and two seamen in the boat.

Senator Smith: Do you know who gave instructions?

Mr. Stengel: I think between Sir Cosmo Duff Gordon and myself we decided which way to go. We followed a light that was to the bow of the ship. . . . Most of the boats rowed toward that light, and after the green lights began to burn I suggested that it was better to turn around and go towards them. They were from another lifeboat. When I got into the boat it was right up against the side of the ship. If it had not been, I would have gone right out into the water because I rolled. I did not step in it; I just simply rolled. There was one of the icebergs particularly that I noticed—a very large one which looked something like the Rock of Gibraltar.

### THE DUFF GORDON EPISODE

Charles Hendricksen, leading fireman (Br. Inq.):

When the ship sank we picked up nobody. The passengers would not listen to our going back. Of the twelve in the boat, seven were of the crew. Symons, who was in charge, said nothing and we all kept our mouths shut. None of the crew objected to going back. It was a woman who objected, Lady Duff Gordon, who said we would be swamped. People screaming for help could be heard by everyone in our boat. I suggested going back. Heard no one else do so. Mr. Duff Gordon upheld his wife.

After we got on the Carpathia Gordon sent for them all and said he would make them a present. He was surprised to receive five pounds from him the day after docking in New York.

Hendricksen recalled.

Witness cross-examined by Sir Cosmo Duff Gordon's counsel.

What did you say about Sir Cosmo's alleged statement preventing you from going back?

Witness: It was up to us to go back.

Did anyone in the boat say anything to you about going back?

Witness: Lady Duff Gordon said something to the effect that if we went back the boat would be swamped.

Who was it that first said anything about Sir Cosmo making a presentation to the crew?

Witness: Fireman Collins came down and said so when we were on board the *Carpathia*.

Before we left the *Carpathia* all the people rescued were photographed together. We members of the crew wrote our names on Lady Duff Gordon's lifebelt. From the time we first left off rowing until the time the vessel sank, Lady Duff Gordon was violently seasick and lying on the oars.

### A. E. Horswell, A. B. (Br. Inq.):

Witness said it would have been quite a safe and proper thing to have gone back and that it was an inhuman thing not to do so, but he had to obey the orders of the coxswain. Two days after boarding the *Carpathia* some gentlemen sent for him and he received a present.

### J. Taylor, fireman (Br. Inq.):

Witness testifies that No. 1 boat stood by about 100 yards to avoid suction and was 200 yards off when the *Titanic* sank. He heard a suggestion made about going back and a lady passenger talked of the boat's being swamped if they did so. Two gentlemen in the boat said it would be dangerous.

Did your boat ever get within reach of drowning people?

Witness: No.

How many more could the boat have taken in?

Witness: Twenty-five or thirty in addition to those already in it.

Did any of the crew object to going back?

Witness: No.

Did you ever hear of a boat's crew consisting of six sailors and one fireman?

Witness: No.

Lord Mersey: What was it that Sir Cosmo Duff Gordon said to you in the boat?

Witness: He said he would write to our homes and to our wives and let them know that we were safe.

Witness said he received five pounds when he was on board the *Carpathia*.

R. W. Pusey, fireman (Br. Inq.):

After the ship went down we heard cries for a quarter of an hour, or twenty minutes. Did not go back in the direction the *Titanic* had sunk. I heard one of the men say: "We have lost our kit," and then someone said: "Never mind, we will give you enough to get a new kit." I was surprised that no one suggested going back. I was surprised that I did not do so, but we were all half dazed. It does occur to me now that we might have gone back and rescued some of the strugglers. I heard Lady Duff Gordon say to Miss Francatelli: "You have lost your beautiful nightdress," and I said: ".Never mind, you have saved your lives; but we have lost our kit"; and then Sir Cosmo offered to provide us with new ones.

Sir Cosmo Duff Gordon (Br. Inq.):

No. 7 was the first boat I went to. It was just being filled. There were only women and the boat was lowered away. No. 3 was partially filled with women, and as there were no more, they filled it up with men. My wife would not go without me. Some men on No. 3 tried to force her away, but she would not go. I heard an officer say: "Man No. 1 boat." I said to him: "May we get in that boat?" He said: "With pleasure; I wish you would." He handed the ladies in and then put two Americans in, and after that he said to two or three firemen that they had better get in. When the boat was lowered I thought the *Titanic* was in a very grave condition. At the time I thought that certainly all the women had gotten off. No notice at all was taken in our boat of these cries. No thought entered my mind about its being possible to go back and try to save some of these people. I made a promise of a present to the men in the boat.

There was a man sitting next to me and about half an hour after the *Titanic* sank a man said to me: "I suppose you have lost everything?" I said: "Yes." He said: "I suppose you can get more." I said: "Yes." He said: "Well, we have lost all our kit, for we shall not get anything out of the Company, and our pay ceases from to-night." I said: "Very well, I will give you five pounds each towards your kit."

Were the cries from the *Titanic* clear enough to hear the words, "My God, My God"?

No. You have taken that from the story in the American papers. Mr. Stengel in his evidence in New York said, "Between Mr. Duff Gordon and myself we decided the direction of the boat."

That's not so; I did not speak to the coxswain in any way.

Lady Duff Gordon (Br. Inq.):

After the three boats had been gotten away my husband and I were left standing on the deck. Then my husband went up and said, might we not get into this boat, and the officer said very politely: "If you will do so I should be very pleased." Then somebody hitched me up at the back, lifted me up and pitched me into the boat. My husband and Miss Francatelli were also pitched into the boat; and then two Americans were also pitched in on top of us. Before the *Titanic* sank I heard terrible cries.

Q. Is it true in an article signed by what purports to be your signature that you heard the last cry which was that of a man shouting, "My God, My God"?

A. Absolutely untrue.

Address by Mr. A. Clement Edwards, M. P., Counsel for Dock Workers' Union (Br. Inq.):

Referring to the Duff Gordon incident he said that the evidence showed that in one of the boats there were only seven seamen and five passengers. If we admitted that, this boat had accommodation for twenty-eight more passengers.

The primary responsibility for this must necessarily be placed on the member of the crew who was in charge of the boat—Symons, no conduct of anyone else in the boat, however reprehensible, relieving that man from such responsibility.

Here was a boat only a short distance from the ship, so near that the cries of those struggling in the water could be heard. Symons had been told to stand by the ship, and that imposed upon him a specific duty. It was shown in Hendricksen's evidence that there was to the fullest knowledge of those in the boat a large number of people in the water, and that someone suggested that they should return and try to rescue them. Then it was proved that one of the ladies, who was shown to be Lady Duff Gordon, had said that the boat might be swamped if they went back, and Sir Cosmo Duff Gordon had admitted that this also represented his mental attitude at the time. He (Mr. Edwards) was going to say, and to say quite fearlessly, that a state of mind which could, while within the hearing of the screams of drowning people, think of so material a matter as the giving of money to replace kits was a state of mind which must have contemplated the fact that there was a possibility of rescuing some of these people, and the danger which might arise if this were attempted.

He was not going to say that there was a blunt, crude bargain, or a deal done with these men: "If you will not go back I will give you five pounds"; but he was going to suggest as a right and true inference that the money was mentioned at that time under these circumstances to give such a sense of ascendancy or supremacy to Sir Cosmo Duff Gordon in the boat that the view to which he gave expression that they should not go back would weigh more with the men than if he had given it as a piece of good advice. There were twenty-eight places on that boat and no one on board had a right to save his own life by avoiding any possible risk involved in filling the vacant places. To say the least of it, it was most reprehensible that there should have been any offer of money calculated to influence the minds of the men or to seduce them from their duty.

From the address of the Attorney-General, Sir Rufus Isaacs, K. C., M. P. (Br. Inq.):

In regard to boat No. 1, I have to make some comment. This was the Emergency boat on the starboard side, which figured somewhat prominently in the inquiry on account of the evidence which was given in the first instance by Hendricksen, and which led to the calling of Sir Cosmo Duff Gordon. Any comment I have to make in regard to that boat is, I wish to say, not directed to Sir Cosmo or his wife. For my part, I would find it impossible to make any harsh or severe comment on the conduct of any woman who, in circumstances such as these, found herself on the water in a small boat on a dark night, and was afraid to go back because she thought there was a danger of being swamped. At any rate, I will make no comment about that, and the only reason I am directing attention to No. 1 boat is that it is quite plain that it was lowered with twelve persons in it instead of forty. I am unable to say why it was that that boat was so lowered with only five passengers and seven of the crew on board, but that circumstance, I contend, shows the importance of boat drill.

As far as he knew from the evidence, no order was given as to the lowering of this boat. He regretted to say that he was quite unable to offer any explanation of it, but he could not see why the boat was lowered under the circumstances. The point of this part of the inquiry was twofold—(1) the importance of a boat drill; (2) that you should have the men ready.

No doubt if there had been proper organization there would have been a greater possibility of saving more passengers. What struck one was that no one seemed to have known what his duty was or how many persons were to be placed in the boat before it was lowered. In all cases no boat had its complement of what could be carried on this particular night. The vessel was on her first passage, and if all her crew had been engaged on the next voyage no doubt things would have been better, but there was no satisfactory organization with regard to calling passengers and getting them on deck. Had these boats had their full complement it would have been another matter, but the worst of them was this boat No. 1, because the man, Symons, in charge did not exercise his duty. No doubt he was told to stand by, but he went quite a distance away. His evidence was unsatisfactory, and gave no proper account why he did not return. He only said that he "exercised his discretion," and that he was "master of the situation." There was, however, no explanation why he went away and why he did not go back except that he would be swamped. That was no explanation. I can see no justification for his not going back. From the evidence, there were no people on the starboard deck at the time. They must have been mistaken in making that statement, because, as they knew, four more boats were subsequently lowered with a number of women and children. The capacity of this boat was forty. No other boat went away with so small a proportion as compared with its capacity, and there was no other boat which went away with a larger number of the crew. I confess it is a thing which I do not understand why that boat was lowered when she was. Speaking generally, the only boats that took their full quantity were four. One had to see what explanation could be given of that. In this particular case it happened that the officers were afraid the boats would buckle. Then they said that no more women were available, and, thirdly, it was contemplated to go back. It struck one as very regrettable that the officers should have doubts in their minds on these points with regard to the capacity of the boats.

## BOAT NO. 9 [1]

No disorder when this boat was loaded and lowered.

*Passengers:* Mesdames Aubert and maid (Mlle. Segesser), Futrelle, Lines; Miss Lines, and second and third-class.

*Men:* Two or three.

*Said good-bye to wife and sank with ship:* Mr. Futrelle.

*Crew:* Seamen: Haines (in charge), Wynne, Q. M., McGough, Peters; Stewards Ward, Widgery and others.

*Total:* 56.

---

[1] The fifth boat lowered on starboard side, 1.20 (Br. Rpt., p. 38).

INCIDENTS

A. Haines, boatswain's mate (Am. Inq., 755):
Officer Murdoch and witness filled boat 9 with ladies. None of the men passengers tried to get into the boats. Officer Murdoch told them to stand back. There was one woman who refused to get in because she was afraid. When there were no more women forthcoming the boat was full, when two or three men jumped into the bow. There were two sailors, three or four stewards, three or four firemen and two or three men passengers. No. 9 was lowered from the Boat Deck with sixty-three people in the boat and lowered all right. Officer Murdoch put the witness in charge and ordered him to row off and keep clear of the ship. When we saw it going down by the head he pulled further away for the safety of the people in the boat: about 100 yards away at first. Cries were heard after the ship went down. He consulted with the sailors about going back and concluded with so many in the boat it was unsafe to do so. There was no compass in the boat, but he had a little pocket lamp. On Monday morning he saw from thirty to fifty icebergs and a big field of ice miles long and large bergs and "growlers," the largest from eighty to one hundred feet high.

W. Wynne, Q. M. (Br. Inq.):
Officer Murdoch ordered witness into boat No. 9. He assisted the ladies and took an oar. He says there were fifty-six all told in the boat, forty-two of whom were women. He saw the light of a steamer—a red light first, and then a white one—about seven or eight miles away. After an interval both lights disappeared. Ten or fifteen minutes afterwards he saw a white light again in the same direction. There was no lamp or compass in the boat.

W. Ward, steward (Am. Inq., 595):
Witness assisted in taking the canvas cover off of boat No. 9 and lowered it to the level of the Boat Deck.[1]
Officer Murdoch, Purser McElroy and Mr. Ismay were near this boat when being loaded. A sailor came along with a bag and threw it into the boat. He said he had been sent to take charge of it by the captain. The boatswain's mate, Haines, was there and ordered him out. He got out. Either Purser McElroy or Officer Murdoch said: "Pass the women and children that are here into that boat." There were several men standing around and they fell back. There were quite a quantity of

[1] Brice, A. B. (Am. Inq., p. 648) and Wheate, assistant second steward (Br. Inq.), say No. 9 was filled from A Deck with women and children only.

women but he could not say how many were helped into the boat. There were no children. One old lady made a great fuss and absolutely refused to enter the boat. She went back to the companionway and forced her way in and would not get into the boat. One woman, a French lady, fell and hurt herself a little. Purser McElroy ordered two more men into the boat to assist the women. When No. 9 was being lowered the first listing of the ship was noticeable.

From the rail to the boat was quite a distance to step down to the bottom of it, and in the dark the women could not see where they were stepping. Purser McElroy told witness to get into the boat to assist the women. Women were called for, but none came along and none were seen on deck at the time. Three or four men were then taken into the boat until the officers thought there were sufficient to lower away with safety.

No. 9 was lowered into the water before No. 11. There was some difficulty in unlashing the oars because for some time no one had a knife. There were four men who rowed all night, but there were some of them in the boat who had never been to sea before and did not know the first thing about an oar, or the bow from the stern. Haines gave orders to pull away. When 200 yards off, rowing was stopped for about an hour. Haines was afraid of suction and we pulled away to about a quarter of a mile from the ship. The ship went down very gradually for a while by the head. We could just see the ports as she dipped. She gave a kind of a sudden lurch forward. He heard a couple of reports like a volley of musketry; not like an explosion at all. His boat was too full and it would have been madness to have gone back. He thinks No. 9 was the fourth or fifth boat picked up by the *Carpathia*. There was quite a big lot of field ice and several large icebergs in amongst the field; also two or three separated from the main body of the field.

J. Widgery, bath steward (Am. Inq., 602):

Witness says that all passengers were out of their cabins on deck before he went up.

When he got to the Boat Deck No. 7 was about to be lowered, but the purser sent him to No. 9. The canvas had been taken off and he helped lower the boat. Purser McElroy ordered him into the boat to help the boatswain's mate pass in women. Women were called for. An elderly lady came along. She was frightened. The boatswain's mate and himself assisted her, but she pulled away and went back to the door (of the companionway) and downstairs. Just before they left the ship the officer gave the order to Haines to keep about 100 yards off. The boat was full as it started to lower away. When they got to the water he was the only one that had a knife to cut loose the oars. He says that the balance of his testimony would be the same as that of Mr. Ward, the previous witness.

## BOAT NO. 11 [1]

No disorder when this boat was loaded and lowered.

*Passengers:* Women: Mrs. Schabert and two others of first cabin; all the rest second and third class. Fifty-eight women and children in all.

*Men:* Mr. Mock, first cabin, and two others.

*Crew:* Seamen: Humphreys (in charge), Brice; Stewards: Wheate, MacKay, McMicken, Thessinger, Wheelton; Fireman ——; Stewardess: Mrs. Robinson.

*Total:* 70.

### INCIDENTS

W. Brice, A. B. (Am. Inq., 648):

This boat was filled from A Deck. An officer said: "Is there a sailor in the boat?" There was no answer. I jumped out and went down the fall into the bow. Nobody was in the stern. I went aft and shipped the rudder. By that time the boat had been filled with women and children. We had a bit of difficulty in keeping the boat clear of a big body of water coming from the ship's side. The after-block got jammed, but I think that must have been on account of the trip not being pushed right down to disconnect the block from the boat. We managed to keep the boat clear from this body of water. It was the pump discharge. There were only two seamen in the boat, a fireman, about six stewards and fifty-one passengers. There were no women and children who tried to get into the boat and were unable to do so. There was no rush and no panic whatever. Everything was done in perfect order and discipline.

Mr. Humphreys, A. B., was in charge of No. 11. There was no light or lantern in our boat. I cut the lashing from the oil bottle and cut rope and made torches. The ship sank bow down first almost perpendicularly. She became a black mass before she made the final plunge when boat was about a quarter of a mile away. Boat No. 9 was packed. Passengers were about forty-five women and about four or five children in arms.

E. Wheelton, steward (Am. Inq.):

As I made along B Deck I met Mr. Andrews, the builder, who was opening the rooms and looking in to see if there was anyone in, and closing the doors again. Nos. 7, 5 and 9 had gone. No. 11 boat was

1 Sixth boat lowered on starboard side, 1.25 (Br. Rpt., p. 38).

hanging in the davits. Mr. Murdoch said: "You go too." He shouted: "Women and children first." He was then on the top deck standing by the taffrail. The boat was loaded with women and children, and I think there were eight or nine men in the boat altogether, including our crew, and one passenger.

"Have you got any sailors in?" asked Mr. Murdoch. I said: "No, sir." He told two sailors to jump into the boat. We lowered away. Everything went very smooth until we touched the water. When we pushed away from the ship's side we had a slight difficulty in hoisting the after block. We pulled away about 300 yards. We rowed around to get close to the other boats. There were about fifty-eight all told in No. 11. It took all of its passengers from A Deck except the two sailors. I think there were two boats left on the starboard side when No. 11 was lowered. The eight or nine men in the boat included a passenger. A quartermaster (Humphreys) was in charge.

C. D. MacKay, steward (Br. Inq.):

No. 11 was lowered to A Deck. Murdoch ordered me to take charge. We collected all the women (40) on the Boat Deck, and on A Deck we collected a few more. The crew were five stewards, one fireman, two sailors, one forward and one aft. There was Wheelton, McMicken, Thessenger, Wheate and myself. The others were strangers to the ship. There were two second-class ladies, one second-glass gentleman, and the rest were third-class ladies. I found out that they were all third-class passengers. We had some difficulty in getting the after-fall away. We went away from the ship about a quarter of a mile. No compass. The women complained that they were crushed up so much and had to stand. Complaints were made against the men because they smoked.

J. T. Wheate, assistant second steward (Br. Inq.):

Witness went upstairs to the Boat Deck where Mr. Murdoch ordered the boats to the A Deck where the witness and seventy of his men helped pass the women and children into boat No. 9, and none but women and children were taken in. He then filled up No. 11 with fifty-nine women and children, three male passengers and a crew of seven stewards, two sailors and one fireman. He could not say how the three male passengers got there. The order was very good. There was nobody on the Boat Deck, so the people were taken off on the A Deck.

Philip E. Mock, first-cabin passenger (letter):

No. 11 carried the largest number of passengers of any boat—about sixty-five. There were only two first-cabin passengers in the boat besides my sister, Mrs. Schabert, and myself. The remainder were second-class or stewards and stewardesses. We were probably a mile away when the *Titanic*'s lights went out. I last saw the ship with her stern high in the air going down. After the noise I saw a huge column of black smoke slightly lighter than the sky rising high into the sky and then flattening out at the top like a mushroom.

I at no time saw any panic and not much confusion. I can positively assert this as I was near every boat lowered on the starboard side up to the time No. 11 was lowered. With the exception of some stokers who pushed their way into boat No. 3 or No. 5, I saw no man or woman force entry into a lifeboat. One of these was No. 13 going down, before we touched the water.

From address of the Attorney-General, Sir Rufus Isaacs, K. C., M. P.:
"No. 11 took seventy, and carried the largest number of any boat."

## BOAT NO. 13 [1]

No disorder when this boat was loaded and lowered.

*Passengers:* Women: Second-cabin, including Mrs. Caldwell and her child Alden. All the rest second and third-class women.

*Men:* Dr. Dodge only first-cabin passenger. Second-cabin, Messrs. Beasley and Caldwell. One Japanese.

*Crew:* Firemen: Barrett (in charge), Beauchamp, Major and two others. Stewards: Ray, Wright and another; also baker ——.

*Total:* 64.

#### INCIDENTS

Mr. Lawrence Beesley's book, already cited, gives an excellent description of No. 13's history, but for further details, see his book, *The Loss of the SS. Titanic*, Houghton, Mifflin Co., Boston.

F. Barrett, leading stoker (Br. Inq.):
Witness then made his escape up the escape ladder and walked aft on to Deck A on the starboard side, where only two boats were left, Nos. 13 and 15. No. 13 was partly lowered when he got there. Five-sixths in the boat were women. No. 15 was lowered about thirty seconds later. When No. 13 got down to the water he shouted: "Let go the after fall," but, as no one took any notice, he had to walk over women and cut the fall himself. No. 15 came down nearly on top of

---

1 Seventh boat lowered on starboard side, 1.25 (Br. Rpt., p. 38).

them, but they just got clear. He took charge of the boat until he got so cold that he had to give up to someone else. A woman put a cloak over him, as he felt so freezing, and he could not remember anything after that. No men waiting on the deck got into his boat. They all stood in one line in perfect order waiting to be told to get into the boat. There was no disorder whatever. They picked up nobody from the sea.

F. D. Ray, steward (Am. Inq., 798):

Witness assisted in the loading of boat No. 9 and saw it and No. 11 boat lowered, and went to No. 13 on A Deck. He saw it about half filled with women and children. A few men were ordered to get in; about nine to a dozen passengers and crew. Dr. Washington Dodge was there and was told that his wife and child had gone away in one of the boats. Witness said to him: "You had better get in here then," and got behind him and pushed him and followed after him. A rather large woman came along crying and saying: "Do not put me in the boat; I don't want to get in one. I have never been in an open boat in my life." He said: "You have got to go and you may as well keep quiet." After that there was a small child rolled in a blanket thrown into the boat to him. The woman that brought it got into the boat afterwards.

We left about three or four men on the deck at the rail and they went along to No. 15 boat. No. 13 was lowered away. When nearly to the water, two or three of them noticed a very large discharge of water coming from the ship's side which he thought was the pumps working. The hole was about two feet wide and about a foot deep with a solid mass of water coming out. They shouted for the boat to be stopped from being lowered and they responded promptly and stopped lowering the boat. They pushed it off from the side of the ship until they were free from this discharge. He thinks there were no sailors or quartermasters in the boat because they apparently did not know how to get free from the tackle. Knives were called for to cut loose. In the meantime they were drifting a little aft and boat No. 15 was being lowered immediately upon them about two feet from their heads and they all shouted again, and they again replied very promptly and stopped lowering boat No. 15. They elected a fireman (Barrett) to take charge. Steward Wright was in the boat; two or three children and a very young baby seven months old. Besides Nos. 9, 11, and 13, No. 15 was lowered to Deck A and filled from it. He saw no male passengers or men of the crew whatever ordered out or thrown out of these lifeboats on the starboard side. Everybody was very orderly and there was no occasion to throw anybody out. In No. 13 there were about four or five firemen, one baker, three stewards; about nine of the crew. Dr. Washington Dodge was the only first-class passenger and the rest were third-class. There was one Japanese. There was no crowd whatever on A Deck while he was loading these boats. No. 13 was full.

Extracts from Dr. Washington Dodge's address: "The Loss of the *Titanic*," a copy of which he kindly sent me:

I heard one man say that the impact was due to ice. Upon one of his listeners questioning the authority of this, he replied: "Go up forward and look down on the fo'castle deck, and you can see for yourself." I at once walked forward to the end of the promenade deck, and looking down could see, just within the starboard rail, small fragments of broken ice, amounting possibly to several cartloads. As I stood there an incident occurred which made me take a more serious view of the situation, than I otherwise would.

Two stokers, who had slipped up onto the promenade deck unobserved, said to me: "Do you think there is any danger, sir?" I replied: "If there is any danger it would be due to the vessel's having sprung a leak, and you ought to know more about it than I." They replied, in what appeared to me to be an alarmed tone: "Well, sir, the water was pouring into the stoke 'old when we came up, sir." At this time I observed quite a number of steerage passengers, who were amusing themselves by walking over the ice, and kicking it about the deck. No ice or iceberg was to be seen in the ocean.

I watched the boats on the starboard side, as they were successively filled and lowered away. At no time during this period, was there any panic, or evidence of fear, or unusual alarm. I saw no women nor children weep, nor were there any evidences of hysteria observed by me.

I watched all boats on the starboard side, comprising the odd numbers from one to thirteen, as they were launched. Not a boat was launched which would not have held from ten to twenty-five more persons. Never were there enough women or children present to fill any boat before it was launched. In all cases, as soon as those who responded to the officers' call were in the boats, the order was given to "Lower away."

What the conditions were on the port side of the vessel I had no means of observing. We were in semi-darkness on the Boat Deck, and owing to the immense length and breadth of the vessel, and the fact that between the port and the starboard side of the Boat Deck, there were officers' cabins, staterooms for passengers, a gymnasium, and innumerable immense ventilators, it would have been impossible, even in daylight, to have obtained a view of but a limited portion of this boat deck. We only knew what was going on within a radius of possibly forty feet.

Boats Nos. 13 and 15 were swung from the davits at about the same moment. I heard the officer in charge of No. 13 say: "We'll lower this boat to Deck A." Observing a group of possibly fifty or sixty about boat 15, a small proportion of which number were women, I descended by means of a stairway close at hand to the deck below, Deck A. Here, as the boat was lowered even with the deck, the women, about eight in number, were assisted by several of us over the rail of the steamer into the boat. The officer in charge then held the boat, and called repeatedly for more women. None appearing, and there being none visible on the deck, which was then brightly illuminated, the men were told to tumble in. Along with those present I entered the boat. Ray was my table steward and called to me to get in.

The boat in which I embarked was rapidly lowered, and as it approached the water I observed, as I looked over the edge of the boat, that the bow, near which I was seated, was being lowered directly into an enormous stream of water, three or four feet in diameter, which was being thrown with great force from the side of the vessel. This was the water thrown out by the condenser pumps. Had our boat been lowered into the same it would have been swamped in an instant. The loud cries which were raised by the occupants of the boat caused those who were sixty or seventy feet above us to cease lowering our boat. Securing an oar with considerable difficulty, as the oars had been firmly lashed together by means of heavy tarred twine, and as in addition they were on the seat running parallel with the side of the lifeboat, with no less than eight or ten occupants of the boat sitting on them, none of whom showed any tendency to disturb themselves—we pushed the bow of the lifeboat, by means of the oar, a sufficient distance away from the side of the _Titanic_ to clear this great stream of water which was gushing forth. We were then safely lowered to the water. During the few moments occupied by these occurrences I felt for the only time a sense of impending danger.

We were directed to pull our lifeboat from the steamer, and to follow a light which was carried in one of the other lifeboats, which had been launched prior to ours. Our lifeboat was found to contain no lantern, as the regulations require; nor was there a single sailor, or officer in the boat. Those who undertook to handle the oars were poor oarsmen, almost without exception, and our progress was extremely slow. Together with two or three other lifeboats which were in the vicinity, we endeavored to overtake the lifeboat which carried the light, in order that we might not drift away and possibly become lost. This light appeared

The *Carpathia*—only ship to come to the *Titanic's* rescue.

Captain Rostron of the *Carpathia,* who supervised the rescue of 705 survivors of the *Titanic* disaster.

to be a quarter of a mile distant, but, in spite of our best endeavors, we were never enabled to approach any nearer to it, although we must have rowed at least a mile.

## BOAT NO. 15 [1]

No disorder in loading or lowering this boat.
*Passengers:* All third-class women and children (53) and
*Men:* Mr. Haven (first-class) and three others (third-class) only. Total: 4.
*Crew:* Firemen: Diamond (in charge), Cavell, Taylor; Stewards: Rule, Hart. Total: 13.
*Grand Total* (Br. Rpt., p. 38): 70.

### INCIDENTS

G. Cavell, trimmer (Br. Inq.):
The officer ordered five of us in the boat. We took on all the women and children and the boat was then lowered. We lowered to the first-class (i. e., A) deck and took on a few more women and children, about five, and then lowered to the water. From the lower deck we took in about sixty. There were men about but we did not take them in. They were not kept back. They were third-class passengers, I think—sixty women, Irish. Fireman Diamond took charge. No other seaman in this boat. There were none left on the third-class decks after I had taken the women.

S. J. Rule, bathroom steward (Br. Inq.):
Mr. Murdoch called to the men to get into the boat. About six got in. "That will do," he said, "lower away to Deck A." At this time the vessel had a slight list to port. We sent scouts around both to the starboard and port sides. They came back and said there were no more women and children. We filled up on A Deck—sixty-eight all told—the last boat to leave the starboard side. There were some left behind. There was a bit of a rush after Mr. Murdoch said we could fill the boat up with men standing by. We very nearly came on top of No. 13 when we lowered away. A man, Jack Stewart, a steward, took charge. Nearly everybody rowed. No lamp. One deckhand in the boat, and men, women and children. Just before it was launched, no more could be found, and about half a dozen men got in. There were sixty-eight in the boat altogether. Seven members of the crew.

[1] Br. Rpt., p. 38, places this next to last lowered on starboard side at 1.35.

J. E. Hart, third-class steward (Br. Inq., 75):

Witness defines the duties and what was done by the stewards, particularly those connected with the steerage.

"Pass the women and children up to the Boat Deck," was the order soon after the collision. About three-quarters of an hour after the collision he took women and children from the C Deck to the first-class main companion. There were no barriers at that time. They were all opened. He took about thirty to boat No. 8 as it was being lowered. He left them and went back for more, meeting third-class passengers on the way to the boats. He brought back about twenty-five more steerage women and children, having some little trouble owing to the men passengers wanting to get to the Boat Deck. These were all third-class people whom we took to the only boat left on the starboard side, viz., No. 15. There were a large number already in the boat, which was then lowered to A Deck, and five women, three children and a man with a baby in his arms taken in, making about seventy people in all, including thirteen or fourteen of the crew and fireman Diamond in charge. Mr. Murdoch ordered witness into the boat. Four men passengers and fourteen crew was the complement of men; the rest were women and children.

When boat No. 15 left the boat deck there were other women and children there—some first-class women passengers and their husbands. Absolute quietness existed. There were repeated cries for women and children. If there had been any more women there would have been found places for them in the boat. He heard some of the women on the A Deck say they would not leave their husbands.

There is no truth in the statement that any of the seamen tried to keep back third-class passengers from the Boat Deck. Witness saw masthead light of a ship from the Boat Deck. He did his very best, and so did all the other stewards, to help get the steerage passengers on the Boat Deck as soon as possible.

## ENGELHARDT BOAT "C" [1]

No disorder in loading or lowering this boat.

*Passengers:* President Ismay, Mr. Carter. Balance women and children.

*Crew:* Quartermaster Rowe (in charge). Steward Pearce. Barber Weikman. Firemen, three.

*Stowaways:* Four Chinamen, or Filipinos.

*Total:* 39.

[1] Br. Rpt., p. 38, makes this last boat lowered on starboard side at 1.40.

INCIDENTS

G. T. Rowe, Q. M. (Am. Inq., p. 519, and Br. Inq.):

To avoid repetition, the testimony of this witness before the two Courts of Inquiry is consolidated:

He assisted the officer (Boxhall) to fire distress signals until about five and twenty minutes past one. At this time they were getting out the starboard collapsible boats. Chief Officer Wilde wanted a sailor. Captain Smith told him to get into the boat "C" which was then partly filled. He found three women and children in there with no more about. Two gentlemen got in, Mr. Ismay and Mr. Carter. Nobody told them to get in. No one else was there. In the boat there were thirty-nine altogether. These two gentlemen, five of the crew (including himself), three firemen, a steward, and near daybreak they found four Chinamen or Filipinos who had come up between the seats. All the rest were women and children.

Before leaving the ship he saw a bright light about five miles away about two points on the port bow. He noticed it after he got into the boat. When he left the ship there was a list to port of six degrees. The order was given to lower the boat, with witness in charge. The rub strake kept on catching on the rivets down the ship's side, and it was as much as we could do to keep off. It took a good five minutes, on account of this rubbing, to get down. When they reached the water they steered for a light in sight, roughly five miles. They seemed to get no nearer to it and altered their course to a boat that was carrying a green light. When day broke, the *Carpathia* was in sight.

In regard to Mr. Ismay's getting into the boat, the witness's testimony before the American Court of Inquiry is cited in full:

Senator Burton: Now, tell us the circumstances under which Mr. Ismay and that other gentleman got into the boat.

Mr. Rowe: When Chief Officer Wilde asked if there were any more women and children, there was no reply, so Mr. Ismay came into the boat.

Senator Burton: Mr. Wilde asked if there were any more women and children? Can you say that there were none?

Mr. Rowe: I could not see, but there were none forthcoming.

Senator Burton: You could see around there on the deck, could you not?

Mr. Rowe: I could see the fireman and steward that completed the boat's crew, but as regards any families I could not see any.

Senator Burton: Were there any men passengers besides Mr. Ismay and the other man?

Mr. Rowe: I did not see any, sir.

Senator Burton: Was it light enough so that you could see anyone near by?

Mr. Rowe: Yes, sir.

Senator Burton: Did you hear anyone ask Mr. Ismay and Mr. Carter to get in the boat?

Mr. Rowe: No, sir.

Senator Burton: If Chief Officer Wilde had spoken to them would you have known it?

Mr. Rowe: I think so, because they got in the after part of the boat where I was.

Alfred Pearce, pantryman, third-class (Br. Inq.):

Picked up two babies in his arms and went into a collapsible boat on the starboard side under Officer Murdoch's order, in which were women and children. There were altogether sixty-six passengers and five of the crew, a quartermaster in charge. The ship had a list on the port side, her lights burning to the last. It was twenty minutes to two when they started to row away. He remembers this because one of the passengers gave the time.

J. B. Ismay, President International Mercantile Marine Co. of America, New Jersey, U. S. A. (Am. Inq., pp. 8, 960):

There were four in the crew—one quartermaster, a pantryman, a butcher and another. The natural order would be women and children first. It was followed as far as practicable. About forty-five in the boat. He saw no struggling or jostling or any attempts by men to get into the boats. They simply picked the women out and put them into the boat as fast as they could—the first ones that were there. He put a great many in—also children. He saw the first lifeboat lowered on the starboard side. As to the circumstances of his departure from the ship, the boat was there. There was a certain number of men in the boat and the officer called and asked if there were any more women, but there was no response. There were no passengers left on the deck, and as the boat was in the act of being lowered away he got into it. The *Titanic* was sinking at the time. He felt the ship going down. He entered because there was room in it. Before he boarded the lifeboat he saw no passengers jump into the sea. The boat rubbed along the ship's side when being lowered, the women helping to shove the boat clear. This was when the ship had quite a list to port. He sat with his back to the ship, rowing all the time, pulling away. He did not wish to see her go down. There were nine or ten men in the boat with him. Mr. Carter, a passenger, was one.

All the other people in the boat, so far as he could see, were third-class passengers.

Examined before the British Court of Inquiry by the Attorney-General, Sir Rufus Isaacs, Mr. Ismay testified:

I was awakened by the impact; stayed in bed a little time and then got up. I saw a steward who could not say what had happened. I put a coat on and went on deck. I saw Captain Smith. I asked him what was the matter and he said we had struck ice. He said he thought it was serious. I then went down and saw the chief engineer, who said that the blow was serious. He thought the pumps would keep the water under control. I think I went back to my room and then to the bridge and heard Captain Smith give an order in connection with the boats. I went to the boat deck, spoke to one of the officers, and rendered all the assistance I could in putting the women and children in. Stayed there until I left the ship. There was no confusion; no attempts by men to get into the boats. So far as I knew all the women and children were put on board the boats and I was not aware that any were left. There was a list of the ship to port. I think I remained an hour and a half on the *Titanic* after the impact. I noticed her going down by the head, sinking. Our boat was fairly full. After all the women and children got in and there were no others on that side of the deck, I got in while the boat was being lowered. Before we got into the boat I do not know that any attempt was made to call up any of the passengers on the Boat Deck, nor did I inquire.

And also examined by Mr. A. C. Edwards, M. P., counsel for the Dock Workers' Union. Mr. Ismay's testimony was taken as follows:

Mr. Edwards: You were responsible for determining the number of boats?

Mr. Ismay: Yes, in conjunction with the ship-builders.

Mr. Edwards: You knew when you got into the boat that the ship was sinking?

Mr. Ismay: Yes.

Mr. Edwards: Had it occurred to you apart perhaps from the captain, that you, as the representative managing director, deciding the number of lifeboats, owed your life to every other person on the ship?

The President: That is not the sort of question which should be put to this witness. You can make comment on it when you come to your speech if you like.

Mr. Edwards: You took an active part in directing women and children into the boats?

Mr. Ismay: I did all I could.

Mr. Edwards: Why did you not go further and send for other people to come on deck and fill the boats?

Mr. Ismay: I put in everyone who was there and I got in as the boat was being lowered away.

Mr. Edwards: Were you not giving directions and getting women and children in?

Mr. Ismay: I was calling to them to come in.

Mr. Edwards: Why then did you not give instructions or go yourself either to the other side of the deck or below decks to get people up?

Mr. Ismay: I understood there were people there sending them up.

Mr. Edwards: But you knew there were hundreds who had not come up?

Lord Mersey: Your point, as I understand it now, is that, having regard for his position as managing director, it was his duty to remain on the ship until she went to the bottom?

Mr. Edwards: Frankly, that is so, and I do not flinch from it; but I want to get it from the witness, inasmuch as he took it upon himself to give certain directions at a certain time, why he did not discharge his responsibility after in regard to other persons or passengers.

Mr. Ismay: There were no more passengers who would have got into the boat. The boat was being actually lowered away.

Examined by Sir Robert Finley for White Star Line:

Mr. Finley: Have you crossed very often to and from America?

Mr. Ismay: Very often.

Mr. Finley: Have you ever, on any occasion, attempted to interfere with the navigation of the vessel on any of these occasions?

Mr. Ismay: No.

Mr. Finley: When you left the deck just before getting into the collapsible boat, did you hear the officer calling out for more women?

Mr. Ismay: I do not think I did; but I heard them calling for women very often.

Mr. Edwards: When the last boat left the *Titanic* you must have known that a number of passengers and crew were still on board?

Mr. Ismay: I did.

Mr. Edwards: And yet you did not see any on the deck?

Mr. Ismay: No, I did not see any, and I could only assume that the other passengers had gone to the other end of the ship.

From an address (Br. Inq.) by Mr. A. Clement Edwards, M. P., Counsel for Dock Workers' Union:

What was Mr. Ismay's duty?

Coming to Mr. Ismay's conduct, Mr. Edwards said it was clear that that gentleman had taken upon himself to assist in getting women and children into the boats. He had also admitted that when he left the *Titanic* he knew she was doomed, that there were hundreds of people in the ship, that he didn't know whether or not there were any women or children left, and that he did not even go to the other side of the Boat Deck to see whether there were any women and children waiting to go. Counsel submitted that a gentleman occupying the position of managing director of the company owning the *Titanic*, and who had taken upon himself the duty of assisting at the boats, had certain special and further duties beyond an ordinary passenger's duties, and that he had no more right to save his life at the expense of any single person on board that ship than the captain would have had. He (Mr. Edwards) said emphatically that Mr. Ismay did not discharge his duty at that particular moment by taking a careless glance around the starboard side of the Boat Deck. He was one of the few persons who at the time had been placed in a position of positive knowledge that the vessel was doomed, and it was his clear duty, under the circumstances, to see that someone made a search for passengers in other places than in the immediate vicinity of the Boat Deck.

Lord Mersey: Moral duty do you mean?

Mr. Edwards: I agree; but I say that a managing director going on board a liner, commercially responsible for it and taking upon himself certain functions, had a special moral obligation and duty more than is possessed by one passenger to another passenger.

Lord Mersey: But how is a moral duty relative to this inquiry? It might be argued that there was a moral duty for every man on board that every woman should take precedence, and I might have to inquire whether every passenger carried out his moral duty.

Mr. Edwards agreed that so far as the greater questions involved in this case were concerned this matter was one of trivial importance.

From address of Sir Robert Finlay, K. C., M. P., Counsel for White Star Company (Br. Inq.):

It has been said by Mr. Edwards that Mr. Ismay had no right to save his life at the expense of any other life. He did not save his life at the expense of any other life. If Mr. Edwards had taken the trouble to look at the evidence he would have seen how unfounded this charge is. There is not the slightest ground for suggesting that any other life would have been saved if Mr. Ismay had not got into the boat. He did not get into the boat until it was being lowered away.

Mr. Edwards has said that it was Mr. Ismay's plain duty to go about the ship looking for passengers, but the fact is that the boat was being lowered. Was it the duty of Mr. Ismay to have remained, though by doing so no other life could have been saved? If he had been impelled to commit suicide of that kind, then it would have been stated that he went to the bottom because he dared not face this inquiry. There is no observation of an unfavorable nature to be made from any point of view upon Mr. Ismay's conduct. There was no duty devolving upon him of going to the bottom with his ship as the captain did. He did all he could to help the women and children. It was only when the boat was being lowered that he got into it. He violated no point of honor, and if he had thrown his life away in the manner now suggested it would be said he did it because he was conscious he could not face this inquiry and so he had lost his life.

## ENGELHARDT BOAT "A"

### Floated off the ship

*Passengers:* T. Beattie,[1] P. D. Daly,[3] G. Rheims, R. N. Williams, Jr., first-class; O. Abelseth,[3] W. J. Mellers, second-class; and Mrs. Rosa Abbott,[3] Edward Lindley,[2] third-class.

*Crew:* Steward: E. Brown. Firemen: J. Thompson, one unidentified body,[1] Seaman: one unidentified body.[1]

An extraordinary story pertains to this boat. At the outset of my research it was called a "boat of mystery," occasioned by the statements of the *Titanic*'s officers. In his conversations with me, as well as in his testimony, Officer Lightoller stated that he was unable to loosen this boat from the ship in time and that he and his men were compelled to abandon their efforts to get it away. The statement in consequence was that this boat "A" was not utilized but went down with the ship. My recent research has disabused his mind of this supposition. There were only four Engelhardt boats in all as we have already learned, and we have fully accounted for "the upset boat B," and "D," the last to leave the ship in the tackles, and boat "C," containing Mr. Ismay, which reached the *Carpathia*'s side and was unloaded there. After all the mystery we have reached the conclusion that boat "A" did not go down with the ship, but was the one whose occupants were rescued by Officer Lowe in the early morning, and then abandoned with three dead bodies in it. This also was the boat picked up nearly one month later by the *Oceanic* nearly 200 miles from the scene of the wreck.

[1] Body found in boat by *Oceanic*.
[2] Died in boat.
[3] Pulled into boat out of sea.

I have made an exhaustive research up to date for the purpose of discovering how Boat A left the ship. Information in regard thereto is obtained from the testimony before the British Court of Inquiry of Steward Edward Brown, from first-class passenger R. N. Williams, Jr., and from an account of William J. Mellers, a second-cabin passenger as related by him to Dr. Washington Dodge. Steward Brown, it will be observed, testified that he was washed out of the boat and yet "did not know whether he went down in the water." As he could not swim, an analysis of his testimony forces me to believe that he held on to the boat and did not have to swim and that boat "A" was the same one that he was in when he left the ship. I am forced to the same conclusion in young Williams' case after an analysis of his statement that he took off his big fur overcoat in the water and cast it adrift while he swam twenty yards to the boat, and in some unaccountable way the fur coat swam after him and also got into the boat. At any rate it was found in the boat when it was recovered later as shown in the evidence.

I also have a letter from Mr. George Rheims, of Paris, indicating his presence on this same boat with Messrs. Williams and Mellers and Mrs. Abbott and others.

### INCIDENTS

Edward Brown, steward (Br. Inq.):

Witness helped with boats 5, 3, 1 and C, and then helped with another collapsible; tried to get it up to the davits when the ship gave a list to port. The falls were slackened but the boat could not be hauled away any further. There were four or five women waiting to get into the boat. The boat referred to was the collapsible boat "A" which they got off the officers' house. They got it down by the planks, but witness does not know where the planks came from. He thinks they were with the bars which came from the other boats; yet he had no difficulty in getting the boat off the house. The ship was then up to the bridge under water, well down by the head. He jumped into the boat then and called out to cut the falls. He cut them at the aft end, but cannot say what happened to the forward fall. He was washed out of the boat *but does not know whether he went down in the water*.[1] He had his lifebelt on and came to the top. People were all around him. They tore his clothes away struggling in the water. He could not swim, but got into the collapsible boat "A." Only men were in it, but they picked up a woman and some men afterwards, consisting of passengers, stewards and crew. There were sixteen men. Fifth Officer Lowe in boat No. 14 picked them up.

---

[1] Italics are mine.—AUTHOR.

O. Abelseth (Am. Inq.):

Witness describes the period just before the ship sank when an effort was made to get out the collapsible boats on the roof of the officers' house. The officer wanted help and called out: "Are there any sailors here?" It was only about five feet to the water when witness jumped off. It was not much of a jump. Before that he could see the people were jumping over. He went under and swallowed some water. A rope was tangled around him. He came on top again and tried to swim. There were lots of men floating around. One of them got him on the neck and pressed him under the water and tried to get on top, but he got loose from him. Then another man hung on to him for a while and let go. Then he swam for about fifteen or twenty minutes. Saw something dark ahead of him; swam towards it and it was one of the Engelhardt boats ("A"). He had a life-preserver on when he jumped from the ship. There was no suction at all. "I will try and see." he thought, "if I can float on the lifebelt without help from swimming," and he floated easily on the lifebelt. When he got on boat "A" no one assisted him, but they said when he got on: "Don't capsize the boat," so he hung on for a little while before he got on.

Some were trying to get on their feet who were sitting or lying down; others fell into the water again. Some were frozen and there were two dead thrown overboard. On the boat he raised up and continuously moved his arms and swung them around to keep warm. There was one lady aboard this raft and she (Mrs. Abbott) was saved. There were also two Swedes and a first-class passenger. He said he had a wife and child. There was a fireman also named Thompson who had burned one of his hands; also a young boy whose name sounded like "Volunteer." He and Thompson were afterwards at St. Vincent's Hospital. In the morning he saw a boat with a sail up, and in unison they screamed together for help. Boat A was not capsized and the canvas was not raised up, and they could not get it up. *They stood all night in about twelve or fourteen inches of water* [1]—their feet in water all the time. Boat No. 14 sailed down and took them aboard and transferred them to the *Carpathia*, he helping to row. There must have been ten or twelve saved from boat A; one man was from New Jersey, with whom he came in company from London. At daybreak he seemed unconscious. He took him by the shoulder and shook him. "Who are you?" he said; "let me be; who are you?" About half an hour or so later he died.

In a recent letter from Dr. Washington Dodge he refers to a young man whom he met on the *Carpathia*, very much exhausted, whom he

[1] Italics are mine.—AUTHOR.

took to his stateroom and gave him medicine and medical attention. This young man was a gentleman's valet and a second-cabin passenger. This answers to the description of William J. Mellers, to whom I have written, but as yet have received no response. Dr. Dodge says he believes this young man's story implicitly: He, Mellers, "was standing by this boat when one of the crew was endeavoring to cut the fastenings that bound it to the vessel just as the onrush of waters came on which tore it loose. It was by clinging to this boat that he was saved."

R. N. Williams, Jr., in his letter writes me as follows:

"I was not under water very long, and as soon as I came to the top I threw off the big fur coat I had on. I had put my lifebelt on under the coat. I also threw off my shoes. About twenty yards away I saw something floating. I swam to it and found it to be a collapsible boat. I hung on to it and after a while got aboard and *stood up in the middle of it. The water was up to my waist.*[1] About thirty of us clung to it. When Officer Lowe's boat picked us up eleven of us were alive; all the rest were dead from cold. My fur coat was found attached to this Engelhardt boat 'A' by the *Oceanic*, and *also a cane marked 'C. Williams.'* This gave rise to the story that my father's body was in this boat, but this, as you see, is not so. How the cane got there I do not know."

Through the courtesy of Mr. Harold Wingate of the White Star Line in letters to me I have the following information pertaining to boat "A":

"One of the bodies found in this boat was that of Mr. Thompson Beattie. We got his watch and labels from his clothes showing his name and that of the dealer, which we sent to the executor. Two others were a fireman and a sailor, both unidentified. The overcoat belonging to Mr. Williams I sent to a furrier to be re-conditioned, but nothing could be done with it except to dry it out, so I sent it to him as it was. *There was no cane in the boat.* The message from the *Oceanic* and the words 'R. N. Williams, *care of Duane Williams,'* were twisted by the receiver of the message to 'Richard N. Williams, *cane of Duane Williams,'* [1] which got into the press, and thus perpetuated the error.

"There was also a ring found in the boat whose owner we eventually traced in Sweden and restored the property to her. We cannot account for its being in the boat, but we know that her husband was a passenger on the *Titanic*—Edward P. Lindell, a third-class passenger. The widow's address is, care of Nels Persson, Helsingborg, Sweden."

Rescue of the occupants of boat "A" at daylight Monday morning is

[1] Italics are mine.—AUTHOR.

recorded in the testimony of Officer Lowe and members of the crew of his boat No. 14 and the other boats 12, 10, 4 and "D" which were tied together. No 14 we recall was emptied of passengers and a crew taken from all the boats referred to went back to the wreck. The substance of the testimony of all of them agrees and I need only cite that of Quartermaster Bright, in charge of boat "D," as follows:

A. Bright, Q. M. (in charge) (Am. Inq., 834):
Just at daylight witness saw from his place in boat "D" one of the other collapsible boats, "A," that was awash just flush with the water. Officer Lowe came and towed witness's boat to the other collapsible one that was just awash and took from it thirteen men and one woman who were in the water up to their ankles. They had been singing out in the dark. As soon as daylight came they could be seen. They were rescued and the boat turned adrift with two dead bodies in it, covered with a lifebelt over their faces.

Admiral Mahan on Ismay's duty:
Rear-Admiral A. T. Mahan, Retired, in a letter which the *Evening Post* publishes, has this to say of J. Bruce Ismay's duty:

In the *Evening Post* of April 24 Admiral Chadwick passes a distinct approval upon the conduct of Mr. Ismay in the wreck of the *Titanic* by characterizing the criticisms passed upon it as the "acme of emotionalism."

Both censure and approval had best wait upon the results of the investigations being made in Great Britain. Tongues will wag, but if men like Admiral Chadwick see fit to publish anticipatory opinions those opinions must receive anticipatory comment.

Certain facts are so notorious that they need no inquiry to ascertain. These are (1) that before the collision the captain of the *Titanic* was solely responsible for the management of the ship; (2) after the collision there were not boats enough to embark more than one-third of those on board, and, (3) for that circumstance the White Star Company is solely responsible, not legally, for the legal requirements were met, but morally. Of this company, Mr. Ismay is a prominent if not the most prominent member.

For all the loss of life the company is responsible, individually and collectively: Mr. Ismay personally, not only as one of the members. He believed the *Titanic* unsinkable; the belief relieves of moral guilt, but not of responsibility. Men bear the consequences of their mistakes as well as of their faults. He—and Admiral Chadwick—justify his leaving over fifteen hundred persons, the death of each one of whom lay on the company, on the ground that it was the last boat half filled; and Mr. Ismay has said, no one else to be seen.

No one to be seen; but was there none to be reached? Mr. Ismay knew there must be many, because he knew the boats could take only a third. The *Titanic* was 882 feet long; 92 broad; say, from Thirty-fourth street to a little north of Thirty-seventh. Within this space were congregated over 1,500 souls, on several decks. True, to find any one person at such a moment in the intricacies of a vessel were a vain hope; but to encounter some stragglers would not seem to be. Read in the *Sun* and *Times* of April 25 Col. Gracie's account of the "mass of humanity, men and women" that suddenly appeared before him after the boats were launched.

In an interview reported in the New York *Times* April 25 Admiral Sir Cyprian Bridge, a very distinguished officer, holds that Mr. Ismay was but a passenger, as other passengers. True, up to a certain point. He is in no sense responsible for the collision; but when the collision had occurred he confronted a wholly new condition for which he was responsible and not the captain, viz., a sinking vessel without adequate provision for saving life. Did no obligation to particularity of conduct rest upon him under such a condition?

I hold that under the conditions, so long as there was a soul that could be saved, the obligation lay upon Mr. Ismay that that one person and not he should have been in the boat. More than 1,500 perished. Circumstances yet to be developed may justify Mr. Ismay's actions completely, but such justification is imperatively required. If this be "the acme of emotionalism" I must be content to bear the imputation.

Admiral Chadwick urges the "preserving a life so valuable to the great organization to which Mr. Ismay belongs." This bestows upon Mr. Ismay's escape a kind of halo of self-sacrifice. No man is indispensable. There are surely brains enough and business capacity enough in the White Star company to run without him. The reports say that of the rescued women thirty-seven were widowed by the accident and the lack of boats. Their husbands were quite as indispensable to them as Mr. Ismay to the company. His duty to the ship's company was clear and primary; that to the White Star company so secondary as to be at the moment inoperative.

We should be careful not to pervert standards. Witness the talk that the result is due to the system. What is a system, except that which individuals have made it and keep it? Whatever thus weakens the sense of individual responsibility is harmful, and so likewise is all condonation of failure of the individual to meet his responsibility.

# Titanic

# TITANIC

*By*

Commander  Lightoller

DEDICATED TO
## MY PERSISTENT WIFE
WHO MADE ME DO IT

The following account originally appeared as
Chapters 30, 31, 32, 33, 34, and 35 of the book
*Titanic and Other Ships*, originally published by Ivor
Nicholson and Watson in 1935. Reprinted through
the kind permission of Mrs. Lightoller.

# LOSS OF THE *TITANIC*

From the *Oceanic* as First, I was appointed to the *Titanic*, of tragic memory, as First, and three very contented chaps took the midnight boat for Belfast, where she was completing. Murdoch, Chief, your humble, First, and Davy Blair, Second; Captain E. J. Smith, Commodore of the Line came over a little later on. Captain Smith, or "E. J." as he was familiarly and affectionately known, was quite a character in the shipping world. Tall, full whiskered, and broad. At first sight you would think to yourself, "Here's a typical Western Ocean Captain." "Bluff, hearty, and I'll bet he's got a voice like a foghorn." As a matter of fact, he had a pleasant, quiet voice and invariable smile. A voice he rarely raised above a conversational tone—not to say he couldn't; in fact, I have often heard him bark an order that made a man come to himself with a bump. He was a great favorite, and a man any officer would give his ears to sail under. I had been with him many years, off and on, in the mail boats, *Majestic*, mainly, and it was an education to see him con his own ship up through the intricate channels entering New York at full speed. One particularly bad corner, known as the South-West Spit, used to make us fairly flush with pride as he swung her round, judging his distances to a nicety; she heeling over to the helm with only a matter of feet to spare between each end of the ship and the banks.

For some time previous to being appointed to the *Titanic* "E. J." had been in command of the *Olympic*—since she was launched in fact. Murdoch also came from the *Olympic*, whilst Blair and I were from the *Oceanic*.

It is difficult to convey any idea of the size of a ship like the *Titanic*, when you could actually walk miles along decks and passages, covering different ground all the time. I was thoroughly familiar with pretty well every type of ship afloat, from a battleship and a barge, but it took me fourteen days before I could with confidence find my way from one part of that ship to another by the shortest route. As an instance of size, there was a huge gangway door through which you could drive a horse and cart on the starboard side aft. Three other officers, joining later, tried for a whole day to find it. No doubt with the help of a plan it would have been fairly simple, but a sailor does not walk round with a plan in his pocket, he must carry his ship in his head, and in an emergency such as fire must be able to get where he wants by sheer instinct—certainly without a chance of getting lost on the way.

Touching on fire, the modern ship's equipment is such that it is almost impossible, with fair play, for a fire to get a serious hold. I say this, despite the fact that quite recently no less than three modern liners have been burned out. Generally speaking, the fire-fighting equipment is based on something like these lines.

Close adjacent to the bridge is the Master Fire Station, where a Fireman in full regalia is on duty night and day, and must never be more than six feet away from the door of his station. In his little cubby hole, he is surrounded with instruments which keep him in close touch with secondary Fire Stations situated in commanding positions through-out the ship. In front of him, in the Master Station, on the bulkhead, is a glass fronted air-tight case, into which are leading numbers of little tubes, coming direct from the Secondary Fire Stations. By suction a current of air is drawn through these tubes and into the case. As the air comes through the tube it impinges on a filament resembling tinfoil, causing this to vibrate, and therefore proves that a current of air is actually passing through. If the other end of the tube should be blocked, or stuffed up by some unconscious humorist, this filament at once becomes stationary.

Now, if anyone were to stand close to the other end of the tube, say smoking a cigarette, the smoke would be drawn into the tube, passed up to the Fire Station, and strike this filament. The smoke would then become exaggerated until it resembled a ball of wool, and would im-mediately catch the notice of the man on duty. It he wishes, he can ascertain for his own satisfaction whether it is just tobacco smoke, or something more dangerous. Probably if he finds it is merely tobacco smoke he will conclude that someone is standing nearby the tube smoking, and may wait a reasonable time for it to disappear. If he is not satisfied he will telephone down, calling that Station; and, the man on duty replying, he will ask, more or less politely, if anyone is smoking near that Detector. Probably the man on the Secondary Station will find that it is just tobacco smoke and report it. If, on the other hand it were, for instance, the result of some careless fool throwing a cigarette down on the carpet, and setting it alight, very few moments would elapse before it was known on the bridge, and communication made to the necessary points.

Hoses are always ready, rigged in readiness and attached to hydrants, so that even in the case of a really serious fire suddenly breaking out, it would be known at headquarters within a very few seconds, "fire stations" signaled, and a Fire Party with hoses, buckets and blankets would be on the spot within three minutes.

In these circumstances it is extremely difficult to arrive at any satisfactory conclusion as to how, with fair play, a fire could break out on a modern ship like say the *Atlantique* without being instantly detected. Admitted there were no passengers on board, yet the ordinary fire precautions would still be in operation. With the *Europa* it was different; she was still in the builders' hands, but judging by what one knows of builders, the fire precautions are just as stringent whilst the ship is being built as they are when she goes to sea; in British shipyards, anyhow, and I don't suppose the Germans are a whit behind us.

But to return to the *Titanic*. Putting a new ship in commission is, at the best of times, a pretty strenuous job. With the *Titanic* it was night and day work, organizing here, receiving stores there, arranging duties, trying and testing out the different contrivances; makers of the hundred-and-one instruments with their chits to be signed certifying that this, that and the other was in perfect working order. All the navigation instruments fell to my lot, as also did firearms and ammunition.

These latter are looked on mostly as ornaments in the modern ship.

Revolvers, rifles, and bayonets, in the Merchant Service, are rather superfluous. A man governs by accepted discipline, tact, his own personality, and good common sense. We have no King's Regulations to back us up; neither do we need them; nor yet do we require firearms, except on the rarest occasions. Curiously enough, the *Titanic* was to prove the only occasion at sea that I have ever seen firearms handed out, and even then it was not Britishers they were used to influence.

After running our trials we finally took over from the builders and proceeded round to Southampton. It was clear to everybody on board that we had a ship that was going to create the greatest stir British shipping circles had ever known. For one thing, she was the first ship to be fitted with a third screw, driven by a low-powered turbine. For maneuvering, the two wing screws alone were used, but once clear of the land, steam from low-pressure cylinders was turned into this turbine, and undoubtedly it gave her a wonderful turn of speed.

Unfortunately, whilst in Southampton, we had a reshuffle amongst the Senior Officers. Owing to the *Olympic* being laid up, the ruling lights of the White Star Line thought it would be a good plan to send the Chief Officer of the *Olympic*, just for the one voyage, as Chief Officer of the *Titanic*, to help, with his experience of her sister ship. This doubtful policy threw both Murdoch and me out of our stride; and, apart from the disappointment of having to step back in our rank, caused quite a little confusion. Murdoch, from Chief, took over my duties as First, I stepped back on Blair's toes, as Second, and picked up the many threads of his job, whilst he—luckily for him as it turned out—was left behind. The other officers remained the same. However, a couple of days in Southampton saw each of us settled in our new positions and familiar with our duties. Board of Trade surveys were carried out to everyone's satisfaction. Lifeboats and all lifesaving equipment tested, exercised and passed. "Fireworks" (distress rockets, distress signals, blue lights, etc.) examined, tried and approved. All these, and a hundred-and-one other details pertaining to a crack Atlantic Liner preparing for sea were gone through. Being a new ship, and the biggest in the world, even more scrupulous care was exercised than is usual, or applies to a ship on her settled run. The Board of Trade Surveyor, Captain Clark, certainly lived up to his reputation of being the best cursed B. O. T. representative in the South of England at that time. Many small details, that another surveyor would have taken in his stride accepting the statement of the officer concerned, was not good enough for Clark. He must see everything, and himself check every item that concerned the survey. He would not accept anyone's word as sufficient—and got heartily cursed in consequence. He did his job, and I'll certainly say he did it thoroughly.

At last sailing day arrived, and from end to end the ship, which for days had been like a nest of bees, now resembled a hive about to swarm.

As "zero" hour drew near, so order could be seen arriving out of chaos. On the stroke of the hour, the gangway was lowered, the whistle blew, ropes were let go, and the tugs took the strain.

She was away.

# LEAVING SOUTHAMPTON

**B**efore she cleared the dock we had a striking example of the power that lay in those engines and propellers.

The *Oceanic* and *St. Paul* were lying moored to the wharf alongside each other. They happened to be in a position where the *Titanic* had to make a slight turn, which necessitated coming astern on her port engine. The terrific suction set up in that shallow water, simply dragged both these great liners away from the wharf. The *St. Paul* broke adrift altogether, and the *Oceanic* was dragged off until a sixty-foot gangway dropped from the wharf into the water. It looked as if nothing could save the *St. Paul* crashing into the *Titanic*'s stern, in fact, it was only Captain Smith's experience and resource that saved her. The *Titanic*, of course, dwarfed these two ships, and made them look like cross-channel boats, and the wash from her screws had a corresponding influence. Just as a collision seemed inevitable, Captain Smith gave the *Titanic* a touch ahead on her port engine, which simply washed the *St. Paul* away, and kept her clear until a couple of tugs, to our unbounded relief, got hold, and took her back alongside the wharf.

To the casual observer the whole incident would have been just a thrill—perhaps not much more even though there had been a collision. For us it would have been something much deeper. It is difficult to describe just exactly where that unity of feeling lies, between a ship and her crew, but it is surely there, in every ship that sails salt water. It is not always a feeling of affection either. A man can hate a ship worse than he can a human being, although he sails on her. Likewise a ship can hate her men, then she frequently becomes known as a "killer," and in the days of sail would regularly kill a man voyage after voyage.

The greatest care had to be taken whilst threading our way down the then comparatively shallow channel of Southampton Water and eventually out to Spithead. There was a general feeling of relief when at last we got her into her proper element, deep water.

We then went across to Cherbourg—a short run which barely warmed her up. Then a longer leg to Queenstown, and finally, the following day, we opened her up on the long run to New York.

Each day, as the voyage went on, everybody's admiration of the ship increased; for the way she behaved, for the total absence of vibration, for her steadiness even with the ever-increasing speed, as she warmed up to her work.

As day followed day, officers and men settled down into the collar, and duty linked up with duty until the watches went by without pause or hitch. We were not out to make a record passage; in fact the White Star Line invariably run their ships at reduced speed for the first few voyages. It tells in the long run, for the engines of a ship are very little different from the engines of a good car, they must be run in. Take the case of the *Oceanic*. She steadily increased her speed from 19½ knots in her early days to 21½ when she was twelve years old. It has often been said that had not the *Titanic* been trying to make a passage, the catastrophe would never have occurred.

Nothing of the kind.

She was certainly making good speed that night of April 12th, but not her best—nothing compared with what she would have been capable, in, say, a couple of years' time. The disaster was just due to a combination of circumstances that never occurred before and can never occur again. That may sound like a sweeping statement, yet it is a fact.

All during that fatal day the sea had been like glass—an unusual occurrence for that time of the year—not that that caused any great worry. Again, there had been an extremely mild winter in the Arctic, owing to which, ice from the ice cap and glaciers had broken away in phenomenal quantities, and official reports say that never before or since has there been known to be such quantities of icebergs, growlers, field ice and float ice, stretching down with the Labrador current. In my fifteen years' experience on the Atlantic I had certainly never seen anything like it—not even in the South Atlantic, when in the old days of sailing ships, we used to sometimes go down to 65° S.

These were just some contributory causes, that combined, and brought into existence, conditions of which the officers of the ship were to a great extent ignorant.

Wireless reports were coming in through the day from various ships, of ice being sighted in different positions. Nor was that anything unusual at this time of the year, and none of the reports indicated the extent of the ice seen. A report would read " Iceberg (or icebergs) sighted in such and such a latitude and longitude." Later on in the day we did get reports of ice sighted in larger quantities, and also two reports of field ice, but they were in positions that did not affect us. The one vital report that came through but which never reached the bridge, was received at 9.40 p. m. from the *Mesaba* stating, " Ice report in Latitude 42° N., to 41° 25' N. Long. 49° to Long. 50° 30' W. Saw much heavy pack ice, and great number large icebergs. Also field ice. Weather good, clear." The position this ship gave was right ahead of us and not many miles distant. The wireless operator was not to know how close we were to this position, and therefore the extreme urgency of the message. That he received the message is known, and it was read by the other operator in his bunk. The operator who received it was busy at the time, working wireless messages to and from Cape Race, also with his accounts, and he put the message under a paper weight at his elbow, just until he squared up what he was doing, and he would then have brought it to the bridge. *That delay proved fatal and was the main contributory cause to the loss of that magnificent ship and hundreds of lives.*

For the last hour of my watch on that never-to-be-forgotten night, I had taken up a stationary position on the bridge, where I had an unobstructed view right ahead, and perhaps a couple of points on either bow. That did not signify that I was *expecting* to see ice, but that there was the *possibility* of seeing ice, as there always is when crossing The Banks; ice *may* be sighted. In point of fact, under normal conditions, we should have proved to be well south of the usual ice limit; only in this case the ice limit had moved very many miles south, due solely to the immense amount of ice released in the Arctic.

In ordinary circumstances the cold current carrying the icebergs south strikes the warm current flowing to the northeast and under-runs it—that is to say the cold current goes under the warm current, on the same principle that warm water always rises. The effect of this is to melt the iceberg around the water line. It soon "calves" or breaks up into smaller pieces, which again break up, continuing to float in the warm surface current for a short time, until completely melted. And so the work of disintegration goes on in an ever-increasing ratio, thereby forming the "ice limit."

It is often said you can tell when you are approaching ice, by the drop in the temperature. The answer to that is, open a refrigerator door when the outside temperature is down, and see how close you have to get before you detect a difference. No, you would have to be uncomfortably close to "smell" ice that way.

Ten p. m. came and with it the change of the officers' Watches. On the bridge, after checking over such things as position, speed and so forth, the officers coming on deck usually have a few minutes' chat with their opposite number, before officially taking over. The Senior Officer, coming on Watch, hunts up his man in the pitch darkness, and just yarns for a few minutes, whilst getting his eyesight after being in the light; when he can see all right he lets the other chap know, and officially "takes over." Murdoch and I were old shipmates, and for a few minutes

—as was our custom—we stood there looking ahead, and yarning over times and incidents past and present. We both remarked on the ship's steadiness, absence of vibration, and how comfortably she was slipping along. Then we passed on to more serious subjects, such as the chances of sighting ice, reports of ice that had been sighted, and the positions. We also commented on the lack of definition between the horizon and the sky—which would make an iceberg all the more difficult to see— particularly if it had a black side, and that should be, by bad luck, turned our way.

The side of an iceberg that has calved or broken away from its parent glacier will usually be black, where the fresh ice is showing, and is consequently more difficult to see at night. After considerable exposure, this side turns white like the rest.

We were then making an easy 22 knots. It was pitch dark and dead cold. Not a cloud in the sky, and the sea like glass. The very smoothness of the sea was, again, another unfortunate circumstance that went to complete the chain.

If there had been either wind or swell, the outline of the berg would have been rendered visible, through the water breaking at the base.

Captain " E. J." was one of the ablest Skippers on the Atlantic, and accusations of recklessness, carelessness, not taking due precautions, or driving his ship at too high a speed, were absolutely, and utterly unfounded; but the armchair complaint is a very common disease, and generally accepted as one of the necessary evils from which the seafarer is condemned to suffer. A dark night, a blinding squall, and a man who has been on the mental rack for perhaps the last forty-eight hours is called on to make an instantaneous decision embodying the safety of his crew and his ship. If he chooses the right course, as nine times out of ten he does, all well and good, but if on the tenth time his judgment is, momentarily, in error, then he may be certain he is coming under the thumb of the armchair judge, who, a thousand to one, has never been called on to make a life-and-death decision in a sudden emergency.

Captain Smith, with every other senior officer (apart from myself), went down, and was lost with the ship, and so escaped that never-to-be-forgotten ordeal carried out in Washington; repeated again in England and finally concluded in the Law Courts.

Murdoch, the First Officer, took over from me in the ordinary way. I passed on the "items of interest," as we called them, course, speed, weather conditions, ice reports, wished him joy of his Watch, and went below. But first of all I had to do the rounds, and in a ship of that size it meant a mile or more of deck, not including a few hundred feet of ladders, staircases, etc.

Being a new ship it was all the more necessary to see that everyone was on the top line. I had been right fore and aft several decks, along a passage known as Park Lane, leading through the bowels of the ship on one side, and bringing me out by a short cut to the after-deck. Here I had to look round to see that the Quartermaster and others were on their stations, and then back to my warm cabin.

The temperature on deck felt somewhere around the zero of Canada, although, actually, it wasn't much below freezing, and I quickly rolled into my blankets. There I lay, turning over my past sins and future punishments, waiting until I could thaw, and get to sleep.

# COLLISION WITH AN ICEBERG

I was just about ready for the land of nod, when I felt a sudden vibrating jar run through the ship. Up to this moment she had been steaming with such a pronounced lack of vibration that this sudden break in the steady running was all the more noticeable. Not that it was by any means a violent concussion, but just a distinct and unpleasant break in the monotony of her motion.

I instantly leapt out of my bunk and ran out on deck, in my pajamas; peered over the port side, but could see nothing there; ran across to the starboard side, but neither was there anything there, and as the cold was cutting like a knife, I hopped back into my bunk.

In any case, to go dashing up to the Bridge in night rig, or even properly clothed, when not on duty, was bound to ensure anything but a hearty welcome. Another thing, to be elsewhere than where you are expected to be found, in a ship like that, would result in the man who is sent to call you, being utterly unable to find you. So I just waited.

The time we struck was 2.20 a. m. April 12th, of tragic memory, and it was about ten minutes later that the Fourth Officer, Boxall, opened my door and, seeing me awake, quietly said, "We've hit an iceberg."

I replied, "I know you've hit something." He then said: "The water is up to F Deck in the Mail Room."

That was quite sufficient. Not another word passed. He went out, closing the door, whilst I slipped into some clothes as quickly as possible, and went out on deck.

The decks in a modern liner are lettered from the boat deck downwards, A, B, C, D, E, and so on. The fact of the water having reached "F" deck showed me that she had been badly holed, but, at the time, although I knew it was serious, I had not a thought that it was likely to prove fatal; that knowledge was to come much later.

Up to this time we had had no chance for boat drill, beyond just lowering some of the boats in Southampton. In any case, officers and men in the Mercantile Marine are always impressed with the vital importance of using their own heads, thinking for themselves and acting on their own initiative in an emergency.

Discipline in a Merchant Ship calls for the highest display of individual intelligence and application. Each man must think for himself.

Whereas, in the Navy, the Bluejacket must do as he is told, nothing more, and nothing less. All perfect in its own way where a man is required to act with machine-like precision, but that won't work in the Merchant Service. If a man does no more than he is told, and makes that an excuse for leaving something undone, unseen or unattended to, he is quickly asked, "What the hell are your brains for?"

The result is that a crew come aboard a strange ship, and everything seems like the pieces of a jigsaw puzzle. But, there is just this difference between the two Services. Whereas each man in the Senior Service must be fell in, and detailed to his own particular job, to which he has probably been trained for years, but by which method each piece of the jigsaw must await the touch of the Master hand; in the Merchant Service the whole of the pieces shake themselves together without being "fell in" and "told off." Thus, in an amazingly short space of time they have all shaken down and become a homogeneous workable unit. If there should be a piece that won't seem to fit, then all I can say is heaven help him!

You may be sure that the crew of the *Titanic* had been put through a fine sieve, and particular care taken that there were no misfits. The result was that when the call came—not the call of bugles, but the call on every man to exhibit the highest individual effort, intelligence and courage, the response was absolutely universal—not a man failed.

The survivors of that night may thank God that our men did not wait for bugles and pipes. Nevertheless, they put up as fine a show as has ever been done in any sea tragedy in history. The final and conclusive proof lay in the fact that every single boat in the ship was cleared, swung out and safely lowered into the water and got away, without a hitch of any kind.

The ship had been running under a big head of steam, therefore the instant the engines were stopped the steam started roaring off at all eight exhausts, kicking up a row that would have dwarfed the row of a thousand railway engines thundering through a culvert.

All the seamen came tumbling up on the boat deck in response to the order "All hands on deck " just following the instinct that told them that it was here they would be required. It was an utter impossibility to convey an order by word of mouth; speech was useless, but a tap on the shoulder and an indication with the hand, dark though it was, was quite sufficient to set the men about the different jobs, clearing away the boat covers, hauling tight the falls and coiling them down on deck, clear and ready for lowering.

The passengers by this time were beginning to flock up on the boat deck, with anxious faces, the appalling din only adding to their anxiety in a situation already terrifying enough in all conscience. In fact it was a marvel how they ever managed to keep their heads at all. All one could do was to give them a cheery smile of encouragement, and hope that the infernal roar would soon stop. My boats were all along the port side, and by the time I had got my Watch well employed, stripping the covers and coiling down, it became obvious to me that the ship was settling. So far she had remained perfectly upright, which was apt to give a false sense of security. Soon the Bosun's Mate came to me and indicated with a wave of his hand that the job I had set him of clearing away was pretty well completed. I nodded, and indicated by a motion of my hand for him to swing out.

The *Titanic* was fitted with a well-known pattern of davit called the "Wellin." In operation it was merely a matter of shipping and manning the handles of the davits and the boats were quickly swung out. By this time it was clear that the ship was seriously damaged and making a lot of water. She struck the berg well forward of the foremast, and evidently there had been a slight shelf protruding below the water. This pierced her bow as she threw her whole weight on the ice, some actually falling on her fore deck. The impact flung her bow off, but only by the whip or spring of the ship. Again she struck, this time a little further aft. Each blow stove in a plate, below the water line, as the ship had not the inherent strength to resist.

Had it been, for instance, the old *Majestic* or even the *Oceanic* the chances are that either of them would have been strong enough to take the blow and be bodily thrown off without serious damage. For instance, coming alongside with the old *Majestic*, it was no uncommon thing for her to hit a knuckle of the wharf a good healthy bump, but beyond perhaps, scraping off the paint, no damage was ever done. The same, to a lesser extent, with the *Oceanic*.

Then ships grew in size, out of all proportion to their strength, till one would see a modern liner brought with all the skill and care possible, fall slowly, and ever so gently on a knuckle, to bend and dent a plate like a piece of tin.

That is exactly what happened to the *Titanic*. She just bump, bump, bumped along the berg, holing herself each time, till she was making water in no less than six compartments, though, unfortunately, we were not to know this until much later. Andrews, the designer, and nephew of the late Lord Pirrie was making the trip with us and it was he, familiar with every nook and corner in her, who made a quick tour of inspection with the Carpenter and reported her condition to Captain Smith.

Actually, the *Titanic* was so constructed and divided into watertight compartments that she would float, with any two compartments full of water; and the margin of safety made it fairly certain that she would still have floated, with even three of the four forward compartments full up. Although the water would have been above the forward watertight bulkheads, it would still have been kept out of the rest of the ship, despite the fact that the forward part of her would have been completely submerged. The whole ship would have assumed a fairly acute and mighty uncomfortable angle, yet, even so, she would, in all probability have floated—at least for some considerable time, perhaps all day. Certainly for sufficient time for everyone to be rescued; and, just possibly, until she could have been beached. But she could not remain afloat when she was holed in the forward stokehold as well. That made the fifth compartment counting from forward, that was smashed in by the iceberg, and this finally sealed her fate.

By the time all the boats were swung out she was well down forward, and the water was practically level with the main deck. Even so I still had no thought that she was actually going to founder. There had been no chance or time to make enquiries, but I figured up in my own mind that she had probably struck the berg a glancing blow with the bluff of her bow and opened up one or perhaps two of the forward compartments, which were filling and putting her down by the head; also that she would go so far, until she balanced her buoyancy, and there she would remain. Bulkheads were all new and sound and should be able to carry the pressure, and there was no reason to suppose they would not be equal to their task. All watertight doors had been closed automatically from the bridge, at the time of the collision—all except one place where there was no door, but which in any case would not have made any ultimate difference.

Although I was fairly confident in my own mind that she would not sink, one has no right to risk an error of judgment that may entail loss of life, particularly when it is the case of the passengers you are carrying. They are your trust, and must at all times be your first consideration, to the total elimination of all personal feelings, or personal impressions. It was fortunate we played for safety, for, as it turned out, she was holed in no less than six compartments along the starboard side, and *nothing* could have saved her.

Having got the boats swung out, I made for the Captain, and happened to meet him near by on the boat deck. Drawing him into a corner, and, cupping both my hands over my mouth and his ear, I yelled at the top of my voice, "Hadn't we better get the women and children into the boats, sir?" He heard me, and nodded reply. One of my reasons for suggesting getting the boats afloat was, that I could see a steamer's steaming lights a couple of miles away on our port bow. If I could get the women and children into the boats, they would be perfectly safe in that smooth sea until this ship picked them up; if the necessity arose. My idea was that I would lower the boats with a few people in each and when safely in the water fill them up from the gangway doors on the lower decks, and transfer them to the other ship.

Although boats and falls were all brand new, it is a risky business at the best of times to attempt to lower a boat between seventy and eighty feet at night time, filled with people who are not "boatwise." It is, unfortunately, the rule rather than the exception for some mishap to occur in lowering boats loaded with people who, through no fault of their own, lack this boat sense. In addition, the strain is almost too much to expect of boats and falls under ordinary conditions.

However, having got Captain Smith's sanction, I indicated to the Bosun's Mate, and we lowered down the first boat level with the boat deck, and, just at this time, thank heaven, the frightful din of escaping steam suddenly stopped, and there was a death-like silence a thousand times more exaggerated, fore and aft the ship. It was almost startling to hear one's own voice again after the appalling din of the last half hour or so.

I got just on forty people into No. 4 boat, and gave the order to "lower away," and for the boat to "go to the gangway door" with the idea of filling each boat as it became afloat, to its full capacity. At the same time I told the Bosun's Mate to take six hands and open the port lower-deck gangway door, which was abreast of No. 2 hatch. He took his men and proceeded to carry out the order, but neither he or the men were ever seen again. One can only suppose that they gave their lives endeavoring to carry out this order, probably they were trapped in the alley-way by a rush of water, for by this time the fo'csle head was within about ten feet of the water. Yet I *still* had hope that we should save her.

Passing along to No. 6 boat to load and lower, I could hear the band playing cheery sort of music. I don't like jazz music as a rule, but I was glad to hear it that night. I think it helped us all.

Wireless signals for help had been broadcast over the ocean ever since the first impact, and ships were coming to our aid. It was excusable that in some cases the Officer of the Watch on some ships could hardly credit his senses, or believe the wireless operator when told that the *Titanic*—that wonder of all mercantile wonders—was *sinking in mid-Atlantic*, and sending out calls for assistance.

The wireless operator of the *Virginian* told me that when he reported the fact to his Officer of the Watch, he was literally chucked off the bridge, for trying to play what the O. O. W. thought was an attempt at

The function of this huge bracket was to hold the propellers of the ship.

The *Titanic* and *Olympic* on the stocks at Belfast. The twin vessels occupied space ordinarily used for three building slips.

a practical joke; it was only as he was being pushed past the chart-room door, preparatory to being shot down the bridge ladder, that he landed out with his foot, and gave a terrific kick on the panel of the door. The wireless operator knew that the Captain was asleep in the chart-room, and that this crash would bring him out with a jump. The Officer of the Watch also realized when the report was officially made to the Captain, that it was no joke, and that the *Titanic* was truly in a bad way. They at once altered course and made all speed towards us.

On the *Titanic*, passengers naturally kept coming up and asking, did I consider the situation serious. In all cases I tried to cheer them up, by telling them "No," but that it was a matter of precaution to get the boats in the water, ready for any emergency. That in any case they were perfectly safe, as there was a ship not more than a few miles away, and I pointed out the lights on the port bow which they could see as well as I could.

At this time we were firing rocket distress signals, which explode with a loud report a couple of hundred feet in the air. Every minute or two one of these went up, bursting overhead with a cascade of stars.

"Why were we firing these signals, if there was no danger?" was the question, to which I replied that we were trying to call the attention of the ship nearby, as we could not get her with wireless. *That ship was the "Californian."* Here again we were to see exemplified, what has become almost proverbial at sea, that in cases of disaster, one ship, the first on the scene, will be in a position to rescue, and yet, through some circumstance or combination of circumstances, fails to make that rescue.

The distress signals we fired were seen by the Officer of the Watch on board the *Californian*, also by several members of her crew. Even the flashes from our Morse lamp were seen but finally judged to be "Just the masthead light flickering." Though at one time the thought evidently did arise that we were trying to call them.

To let pass the possibility of a ship calling by Morse, in the existing circumstances then surrounding her, was bad enough; but to mistake distress signals was inexcusable, and to ignore them, criminal. In point of fact the O. O. W. alone saw, and counted, five distress signals (or, as he reported them to Captain Lord, "five white rockets"). Evidently the Captain's curiosity was more than a little aroused for him to ask, "Are they company's signals?" To which the O. O. W. replied that he did not know, but they "Appear to me to be white rockets." Captain Lord merely told him to "go on Morsing," and if he received any further information to send it down to him.

It is an unqualified fact that every single one of our distress signals—unmistakable and urgent calls for help, were clearly seen by the

*Californian.* These signals are never made, except in cases of dire necessity. The O. O. W. of the *Californian* fully appreciated this fact as was evidenced by his remark to the Apprentice on watch with him, "A ship is not going to fire rockets at sea for nothing."

Shortly after counting eight "rockets" he again sent down word to the Captain, with the added rider to the Apprentice, "be sure and wake him and tell him that altogether we have seen eight of these white lights, like rockets, in the direction of this other steamer."

Precisely at 2.40 a. m. this Officer of the Watch again called Captain Lord, this time by voice pipe, and told him that the ship from which he had seen the rockets, had disappeared.

He spoke truly. *A great sea tragedy had been consummated before his very eyes.*

# WOMEN AND CHILDREN—ONLY

The quiet orderliness amongst the passengers, and the discipline amongst the crew, is a thing never to be forgotten. Many of the former came quietly with offers of help. The Bosun's Mate and six of the Watch having been lost to me, the work had become very heavy, and still heavier as I detailed two of the remaining Watch to go away with each boat as it was lowered. The practise was, to lower each boat until the gunwale was level with the boat deck, then, standing with one foot on the deck and one in the boat, the women just held out their right hand, the wrist of which I grabbed with my right hand, hooking my left arm underneath their arm, and so practically lifted them over the gap between the boat's gunwale and the ship's side, into the boat.

Between one boat being lowered away and the next boat being prepared, I usually nipped along to have a look down the very long emergency staircase leading direct from the boat deck down to "C" deck. Actually, built as a short cut for the crew, it served my purpose now to gauge the speed with which the water was rising, and how high it had got. By now the fore deck was below the surface. That cold, green water, crawling its ghostly way up that staircase, was a sight that stamped itself indelibly on my memory. Step by step, it made its way up, covering the electric lights, one after the other, which, for a time, shone under the surface with a horribly weird effect.

Still, it served a very good purpose, and enabled me to form an accurate judgment as to how far she had gone, and how quickly she was going down. Dynamos were still running, and deck lights on, which, though dim, helped considerably with the work; more than could be said of one very good lady who achieved fame by waving an electric light and successfully blinding us as we worked on the boats. It puzzled me until I found she had it installed in the head of her walking stick! I am afraid she was rather disappointed on finding out that her precious light was not a bit appreciated. Arriving in safety on board the *Carpathia*, she tried to make out that someone had stolen her wretched stick, whereas it had been merely taken from her, in response to my request that someone would throw the damn thing overboard.

It had now become apparent that the ship was doomed, and in consequence I began to load the boats to the utmost capacity that I dared.

My scheme for filling up at the lower deck doors had gone by the board —they were under water.

Many were the instances of calm courage.

One young couple walked steadily up and down the boat deck throughout pretty well the whole of the proceedings. Once or twice the young chap asked if he could help. He was a tall, clean-bred Britisher, on his honeymoon I should say. The girl—she was little more—never made the slightest attempt to come towards the boats, much less to be taken on board, although I looked towards her several times with a sort of silent invitation, but no, she was not going to be parted from her man.

The order implicitly obeyed was, "Women and children only." The very highest tribute that it was possible for a human being to pay would hardly do justice to or give the praise due to the sheer calm courage shown by men, women and children amongst the passengers on that ship, individually and collectively. It made me unutterably proud of the English-speaking race. The conditions were all strange; the ship was sinking and the boats were leaving, yet, neither man nor woman attempted to get into a boat without being ordered.

In the case of a Major Peuchen, a Canadian by birth, who went away in one of the boats, unwarrantable blame was attached, at a later date.

I was reduced to sending one seaman away in a boat, and on an occasion, after ordering away a sailor to take charge, I turned round to find there was only one left to attend the boat falls, for lowering away.

"Someone for that after-fall," I called, and the next thing a man who had sailed with me for many years, Hemming by name, replied, "Aye, aye, sir! all ready." Unknown to me he had stepped out of the boat, back on board, to carry out what he considered the more important duty. Bravery and self-sacrifice such as this was of common occurrence throughout the night.

The boat was half way down when someone hailed me, saying, "We've no seamen in the boat," and at that moment I had no one available. I called to the people standing around, "Any seaman there?" No reply, and it was then that Major Peuchen, when he saw that there were none of the ship's crew available, said, "I'm not a seaman, but I'm a yachtsman, if I can be of any use to you."

The boat's falls, or ropes, by which the boat is lowered, hang up and down from the davit head, about nine or ten feet away from the ship's side. I said to him, "If you're seaman enough to get out on those falls, and get down into the boat you may go ahead." He did, and has been very unfairly criticized for carrying out what was a direct order.

It was about this time that the Chief Officer came over from the starboard side and asked, did I know where the firearms were?

As I pointed out before, it was the *First* Officer's responsibility to receive firearms, navigation instruments, and so forth. I have also said firearms on merchant ships are looked on as ornamental more than useful, and as First Officer I had simply hove the lot, revolvers and ammunition into a locker, in my original cabin, a locker that was of little use owing to its inaccessibility.

Then, later on, had come the "general post," whereby Murdoch, who was now First Officer, knew nothing about the firearms, and couldn't find them, when they were wanted—I say wanted, rather than needed, because I still don't believe that they were actually needed.

I told the Chief Officer, "Yes, I know where they are. Come along and I'll get them for you," and into the First Officer's cabin we went— the Chief, Murdoch, the Captain and myself—where I hauled them out, still in all their pristine newness and grease.

I was going out when the Chief shoved one of the revolvers into my hands, with a handful of ammunition, and said, "Here you are, you may need it." On the impulse, I just slipped it into my pocket, along with the cartridges, and returned to the boats. The whole incident had not taken three minutes, though it seemed barely worth that precious time.

As I returned along the deck, I passed Mr. and Mrs. Strauss leaning up against the deck house, chatting quite cheerily. I stopped and asked Mrs. Strauss, "Can I take you along to the boats?" She replied, "I think I'll stay here for the present." Mr. Strauss, calling her by her Christian name said, smilingly, "Why don't you go along with him, dear?" She just smiled, and said, "No, not yet." I left them, and they went down together. To another couple, evidently from the Western States, that I found sitting on a fan casing I asked the girl, "Won't you let me put you in one of the boats?" She replied with a frank smile, "Not on your life. We started together, and if need be, we'll finish together." It was typical of the spirit throughout.

Boat after boat was safely lowered into the water, with its human freight of women and children, each with an ever-increasing cargo as it became more and more evident that the *Titanic* was doomed, and that the ship to which we had looked for immediate help, was also a false hope. Time and again I had used her lights as a means to buoy up the hopes of the many that I now knew only too well, were soon to find themselves struggling in that icy water.

Why *couldn't* she hear our wireless calls? Why *couldn't* her Officer of the Watch or some one of her crew, see our distress signals with their showers of stars, visible for miles and miles around?—a signal that is never used except when a ship is in dire need of assistance. What wouldn't I have given for a six-inch gun and a couple of shells to wake them up. I had assured and reassured the passengers throughout these anxious hours, "She cannot help but see these signals, and must soon steam over and pick everyone up." And what an absolutely unique opportunity Captain Lord, of the *Californian*, had that night of rendering aid and saving close on 1,500 lives. Nothing could have been easier than to have laid his ship actually alongside the *Titanic* and taken every soul on board. Yet, not a thing was done, not even was their wireless operator aroused to see if there *were* any distress calls.

There are no police, fire brigades or lifeboats out at sea, therefore it becomes nothing less than a fetish—the tenet above all tenets in the religion among sailors, that absolutely no effort shall be spared in an endeavor to save life at sea. A man must even be prepared to hazard his ship and his life.

Just before launching the last two lifeboats, I had made my final hurried visit to the stairway. It was then conclusively evident that not only *was* she going, but that she was going *very soon*, and if we were to avoid the unutterable disgrace of going down with lifeboats still hanging to the davits, there was not one single moment to lose.

Hurrying back to the two remaining lifeboats still hanging in their davits, I met the Purser, Assistant Purser, and the Senior and Junior Surgeons—the latter a noted wag—even in the face of tragedy, couldn't resist his last mild joke, "Hello, Lights, are you warm?" The idea of anyone being warm in that temperature was a joke in itself, and I suppose it struck him as odd to meet me wearing a sweater, no coat or overcoat. I had long since discarded my greatcoat, even in pants and sweater over pajamas alone I was in a bath of perspiration. There was only time to pass a few words, then they all shook hands and said "Good-bye." Frankly, I didn't feel at all like "Good-bye," although I knew we shouldn't have the ship under us much longer. The thing was to get these boats away at all costs. Eventually, and to my great relief, they were all loaded and safely lowered into the water.

The last lifeboat having got away, there remained No. 2 boat, which was actually a small sea boat used for emergency purposes (in fact often termed "The Emergency Boat"), hanging in the davits.

About this time I met all the engineers, as they came trooping up from below. Most of them I knew individually, and had been shipmates with them on different ships of the Line. They had all loyally stuck to their guns, long after they could be of any material assistance. Much earlier on the engine-room telegraphs had been "Rung off—" the last ring made on board ships at sea, and which conveys to the engine-room staff the final information that their services below can be of no further use, that the case (from whatever cause) is hopeless. At the same time it releases engineers and stokers from duty, leaving them free to make the best of their way to the boats. Of course, in theory, each has his appointed place in a given boat.

Since the *Titanic* disaster, each undoubtedly has. But before that tragedy brought home to the world the utter fallacy of the "unsinkable ship" I'm afraid that many "appointed places"—as far as lifesaving equipment was concerned—were just so much theory, concocted ashore with a keen eye to dividends.

Certainly there was no sailor who ever sailed salt water but who smiled—and still smiles—at the idea of the "unsinkable ship."

There was little opportunity to say more than a word or two to the engineers. Up to that time they had known little of what was going on, and it was surely a bleak and hopeless spectacle that met their eyes. Empty falls hanging loosely from every davit head, and not a solitary hope for any one of them.

In point of fact, they were lost to a man, *not one single survivor* out of the whole thirty-five.

# SHE FOUNDERS

Arriving alongside the emergency boat, someone spoke out of the darkness, and said, "There are men in that boat." I jumped in, and regret to say that there actually were—but they weren't British, nor of the English-speaking race. I won't even attribute any nationality to them, beyond saying that they come under the broad category known to sailors as "Dagoes." They hopped out mighty quickly, and I encouraged them verbally, also by vigorously flourishing my revolver. They certainly thought they were between the devil and the deep sea in more senses than one, and I had the satisfaction of seeing them tumbling head over heels onto the deck, preferring the uncertain safety of the deck, to the cold lead which I suppose they fully imagined would follow their disobedience—so much for imagination—the revolver was not even loaded!

"Any more women and children?" was the cry, and we had the greatest difficulty in finding sufficient to fill even this small boat—of those who were willing to go and leave others behind. Eventually, she was filled, and we lowered her away.

There now only remained two folded boats of the Engleheart type, with collapsible canvas sides, one on the deck by the davits of No. 2 emergency and one on top of the officers' quarters, both firmly lashed down. The rope falls of No. 2 were hurriedly rounded up and one collapsible boat hooked on and swung out ready for lowering.

I stood partly in the boat, owing to the difficulty of getting the womenfolk over a high bulwark rail just here. As we were ready for lowering the Chief came over to my side of the deck and, seeing me in the boat and no seaman available said, "You go with her, Lightoller."

Praises be, I had just sufficient sense to say, "Not damn likely," and jump back on board; not with any idea of self-imposed martyrdom—far from it—it was just pure impulse of the moment, and an impulse for which I was to thank my lucky stars a thousand times over, in the days to come. I had taken my chance and gone down with the rest, consequently I didn't have to take any old back-chat from anyone.

As this boat was being lowered, two men passengers jumped into her from the deck below. This, as far as I know, was the only instance of men getting away in boats from the port side. I don't blame them, the boat wasn't full, for the simple reason we couldn't find sufficient women, and there was no time to wait—the water was then actually lapping round their feet on "A" deck, so they jumped for it and got away. Good luck to them.

With one other seaman I started to cast adrift the one remaining Engleheart on top of the officers' quarters. We cut and threw off the lashings, jumped round to the inboard side ready to pick up the gunwale together and throw her bodily down on to the boat deck. The seaman working with me called:

"All ready, sir," and I recognized Hemmings' voice—the chap I had ordered away long before, and who returned on board to tend the falls, and in whose place I sent Major Peuchen.

"Hello, is that you, Hemming?"

"Yes, sir."

"Why haven't you gone?" I asked.

"Oh, plenty of time yet, sir," he replied cheerily. Apparently the chap had loyally stuck by me all through, though it had been too dark to recognize him. Stout fellow. Later, he slid down one of the falls, swam for it and was saved.

We had just time to tip the boat over, and let her drop into the water that was now above the boat deck, in the hope that some few would be able to scramble on to her as she floated off. Hemming and I then, as every single boat was now away from the port side, went over to the starboard side, to see if there was anything further to be done there. But all the boats on this side had also been got away, though there were still crowds of people on the deck.

Just then the ship took a slight but definite plunge—probably a bulkhead went—and the sea came rolling up in a wave, over the steel-fronted bridge, along the deck below us, washing the people back in a dreadful huddled mass. Those that didn't disappear under the water right away, instinctively started to clamber up that part of the deck still out of water, and work their way towards the stern, which was rising steadily out of the water as the bow went down. A few of the more agile leapt up on top of the officers' quarters where Hemming and I were at the moment. It was a sight that doesn't bear dwelling on—to stand there, above the wheelhouse, and on our quarters, watching the frantic struggles to climb up the sloping deck, utterly unable to even hold out a helping hand.

I knew, only too well, the utter futility of following that driving instinct of self-preservation and struggling up towards the stern. It would only be postponing the plunge, and prolonging the agony—even lessening one's already slim chances, by becoming one of a crowd.

It came home to me very clearly how fatal it would be to get amongst those hundreds and hundreds of people who would shortly be struggling for their lives in that deadly cold water. There was only one thing to do, and I might just as well do it and get it over, so, turning to the fore part of the bridge, I took a header. Striking the water, was like a thousand knives being driven into one's body, and, for a few moments, I completely lost grip of myself—and no wonder for I was perspiring freely, whilst the temperature of the water was 28°, or 4° below freezing.

Ahead of me the lookout cage on the foremast was visible just above the water—in normal times it would be a hundred feet above. I struck out blindly for this, but only for a short while, till I got hold of myself again and realized the futility of seeking safety on anything connected with the ship. I then turned to starboard, away from the ship altogether.

For a time I wondered what was making it so difficult for me to keep my head above the water. Time and again I went under, until it dawned on me that it was the great Webley revolver, still in my pocket, that was dragging me down. I soon sent that on its downward journey.

The water was now pouring down the stokeholds, by way of the fiddley gratings abaft the bridge, and round the forward funnel.

On the boat deck, above our quarters, on the fore part of the forward funnel, was a huge rectangular air shaft and ventilator, with an opening about twenty by fifteen feet. On this opening was a light wire grating to prevent rubbish being drawn down or anything else being thrown down. This shaft led direct to No. 3 stokehold, and was therefore a sheer drop of close on hundred feet, right to the bottom of the ship.

I suddenly found myself drawn, by the sudden rush of the surface water now pouring down this shaft, and held flat and firmly up against this wire netting with the additional full and clear knowledge of what would happen if this light wire carried away. The pressure of the water just glued me there whilst the ship sank slowly below the surface.

Although I struggled and kicked for all I was worth, it was impossible to get away, for as fast as I pushed myself off I was irresistibly dragged back, every instant expecting the wire to go, and to find myself shot down into the bowels of the ship.

Apart from that, I was drowning, and a matter of another couple of minutes would have seen me through. I was still struggling and fighting when suddenly a terrific blast of hot air came up the shaft, and blew me right away from the air shaft and up to the surface.

The water was now swirling round, and the ship sinking rapidly, when once again I was caught and sucked down by an inrush of water, this time adhering to one of the fiddley gratings. Just how I got clear of that,

I don't know, as I was rather losing interest in things, but I eventually came to the surface once again, this time alongside that last Engleheart boat which Hemming and I had launched from on top of the officers' quarters on the opposite side—for I was now on the starboard side, near the forward funnel.

There were many around in the water by this time, some swimming, others (mostly men, thank God), definitely drowning—an utter nightmare of both sight and sound. In the circumstances I made no effort to get on top of the upturned boat, but, for some reason, was content to remain floating alongside, just hanging on to a small piece of rope.

The bow of the ship was now rapidly going down and the stern rising higher and higher out of the water, piling the people into helpless heaps around the steep decks, and by the score into the icy water. Had the boats been around many might have been saved, but of them, at this time there was no sign. Organized help, or even individual help, was quite impossible. All one could do was just wait on events, and try and forget the icy cold grip of the water.

The terrific strain of bringing the after-end of that huge hull clear out of the water, caused the expansion joint abaft No. 1 funnel to open up. (These expansion joints were found necessary in big ships to allow the ship to "work" in a seaway.) The fact that the two wire stays to this funnel, on the after-part, led over and abaft the expansion joint, threw on them an extraordinary strain, eventually carrying away the port wire guy, to be followed almost immediately by the starboard one. Instantly the port one parted, the funnel started to fall, but the fact that the starboard one held a moment or two longer, gave this huge structure a pull over to that side of the ship, causing it to fall, with its scores of tons, right amongst the struggling mass of humanity already in the water. It struck the water between the Engleheart and the ship, actually missing me by inches.

Amongst the many historic and, what in less tragic circumstances would have been humorous—questions, asked by Senator Smith at the Washington Enquiry was, "Did it hurt anyone?"

One effect of the funnel crashing down on the sea, was to pick up the Engleheart, in the wash so created, and fling it well clear of the sinking ship.

When I again recognized my surroundings, we were full fifty yards clear of the ship. The piece of rope was still in my hand, with old friend Engleheart upturned and attached to the other end, with several men by now standing on it. I also scrambled up, after spending longer than I like to remember in that icy water. Lights on board the *Titanic* were still burning, and a wonderful spectacle she made, standing out black and massive against the starlit sky; myriads of lights still gleaming through the portholes, from that part of the decks still above water.

The fore part, and up to the second funnel was by this time completely submerged, and as we watched this terribly awe-inspiring sight, suddenly all lights went out and the huge bulk was left in black darkness, but clearly silhouetted against the bright sky. Then, the next moment, the massive boilers left their beds and went thundering down with a hollow rumbling roar, through the bulkheads, carrying everything with them that stood in their way. This unparalleled tragedy that was being enacted before our very eyes, now rapidly approached its finale, as the huge ship slowly but surely reared herself on end and brought rudder and propellers clear of the water, till, at last, she assumed *an absolute perpendicular position.* In this amazing attitude she remained for the space of half a minute. Then with impressive majesty and ever-increasing momentum, she silently took her last tragic dive to seek a final resting place in the unfathomable depths of the cold gray Atlantic.

Almost like a benediction everyone round me on the upturned boat breathed the two words, "She's gone."

Fortunately, the scene that followed was shrouded in darkness. Less fortunately, the calm still silence carried every sound with startling distinctness. To enter into a description of those heartrending, never-to-be-forgotten sounds would serve no useful purpose. I never allowed my thoughts to dwell on them, and there are some that would be alive and well to-day had they just determined to erase from their minds all memory of those ghastly moments, or at least until time had somewhat dimmed the memory of that awful tragedy.

# THE RESCUE

However anyone that had sought refuge on that upturned Engle-heart survived the night is nothing short of miraculous. If ever human endurance was taxed to the limit, surely it was during those long hours of exposure in a temperature below freezing, standing motionless in our wet clothes. That the majority were still standing when the first faint streaks of dawn appeared, is proof that whilst there is life there is still some hope.

Hour by hour the compartments in this collapsible boat were surely filling with water, due, no doubt to the rough-and-ready treatment she had received when dumped incontinently from the top of our quarters, with a crash on to the boat deck, there to float off of her own sweet will.

The fact remains we were painfully conscious of that icy cold water, slowly but surely creeping up our legs.

Some quietly lost consciousness, subsided into the water, and slipped overboard, there being nothing on the smooth flat bottom of the boat to hold them. No one was in a condition to help, and the fact that a slight but distinct swell had started to roll up, rendered help from the still living an impossibility.

It was only by the grace of being huddled together that most of us didn't add to the many that lost their lives that night.

Another thing, with the rising sea I realized that without concerted action, we were *all* going to be pitched headlong into the sea, and that would spell finish for everyone. So I made everyone face one way, and then, as I felt the boat under our feet lurch to the sea, one way or the other, I corrected it by the order, "Lean to the right," "Stand upright," or "Lean to the left," as the case might be.

In this way we managed to maintain our foothold on the slippery planks by now well under water.

We knew that ships were racing to our rescue, though the chances of our keeping up our efforts of balancing until one came along seemed very, very remote. Phillips, the senior wireless operator, standing near me, told me the different ships that had answered our call. Of these, according to their positions, undoubtedly the *Carpathia* was nearest and should be up with the position where the *Titanic* sank, by daylight.

For encouragement, I passed on to those around, my rough

calculation and it certainly helped the struggle to keep up. As it turned out, the information from Phillips, and the calculation, were about right, though poor old Phillips did not live to benefit by it. He hung on till daylight came in and we sighted one of the lifeboats in the distance. We were beyond making her hear with our shouting, but I happened to have in my pocket the ordinary whistle which every officer of the Watch carries. This piercing sound carried, and likewise carried the information (for what it was worth) that it was an officer making the call.

Slowly—oh how slow it seemed—she worked her way towards us. Meantime the boat under us showed unmistakable signs of leaving us altogether. I think it must have been the final and terrible anxiety that tipped the beam with Phillips, for he suddenly slipped down, sitting in the water, and though we held his head up, he never recovered. I insisted on taking him into the lifeboat with us, hoping there still might be life, but it was too late. Altogether there were thirty of us boarded the lifeboat, and later on I counted seventy-five living, apart from those lying on the bottom boards. If a sea got up it was going to take all my knowledge of boat-craft to keep *her* afloat.

As daylight increased we had the thrice welcome sight of the Cunard Liner *Carpathia* cautiously picking her way through the ice towards us. We saw boat by boat go alongside, but the question was, would she come our way in time? Sea and wind were rising. Every wave threatened to come over the bows of our overloaded lifeboat and swamp us. All were women and children in the boat apart from those of us men from the Engleheart. Fortunately, none of them realized how near we were to being swamped.

I trimmed the boat down a little more by the stern, and raised the bow, keeping her carefully bow-on to the sea, and hoping against hope she would continue to rise. Sluggishly, she lifted her bows, but there was no life in her with all that number on board.

Then, at long last, the *Carpathia* definitely turned her head towards us, rounding to about 100 yards to windward. Now to get her safely alongside! We couldn't last many minutes longer, and round the *Carpathia*'s bows was a scurry of wind and waves that looked like defeating all my efforts after all. One sea lopped over the bow and the next one far worse. The following one she rode, and then, to my unbounded relief, she came through the scurry into calm water under the *Carpathia*'s lee.

Quickly the bosun's chairs were lowered for those unable to climb the sheer side by a swinging rope ladder, and little enough ceremony was shown in bundling old and young, fat and thin, onto that bit of wood constituting the "Boatswain's Chair."

A funnel of the *Olympic*, sister ship of the *Titanic*. The *Titanic* carried four such funnels, one of which fell upon scores of persons struggling in the water as the ship sank.

J. Bruce Ismay, chairman and managing director of the White Star Line and passenger aboard the *Titanic*.

Once the word was given to "hoist away" and up into the air they went. There were a few screams, but on the whole, they took it well, in fact many were by now in a condition that rendered them barely able to hang on, much less scream.

When all were on board we counted the cost. There were a round total of 711 saved out of 2,201 on board. Fifteen hundred of all ranks and classes had gone to their last account. Apart from four junior officers ordered away in charge of boats, I found I was the solitary survivor of over fifty officers and engineers who went down with her. Hardly one amongst the hundreds of surviving passengers, but had lost someone near and dear.

Then came the torment of being unable to hold out a vestige of hope.

"Could not another ship have picked them up?"

"Could they not possibly be in some boat overlooked by the *Carpathia*?"

"Was it not possible that he might have climbed on to an iceberg?"

After serious consideration it seemed the kindest way to be perfectly frank and give the one reply possible. What kindness was there in holding out a hope, knowing full well there was not even the *shadow* of hope. Cold comfort, and possibly cruel, but I could see no help for it.

Countess Rothes was one of the foremost amongst those trying to carry comfort to others, and through that sad trip to New York, there were very many quiet acts of self-denial.

Everybody's hope, so far as the crew were concerned, was that we might arrive in New York in time to catch the *Celtic* back to Liverpool and so escape the inquisition that would otherwise be awaiting us. Our luck was distinctly out. We were served with Warrants, immediately on arrival. It was a colossal piece of impertinence that served no useful purpose and elicited only a garbled and disjointed account of the disaster; due in the main to a total lack of co-ordination in the questioning in conjunction with an abysmal ignorance of the sea.

In Washington our men were herded into a second-rate boarding house, which might have suited some, but certainly not such men as formed the crew of the *Titanic*. In the end they point-blank refused to have anything more to do with either the enquiry or the people, whose only achievement was to make our Seamen, Quartermasters and Petty Officers look utterly ridiculous. It was only with the greatest difficulty I was able to bring peace into the camp—mainly due to the tact exhibited by the British Ambassador, Lord Percy, and Mr. P. A. Franklyn, President of the International Mercantile Marine Co.

With all the goodwill in the world, the "Enquiry" could be called nothing but a complete farce, wherein all the traditions and customs of the sea were continuously and persistently flouted.

Such a contrast to the dignity and decorum of the Court held by Lord Mersey in London, where the guiding spirit was a sailor in essence, and who insisted, when necessary, that any cross-questioner should at any rate be familiar with at least the rudiments of the sea. Sir Rufus Isaacs —as he was then—had started his career as a sailor. One didn't need to explain that "going down by the bow" and "going down by the head" was one and the same thing. Nor, that water-tight compartments, dividing the ship, were not necessarily places of refuge in which passengers could safely ensconce themselves, whilst the ship went to the bottom of the Atlantic, to be rescued later, as convenient. Neither was it necessary to waste precious time on lengthy explanations as to how and why a sailor was not an officer, though an officer was a sailor.

In Washington it was of little consequence, but in London it was very necessary to keep one's hand on the whitewash brush.

Sharp questions that needed careful answers if one was to avoid a pitfall, carefully and subtly dug, leading to a pinning down of blame on to someone's luckless shoulders. How hard Mr. Scanlan and the legal luminary, representing the interests of the Seamen and Firemen, tried to prove there were not enough seamen to launch and man the boats. The same applied to the passengers, and quite truly.

But it was inadvisable to admit it then and there, hence the hard-fought verbal duels between us. Mr. Scanlan's conquest of the higher legal spheres of recent years proves he was no mean antagonist to face. His aim was to force the admission that I had not sufficient seamen to give adequate help with the boats, and consequently that the ship was undermanned. How many men did I consider necessary to launch a lifeboat?

"What size lifeboat?"

"Take one of the *Titanic*'s lifeboats."

"Well," I pointed out, "it would depend greatly on weather conditions."

"Make your own conditions," replied my legal opponent impatiently.

I suggested, as an example, we should take the wind as force six Beaufort's scale.

"Yes," he agreed.

"Then," I added, "there would be an accompanying sea, of course."

"Yes, yes," he again agreed, and fell into the trap which Lord Mersey proceeded to spring, by informing Mr. Scanlan that in the circumstances described it would be impossible to launch any boat.

So the legal battle went on.

Still, I think we parted very good friends.

A washing of dirty linen would help no one. The Board of Trade had passed that ship as in all respects fit for sea, in every sense of the word, with sufficient margin of safety for everyone on board. Now the Board of Trade was holding an enquiry into the loss of that ship—hence the whitewash brush. Personally, I had no desire that blame should be attributed either to the Board of Trade or the White Star Line, though in all conscience it was a difficult task, when handled by some of the cleverest legal minds in England, striving tooth and nail to prove the inadequacy here, the lack there, when one had known, full well, and for many years, the ever-present possibility of just such a disaster. I think in the end the Board of Trade and the White Star Line won.

The very point, namely the utter inadequacy of the lifesaving equipment then prevailing, which Mr. Scanlan and his confrères had been fighting tooth and nail to prove, has since been wholly, frankly, and fully admitted by the stringent rules now governing British ships, "Going Foreign."

No longer is the Boat-Deck almost wholly set aside as a recreation ground for passengers, with the smallest number of boats relegated to the least possible space.

In fact, the pendulum has swung to the other extreme and the margin of safety reached the ridiculous.

Be that as it may, I am never likely to forget that long-drawn-out battle of wits, where it seemed that I must hold that unenviable position of whipping boy to the whole lot of them. Pull devil, pull baker, till it looked as if they would pretty well succeed in pulling my hide off completely, each seemed to want his bit. I know when it was all over I felt more like a legal doormat than a Mail Boat Officer.

Perhaps the heads of the White Star Line didn't quite realize just what an endless strain it had all been, falling on one man's luckless shoulders, as it needs must, being the sole survivor out of so many departments—fortunately they were broad.

Still, just that word of thanks which was lacking, which when the *Titanic* Enquiry was all over would have been very much appreciated. It must have been a curious psychology that governed the managers of that magnificent Line. Promotion and service in their Western Ocean Mail Boats was the mark of their highest approval. Both these tokens came my way, and fifteen of my twenty years under the red Burgee, with its silver star, were spent in the Atlantic Mail. Yet, when after completing my twentieth year of service I came to bury my anchor, and awaited their pleasure at headquarters, for the last time, there was a brief:

"Oh, you are leaving us, are you. Well, Good-bye."

A curious people!

However, that was not to be for some years, and I was yet to see another of the Line, my old favorite, the *Oceanic*, swallowed up by the insatiable sea.

Having at last finished with the "*Titanic* Enquiry," I again set about picking up the threads and found myself once more signing Articles on the *Oceanic* with many that had survived the *Titanic*. One well-known figure was missing from the Shipping Office about this time and that was "Old Ned," known to all and sundry as just "Ned." Actually, he was responsible for the stokehold crowd, and a tougher bunch than the firemen on a Western Ocean Mail boat it would be impossible to find. Bootle seemed to specialize in the Liverpool Irishman, who was accounted to be the toughest of the tough, and prominent amongst the few that could stand up to the life, where life below consisted of one endless drive. Even the engineers seemed to get tainted with that unqualified "toughness," for they must be able to hold their own with the worst. This type reached its peak in the days of the old *Majestic* and *Teutonic*. The conditions under which firemen labored in these boats, were inhuman. Little blame if the men did become brutes. The heat of the stokehold alone, when driving under the last ounce of steam, was terrible. Added to this, when in the Gulf Stream, was the intense humidity.

It was no uncommon sight to see a man, sometimes two, three or even four in a watch, hoisted up the ash-shoot with the bucket chain hooked roughly round under their arm-pits, to be dumped on deck unconscious. A few buckets of water over them and then they were left to recover. Neither must they be long about it, or up comes the Leading Fireman, who, with strict impartiality, will apply both boot and fist to drive his dogs of war below again.

The instructions were to keep up that "arrow," indicating the steam pressure, at all costs, regardless of body or bones. Small wonder at the tales that used to creep about, of men gone missing after a free fight, when sharp shovels are used as flails.

"So and so missing. He must have gone overboard during the night. Caught with the heat, poor beggar."

Yes, caught all right, but perhaps with the sharp edge of a shovel.

An engineer at one time was seen to go into the stokehold, and never seen to come out, nor yet seen on deck. He was a particularly powerful type of man and brutal withal, who hazed his watch to the limit in the demand for steam, till the stokehold was Bedlam let loose. From that day till this—though never mentioned ashore—his disappearance was frankly attributed to the swift cut of a shovel from behind, and his body shot into a furnace. The truth will never be known, but from then on, an engineer never went into the stokehold unaccompanied by his leading hand.

These were the type of men "Old Ned" was called upon to supply and handle. Originally a fireman himself, he knew all the tricks, and feared none. Tall, keen alert. Perfect athletic build. A hawk-like eye, and monstrous aquiline nose, that had been broken more times than even he could remember. Slow of movement and quiet of speech, with a voice that came rumbling from way down in his chest.

A couple of hundred toughs, crowding and jostling together, waiting to sign on. "Ned," towering above the tallest, comes through the door-way and makes his way with hardly a check, surging through, and throwing aside the Bootle toughs like a ship contemptuously flinging off the little waves that would hold her. A shoulder here, an elbow there. Nor would he hesitate to put the flat of that huge hand of his on the flat of some more than usually objectionable face, with the base of his wrist tucked neatly under the chin. If the man was sensible, he stepped back, quickly and sharply, regardless of the curses of those behind him, or how they might retaliate. Arriving at the table, "Ned" quickly says, "*Stand back*" to those who would crowd in with their Discharge books held out. For be it known there will be a full score and more eager to accept every single vacancy. Even "Brutal Bootle" looks with respect on a man who has gained that giddy height, and been chosen by "Ned" for "The Mail Boat." A vicious and resentful crowd they were, and though master of the situation at the pay table, it was a different matter when turning a dark corner in Dockland, as old "Ned" had known to his cost, many a time and often. On the other hand, there was not a pub within a mile or more radius, that he could not walk into and call for enough beer to drown a man, had he wished. No fireman came ashore from the Mail Boat, with his pay in his pocket but "chalked one up for Ned." Even a Chicago gangster might have envied the cortège that finally followed "Old Ned" after signing his last ship.

With the *Oceanic*'s comfortable quarters, and bathrooms, there was no call for the tough element, in fact it did not exist in Southampton, where the mail boats were now running from. Again, she introduced a reserve of power that enabled a steady speed to be kept. In fact, the *Oceanic*'s records for steady and consistent running have never been beaten. Two consecutive runs of over three thousand miles and not one minute of difference. Three consecutive voyages and only one minute of difference between the times of leaving Sandy Hook, New York, and passing the Wolf Rock off the Scillies.

We were bound home on that fateful August 4th, 1914, when we got the brief message that hostilities had broken out and were advised to "deviate from the recognized tracks." We did deviate, too, for we saw no fun in being captured in a fine ship like the *Oceanic*, right at the outbreak of war. Judge our anxiety when nearing the Irish Coast, on seeing the masts and funnels of two ships coming above the horizon—ships obviously of the cruiser variety. The only question was, *whose* cruisers? Well, anyway, we had to get in sometime, and the chances were they were not Germans—so we'd better risk it. All the same, it was an undoubted relief when at last the white ensign also came above the rim of the sea.

Thrilling Tale by Titanic's
Surviving Wireless Man

THRILLING TALE BY TITANIC'S
# SURVIVING
# WIRELESS MAN
as told in New York Times, April 28,
1912

*by*

Harold  Bride

# Bride Tells How He and Phillips Worked and How He Dealt with a Stoker Who Tried to Steal Phillips's Life Belt—Titanic's Band Played "Autumn" as She Went Down

(*This statement was dictated by Mr. Bride to a reporter for THE NEW YORK TIMES, who visited him with Mr. Marconi in the wireless cabin of the Carpathia a few minutes after the steamship touched her pier. It is reprinted here from THE TIMES of April* 19 *at the request of many readers.*) *It is the most graphic and most important story published during the tense days that followed the disaster.*

*By HAROLD BRIDE, Surviving Wireless Operator of the Titanic.*

In the first place, the public should not blame anybody because more wireless messages about the disaster to the *Titanic* did not reach shore from the *Carpathia*. I positively refused to send press dispatches because the bulk of personal messages with touching words of grief was so large. The wireless operators aboard the *Chester* got all they asked for. And they were wretched operators.

They knew American Morse, but not Continental Morse sufficiently to be worth while. They taxed our endurance to the limit.

I had to cut them out at last, they were so insufferably slow, and go ahead with our messages of grief to relatives. We sent 119 personal messages to-day, and 50 yesterday.

When I was dragged aboard the *Carpathia* I went to the hospital at first. I stayed there for ten hours. Then somebody brought word that the *Carpathia*'s wireless operator was "getting queer" from the work.

They asked me if I could go up and help. I could not walk. Both my feet were broken or something, I don't know what. I went up on crutches with somebody helping me.

I took the key, and I never left the wireless cabin after that. Our meals were brought to us. We kept the wireless working all the time.

The navy operators were a great nuisance. I advise them all to learn the Continental Morse and learn to speed up in it if they ever expect to be worth their salt. The *Chester*'s man thought he knew it, but he was as slow as Christmas coming.

We worked all the time. Nothing went wrong. Sometimes the *Carpathia* man sent, and sometimes I sent. There was a bed in the wireless cabin. I could sit on it and rest my feet while sending sometimes.

To begin at the beginning, I joined the *Titanic* at Belfast. I was born at Nunhead, England, twenty-two years ago, and joined the Marconi forces last July. I first worked on the *Hoverford*, and then on the *Lusitania*. I joined the *Titanic* at Belfast.

## ASLEEP WHEN CRASH CAME

I didn't have much to do aboard the *Titanic* except to relieve Phillips from midnight until some time in the morning, when he should be through sleeping. On the night of the accident I was not sending, but was asleep. I was due to be up and relieve Phillips earlier than usual. And that reminds me—if it hadn't been for a lucky thing, we never could have sent any call for help.

The lucky thing was that the wireless broke down early enough for us to fix it before the accident. We noticed something wrong on Sunday, and Phillips and I worked seven hours to find it. We found a " secretary" burned out, at last, and repaired it just a few hours before the iceberg was struck.

Phillips said to me as he took the night shift, " You turn in, boy, and get some sleep, and go up as soon as you can and give me a chance. I'm all done for with this work of making repairs."

There were three rooms in the wireless cabin. One was a sleeping room, one a dynamo room, and one an operating room. I took off my clothes and went to sleep in bed. Then I was conscious of waking up and hearing Phillips sending to Cape Race. I read what he was sending. It was traffic matter.

I remembered how tired he was, and I got out of bed without my clothes on to relieve him. I didn't even feel the shock. I hardly knew it had happened after the Captain had come to us. There was no jolt whatever.

I was standing by Phillips telling him to go to bed when the Captain put his head in the cabin.

"We've struck an iceberg," the Captain said, "and I'm having an inspection made to tell what it has done for us. You better get ready to send out a call for assistance. But don't send it until I tell you."

The Captain went away and in ten minutes, I should estimate the time, he came back. We could hear a terrible confusion outside, but there was not the least thing to indicate that there was any trouble. The wireless was working perfectly.

"Send the call for assistance," ordered the Captain, barely putting his head in the door.

"What call should I send?" Phillips asked.

"The regulation international call for help. Just that."

Then the Captain was gone. Phillips began to send "C. Q. D." He flashed away at it and we joked while he did so. All of us made light of the disaster.

## JOKED AT DISTRESS CALL

We joked that way while he flashed signals for about five minutes. Then the Captain came back.

"What are you sending?" he asked.

"C. Q. D.," Phillips replied.

The humor of the situation appealed to me. I cut in with a little remark that made us all laugh, including the Captain.

"Send 'S. O. S.,'" I said. "It's the new call, and it may be your last chance to send it."

Phillips with a laugh changed the signal to "S. O. S." The Captain told us we had been struck amidships, or just back of amidships. It was ten minutes, Phillips told me, after he had noticed the iceberg that the slight jolt that was the collision's only signal to us occurred. We thought we were a good distance away.

We said lots of funny things to each other in the next few minutes. We picked up first the steamship *Frankfurd*. We gave her our position and said we had struck an iceberg and needed assistance. The *Frankfurd* operator went away to tell his Captain.

He came back, and we told him we were sinking by the head. By that time we could observe a distinct list forward.

The *Carpathia* answered our signal. We told her our position and said we were sinking by the head. The operator went to tell the Captain, and in five minutes returned and told us that the Captain of the *Carpathia* was putting about and heading for us.

## GREAT SCRAMBLE ON DECK

Our Captain had left us at this time and Phillips told me to run and tell him what the *Carpathia* had answered. I did so, and I went through an awful mass of people to his cabin. The decks were full of scrambling men and women. I saw no fighting, but I heard tell of it.

I came back and heard Phillips giving the *Carpathia* fuller directions. Phillips told me to put on my clothes. Until that moment I forgot that I was not dressed.

I went to my cabin and dressed. I brought an overcoat to Phillips. It was very cold. I slipped the overcoat upon him while he worked.

Every few minutes Phillips would send me to the Captain with little messages. They were merely telling how the *Carpathia* was coming our way and gave her speed.

I noticed as I came back from one trip that they were putting off women and children in lifeboats. I noticed that the list forward was increasing.

Phillips told me the wireless was growing weaker. The Captain came and told us our engine rooms were taking water and that the dynamos might not last much longer. We sent that word to the *Carpathia*.

I went out on deck and looked around. The water was pretty close up to the boat deck. There was a great scramble aft, and how poor Phillips worked through it I don't know.

He was a brave man. I learned to love him that night, and I suddenly felt for him a great reverence to see him standing there sticking to his work while everybody else was raging about. I will never live to forget the work of Phillips for the last awful fifteen minutes.

I thought it was about time to look about and see if there was anything detached that would float. I remembered that every member of the crew had a special lifebelt and ought to know where it was. I remembered mine under my bunk. I went and got it. Then I thought how cold the water was.

I remembered I had some boots, and I put those on, and an extra jacket and I put that on. I saw Phillips standing out there still sending away, giving the *Carpathia* details of just how we were doing.

We picked up the *Olympic* and told her we were sinking by the head and were about all down. As Phillips was sending the message I strapped his lifebelt to his back. I had already put on his overcoat.

I wondered if I could get him into his boots. He suggested with a sort of laugh that I look out and see if all the people were off in the boats, or if any boats were left, or how things were.

I saw a collapsible boat near a funnel and went over to it. Twelve men were trying to boost it down to the boat deck. They were having an awful time. It was the last boat left. I looked at it longingly a few minutes. Then I gave them a hand, and over she went. They all started to scramble in on the boat deck, and I walked back to Phillips. I said the last raft had gone.

Then came the Captain's voice: "Men you have done your full duty.

You can do no more. Abandon your cabin. Now it's every man for himself. You look out for yourselves. I release you. That's the way of it at this kind of a time. Every man for himself."

I looked out. The boat deck was awash. Phillips clung on sending and sending. He clung on for about ten minutes, or maybe fifteen minutes, after the Captain had released him. The water was then coming into our cabin.

While he worked something happened I hate to tell about. I was back in my room getting Phillip's money for him, and as I looked out the door I saw a stoker, or somebody from below decks, leaning over Phillips from behind. He was too busy to notice what the man was doing. The man was slipping the lifebelt off Phillips's back.

He was a big man, too. As you can see, I am very small. I don't know what it was I got hold of. I remembered in a flash the way Phillips had clung on—how I had to fix that lifebelt in place because he was too busy to do it.

I knew that man from below decks had his own lifebelt and should have known where to get it.

I suddenly felt a passion not to let that man die a decent sailors' death. I wished he might have stretched rope or walked a plank. I did my duty. I hope I finished him. I don't know. We left him on the cabin floor of the wireless room, and he was not moving.

## BAND PLAYS IN RAG-TIME

From aft came the tunes of the band. It was a rag-time tune, I don't know what. Then there was "Autumn." Phillips ran aft, and that was the last I ever saw of him alive.

I went to the place I had seen the collapsible boat on the boat deck, and to my surprise I saw the boat and the men still trying to push it off. I guess there wasn't a sailor in the crowd. They couldn't do it. I went up to them and was just lending a hand when a large wave came awash of the deck.

The big wave carried the boat off. I had hold of an oarlock, and I went off with it. The next I knew I was in the boat.

But that was not all. I was in the boat, and the boat was upside down, and I was under it. And I remember realizing that I was wet through, and that whatever happened I must not breathe, for I was under water.

I know I had to fight for it, and I did. How I got out from under the boat I do not know, but I felt a breath of air at last.

There were men all around me—hundreds of them. The sea was dotted with them, all depending on their lifebelts. I felt I simply had to get away from the ship. She was a beautiful sight then.

Smoke and sparks were rushing put of her funnel. There must have been an explosion, but we had heard none. We only saw the big stream of sparks. The ship was gradually turning on her nose—just like a duck does that goes down for a dive. I had only one thing on my mind—to get away from the suction. The band was still playing. I guess all of the band went down.

They were playing "Autumn" then. I swam with all my might. I suppose I was 150 feet away when the *Titanic* on her nose, with her afterquarter sticking straight up in the air, began to settle—slowly.

## PULLED INTO A BOAT

When at last the waves washed over her rudder there wasn't the least bit of suction I could feel. She must have kept going just so slowly as she had been.

I forgot to mention that, besides the *Olympic* and *Carpathia*, we spoke some German boat, I don't know which, and told them how we were. We also spoke to the *Baltic*. I remembered those things as I began to figure what ships would be coming towards us.

I felt, after a little while, like sinking. I was very cold. I saw a boat of some kind near me and put all my strength into an effort to swim to it. It was hard work. I was all done when a hand reached out from the boat and pulled me aboard. It was our same collapsible. The same crowd was on it.

There was just room for me to roll on the edge. I lay there, not caring what happened. Somebody sat on my legs. They were wedged in between slats and were being wrenched. I had not the heart left to ask the man to move. It was a terrible sight all around—men swimming and sinking.

I lay where I was, letting the man wrench my feet out of shape. Others came near. Nobody gave them a hand. The bottom-up boat already had more men than it would hold and it was sinking.

At first the larger waves splashed over my clothing. Then they began to splash over my head, and I had to breathe when I could.

As we floated around on our capsized boat, and I kept straining my eyes for a ship's lights, somebody said, "Don't the rest of you think we ought to pray?" The man who made the suggestion asked what the religion of the others was. Each man called out his religion. One was a Catholic, one a Methodist, one a Presbyterian.

It was decided the most appropriate prayer for all was the Lord's Prayer. We spoke it over in chorus with the man who first suggested that we pray as the leader.

Some splendid people saved us. They had a right-side-up boat, and it was full to its capacity. Yet they came to us and loaded us all into it. I saw some lights off in the distance and knew a steamship was coming to our aid.

I didn't care what happened. I just lay and gasped when I could and felt the pain in my feet. At last the *Carpathia* was alongside and the people were being taken up a rope ladder. Our boat drew near and one by one the men were taken off of it.

## ONE DEAD ON THE RAFT

One man was dead. I passed him and went to the ladder, although my feet pained terribly. The dead man was Phillips. He had died on the raft from exposure and cold, I guess. He had been all in from work before the wreck came. He stood his ground until the crisis had passed, and then he had collapsed, I guess.

But I hardly thought that then. I didn't think much of anything. I tried the rope ladder. My feet pained terribly, but I got to the top and felt hands reaching out to me. The next I knew a woman was leaning over me in a cabin, and I felt her hand waving back my hair and rubbing my face.

I felt somebody at my feet and felt the warmth of a jolt of liquor. Somebody got me under the arms. Then I was hustled down below to the hospital. That was early in the day, I guess. I lay in the hospital until near night, and they told me the *Carpathia*'s wireless man was getting "queer," and would I help.

After that I never was out of the wireless room, so I don't know what happened among the passengers. I saw nothing of Mrs. Astor or any of them. I just worked wireless. The splutter never died down. I knew it soothed the hurt and felt like a tie to the world of friends and home.

How could I, then, take news queries? Sometimes I let a newspaper ask a question and get a long string of stuff asking for full particulars about everything. Whenever I started to take such a message I thought of the poor people waiting for their messages to go—hoping for answers to them.

I shut off the inquirers, and sent my personal messages. And I feel I did the white thing.

If the *Chester* had had a decent operator I could have worked with him longer, but he got terribly on my nerves with his insufferable incompetence. I was still sending my personal messages when Mr. Marconi and *The Times* reporter arrived to ask that I prepare this statement.

There were, maybe, 100 left. I would like to send them all, because I could rest easier if I knew all those messages had gone to the friends waiting for them. But an ambulance man is waiting with a stretcher, and I guess I have got to go with him. I hope my legs get better soon.

The way the band kept playing was a noble thing. I heard it first while still we were working wireless, when there was a ragtime tune for us, and the last I saw of the band, when I was floating out in the sea with my lifebelt on, it was still on deck playing "Autumn." How they ever did it I cannot imagine.

That and the way Phillips kept sending after the Captain told him his life was his own, and to look out for himself, are two things that stand out in my mind over all the rest.

A CATALOG OF SELECTED
## DOVER BOOKS
IN ALL FIELDS OF INTEREST

# A CATALOG OF SELECTED DOVER
# BOOKS IN ALL FIELDS OF INTEREST

CONCERNING THE SPIRITUAL IN ART, Wassily Kandinsky. Pioneering work by father of abstract art. Thoughts on color theory, nature of art. Analysis of earlier masters. 12 illustrations. 80pp. of text. 5⅜ x 8½.                           23411-8 Pa. $3.95

ANIMALS: 1,419 Copyright-Free Illustrations of Mammals, Birds, Fish, Insects, etc., Jim Harter (ed.). Clear wood engravings present, in extremely lifelike poses, over 1,000 species of animals. One of the most extensive pictorial sourcebooks of its kind. Captions. Index. 284pp. 9 x 12.                           23766-4 Pa. $12.95

CELTIC ART: The Methods of Construction, George Bain. Simple geometric techniques for making Celtic interlacements, spirals, Kells-type initials, animals, humans, etc. Over 500 illustrations. 160pp. 9 x 12. (USO)                           22923-8 Pa. $9.95

AN ATLAS OF ANATOMY FOR ARTISTS, Fritz Schider. Most thorough reference work on art anatomy in the world. Hundreds of illustrations, including selections from works by Vesalius, Leonardo, Goya, Ingres, Michelangelo, others. 593 illustrations. 192pp. 7⅛ x 10¼.                           20241-0 Pa. $9 95

CELTIC HAND STROKE-BY-STROKE (Irish Half-Uncial from "The Book of Kells"): An Arthur Baker Calligraphy Manual, Arthur Baker. Complete guide to creating each letter of the alphabet in distinctive Celtic manner. Covers hand position, strokes, pens, inks, paper, more. Illustrated. 48pp. 8¼ x 11.                           24336-2 Pa. $3.95

EASY ORIGAMI, John Montroll. Charming collection of 32 projects (hat, cup, pelican, piano, swan, many more) specially designed for the novice origami hobbyist. Clearly illustrated easy-to-follow instructions insure that even beginning papercrafters will achieve successful results. 48pp. 8¼ x 11.                           27298-2 Pa. $2.95

THE COMPLETE BOOK OF BIRDHOUSE CONSTRUCTION FOR WOOD-WORKERS, Scott D. Campbell. Detailed instructions, illustrations, tables. Also data on bird habitat and instinct patterns. Bibliography. 3 tables. 63 illustrations in 15 figures. 48pp. 5¼ x 8½.                           24407-5 Pa. $2.50

BLOOMINGDALE'S ILLUSTRATED 1886 CATALOG: Fashions, Dry Goods and Housewares, Bloomingdale Brothers. Famed merchants' extremely rare catalog depicting about 1,700 products: clothing, housewares, firearms, dry goods, jewelry, more. Invaluable for dating, identifying vintage items. Also, copyright-free graphics for artists, designers. Co-published with Henry Ford Museum & Greenfield Village. 160pp. 8¼ x 11.                           25780-0 Pa. $9.95

HISTORIC COSTUME IN PICTURES, Braun & Schneider. Over 1,450 costumed figures in clearly detailed engravings–from dawn of civilization to end of 19th century. Captions. Many folk costumes. 256pp. 8⅜ x 11¾.                           23150-X Pa. $12.95

STICKLEY CRAFTSMAN FURNITURE CATALOGS, Gustav Stickley and L. & J. G. Stickley. Beautiful, functional furniture in two authentic catalogs from 1910. 594 illustrations, including 277 photos, show settles, rockers, armchairs, reclining chairs, bookcases, desks, tables. 183pp. 6½ x 9¼.                    23838-5 Pa. $9.95

AMERICAN LOCOMOTIVES IN HISTORIC PHOTOGRAPHS: 1858 to 1949, Ron Ziel (ed.). A rare collection of 126 meticulously detailed official photographs, called "builder portraits," of American locomotives that majestically chronicle the rise of steam locomotive power in America. Introduction. Detailed captions. xi + 129pp. 9 x 12.                    27393-8 Pa. $12.95

AMERICA'S LIGHTHOUSES: An Illustrated History, Francis Ross Holland, Jr. Delightfully written, profusely illustrated fact-filled survey of over 200 American lighthouses since 1716. History, anecdotes, technological advances, more. 240pp. 8 x 10¾.
                    25576-X Pa. $12.95

TOWARDS A NEW ARCHITECTURE, Le Corbusier. Pioneering manifesto by founder of "International School." Technical and aesthetic theories, views of industry, economics, relation of form to function, "mass-production split" and much more. Profusely illustrated. 320pp. 6⅛ x 9¼. (USO)                    25023-7 Pa. $9.95

HOW THE OTHER HALF LIVES, Jacob Riis. Famous journalistic record, exposing poverty and degradation of New York slums around 1900, by major social reformer. 100 striking and influential photographs. 233pp. 10 x 7⅞.
                    22012-5 Pa. $10.95

FRUIT KEY AND TWIG KEY TO TREES AND SHRUBS, William M. Harlow. One of the handiest and most widely used identification aids. Fruit key covers 120 deciduous and evergreen species; twig key 160 deciduous species. Easily used. Over 300 photographs. 126pp. 5⅜ x 8½.                    20511-8 Pa. $3.95

COMMON BIRD SONGS, Dr. Donald J. Borror. Songs of 60 most common U.S. birds: robins, sparrows, cardinals, bluejays, finches, more—arranged in order of increasing complexity. Up to 9 variations of songs of each species.
                    Cassette and manual 99911-4 $8.95

ORCHIDS AS HOUSE PLANTS, Rebecca Tyson Northen. Grow cattleyas and many other kinds of orchids—in a window, in a case, or under artificial light. 63 illustrations. 148pp. 5⅜ x 8½.                    23261-1 Pa. $4.95

MONSTER MAZES, Dave Phillips. Masterful mazes at four levels of difficulty. Avoid deadly perils and evil creatures to find magical treasures. Solutions for all 32 exciting illustrated puzzles. 48pp. 8¼ x 11.                    26005-4 Pa. $2.95

MOZART'S DON GIOVANNI (DOVER OPERA LIBRETTO SERIES), Wolfgang Amadeus Mozart. Introduced and translated by Ellen H. Bleiler. Standard Italian libretto, with complete English translation. Convenient and thoroughly portable—an ideal companion for reading along with a recording or the performance itself. Introduction. List of characters. Plot summary. 121pp. 5¼ x 8½.
                    24944-1 Pa. $2.95

TECHNICAL MANUAL AND DICTIONARY OF CLASSICAL BALLET, Gail Grant. Defines, explains, comments on steps, movements, poses and concepts. 15-page pictorial section. Basic book for student, viewer. 127pp. 5⅜ x 8½.
                    21843-0 Pa. $4.95

BRASS INSTRUMENTS: Their History and Development, Anthony Baines. Authoritative, updated survey of the evolution of trumpets, trombones, bugles, cornets, French horns, tubas and other brass wind instruments. Over 140 illustrations and 48 music examples. Corrected and updated by author. New preface. Bibliography. 320pp. 5⅜ x 8½. 27574-4 Pa. $9.95

HOLLYWOOD GLAMOR PORTRAITS, John Kobal (ed.). 145 photos from 1926-49. Harlow, Gable, Bogart, Bacall; 94 stars in all. Full background on photographers, technical aspects. 160pp. 8⅜ x 11¼. 23352-9 Pa. $11.95

MAX AND MORITZ, Wilhelm Busch. Great humor classic in both German and English. Also 10 other works: "Cat and Mouse," "Plisch and Plumm," etc. 216pp. 5⅜ x 8½. 20181-3 Pa. $6.95

THE RAVEN AND OTHER FAVORITE POEMS, Edgar Allan Poe. Over 40 of the author's most memorable poems: "The Bells," "Ulalume," "Israfel," "To Helen," "The Conqueror Worm," "Eldorado," "Annabel Lee," many more. Alphabetic lists of titles and first lines. 64pp. 5³⁄₁₆ x 8¼. 26685-0 Pa. $1.00

PERSONAL MEMOIRS OF U. S. GRANT, Ulysses Simpson Grant. Intelligent, deeply moving firsthand account of Civil War campaigns, considered by many the finest military memoirs ever written. Includes letters, historic photographs, maps and more. 528pp. 6⅛ x 9¼. 28587-1 Pa. $11.95

AMULETS AND SUPERSTITIONS, E. A. Wallis Budge. Comprehensive discourse on origin, powers of amulets in many ancient cultures: Arab, Persian Babylonian, Assyrian, Egyptian, Gnostic, Hebrew, Phoenician, Syriac, etc. Covers cross, swastika, crucifix, seals, rings, stones, etc. 584pp. 5⅜ x 8½. 23573-4 Pa. $12.95

RUSSIAN STORIES/PYCCKNE PACCKA3bl: A Dual-Language Book, edited by Gleb Struve. Twelve tales by such masters as Chekhov, Tolstoy, Dostoevsky, Pushkin, others. Excellent word-for-word English translations on facing pages, plus teaching and study aids, Russian/English vocabulary, biographical/critical introductions, more. 416pp. 5⅜ x 8½. 26244-8 Pa. $8.95

PHILADELPHIA THEN AND NOW: 60 Sites Photographed in the Past and Present, Kenneth Finkel and Susan Oyama. Rare photographs of City Hall, Logan Square, Independence Hall, Betsy Ross House, other landmarks juxtaposed with contemporary views. Captures changing face of historic city. Introduction. Captions. 128pp. 8¼ x 11. 25790-8 Pa. $9.95

AIA ARCHITECTURAL GUIDE TO NASSAU AND SUFFOLK COUNTIES, LONG ISLAND, The American Institute of Architects, Long Island Chapter, and the Society for the Preservation of Long Island Antiquities. Comprehensive, well-researched and generously illustrated volume brings to life over three centuries of Long Island's great architectural heritage. More than 240 photographs with authoritative, extensively detailed captions. 176pp. 8¼ x 11. 26946-9 Pa. $14.95

NORTH AMERICAN INDIAN LIFE: Customs and Traditions of 23 Tribes, Elsie Clews Parsons (ed.). 27 fictionalized essays by noted anthropologists examine religion, customs, government, additional facets of life among the Winnebago, Crow, Zuni, Eskimo, other tribes. 480pp. 6⅛ x 9¼. 27377-6 Pa. $10.95

FRANK LLOYD WRIGHT'S HOLLYHOCK HOUSE, Donald Hoffmann. Lavishly illustrated, carefully documented study of one of Wright's most controversial residential designs. Over 120 photographs, floor plans, elevations, etc. Detailed perceptive text by noted Wright scholar. Index. 128pp. 9¼ x 10¾. 27133-1 Pa. $11.95

THE MALE AND FEMALE FIGURE IN MOTION: 60 Classic Photographic Sequences, Eadweard Muybridge. 60 true-action photographs of men and women walking, running, climbing, bending, turning, etc., reproduced from rare 19th-century masterpiece. vi + 121pp. 9 x 12. 24745-7 Pa. $10.95

1001 QUESTIONS ANSWERED ABOUT THE SEASHORE, N. J. Berrill and Jacquelyn Berrill. Queries answered about dolphins, sea snails, sponges, starfish, fishes, shore birds, many others. Covers appearance, breeding, growth, feeding, much more. 305pp. 5¼ x 8¼. 23366-9 Pa. $8.95

GUIDE TO OWL WATCHING IN NORTH AMERICA, Donald S. Heintzelman. Superb guide offers complete data and descriptions of 19 species: barn owl, screech owl, snowy owl, many more. Expert coverage of owl-watching equipment, conservation, migrations and invasions, etc. Guide to observing sites. 84 illustrations. xiii + 193pp. 5⅜ x 8½. 27344-X Pa. $8.95

MEDICINAL AND OTHER USES OF NORTH AMERICAN PLANTS: A Historical Survey with Special Reference to the Eastern Indian Tribes, Charlotte Erichsen-Brown. Chronological historical citations document 500 years of usage of plants, trees, shrubs native to eastern Canada, northeastern U.S. Also complete identifying information. 343 illustrations. 544pp. 6½ x 9¼. 25951-X Pa. $12.95

STORYBOOK MAZES, Dave Phillips. 23 stories and mazes on two-page spreads: Wizard of Oz, Treasure Island, Robin Hood, etc. Solutions. 64pp. 8¼ x 11. 23628-5 Pa. $2.95

NEGRO FOLK MUSIC, U.S.A., Harold Courlander. Noted folklorist's scholarly yet readable analysis of rich and varied musical tradition. Includes authentic versions of over 40 folk songs. Valuable bibliography and discography. xi + 324pp. 5⅜ x 8½. 27350-4 Pa. $7.95

MOVIE-STAR PORTRAITS OF THE FORTIES, John Kobal (ed.). 163 glamor, studio photos of 106 stars of the 1940s: Rita Hayworth, Ava Gardner, Marlon Brando, Clark Gable, many more. 176pp. 8⅜ x 11¼. 23546-7 Pa. $12.95

BENCHLEY LOST AND FOUND, Robert Benchley. Finest humor from early 30s, about pet peeves, child psychologists, post office and others. Mostly unavailable elsewhere. 73 illustrations by Peter Arno and others. 183pp. 5⅜ x 8½. 22410-4 Pa. $6.95

YEKL and THE IMPORTED BRIDEGROOM AND OTHER STORIES OF YIDDISH NEW YORK, Abraham Cahan. Film Hester Street based on Yekl (1896). Novel, other stories among first about Jewish immigrants on N.Y.'s East Side. 240pp. 5⅜ x 8½. 22427-9 Pa. $6.95

SELECTED POEMS, Walt Whitman. Generous sampling from *Leaves of Grass*. Twenty-four poems include "I Hear America Singing," "Song of the Open Road," "I Sing the Body Electric," "When Lilacs Last in the Dooryard Bloom'd," "O Captain! My Captain!"—all reprinted from an authoritative edition. Lists of titles and first lines. 128pp. 5³⁄₁₆ x 8¼. 26878-0 Pa. $1.00

THE BEST TALES OF HOFFMANN, E. T. A. Hoffmann. 10 of Hoffmann's most important stories: "Nutcracker and the King of Mice," "The Golden Flowerpot," etc. 458pp. 5⅜ x 8½. 21793-0 Pa. $9.95

FROM FETISH TO GOD IN ANCIENT EGYPT, E. A. Wallis Budge. Rich detailed survey of Egyptian conception of "God" and gods, magic, cult of animals, Osiris, more. Also, superb English translations of hymns and legends. 240 illustrations. 545pp. 5⅜ x 8½. 25803-3 Pa. $11.95

FRENCH STORIES/CONTES FRANÇAIS: A Dual-Language Book, Wallace Fowlie. Ten stories by French masters, Voltaire to Camus: "Micromegas" by Voltaire; "The Atheist's Mass" by Balzac; "Minuet" by de Maupassant; "The Guest" by Camus, six more. Excellent English translations on facing pages. Also French-English vocabulary list, exercises, more. 352pp. 5⅜ x 8½. 26443-2 Pa. $8.95

CHICAGO AT THE TURN OF THE CENTURY IN PHOTOGRAPHS: 122 Historic Views from the Collections of the Chicago Historical Society, Larry A. Viskochil. Rare large-format prints offer detailed views of City Hall, State Street, the Loop, Hull House, Union Station, many other landmarks, circa 1904-1913. Introduction. Captions. Maps. 144pp. 9⅜ x 12¼. 24656-6 Pa. $12.95

OLD BROOKLYN IN EARLY PHOTOGRAPHS, 1865-1929, William Lee Younger. Luna Park, Gravesend race track, construction of Grand Army Plaza, moving of Hotel Brighton, etc. 157 previously unpublished photographs. 165pp. 8⅞ x 11¾. 23587-4 Pa. $13.95

THE MYTHS OF THE NORTH AMERICAN INDIANS, Lewis Spence. Rich anthology of the myths and legends of the Algonquins, Iroquois, Pawnees and Sioux, prefaced by an extensive historical and ethnological commentary. 36 illustrations. 480pp. 5⅜ x 8½. 25967-6 Pa. $8.95

AN ENCYCLOPEDIA OF BATTLES: Accounts of Over 1,560 Battles from 1479 B.C. to the Present, David Eggenberger. Essential details of every major battle in recorded history from the first battle of Megiddo in 1479 B.C. to Grenada in 1984. List of Battle Maps. New Appendix covering the years 1967-1984. Index. 99 illustrations. 544pp. 6½ x 9¼. 24913-1 Pa. $14.95

SAILING ALONE AROUND THE WORLD, Captain Joshua Slocum. First man to sail around the world, alone, in small boat. One of great feats of seamanship told in delightful manner. 67 illustrations. 294pp. 5⅜ x 8½. 20326-3 Pa. $5.95

ANARCHISM AND OTHER ESSAYS, Emma Goldman. Powerful, penetrating, prophetic essays on direct action, role of minorities, prison reform, puritan hypocrisy, violence, etc. 271pp. 5⅜ x 8½. 22484-8 Pa. $6.95

MYTHS OF THE HINDUS AND BUDDHISTS, Ananda K. Coomaraswamy and Sister Nivedita. Great stories of the epics; deeds of Krishna, Shiva, taken from puranas, Vedas, folk tales; etc. 32 illustrations. 400pp. 5⅜ x 8½. 21759-0 Pa. $10.95

BEYOND PSYCHOLOGY, Otto Rank. Fear of death, desire of immortality, nature of sexuality, social organization, creativity, according to Rankian system. 291pp. 5⅜ x 8½. 20485-5 Pa. $8.95

A THEOLOGICO-POLITICAL TREATISE, Benedict Spinoza. Also contains unfinished Political Treatise. Great classic on religious liberty, theory of government on common consent. R. Elwes translation. Total of 421pp. 5⅜ x 8½. 20249-6 Pa. $9.95

MY BONDAGE AND MY FREEDOM, Frederick Douglass. Born a slave, Douglass became outspoken force in antislavery movement. The best of Douglass' autobiographies. Graphic description of slave life. 464pp. 5⅜ x 8½. 22457-0 Pa. $8.95

FOLLOWING THE EQUATOR: A Journey Around the World, Mark Twain. Fascinating humorous account of 1897 voyage to Hawaii, Australia, India, New Zealand, etc. Ironic, bemused reports on peoples, customs, climate, flora and fauna, politics, much more. 197 illustrations. 720pp. 5⅜ x 8½. 26113-1 Pa. $15.95

THE PEOPLE CALLED SHAKERS, Edward D. Andrews. Definitive study of Shakers: origins, beliefs, practices, dances, social organization, furniture and crafts, etc. 33 illustrations. 351pp. 5⅜ x 8½. 21081-2 Pa. $8.95

THE MYTHS OF GREECE AND ROME, H. A. Guerber. A classic of mythology, generously illustrated, long prized for its simple, graphic, accurate retelling of the principal myths of Greece and Rome, and for its commentary on their origins and significance. With 64 illustrations by Michelangelo, Raphael, Titian, Rubens, Canova, Bernini and others. 480pp. 5⅜ x 8½. 27584-1 Pa. $9.95

PSYCHOLOGY OF MUSIC, Carl E. Seashore. Classic work discusses music as a medium from psychological viewpoint. Clear treatment of physical acoustics, auditory apparatus, sound perception, development of musical skills, nature of musical feeling, host of other topics. 88 figures. 408pp. 5⅜ x 8½. 21851-1 Pa. $10.95

THE PHILOSOPHY OF HISTORY, Georg W. Hegel. Great classic of Western thought develops concept that history is not chance but rational process, the evolution of freedom. 457pp. 5⅜ x 8½. 20112-0 Pa. $9.95

THE BOOK OF TEA, Kakuzo Okakura. Minor classic of the Orient: entertaining, charming explanation, interpretation of traditional Japanese culture in terms of tea ceremony. 94pp. 5⅜ x 8½. 20070-1 Pa. $3.95

LIFE IN ANCIENT EGYPT, Adolf Erman. Fullest, most thorough, detailed older account with much not in more recent books, domestic life, religion, magic, medicine, commerce, much more. Many illustrations reproduce tomb paintings, carvings, hieroglyphs, etc. 597pp. 5⅜ x 8½. 22632-8 Pa. $11.95

SUNDIALS, Their Theory and Construction, Albert Waugh. Far and away the best, most thorough coverage of ideas, mathematics concerned, types, construction, adjusting anywhere. Simple, nontechnical treatment allows even children to build several of these dials. Over 100 illustrations. 230pp. 5⅜ x 8½. 22947-5 Pa. $7.95

DYNAMICS OF FLUIDS IN POROUS MEDIA, Jacob Bear. For advanced students of ground water hydrology, soil mechanics and physics, drainage and irrigation engineering, and more. 335 illustrations. Exercises, with answers. 784pp. 6⅛ x 9¼. 65675-6 Pa. $19.95

SONGS OF EXPERIENCE: Facsimile Reproduction with 26 Plates in Full Color, William Blake. 26 full-color plates from a rare 1826 edition. Includes "The Tyger," "London," "Holy Thursday," and other poems. Printed text of poems. 48pp. 5¼ x 7. 24636-1 Pa. $4.95

OLD-TIME VIGNETTES IN FULL COLOR, Carol Belanger Grafton (ed.). Over 390 charming, often sentimental illustrations, selected from archives of Victorian graphics—pretty women posing, children playing, food, flowers, kittens and puppies, smiling cherubs, birds and butterflies, much more. All copyright-free. 48pp. 9¼ x 12¼. 27269-9 Pa. $5.95

PERSPECTIVE FOR ARTISTS, Rex Vicat Cole. Depth, perspective of sky and sea, shadows, much more, not usually covered. 391 diagrams, 81 reproductions of drawings and paintings. 279pp. 5⅜ x 8½. 22487-2 Pa. $6.95

DRAWING THE LIVING FIGURE, Joseph Sheppard. Innovative approach to artistic anatomy focuses on specifics of surface anatomy, rather than muscles and bones. Over 170 drawings of live models in front, back and side views, and in widely varying poses. Accompanying diagrams. 177 illustrations. Introduction. Index. 144pp. 8⅜ x11¼. 26723-7 Pa. $8.95

GOTHIC AND OLD ENGLISH ALPHABETS: 100 Complete Fonts, Dan X. Solo. Add power, elegance to posters, signs, other graphics with 100 stunning copyright-free alphabets: Blackstone, Dolbey, Germania, 97 more—including many lower-case, numerals, punctuation marks. 104pp. 8⅛ x 11. 24695-7 Pa. $8.95

HOW TO DO BEADWORK, Mary White. Fundamental book on craft from simple projects to five-bead chains and woven works. 106 illustrations. 142pp. 5⅜ x 8. 20697-1 Pa. $4.95

THE BOOK OF WOOD CARVING, Charles Marshall Sayers. Finest book for beginners discusses fundamentals and offers 34 designs. "Absolutely first rate . . . well thought out and well executed."—E. J. Tangerman. 118pp. 7¾ x 10⅝. 23654-4 Pa. $6.95

ILLUSTRATED CATALOG OF CIVIL WAR MILITARY GOODS: Union Army Weapons, Insignia, Uniform Accessories, and Other Equipment, Schuyler, Hartley, and Graham. Rare, profusely illustrated 1846 catalog includes Union Army uniform and dress regulations, arms and ammunition, coats, insignia, flags, swords, rifles, etc. 226 illustrations. 160pp. 9 x 12. 24939-5 Pa. $10.95

WOMEN'S FASHIONS OF THE EARLY 1900s: An Unabridged Republication of "New York Fashions, 1909," National Cloak & Suit Co. Rare catalog of mail-order fashions documents women's and children's clothing styles shortly after the turn of the century. Captions offer full descriptions, prices. Invaluable resource for fashion, costume historians. Approximately 725 illustrations. 128pp. 8⅜ x 11¼. 27276-1 Pa. $11.95

THE 1912 AND 1915 GUSTAV STICKLEY FURNITURE CATALOGS, Gustav Stickley. With over 200 detailed illustrations and descriptions, these two catalogs are essential reading and reference materials and identification guides for Stickley furniture. Captions cite materials, dimensions and prices. 112pp. 6½ x 9¼. 26676-1 Pa. $9.95

EARLY AMERICAN LOCOMOTIVES, John H. White, Jr. Finest locomotive engravings from early 19th century: historical (1804–74), main-line (after 1870), special, foreign, etc. 147 plates. 142pp. 11⅜ x 8¼. 22772-3 Pa. $10.95

THE TALL SHIPS OF TODAY IN PHOTOGRAPHS, Frank O. Braynard. Lavishly illustrated tribute to nearly 100 majestic contemporary sailing vessels: Amerigo Vespucci, Clearwater, Constitution, Eagle, Mayflower, Sea Cloud, Victory, many more. Authoritative captions provide statistics, background on each ship. 190 black-and-white photographs and illustrations. Introduction. 128pp. 8⅞ x 11¾. 27163-3 Pa. $13.95

EARLY NINETEENTH-CENTURY CRAFTS AND TRADES, Peter Stockham (ed.). Extremely rare 1807 volume describes to youngsters the crafts and trades of the day: brickmaker, weaver, dressmaker, bookbinder, ropemaker, saddler, many more. Quaint prose, charming illustrations for each craft. 20 black-and-white line illustrations. 192pp. 4⅝ x 6. 27293-1 Pa. $4.95

VICTORIAN FASHIONS AND COSTUMES FROM HARPER'S BAZAR, 1867–1898, Stella Blum (ed.). Day costumes, evening wear, sports clothes, shoes, hats, other accessories in over 1,000 detailed engravings. 320pp. 9⅜ x 12¼.
22990-4 Pa. $14.95

GUSTAV STICKLEY, THE CRAFTSMAN, Mary Ann Smith. Superb study surveys broad scope of Stickley's achievement, especially in architecture. Design philosophy, rise and fall of the Craftsman empire, descriptions and floor plans for many Craftsman houses, more. 86 black-and-white halftones. 31 line illustrations. Introduction 208pp. 6½ x 9¼. 27210-9 Pa. $9.95

THE LONG ISLAND RAIL ROAD IN EARLY PHOTOGRAPHS, Ron Ziel. Over 220 rare photos, informative text document origin (1844) and development of rail service on Long Island. Vintage views of early trains, locomotives, stations, passengers, crews, much more. Captions. 8⅞ x 11¾. 26301-0 Pa. $13.95

THE BOOK OF OLD SHIPS: From Egyptian Galleys to Clipper Ships, Henry B. Culver. Superb, authoritative history of sailing vessels, with 80 magnificent line illustrations. Galley, bark, caravel, longship, whaler, many more. Detailed, informative text on each vessel by noted naval historian. Introduction. 256pp. 5⅜ x 8½.
27332-6 Pa. $7.95

TEN BOOKS ON ARCHITECTURE, Vitruvius. The most important book ever written on architecture. Early Roman aesthetics, technology, classical orders, site selection, all other aspects. Morgan translation. 331pp. 5⅜ x 8½. 20645-9 Pa. $8.95

THE HUMAN FIGURE IN MOTION, Eadweard Muybridge. More than 4,500 stopped-action photos, in action series, showing undraped men, women, children jumping, lying down, throwing, sitting, wrestling, carrying, etc. 390pp. 7⅞ x 10⅝.
20204-6 Clothbd. $25.95

TREES OF THE EASTERN AND CENTRAL UNITED STATES AND CANADA, William M. Harlow. Best one-volume guide to 140 trees. Full descriptions, woodlore, range, etc. Over 600 illustrations. Handy size. 288pp. 4½ x 6⅜.
20395-6 Pa. $5.95

SONGS OF WESTERN BIRDS, Dr. Donald J. Borror. Complete song and call repertoire of 60 western species, including flycatchers, juncoes, cactus wrens, many more–includes fully illustrated booklet. Cassette and manual 99913-0 $8.95

GROWING AND USING HERBS AND SPICES, Milo Miloradovich. Versatile handbook provides all the information needed for cultivation and use of all the herbs and spices available in North America. 4 illustrations. Index. Glossary. 236pp. 5⅜ x 8½.
25058-X Pa. $6.95

BIG BOOK OF MAZES AND LABYRINTHS, Walter Shepherd. 50 mazes and labyrinths in all–classical, solid, ripple, and more–in one great volume. Perfect inexpensive puzzler for clever youngsters. Full solutions. 112pp. 8⅛ x 11.
22951-3 Pa. $4.95

PIANO TUNING, J. Cree Fischer. Clearest, best book for beginner, amateur. Simple repairs, raising dropped notes, tuning by easy method of flattened fifths. No previous skills needed. 4 illustrations. 201pp. 5⅜ x 8½. 23267-0 Pa. $6.95

A SOURCE BOOK IN THEATRICAL HISTORY, A. M. Nagler. Contemporary observers on acting, directing, make-up, costuming, stage props, machinery, scene design, from Ancient Greece to Chekhov. 611pp. 5⅜ x 8½. 20515-0 Pa. $12.95

THE COMPLETE NONSENSE OF EDWARD LEAR, Edward Lear. All nonsense limericks, zany alphabets, Owl and Pussycat, songs, nonsense botany, etc., illustrated by Lear. Total of 320pp. 5⅜ x 8½. (USO) 20167-8 Pa. $6.95

VICTORIAN PARLOUR POETRY: An Annotated Anthology, Michael R. Turner. 117 gems by Longfellow, Tennyson, Browning, many lesser-known poets. "The Village Blacksmith," "Curfew Must Not Ring Tonight," "Only a Baby Small," dozens more, often difficult to find elsewhere. Index of poets, titles, first lines. xxiii + 325pp. 5⅝ x 8¼. 27044-0 Pa. $8.95

DUBLINERS, James Joyce. Fifteen stories offer vivid, tightly focused observations of the lives of Dublin's poorer classes. At least one, "The Dead," is considered a masterpiece. Reprinted complete and unabridged from standard edition. 160pp. 5³⁄₁₆ x 8¼. 26870-5 Pa. $1.00

THE HAUNTED MONASTERY and THE CHINESE MAZE MURDERS, Robert van Gulik. Two full novels by van Gulik, set in 7th-century China, continue adventures of Judge Dee and his companions. An evil Taoist monastery, seemingly supernatural events; overgrown topiary maze hides strange crimes. 27 illustrations. 328pp. 5⅜ x 8½. 23502-5 Pa. $8.95

THE BOOK OF THE SACRED MAGIC OF ABRAMELIN THE MAGE, translated by S. MacGregor Mathers. Medieval manuscript of ceremonial magic. Basic document in Aleister Crowley, Golden Dawn groups. 268pp. 5⅜ x 8½. 23211-5 Pa. $8.95

NEW RUSSIAN-ENGLISH AND ENGLISH-RUSSIAN DICTIONARY, M. A. O'Brien. This is a remarkably handy Russian dictionary, containing a surprising amount of information, including over 70,000 entries. 366pp. 4½ x 6⅛. 20208-9 Pa. $9.95

HISTORIC HOMES OF THE AMERICAN PRESIDENTS, Second, Revised Edition, Irvin Haas. A traveler's guide to American Presidential homes, most open to the public, depicting and describing homes occupied by every American President from George Washington to George Bush. With visiting hours, admission charges, travel routes. 175 photographs. Index. 160pp. 8¼ x 11. 26751-2 Pa. $11.95

NEW YORK IN THE FORTIES, Andreas Feininger. 162 brilliant photographs by the well-known photographer, formerly with *Life* magazine. Commuters, shoppers, Times Square at night, much else from city at its peak. Captions by John von Hartz. 181pp. 9¼ x 10¾. 23585-8 Pa. $12.95

INDIAN SIGN LANGUAGE, William Tomkins. Over 525 signs developed by Sioux and other tribes. Written instructions and diagrams. Also 290 pictographs. 111pp. 6⅛ x 9¼. 22029-X Pa. $3.95

ANATOMY: A Complete Guide for Artists, Joseph Sheppard. A master of figure drawing shows artists how to render human anatomy convincingly. Over 460 illustrations. 224pp. 8⅜ x 11¼. 27279-6 Pa. $10.95

MEDIEVAL CALLIGRAPHY: Its History and Technique, Marc Drogin. Spirited history, comprehensive instruction manual covers 13 styles (ca. 4th century thru 15th). Excellent photographs; directions for duplicating medieval techniques with modern tools. 224pp. 8⅜ x 11¼. 26142-5 Pa. $11.95

DRIED FLOWERS: How to Prepare Them, Sarah Whitlock and Martha Rankin. Complete instructions on how to use silica gel, meal and borax, perlite aggregate, sand and borax, glycerine and water to create attractive permanent flower arrangements. 12 illustrations. 32pp. 5⅜ x 8½. 21802-3 Pa. $1.00

EASY-TO-MAKE BIRD FEEDERS FOR WOODWORKERS, Scott D. Campbell. Detailed, simple-to-use guide for designing, constructing, caring for and using feeders. Text, illustrations for 12 classic and contemporary designs. 96pp. 5⅜ x 8½. 25847-5 Pa. $2.95

SCOTTISH WONDER TALES FROM MYTH AND LEGEND, Donald A. Mackenzie. 16 lively tales tell of giants rumbling down mountainsides, of a magic wand that turns stone pillars into warriors, of gods and goddesses, evil hags, powerful forces and more. 240pp. 5⅜ x 8½. 29677-6 Pa. $6.95

THE HISTORY OF UNDERCLOTHES, C. Willett Cunnington and Phyllis Cunnington. Fascinating, well-documented survey covering six centuries of English undergarments, enhanced with over 100 illustrations: 12th-century laced-up bodice, footed long drawers (1795), 19th-century bustles, 19th-century corsets for men, Victorian "bust improvers," much more. 272pp. 5⅜ x 8¼. 27124-2 Pa. $9.95

ARTS AND CRAFTS FURNITURE: The Complete Brooks Catalog of 1912, Brooks Manufacturing Co. Photos and detailed descriptions of more than 150 now very collectible furniture designs from the Arts and Crafts movement depict davenports, settees, buffets, desks, tables, chairs, bedsteads, dressers and more, all built of solid, quarter-sawed oak. Invaluable for students and enthusiasts of antiques, Americana and the decorative arts. 80pp. 6½ x 9¼. 27471-3 Pa. $7.95

HOW WE INVENTED THE AIRPLANE: An Illustrated History, Orville Wright. Fascinating firsthand account covers early experiments, construction of planes and motors, first flights, much more. Introduction and commentary by Fred C. Kelly. 76 photographs. 96pp. 8¼ x 11. 25662-6 Pa. $8.95

THE ARTS OF THE SAILOR: Knotting, Splicing and Ropework, Hervey Garrett Smith. Indispensable shipboard reference covers tools, basic knots and useful hitches; handsewing and canvas work, more. Over 100 illustrations. Delightful reading for sea lovers. 256pp. 5⅜ x 8½. 26440-8 Pa. $7.95

FRANK LLOYD WRIGHT'S FALLINGWATER: The House and Its History, Second, Revised Edition, Donald Hoffmann. A total revision—both in text and illustrations—of the standard document on Fallingwater, the boldest, most personal architectural statement of Wright's mature years, updated with valuable new material from the recently opened Frank Lloyd Wright Archives. "Fascinating"—*The New York Times*. 116 illustrations. 128pp. 9¼ x 10¾. 27430-6 Pa. $11.95

AUTOBIOGRAPHY: The Story of My Experiments with Truth, Mohandas K. Gandhi. Boyhood, legal studies, purification, the growth of the Satyagraha (nonviolent protest) movement. Critical, inspiring work of the man responsible for the freedom of India. 480pp. 5⅜ x 8½. (USO)                    24593-4 Pa. $8.95

CELTIC MYTHS AND LEGENDS, T. W. Rolleston. Masterful retelling of Irish and Welsh stories and tales. Cuchulain, King Arthur, Deirdre, the Grail, many more. First paperback edition. 58 full-page illustrations. 512pp. 5⅜ x 8½.          26507-2 Pa. $9.95

THE PRINCIPLES OF PSYCHOLOGY, William James. Famous long course complete, unabridged. Stream of thought, time perception, memory, experimental methods; great work decades ahead of its time. 94 figures. 1,391pp. 5⅜ x 8½. 2-vol. set.
Vol. I: 20381-6 Pa. $12.95
Vol. II: 20382-4 Pa. $12.95

THE WORLD AS WILL AND REPRESENTATION, Arthur Schopenhauer. Definitive English translation of Schopenhauer's life work, correcting more than 1,000 errors, omissions in earlier translations. Translated by E. F. J. Payne. Total of 1,269pp. 5⅜ x 8½. 2-vol. set.
Vol. 1: 21761-2 Pa. $11.95
Vol. 2: 21762-0 Pa. $11.95

MAGIC AND MYSTERY IN TIBET, Madame Alexandra David-Neel. Experiences among lamas, magicians, sages, sorcerers, Bonpa wizards. A true psychic discovery. 32 illustrations. 321pp. 5⅜ x 8½. (USO)          22682-4 Pa. $8.95

THE EGYPTIAN BOOK OF THE DEAD, E. A. Wallis Budge. Complete reproduction of Ani's papyrus, finest ever found. Full hieroglyphic text, interlinear transliteration, word-for-word translation, smooth translation. 533pp. 6½ x 9¼.
21866-X Pa. $10.95

MATHEMATICS FOR THE NONMATHEMATICIAN, Morris Kline. Detailed, college-level treatment of mathematics in cultural and historical context, with numerous exercises. Recommended Reading Lists. Tables. Numerous figures. 641pp. 5⅜ x 8½.
24823-2 Pa. $11.95

THEORY OF WING SECTIONS: Including a Summary of Airfoil Data, Ira H. Abbott and A. E. von Doenhoff. Concise compilation of subsonic aerodynamic characteristics of NACA wing sections, plus description of theory. 350pp. of tables. 693pp. 5⅜ x 8½.                    60586-8 Pa. $14.95

THE RIME OF THE ANCIENT MARINER, Gustave Doré, S. T. Coleridge. Doré's finest work; 34 plates capture moods, subtleties of poem. Flawless full-size reproductions printed on facing pages with authoritative text of poem. "Beautiful. Simply beautiful."–*Publisher's Weekly.* 77pp. 9¼ x 12.          22305-1 Pa. $6.95

NORTH AMERICAN INDIAN DESIGNS FOR ARTISTS AND CRAFTSPEOPLE, Eva Wilson. Over 360 authentic copyright-free designs adapted from Navajo blankets, Hopi pottery, Sioux buffalo hides, more. Geometrics, symbolic figures, plant and animal motifs, etc. 128pp. 8⅜ x 11. (EUK)          25341-4 Pa. $8.95

SCULPTURE: Principles and Practice, Louis Slobodkin. Step-by-step approach to clay, plaster, metals, stone; classical and modern. 253 drawings, photos. 255pp. 8⅛ x 11.
22960-2 Pa. $10.95

PHOTOGRAPHIC SKETCHBOOK OF THE CIVIL WAR, Alexander Gardner. 100 photos taken on field during the Civil War. Famous shots of Manassas Harper's Ferry, Lincoln, Richmond, slave pens, etc. 244pp. 10⅝ x 8¼.        22731-6 Pa. $9.95

FIVE ACRES AND INDEPENDENCE, Maurice G. Kains. Great back-to-the-land classic explains basics of self-sufficient farming. The one book to get. 95 illustrations. 397pp. 5⅜ x 8½.        20974-1 Pa. $7.95

SONGS OF EASTERN BIRDS, Dr. Donald J. Borror. Songs and calls of 60 species most common to eastern U.S.: warblers, woodpeckers, flycatchers, thrushes, larks, many more in high-quality recording.        Cassette and manual 99912-2 $8.95

A MODERN HERBAL, Margaret Grieve. Much the fullest, most exact, most useful compilation of herbal material. Gigantic alphabetical encyclopedia, from aconite to zedoary, gives botanical information, medical properties, folklore, economic uses, much else. Indispensable to serious reader. 161 illustrations. 888pp. 6½ x 9¼. 2-vol. set. (USO)        Vol. I: 22798-7 Pa. $9.95
        Vol. II: 22799-5 Pa. $9.95

HIDDEN TREASURE MAZE BOOK, Dave Phillips. Solve 34 challenging mazes accompanied by heroic tales of adventure. Evil dragons, people-eating plants, blood-thirsty giants, many more dangerous adversaries lurk at every twist and turn. 34 mazes, stories, solutions. 48pp. 8¼ x 11.        24566-7 Pa. $2.95

LETTERS OF W. A. MOZART, Wolfgang A. Mozart. Remarkable letters show bawdy wit, humor, imagination, musical insights, contemporary musical world; includes some letters from Leopold Mozart. 276pp. 5⅜ x 8½.        22859-2 Pa. $7.95

BASIC PRINCIPLES OF CLASSICAL BALLET, Agrippina Vaganova. Great Russian theoretician, teacher explains methods for teaching classical ballet. 118 illus-trations. 175pp. 5⅜ x 8½.        22036-2 Pa. $5.95

THE JUMPING FROG, Mark Twain. Revenge edition. The original story of The Celebrated Jumping Frog of Calaveras County, a hapless French translation, and Twain's hilarious "retranslation" from the French. 12 illustrations. 66pp. 5⅜ x 8½.        22686-7 Pa. $3.95

BEST REMEMBERED POEMS, Martin Gardner (ed.). The 126 poems in this superb collection of 19th- and 20th-century British and American verse range from Shelley's "To a Skylark" to the impassioned "Renascence" of Edna St. Vincent Millay and to Edward Lear's whimsical "The Owl and the Pussycat." 224pp. 5⅜ x 8½.
        27165-X Pa. $4.95

COMPLETE SONNETS, William Shakespeare. Over 150 exquisite poems deal with love, friendship, the tyranny of time, beauty's evanescence, death and other themes in language of remarkable power, precision and beauty. Glossary of archaic terms. 80pp. 5³⁄₁₆ x 8¼.        26686-9 Pa. $1.00

BODIES IN A BOOKSHOP, R. T. Campbell. Challenging mystery of blackmail and murder with ingenious plot and superbly drawn characters. In the best tradition of British suspense fiction. 192pp. 5⅜ x 8½.        24720-1 Pa. $6.95

THE WIT AND HUMOR OF OSCAR WILDE, Alvin Redman (ed.). More than 1,000 ripostes, paradoxes, wisecracks: Work is the curse of the drinking classes; I can resist everything except temptation; etc. 258pp. 5⅜ x 8½.          20602-5 Pa. $5.95

SHAKESPEARE LEXICON AND QUOTATION DICTIONARY, Alexander Schmidt. Full definitions, locations, shades of meaning in every word in plays and poems. More than 50,000 exact quotations. 1,485pp. 6½ x 9¼. 2-vol. set.
Vol. 1: 22726-X Pa. $16.95
Vol. 2: 22727-8 Pa. $16.95

SELECTED POEMS, Emily Dickinson. Over 100 best-known, best-loved poems by one of America's foremost poets, reprinted from authoritative early editions. No comparable edition at this price. Index of first lines. 64pp. 5³⁄₁₆ x 8¼.
26466-1 Pa. $1.00

CELEBRATED CASES OF JUDGE DEE (DEE GOONG AN), translated by Robert van Gulik. Authentic 18th-century Chinese detective novel; Dee and associates solve three interlocked cases. Led to van Gulik's own stories with same characters. Extensive introduction. 9 illustrations. 237pp. 5⅜ x 8½.          23337-5 Pa. $6.95

THE MALLEUS MALEFICARUM OF KRAMER AND SPRENGER, translated by Montague Summers. Full text of most important witchhunter's "bible," used by both Catholics and Protestants. 278pp. 6⅝ x 10.          22802-9 Pa. $12.95

SPANISH STORIES/CUENTOS ESPAÑOLES: A Dual-Language Book, Angel Flores (ed.). Unique format offers 13 great stories in Spanish by Cervantes, Borges, others. Faithful English translations on facing pages. 352pp. 5⅜ x 8½.
25399-6 Pa. $8.95

THE CHICAGO WORLD'S FAIR OF 1893: A Photographic Record, Stanley Appelbaum (ed.). 128 rare photos show 200 buildings, Beaux-Arts architecture, Midway, original Ferris Wheel, Edison's kinetoscope, more. Architectural emphasis; full text. 116pp. 8¼ x 11.          23990-X Pa. $9.95

OLD QUEENS, N.Y., IN EARLY PHOTOGRAPHS, Vincent F. Seyfried and William Asadorian. Over 160 rare photographs of Maspeth, Jamaica, Jackson Heights, and other areas. Vintage views of DeWitt Clinton mansion, 1939 World's Fair and more. Captions. 192pp. 8⅞ x 11.          26358-4 Pa. $12.95

CAPTURED BY THE INDIANS: 15 Firsthand Accounts, 1750-1870, Frederick Drimmer. Astounding true historical accounts of grisly torture, bloody conflicts, relentless pursuits, miraculous escapes and more, by people who lived to tell the tale. 384pp. 5⅜ x 8½.          24901-8 Pa. $8.95

THE WORLD'S GREAT SPEECHES, Lewis Copeland and Lawrence W. Lamm (eds.). Vast collection of 278 speeches of Greeks to 1970. Powerful and effective models; unique look at history. 842pp. 5⅜ x 8½.          20468-5 Pa. $14.95

THE BOOK OF THE SWORD, Sir Richard F. Burton. Great Victorian scholar/adventurer's eloquent, erudite history of the "queen of weapons"—from prehistory to early Roman Empire. Evolution and development of early swords, variations (sabre, broadsword, cutlass, scimitar, etc.), much more. 336pp. 6⅛ x 9¼.
25434-8 Pa. $9.95

THE INFLUENCE OF SEA POWER UPON HISTORY, 1660–1783, A. T. Mahan. Influential classic of naval history and tactics still used as text in war colleges. First paperback edition. 4 maps. 24 battle plans. 640pp. 5⅜ x 8½.    25509-3 Pa. $12.95

THE STORY OF THE TITANIC AS TOLD BY ITS SURVIVORS, Jack Winocour (ed.). What it was really like. Panic, despair, shocking inefficiency, and a little heroism. More thrilling than any fictional account. 26 illustrations. 320pp. 5⅜ x 8½.
20610-6 Pa. $8.95

FAIRY AND FOLK TALES OF THE IRISH PEASANTRY, William Butler Yeats (ed.). Treasury of 64 tales from the twilight world of Celtic myth and legend: "The Soul Cages," "The Kildare Pooka," "King O'Toole and his Goose," many more. Introduction and Notes by W. B. Yeats. 352pp. 5⅜ x 8½.    26941-8 Pa. $8.95

BUDDHIST MAHAYANA TEXTS, E. B. Cowell and Others (eds.). Superb, accurate translations of basic documents in Mahayana Buddhism, highly important in history of religions. The Buddha-karita of Asvaghosha, Larger Sukhavativyuha, more. 448pp. 5⅜ x 8½.    25552-2 Pa. $9.95

ONE TWO THREE . . . INFINITY: Facts and Speculations of Science, George Gamow. Great physicist's fascinating, readable overview of contemporary science: number theory, relativity, fourth dimension, entropy, genes, atomic structure, much more. 128 illustrations. Index. 352pp. 5⅜ x 8½.    25664-2 Pa. $8.95

ENGINEERING IN HISTORY, Richard Shelton Kirby, et al. Broad, nontechnical survey of history's major technological advances: birth of Greek science, industrial revolution, electricity and applied science, 20th-century automation, much more. 181 illustrations. ". . . excellent . . ."–Isis. Bibliography. vii + 530pp. 5⅜ x 8¼.
26412-2 Pa. $14.95

DALÍ ON MODERN ART: The Cuckolds of Antiquated Modern Art, Salvador Dalí. Influential painter skewers modern art and its practitioners. Outrageous evaluations of Picasso, Cézanne, Turner, more. 15 renderings of paintings discussed. 44 calligraphic decorations by Dalí. 96pp. 5⅜ x 8½. (USO)    29220-7 Pa. $4.95

ANTIQUE PLAYING CARDS: A Pictorial History, Henry René D'Allemagne. Over 900 elaborate, decorative images from rare playing cards (14th–20th centuries): Bacchus, death, dancing dogs, hunting scenes, royal coats of arms, players cheating, much more. 96pp. 9¼ x 12¼.    29265-7 Pa. $11.95

MAKING FURNITURE MASTERPIECES: 30 Projects with Measured Drawings, Franklin H. Gottshall. Step-by-step instructions, illustrations for constructing handsome, useful pieces, among them a Sheraton desk, Chippendale chair, Spanish desk, Queen Anne table and a William and Mary dressing mirror. 224pp. 8⅛ x 11¼.
29338-6 Pa. $13.95

THE FOSSIL BOOK: A Record of Prehistoric Life, Patricia V. Rich et al. Profusely illustrated definitive guide covers everything from single-celled organisms and dinosaurs to birds and mammals and the interplay between climate and man. Over 1,500 illustrations. 760pp. 7½ x 10⅛.    29371-8 Pa. $29.95

*Prices subject to change without notice.*

Available at your book dealer or write for free catalog to Dept. GI, Dover Publications, Inc., 31 East 2nd St., Mineola, N.Y. 11501. Dover publishes more than 500 books each year on science, elementary and advanced mathematics, biology, music, art, literary history, social sciences and other areas.